THE RACIAL PROBLEM
in the Works of
RICHARD WRIGHT
and
JAMES BALDWIN

THE RACIAL PROBLEM
in the Works of
RICHARD WRIGHT
and
JAMES BALDWIN

JEAN-FRANÇOIS GOUNARD

Translated by JOSEPH J. RODGERS, JR.

Foreword by Jean F. Béranger

Contributions in Afro-American and African Studies,
Number 140

GREENWOOD PRESS _____
Westport, Connecticut • London

Library of Congress Cataloging-in-Publication Data

Gounard, Jean-François, 1939-
    [Problème noir dans les œuvres de Richard Wright et de James Baldwin. English]
    The racial problem in the works of Richard Wright and James Baldwin / Jean-François Gounard ; translated by Joseph J. Rodgers, Jr. ; foreword by Jean F. Béranger.
        p.   cm.—(Contributions in Afro-American and African studies, ISSN 0069-9624 ; no. 140)
    Translation of: Le problème noir dans les œuvres de Richard Wright et de James Baldwin.
    Includes bibliographical references and index.
    ISBN 0-313-27308-1 (lib. bdg. : alk. paper)
    1. American literature—Afro-American authors—History and criticism.   2. Wright, Richard, 1908-1960—Political and social views.   3. Baldwin, James, 1924-   —Political and social views.
    4. American literature—20th century—History and criticism.
    5. Afro-Americans in literature.   6. Race relations in literature.
    7. Racism in literature.   I. Title.   II. Series.
    PS153.N5G6813   1992
    810.9'3520396073—dc20   90-43379

British Library Cataloguing in Publication Data is available.

Library of Congress Catalog Card Number: 90-43379
ISBN: 0-313-27308-1
ISSN: 0069-9624

First published in 1992

Greenwood Press, 88 Post Road West, Westport, CT 06881
An imprint of Greenwood Publishing Group, Inc.

Printed in the United States of America

The paper used in this book complies with the Permanent Paper Standard issued by the National Information Standards Organization (Z39.48-1984).

10 9 8 7 6 5 4 3 2 1

Copyright Acknowledgments

The author and publisher are grateful to the following sources for granting permission to use copyright material.

"Hokku Poems" by Richard Wright, in *American Negro Poetry*, ed. Arna Bontemps (New York: Hill and Wang, 1963). Copyright © Richard Wright. Reprinted by permission of John Hawkins & Associates, Inc.

"Fourteen Haikus" by Richard Wright, in *Studies in Black Literature* 1 (Fall 1970). Reprinted by permission of Mary Washington College and John Hawkins & Associates, Inc.

Haikus by Richard Wright, in *The Unfinished Quest of Richard Wright*, by Michael Fabre (New York: William Morrow and Company, 1973). Reprinted by permission of John Hawkins & Associates, Inc.

Haikus by Richard Wright, in *Richard Wright: A Biography*, by Constance Webb (New York: G. P. Putnam's Sons, 1968). Reprinted by permission of John Hawkins & Associates, Inc.

This book is dedicated to
my father, my mother, and my daughters,
Anne-Marie and Emilie,
who were a great moral support to me
during its development.
                    Jean-F. Gounard

It is also dedicated to
Carolyn Burnett and Cynthia Kelly,
without whose expert assistance this
work might still be unavailable in
English.
                    Joseph J. Rodgers

Special thanks are due to Sue Smock
for her superb Richard Wright and James Baldwin woodcut prints.

The French version of this book was approved by the Groupe d'Etudes des Livres et des Publications of the French Ministry of National Education in the November-December 1985 issue (numbers 304/305) of the bibliographical bulletin, Les Livres, published by the Centre National de Documentation Pédagogique for use by all faculty and students of French high schools, colleges and universities.

Partial funding for the publication
of the English version of this study was provided by a Lilly Foundation
grant awarded to Lincoln University (Pennsylvania).

CONTENTS

FOREWORD

The result of lengthy and deep thought about the plight of blacks in the United States, this academic study by a Frenchman, who has spent much time in North America and who has settled there, contains one thesis: the complementary relationship between Richard Wright and James Baldwin.

Based on a very wide knowledge of early or recently published works on the racial question (as the extensive bibliography attests) this book, constructed according to a rigorous plan of traditional structure, relies on biographical elements and on textual analysis to retrace, meticulously and reliably, the careers of two American writers who deeply influenced their era. This analytical work covers both the literary works and the political and philosophical essays of the two men, thus combining in the same undertaking the attempt at aesthetic dramatization of the racial problem and the political involvement of the authors. Pragmatic in his approach, Jean-François Gounard has recourse to the history of ideas and social questions, to literary history, to psychology, to basic psychoanalytical sketches in order to carry out his work successfully. The two monographs, constructed on the same pattern, echo each other in a dialectic movement which emphasizes the author's opinions on the racial situation. For Jean-François Gounard, Richard Wright's violent revolt is counterbalanced by James Baldwin's words of love and peace. The differences between the two authors are clearly delineated, both from the literary and the human angle.

In his conclusion, the author expresses the profound wish that the spokesmen of the new revolt such as LeRoi Jones will not get the upper hand, and that white and black children will have peace, which may contribute to bringing social integration into primary and secondary schools. This generous remark is stamped with the seal of the preoccupations and the experience of the early 1970s. The whole book raises questions to which the changes of these last few years seem not to have given any definitive and clearly hopeful answers. The United States continues to bear the burden of the racial problem, even if the face of violence has changed. This is what makes reading the two great classics, Richard Wright and James Baldwin, still current.

Jean F. Béranger

FOREWORD TO THE
ENGLISH EDITION

The legendary singer Josephine Baker proclaimed in song: "Two loves have I, my own country and Paris." Like Josephine, their expatriate predecessor, Wright and Baldwin also had "two loves," the United States and France. And to prove their unwavering fidelity to both, they changed the mutually exclusive alternatives, "America: Love it or leave it," into a tripartite plan of action: "America, love it, leave it, change it." Wright and Baldwin left their native land not to forget but to change it, for they knew that, in their day, the only way for them to continue to love and serve their country was by physical separation. Although their exile was voluntary and self-imposed, the general racial climate of the times conduced to its realization. From afar, Baldwin and Wright hoped to get a panoramic view of the racial problem, achieve greater objectivity, gain a broader perspective and find viable, workable solutions. They also needed a truce, a respite from the stranglehold of America's racism.

As pervasive as it is despotic, racism compels every American to take a stand -- to choose between two equally challenging and extreme options. It excludes neutrality and exempts no one. Under the tyranny of racism, one succumbs or one survives. There is no middle ground: one is victor or victim. Whatever the choice, racism challenges all Americans to a fierce duel to the death.

Choosing the path of exile and survival, Wright (in the early 40s) and Baldwin (in the late 40s) valiantly resisted racism. In the final days of the twentieth century, the chameleonic beast, ever renewing, camouflaging and presenting itself under increasingly subtle but alluring guises, exacts a disproportionately high toll among its African-American victims. Casting off the fetters and shackles of slavery only to hurl themselves into more enticing but equally oppressive forms of servitude, many African-Americans have traded futile action and the stone of Sisyphus for seductive and facile siren songs that offer intoxicating old wine in shiny new bottles. The siren call of racism exhorts them to assimilate rapidly the most negative psychic environment and the most debilitated and deleterious aspects of American mainstream society. Increasingly today, there is a high degree of identification among African-Americans with the negative aspects of mainstream society. That society itself clearly suffers from a severe case of inverted or conflicting moral and ethical values, i.e., the state-sponsored apotheosis by the United States Postal Service of a rock star whose music and lifestyle doubtlessly contributed to today's rampant drug culture, the corruption and destruction of America's youth, promiscuity, and the nation's degenerative, evanescent morals and ethics. Far too many blacks fail to understand that accommodation implies selective assimilation, not blind, uncritical acceptance and adoption of America's most bizarre.

To ward off the grim effects of the defeat by racism, other African-Americans have recourse to introjection, one of the most pernicious of the ego defenses. By this circuitous means, they hope to avenge themselves on their oppressors, who constantly remind them that they are "minorities" (and thus less than) and who often fail to accord them even the essentials of external respect. These unfortunate African-Americans, by way of substitution, psychically incorporate, assimilate and identify themselves with their oppressors, substitute themselves for their opponents, and then punish themselves, thinking that, through this method of introjection, retaliation can be attained against their persecutors. When such people accede to positions of power and influence, they often reveal themselves as exaggerated carbon copies of the hated role models whose mentality they have introjected unwittingly. These vengeful souls seem unaware that the heaviest toll is the one they exact on themselves -- determined as they are to win a psychological victory, albeit a Phyrric one.

The number of Americans -- of any hue -- who truly overcome racism is abysmally low, for survival requires that one wage a sustained battle while keeping victory in focal awareness. Racism is so intricately ingrained and interwoven into the very fabric of American society and so deeply incorporated into the psyche of Americans -- black and white alike -- that only a conscious change of the heart and a deliberate act of the will can dismantle it. Racism will never be defeated until all Americans -- black and white -- understand its insidious nature and resolve, by a collective and conscious act of the will and a radical change of the heart, to destroy that blotch on our national conscience. Instead of choosing the easy path of identification and introjection, African-Americans must develop new paradigms of leadership, interaction and management styles based on unconditional love and the fundamental truth that people are all equally human and deserve to be treated as such. Perhaps these salvific models may serve as the prototype ultimately leading to the healing of the nation. Otherwise, having broken with history, African-Americans will be forever doomed to the fate of Sisyphus. They will tire quickly, abandon the stone and all efforts to affect their destiny, and follow the first Janus-faced siren that beckons.

Wright and Baldwin were two dreamers who have now become symbols of perennial hope for all Americans as regards race relations. The dreamers are gone but their dreams live on. Did Wright and Baldwin make a difference? We must exercise caution in answering that question, taking care not to confuse motion with progress. The concept of progress entails a directional, quantitative, and qualitative dimension. Movement must be forward, discernible and substantive or it is merely the illusion of progress. Only the test of time will assess the full impact of Wright and Baldwin. One thing is certain, however: like the corn seed, they tried -- and tried to the bitter end. Perhaps, as is the lot of many dreamers and visionaries, they will achieve more in death than life ever permitted them. Therein lies America's hope for improved race relations, but only if African-Americans develop alternative paradigms of leadership and interaction and devise conscious techniques to defeat racism. Concomitantly, mainstream America must undergo a comprehensive identity crisis resulting in its realization that all people are equally human and the resolve to treat them as such. For there is a fundamental truism regarding human behavior: when men and women begin to think, they can always think of a better way. Coupled with the infinite capacity of humans for adjustment and their aptness to survive, this basic characteristic enables humankind to overcome all adversity. What has held America back? What has kept racism alive and robust in America for well over three centuries is an absence of love, of dreams, a resolve, the collective national will -- black and white -- to change.

That the creator of the English version of this work is himself an African-American Francophile seems to suggest that poetic justice is more than a mere literary notion. A product of the seething sixties, this writer first went to France to study as a teenager on the eve of the demonstrations in Greensboro, North Carolina, and found himself torn between his "two loves," his own country and France. He yearned, on the one hand, to return home to be an eyewitness to, and a participant in, a historic moment. On the other, his new-found love, France, tugged at his heart, caressed and beseeched him to stay, complete his studies and get better acquainted. Once back in the United States during the first summer of the incipient sixties, the writer knew he had made the right decision in remaining in France to perfect his French and acclimate himself to his second home. Some thirty years later, The Racial Problem in the Works of Richard Wright and James Baldwin thus appears as both confirmation and fruit of a lifelong "ménage à trois." But true love is not blind, nor does it preclude objectivity, as Wright and Baldwin never ceased to remind us. Paradoxically, both Wright and Baldwin had to leave their homeland in order to love it to the fullest extent, for American racism forced them to choose. Fortunately, this writer has not yet been compelled to seek refuge in exile in order to remain faithful to his "two loves." Nonetheless, racism still exerts a dynamic influence upon American society. Like a kaleidoscope, it is continually changing its forms, patterns and guises. But when properly understood and fully displayed, racism may, within due limits, serve as a spurt of activity propelling the resources of the African-American spirit to maximum development. For those who still dare to dream, like Wright and Baldwin, to excel, to risk, to care, to expect -- in short -- to hope, the future still holds great promise. The possession of two legitimate loves, France and one's own country, is a luxury that surely enhances the odds in one's favor. Tragically, however, most African-Americans are still in search of one requited national love. Racism offers no easy solutions. One emerges from it, as from the simmering sixties -- whole and more aware or frayed, scarred, bruised and piteously fragmented. Any victory proclaimed is necessarily a Cadmean one serving only to underscore the common humanity of the victor and the vanquished. Undying racism -- more than any other single factor -- explains why one third of the nation is still at risk, brilliant minds are wasted and countless talents untapped. It is the twentieth-century "mal du siècle," the world-weariness that is warping the national psyche and sabotaging this country's moral core. To regain its status as the ultimate world-class super power, the United States must establish and implement a domestic Marshall Plan to energize and develop the full complement of its citizenry -- white, black, yellow, brown and red alike. The state of the union (or disunion) in race relations must be officially recognized as nothing short of a national disaster and a dire emergency. Finally, a Presidential declaration of war must be promulgated, and all Americans of goodwill, irrespective of color, must be enlisted. Only then will the hideous hydra called racism be slain, permanently laid to rest, and an epitaph erected proclaiming: "RACISM EXTINCT." Perhaps then, too, will Wright and Baldwin find the object of their lifelong quest -- peace for their beloved country and for their tormented souls.

Joseph J. Rodgers

INTRODUCTION

The black American problem has always lain heavy on the conscience of white America, ill at ease about the moral conflict created by its racism and its democratic ideals. The less it talks about black Americans, the less it feels guilty about the fate that it reserves for them within the American nation. The aim of this study is to show the part played by two black American writers: Richard Wright and James Baldwin. Both succeeded in making white America understand that it could no longer ignore the reality of the racial problem, and that it had to try to solve it. Otherwise, the United States would risk being drawn into a civil war capable of jeopardizing the country's very existence.

The most important works of Richard Wright span the forties and the fifties, whereas James Baldwin's encompass the fifties and the sixties. The fifties mark a period of transition and change not only in these two authors, but also in race relations in America. It was on May 17, 1954, that the Supreme Court of the United States officially put an end to school segregation. The boycott of the Montgomery buses by blacks in the state of Alabama from December 1955 to December 1956 led the U.S. Supreme Court to abolish segregation in public facilities. These two important events made black Americans aware of their voice within America. They also realized that they were one of the last peoples of color still colonized.

During the forties, blacks had become aware of their position as a second-class citizen in American society. The political climate of the time was not conducive to improving their plight, and white America's anti-Fascist and anti-Communist sentiments denied them, in advance, any vague desire for resistance. They had to wait for the fifties, capitalizing on the Cold War between the United States and the U.S.S.R., to attempt to claim their rights as full American citizens.

Realizing that it would take many years to obtain what they wanted, blacks first decided to use peaceful means in order to achieve their integration into American society. The creation of various civil rights movements was the outcome. Since white America did not take them seriously, they switched to direct action. The riots that then tore Harlem, Watts, Newark, and other large American urban centers apart in the sixties were cogent proof that blacks had lost their patience and were demanding positive results immediately.

White America, surprised, became frightened and began to understand blacks' attitudes. Thus the American Congress adopted the Civil Rights Act in 1964, the Voting Rights Act in 1965 and the Open

Housing Act in 1968. Black Americans were now officially full citizens. For the third time in the history of the United States, a black man, Edward W. Brooke, from the state of Massachusetts, was elected to the Senate in November 1966, while, at the same time, a dozen black men were elected to the House of Representatives.[1]

No country in all the world could understand the living conditions imposed on black Americans in the most powerful and the wealthiest democratic country. It was thus, in large measure, because of the negative attitudes of many nations toward it that white America decided to improve black people's lot. In reality, whites' behavior towards blacks did not change immediately, however. In the forties and the fifties, Richard Wright had said time and time again that the United States was a fundamentally racist nation, and that it would take a change of attitude and of intention on the part of whites and the government for the black man to feel finally at home in America. The publication of his novel <u>Native Son</u>, in 1940, had had a tremendous impact upon the whites who had become aware that the black man was a man like all other men.[2] The appearance of this novel marked a new stage in race relations in the United States, and Richard Wright's voice dominated for twenty years the black authors who, like him, embarked on that course. Taking into consideration the political climate of the forties and the fifties, Richard Wright had to be content with protesting against the way the black man was treated. He formulated demands. In order to have greater freedom of expression, Wright exiled himself to France.

Richard Wright's literary protest demonstrated that the integration of black Americans into American society was slow. Though he had said many times that blacks would end up losing their patience, Wright never incited them to rebellion. His repeated warnings, nonetheless, showed that he feared it.

In the early sixties, the growth of many civil rights movements emphasized the need to rethink and reexamine the democratic principles of a nation whose freedom and prestige were at stake abroad and under discussion at home. Richard Wright was dead, but his protest work had not been written in vain since America had decided to bring about some changes in favor of blacks. By exiling himself to France, Wright had shown that he did not harbor any hope for the future of race relations in the United States. In a way, he had placed himself on the fringes of the American community and had lost all hope of seeing any change whatsoever for blacks. That is where, in the fifties, he broke with James Baldwin's prophetic action. Baldwin had not lost the hope of a better world in his country's race relations.

Richard Wright and James Baldwin viewed the black problem differently, particularly for the following reasons. Wright was from the South; Baldwin from the North. They belonged to two different generations, their backgrounds were not similar, and they had not had the same experiences in life. Finally, if Wright lost all direct contact with America while staying in France, Baldwin always remained in touch with his original environment. Although different from each other, Wright and Baldwin were complementary because they were intimately linked by their involvement in race relations. Thus, in <u>Native Son</u>, Wright aroused whites' conscience whereas Baldwin, in his essays, made white America feel guilty.

This complementary relationship between Wright and Baldwin and their leading roles in American race relations make their actions important and worthy of our complete attention. There are many black American authors whose works are comparable to Wright's or Baldwin's, but no two black authors complement each other like Wright and Baldwin. They are the descendants of a long line of black American writers who, through the centuries, have always tried to make their hopes known. In 1829, David Walker published his <u>Appeal,</u> in which he incited the black slaves to a bloody rebellion, while at the same time condemning the whites' racism.[3] In 1881, Frederick Douglass had published <u>The Life and Times of Frederick Douglass,</u> in which he talked about his adventures as a slave and as a free man.[4] In his novel, <u>The Marrow of Tradition</u> . . . , published in 1901, Charles W. Chesnutt tried to analyze the relationship between black and white Americans.[5] In short, black American literature has always included protest works in which the individual was filled with indignation about the way he was treated.

Actually, Wright's and Baldwin's works lead toward a reconciliation between black and white Americans. These works cover a thirty-year period and place Wright and Baldwin in a limited historical position.Since 1970, black leadership has shifted. The year 1970 marks, indeed, an era of transition and announces a decade much calmer but no less important than the former one. As the understanding of the evolution of Wright's and Baldwin's ideas is essential to an understanding of the evolution of the race problem in America, this study will attempt to stress these ideas in the essays, articles, and interviews of both authors. We shall also emphasize how those ideas have been applied in Wright's and Baldwin's novels, short stories, plays,and poems. Finally, a better understanding of these two authors and of their ideas will be made possible through the introduction of the points of view of various critics. The plan adopted begins with a study of Richard Wright's works and ends with James Baldwin's. The first writer shows the black American's struggle to survive in a hostile environment, while the second indicates, on one hand, a noticeable improvement in the black American situation and, on the other, the anguish of an American who, seized by the problem, wishes that whites and blacks will come to understand one another. This plan also has the advantage of following the chronological order of the events and writings.

NOTES

1. It was during the "Reconstruction" years in the South that the U.S. Senate had its first two black members. The first one, Hiram Revels, represented the state of Mississippi from 1870 to 1871, and the second, Blanche K. Bruce, also presented Mississippi from 1875 to 1881.

2. Richard Wright, <u>Native Son</u> (New York: Harper and Brothers, 1940).

3. David Walker, <u>Appeal in Four Articles</u>: <u>Together with a Preamble</u>, <u>to the Colored Citizens of the World</u>, <u>but in Particular</u>, <u>and Very Expressly</u>, <u>to those of the United States of America</u> (Boston: D. Walker, 1829).

4. Frederick Douglass, <u>The Life and Times of Frederick Douglass</u> (Hartford, Connecticut: Park Publishing Co., 1881).

5. Charles W. Chesnutt, <u>The Marrow of Tradition</u> (New York: Houghton Mifflin and Co., 1901).

I
Richard Wright

"Richard Wright," woodcut by Sue Smock. Used with
permission.

1

THE LIFE OF RICHARD NATHANIEL WRIGHT (1908–1960)

Richard Nathaniel Wright was born on September 4, 1908, near the little town of Natchez, Mississippi. His parents were from a very humble background. His father, Nathan, who came from a poor family of black sharecroppers, was illiterate and worked as a farmhand on a plantation. His mother, Ella, was a teacher in a black elementary school when she met her future husband. She was from a family of nine children. Her family lived in a respectable black neighborhood in Natchez. One of her brothers, Tom, and one of her sisters, Addie, were also elementary schoolteachers. Since the Bureau of Vital Statistics in Natchez did not begin to issue birth certificates until 1912, it had always been impossible for Richard Wright to obtain documentary proof that he was born in 1908. But as is the custom in Southern black families, the date of his birth is recorded in the family Bible.

From his early childhood, Richard Wright lived under the all-powerful influence of his very authoritarian grandmother, Margaret Bolden Wilson. She had white skin, inherited from her numerous Irish, French, and Scottish ancestors who had mixed their blood with that of blacks they came across. This played an important and positive role in Richard Wright's life and conduct, for he soon got used to not fearing white people. He had associated the color white with authority.

Richard had a brother, Leon Alan, born in 1910, who was much darker than he. Since he had realized this difference in pigmentation, Wright was proud to be white like his grandmother. Very aggressive by nature, his first actions and reactions toward everything white were surprising. In 1912, when he was barely four years old, he set fire to his grandmother's white curtains. This act was probably the result of conversations he had heard about the evil power of whites. In Black Boy: A Record of Childhood and Youth he says: "Tension would set in at the mere mention of whites and a vast complex of emotions, involving the whole of my personality, would be aroused. It was as though I was continuously reacting to the threat of some natural force whose hostile behavior could not be predicted,"[1] he had already understood that the white world was a blind force which controlled and mistreated blacks.

Still in 1912, his parents, thinking they would find a new life, left Mississippi to settle down in Memphis, Tennessee. The trip, taken on the Kate Adams, one of the last Mississippi paddle boats, made a strong impression on Richard Wright. After a few months, unable to support his family, Nathan Wright started drinking; then he left his wife to go live with another woman. This was in 1913. Then began one long painful agony for Richard Wright's mother. To feed her two sons, she took a job as a cook for a white family. But that job kept her away from her children during the day. This kind of situation was common in those days, for the direct result of racial discrimination in the South was the perpetual unemployment of black men. Most black families subsisted only because of the hard labor of black women.

In 1914, left to himself, Richard Wright began frequenting the disreputable bars in his neighborhood and on Beale Street. He started drinking and learned to use coarse language. But Ella Wright put an end to such behavior by placing her sons in a black orphanage in Memphis. This unhappy life in a boarding house, where the two brothers endured hunger and cold, was very brief. After several attempts to escape, Richard Wright and his mother went to Nathan Wright to ask him for money to go to Arkansas, where some relatives were living. But Richard's father openly laughed at his wife and son in front of his mistress and did not give them anything. This event left an indelible mark on Wright, who still remembered it twenty-five years later when he saw his father again.[2] This painful incident also convinced Richard to count no longer on his father nor on that poor and ignorant side of his family.

Not long after that cruel humiliation, Ella Wright, exhausted from fatigue, became seriously ill. But, thanks to grandmother Wilson's valuable help, Richard Wright, his brother, and his mother went to Jackson, Mississippi, to live with his maternal grandparents, who has just settled there. A black elementary school teacher, Ella was then living at the Wilsons'. Prompted by the solitude that surrounded him, Richard Wright, however, succeeded in winning her friendship; and one day she told him the story of Bluebeard and his seven wives. This tale made a deep impression on Richard. From then on, he started to become interested in reading and to understand that books could contain a world different from his. As she considered every book to be the work of the devil, the grandmother accused Ella of trying to corrupt her grandson and ordered her to leave the house immediately.

Richard was very much affected by his grandmother's life-style and her inflexible character.   Without her, it is unlikely that Ella Wright could have continued bearing life's burdens.   Grandmother Wilson got that attitude from the religious faith, Seventh-Day Adventism, which she had always known and fervently practiced.   Under her influence, Richard's mother was encouraged to seek consolation in religion.

In 1917, Richard and his mother went to visit his Aunt Maggie and his rich Uncle Hoskins, who were living near Elaine, Arkansas. Ella Wright was three years older than her sister Maggie and she was very close to her. Uncle Hoskins, owner of a very profitable bar, had always refused to be submissive to whites, who were jealous of him. Only a few days after Richard and his mother's arrival, Uncle Hoskins was killed by a white in his bar. Despite his tender age (he was nine) Wright found the strength to comfort his aunt and his mother before a hurried trip back to Jackson. Aunt Maggie did not dare say or ask for anything after her husband's murder. She simply disappeared quietly and left all her belongings to the whites. This behavior was then common among Southern blacks, who knew they could do nothing about the inhumane acts of whites. The only thing to do in such cases was to flee in silence. Indeed, in those days, whites could kill a black under any pretext. They knew that justice would always be on their side.

A few months later, Richard, his mother, and his Aunt Maggie, having recovered from their painful emotional ordeal, moved to West Helena, Arkansas. That is where Richard became involved in a black youth gang that was constantly fighting with whites of the same age.

In 1919, exhausted from working, Ella Wright was stricken with paralysis and Richard had to spend some time at his Uncle Clark's in Greenwood, Mississippi. Aunt Maggie, having got over her mourning, had gone to live in the North, in Detroit, with a certain Professor Matthews. Back at his grandmother Wilson's in Jackson in 1920, Wright had changed a lot; disenchantment had taken hold of his soul: "The spirit I had caught gave me insight into the sufferings of others, made me gravitate toward those whose feelings were like my own, made me sit for hours while others told me their lives, made me strangely tender and cruel, violent and peaceful."[3] He had just discovered that the cruel daily reality created by whites reigned supreme.

Richard started writing around that time. He wrote a short story about a young, mysterious Indian girl who drowns in the Mississippi waters. This short story has left no traces of its existence. But it is proof that, already at twelve, Wright was attempting to escape from his environment by trying to write fiction.

For the first time in his life, from September 1920, Richard regularly attended a black elementary school. This school, located in Jackson, was Adventist. His Aunt Addie taught there. But this extremely rigid and religious environment hardly suited him, since he was constantly in conflict with his strict aunt. In September 1921, still in Jackson, he entered a black public school, the Jim Hill Public School. Although he was two years behind his classmates, Richard Wright did not take long to make up for lost time and win his teachers' esteem. By June 1923 he had finished elementary school.

His attention was then captivated by his maternal grandfather, Richard Wilson. He had fought in the Northern ranks during the Civil War, in which he had been wounded. Since then, he had been trying hard to get a disability pension from the American government. Despite all the possible details he had given about his numerous military activities, the grandfather's efforts met a dead-end. These troubles were caused by the name "Wilson," misunderstood by an officer of the Northern army, who had spelled it "Vinson."[4] This wrong was never redressed.

Ella Wright never completely recovered from her paralysis. Since she was feeling slightly better, Richard agreed to accompany her to a black Methodist church in Jackson, where he let them baptize him at the age of thirteen, more out of the desire to please his mother than through religious conviction. For him, the church and its peculiar rites made no sense. He only went there to meet his playmates.

In September 1923, Richard Wright entered a black high school in Jackson, the Smith-Robinson High School, which offered its students only two years of instruction. Though living in a black neighborhood and having attended only black schools, Richard had already been exposed to brutality in Jackson when he had worked during the summer and even during the school year in order to help support his family. Of a sensitive nature, and suffering much from the injustices of the white world, Richard Wright found refuge in reading Horatio Alger's novels. Although an adolescent, he dreamed of becoming rich and famous one day, like Alger's young heroes. During the spring of 1924, he wrote a story of more than three thousands words, "The Voodoo of Hell's Half Acre," published in three installments in Jackson's black newspaper, the Southern Register.[5] "The Voodoo of Hell's Half Acre," now lost, told the story of a hoodlum who wanted to get hold of the house and belongings of a poor, defenseless widow. This first venture into the literary world resulted only in baffling Richard Wright's little friends, who "could not understand why anyone would want to write a story; . . . The mood out of which a story was written was the most alien thing conceivable to them. They looked at me with new eyes, and a distance, a suspiciousness came between us."[6] This publication also provoked a violent reaction in grandmother Wilson, for whom any fictional work was synonymous with capital sin. But "The Voodoo of Hell's Half Acre" met with such a success within the black community of Jackson that Richard understood that he could communicate his feelings by writing. He had found there a means of giving free rein to his ideas without incurring the destructive wrath of whites.

Southern blacks were then frequently lynched, and Jackson's black community often suffered the blind violence of whites. Bob Greenley, the brother of one of Wright's classmates, was the victim of an atrocious murder because he had violated a racial taboo by sleeping with a white prostitute at the hotel where he was working. After having savagely beaten and tortured him, the whites had finished him off with a bullet in the head. This incident taught Wright that whites were capable of doing anything in order to subject blacks to their will.

In June 1925, Wright interrupted his secondary studies and started looking for a job in Jackson. A new life was beginning. It was going to be the source of numerous experiences that hardened his already wounded soul. He quickly learned the proper way to behave with respect to the racist and segregationist laws of the South in order to protect his person and his pride. After having been successively a janitor in a store, a messenger, a worker in an optical goods firm, a street cleaner, a bellboy, and an usher in a movie theater, he understood that this kind of life would be a dead end for him. He then decided to save as much money as possible and to leave Mississippi for somewhere else. He did not want to depend any longer on the pity and generosity of whites in order to make a living. To hasten this long-awaited departure, he even stole a gun and some canned goods to sell on the sly.

Richard Wright finally managed to leave Jackson in November 1925. He went to Memphis, the first stop on his trip to the North. He had only just arrived in town when he rented a room in the home of a certain Mrs. Moss, who wanted to make him marry her daughter, Bess. But Richard Wright's cold and distant attitude was convincing enough to make his hostess change her mind. However, he was not obliged to leave his new home.

After a short while he found a job with an optical goods company, where whites did not make things very easy for him. But thanks to one of them who lent him his library card, he could get books from the Memphis city library, the Cossitt Library, which was then closed to blacks. He could thus escape from reality by reading detective novels and especially the Edgar Allan Poe tales. As he regularly read the Memphis morning newspaper, The Memphis Commercial Appeal, he noticed several times that H. L. Mencken was criticized by Southern whites. So he hastened to read Mencken's Prejudices and A Book of Prefaces, which fascinated him and exerted a strong influence on his literary development.[7]

Mencken's wise advice was followed literally by Wright, who had everything to learn about literature. He started reading Theodore Dreiser, Sinclair Lewis, and Sherwood Anderson. With a job and something to live on, Wright sent for his mother and his brother. Since she had lost her male friend in Detroit, Aunt Maggie joined them somewhat later.

Richard Wright's family situation (in which there was no father and the mother held the children's complete attention) was common among Southern blacks. It had its origin in slavery, which had always promoted this state of affairs. Richard Wright was very attached to his mother and had fulfilled the responsibilities toward her that his father had refused to assume. Ella Wright had also always encouraged him to read and write. Since she had been a primary schoolteacher, she knew exactly what to say and do to encourage a child to work hard. Her maternal instinct had made her aware of her son's desire to educate himself at all costs. The five years of instruction that one received in Jackson's schools were not designed to produce a literary genius. In fact, black schools have always been definitely inferior to white schools. The direct cause of this situation was the segregationist policy of the South.

Since he understood the necessity of leaving the South if he wanted to be respected, Richard Wright decided to go north in November 1927. He had great difficulty convincing his white boss that he had to leave for family reasons. Southern whites have always been suspicious of blacks who go north. A few days later, Richard Wright and his Aunt Maggie were taking the train to Chicago, where Aunt Cleo, Richard Wright's mother's oldest sister, was awaiting them. Ella Wright and her younger son, Leon Alan, stayed on in Memphis for some time.

Richard Wright thought he would discover an ideal democracy when he reached Chicago. Like all Southern blacks in search of the Northern Eldorado, he landed in the destitution and poverty of the South Side, the black ghetto in Chicago. A week after his arrival, he had to get out of this human jail to look for a job in a white town. He rapidly found a job in a delicatessen. His bosses, Mr. and Mrs. Hoffman, Jewish immigrants, had an accent that was hard to understand. At first, their way of talking caused some problems for Richard Wright, who had been accustomed thus far to the slow pronunciation of Southerners. But he got used to his work, which consisted of shopping, delivering packages, and looking after the store.

In order to take the civil service exam for a job at the Chicago post office, Richard Wright left for three days without saying anything to his bosses. When he came back to work, he was surprised to find Mr. and Mrs. Hoffman as nice as usual. They did not believe him when, to explain his absence, he told them that his mother had died suddenly and that he had had to leave Chicago without having the time to inform them. Richard Wright was extremely ill at ease when Mr. Hoffman accused him of lying but did not fire him, nevertheless. Not knowing what to do, Richard Wright decided not to see them any more. He had not understood that not all whites were alike. Lying, one of his ready-made defense reactions toward whites, had had no effect on the Hoffmans.

Since he had settled in an environment very different from his, Richard Wright could not understand why Northern whites also had racial prejudices toward blacks. The situation drove him to hate himself, hate other blacks, and even made him expose himself to self-destruction. He avoided catastrophe by imagining a brilliant future for himself as a writer. To escape daily reality, he kept reading voraciously and started writing industriously. He decided to remain calm and detached in the company of both whites and blacks in order to protect his intellectual independence. Reading and learning to be a writer were for him a world that one could penetrate. He talked to nobody about what he was reading or writing and applied himself to this fascinating work every evening and sometimes for whole nights.

Aunt Maggie had found a small apartment and he was living at her place. She could not understand that a person could read and write so often without having a definite goal in mind. But after Ella and Leon Alan's arrival, Richard Wright was free to do what he pleased; even if he had to share his room with his mother and brother. Beginning in 1929, he very often went to the George Cleveland Hall Branch Library on the South Side, where he discovered <u>Three Lives</u> by Gertrude Stein, <u>The Red Badge of Courage</u> by Stephen Crane, and <u>The Possessed</u> by Fedor Dostoyevski.[8] These three books had a great influence on his literary character, then fully developing.

But meanwhile it was necessary to earn a living and to support his family. After leaving the Hoffmans, he found a job in a white restaurant which had just opened. One day the white boss caught him in the kitchen reading <u>The American Mercury</u> and did not hide her surprise at seeing him with such a magazine in his possession. Through fear of losing his job, Richard Wright told her he had found the magazine. That lie allowed him not to compromise himself in a delicate situation. He knew, in fact, that whites were convinced that blacks were incapable of thinking. Richard Wright did not want to give an impression contrary to the one the majority of whites had about black people.

From the time he started working in the restaurant, Richard Wright had been intimidated by the attitude of the young white waitresses and the Finnish cook, Tillie, who treated him like a friend. One day he was extremely ill at ease when a white waitress, who had arrived late and was in a hurry, asked him to tie her apron. His numerous experiences in the South had strictly forbidden him, under penalty of death, from coming into physical contact with white women. This uneasiness had been provoked by the harsh racism he had experienced before coming to Chicago. The racial prejudices encountered in the North were different from those experienced in the South. But the effects were the same, since Richard Wright suffered a great deal from them. The only difference was that the South was direct with blacks, whereas the North was more subtle.

One morning Richard Wright caught Tillie spitting in the soup she was preparing. Horrified, he told a black waitress, who, after having secretly observed the cook's strange ritual, went to complain to the white proprietress. Though not disposed to believe everything she heard, the boss started nevertheless to keep an eye on the cook. Eventually she caught her in the act and dismissed her forthwith. Since she had never trusted blacks, the white boss had hesitated to believe what the black waitress and Richard Wright had told her. She had been convinced only after witnessing the cook's strange behavior in person. The lesson Richard Wright drew from this experience was that it would always be difficult for blacks to win the complete trust of whites.

In 1928, Wright worked for a few months at the Chicago post office. During that short period, he also had to take care of his Aunt Cleo, who had heart disease; of his brother, who had stomach ulcers; and of his mother, whose paralysis had gotten worse. After that, Wright worked for a funeral parlor managed by a cousin, who gave him the job of selling insurance policies to blacks who were mainly poor and illiterate. That was a completely new and often distressing experience, for, to earn a living, Richard Wright had to take advantage shamelessly of the gullibility of blacks. He got involved for a while with a simple-minded young black woman whose only desire was to go to the circus. This young woman had a child but was not sure who the father had been. She did not try to hide the fact that she had other lovers. The human degeneration of the South Side revealed itself then to Richard Wright in all its harshness. But the crisis of 1929 erupted and he found himself jobless.

Like thousands of other hungry blacks, he was reduced to going to the public welfare office to seek help and employment. In order to earn a living, he had to sweep the streets and look after the parks of Chicago. Surrounded by an immense crowd of dissatisfied blacks, Wright realized that such a mass could exert a decisive influence on American social policy. In April 1931, "Superstition" was published in Abbot's Monthly, a magazine popular among blacks in Chicago.[9] This short story, the fruit of hard labor, was blatant proof of Richard Wright's will to become a writer. He had it published with the sole aim of earning a little money. He was never to be paid, the economic crisis having suddenly put an end to the magazine's publication.

Toward the end of 1931, Richard Wright worked at the Chicago post office. The economic situation of America at that time had drawn blacks and whites closer together, and in many cases, racial prejudices had become blurred in order to make room for a common social struggle. Since he intrigued his white co-workers at the post office with his ideas, Richard Wright was invited to their homes. One of them, a Jew, invited him to attend meetings of the John Reed Club of Chicago, known for its revolutionary ideas and activities. At that time there were more than thirty of those clubs in the United States. John Reed had been a militant American Communist who had died in the Soviet Union in 1920. One Saturday evening in January 1932, Wright went, out of sheer curiosity, to the address his Jewish friend had given him. The moment he arrived, he was given several issues of various Communist magazines, such as International Literature and New Masses.

After attending a few meetings of the John Reed Club, Richard Wright became an official member and, a few weeks later, the secretary of the organization. Since most members of the club were Communists, Richard Wright understood that, in order to remain secretary, he too would have to become a party member. He was twenty-three years old and it was March 1932.[10] Richard Wright had decided to adhere to Communism because he saw in it a means rather than an end in itself. He had finally found an organization that not only recognized his humanity, but was also going to permit him to express himself freely in its official publications. Even before becoming a member of the John Reed Club, Richard Wright had been fascinated by the Communist ideology as he had understood it after reading the magazines he had been given. He had felt that "here at last, in the realm of revolutionary expression, Negro experience could find a home, a functioning value and role."[11] But the distrustful attitude of his black and white Communist friends made him quickly realize that he had made a mistake, for they wished to see in him only a dangerous intellectual. How, he wondered, with rage, could they accuse him of being a fearsome intellectual when he had not even finished high school and was once more forced to sweep the streets of Chicago to earn a living? The black Communists to whom he spoke about his work, his ideas, and his plans did not understand him and accused him of being a selfish bourgeois who cared little for the proletariat. From the end of 1932, Richard Wright knew that if he were to be a Communist, he would be one in his own way. He wanted in no way to lose his identity and abandon his hopes of becoming a writer. From 1933 to 1939, he wrote a score of poems revealing Communist leanings that were published in Left Front, a magazine of the John Reed Club of Chicago, The Anvil, New Masses, Midland Left, and International Literature.[12]

When he lost his job as a street cleaner, Wright was placed by the office of public welfare in an institute for medical research at a large Chicago hospital, the Michael Reese Hospital. It was at the beginning of 1933. His job consisted of cleaning the operating rooms, scouring cages containing all sorts of little animals, and feeding the guinea pigs. Working with him were three other blacks. Two of them, Brand and Cooke, did not get along.

Often Richard Wright helped the doctors cut the vocal cords of dogs that were too noisy. Contemptuous of Wright, those doctors never told him anything about the nature of the operations. Just like the dogs deprived of their voices, Wright had to suffer in silence. One day, a Jewish employee calculated with a stopwatch the amount of time it took Wright to mop the wooden floor and the stairs of a section of the institute. This was to improve job efficiency in the hospital. The vexations that Wright suffered because of the color of his skin had made him suspicious. Refusing to believe that he belonged to a class of inferior beings, he lived only for his readings and his future works.

One freezing cold winter day, the bad blood between Brand and Cooke rose to a such a violent level that the results were disastrous for the animals in the institute. It was noon and Richard Wright and his co-workers were having lunch in a room filled with caged animals. Cooke was reading the Chicago Daily Tribune and remarked out loud that the weather had never been so cold. Brand retorted immediately that it was not true because the Chicago Herald and Examiner, which he was reading, did not say the same thing. These two newspapers are well known in Chicago and have always tried to compete with each other. The verbal exchange between Brand and Cooke grew more bitter and the two men quickly came to blows. In their struggle they knocked over some cages which crashed on the floor, killing or wounding several animals. After a quick return to calm, the black men then realized that the situation was alarming because all the animals were closely observed by the hospital doctors. They knew that if the damages were discovered, they would be fired on the spot. Of a common accord, they decided to straighten up the room as well as could be expected. They put the animals back in their cages and replaced the dead with living ones. To their great joy, the doctors noticed nothing and continued their scientific experiments with the same diligence as before. From this incident, Richard Wright concluded that black America exerted an invisible and determining influence over the American white.

After having worked at Michael Reese Hospital, Wright was placed by the Works Progress Administration in the South Side Boys Club, where idle young blacks from the black Chicago ghetto got together.[13] Richard

Wright was twenty-four years old. Far from his Communist friends, he could relax there and listen attentively to the conversations of young people from the South Side. It was in the same club that the idea for a future novel, Native Son, germinated.[14] Richard Wright took notes, understanding all the while the negative meaning those young blacks gave to life. He felt pity for their plight, for "They were a wild and homeless lot, culturally lost, spiritually disinherited, candidates for the clinics, morgues, prisons, reformatories, and the electric chair of the state's death house."[15] In this environment, Wright found himself closely linked to his past and to his own experience.

During the summer of 1934, the Congress of Communist Writers from the central region of the United States was held in Chicago. After attending numerous political and literary debates, Wright realized the distance that separated him from the Marxist movement. "It was whispered that I was trying to lead a secret group in opposition to the party. I had learned that denial of accusations was useless. It was now painful to meet a Communist, for I did not know what his attitude would be."[16] That same summer, the National Congress of John Reed Clubs also met in Chicago. All the leftist writers were there. Richard Wright's attitude was poorly regarded and misinterpreted because he desired above all to be a writer and because no one wanted to take the trouble to understand him. He had already begun to write two autobiographical novels. The first, then entitled "Cesspool," was published in 1963 under the title of Lawd Today.[17] The second, "Tarbaby's Dawn," was never published. Only a part of it appeared in January 1940 under the title of "Almos' A Man."[18]

During the summer of 1935, Richard Wright went to New York to take part in the Congress of American Writers. He had great difficulty in finding a room because of racial discrimination. Thus he was disappointed to see that even the communist whites could not help him. His disillusionment was all the more bitter since the John Reed Clubs were dissolved. In October 1935, his first article, "Joe Louis Uncovers Dynamite," was published in New Masses.[19] In the introduction preceding the article, the newspaper's editorial staff introduces Wright as a young black poet from Chicago. The lively style of the article seemed to promise Richard Wright a brilliant future as a writer. A few months later, he was publishing a short story, "Big Boy Leaves Home."[20] At that time, he met Buddy Nealson, an influential black Communist, who accused him of socializing too much with whites. Wright was criticized and misunderstood on both sides, black and white alike.

In 1936, the Works Progress Administration found him a job as an advertising executive in a black theatrical company, the Federal Negro Theater. Since he wanted to help black actors, Richard Wright obtained the invaluable assistance of a very talented Jewish producer, Charles DeSheim. But after the rehearsal of a one-act play by Paul Green, Hymn to the Rising Sun, Wright and DeSheim were forced to leave the Federal Negro Theater with all possible speed.[21] Offended by the play, which dealt with the atrocious living conditions in black penitentiaries in the South, the black actors had threatened to kill them if they did not leave immediately. The actors wanted to put on only plays that would endear them to the American white public. Richard Wright's goodwill had been misinterpreted by his own people and had even endangered his life. The incident taught him that most blacks preferred to please whites rather than remind them of past and present sufferings. Those blacks wanted to do everything to avoid irritating whites and incurring their contempt.

After this misadventure, the Works Progress Administration placed Richard Wright in a white theatrical company, the Federal Experimental Theater, where he worked as an advertising executive. At that time, he attended the trial of one of his black friends, Ross, falsely accused by the Communist Party of militant and subversive actions. The resigned submission of Ross, forced to confess his guilt in public, gave Wright a feeling of horror and despair. He had before him the sad spectacle of Communism, which, blind and pitiless, was striking down an innocent victim. It was largely due to the stories Ross, a native of the South, had told him that Wright had been able to write "Big Boy Leaves Home."

Since it had considered Richard Wright as having discharged his duties well at the Federal Experimental Theater, the Works Progress Administration placed him with the Federal Writers' Project, where he was asked to do research on the state of Illinois and on blacks in Chicago.[22] Wright wrote an essay, "Ethnographical Aspects of Chicago's Black Belt," showing the social and historical interest he had in the black community of Chicago.[23] He also composed a long bibliography on Chicago blacks, "Bibliography on the Negro in Chicago, 1936."[24] Richard Wright did such a good job that the Works Progress Administration asked him to edit essays written by members of the Federal Writers' Project. That honor aroused the jealousy of his Communist co-workers, who tried to have him fired for incompetence. But all their attempts failed.

The animosity that most Communists in Chicago felt toward Richard Wright materialized on May 1, 1936, May Day.[25] Wright had been invited to join the South Side Communist section for the traditional parade. But he was manhandled and thrown to the ground by two white Communists before the eyes of blacks, who made no attempt to intervene. That incident deeply affected Wright. He understood that the hope placed by the American black in the Marxist ideology was only a deceptive utopia.[26] A few weeks later, he was to declare before the Congress of Communist Writers from the central region of the United States, meeting in Chicago:

> There is among the petty bourgeois writers no class solidarity, no economic interests to preserve, no ideology or psychology to maintain. They have only themselves and that consciousness of themselves as being between two worlds, one rising and the other falling; and the consciousness that their values and hopes are receding. Therefore, the only expression possible in the initial stages is one of personal protest, or personalism.[27]

While trying to explain his attitude toward the world, Richard Wright had set forth the broad lines of existentialism. Nearly ten years before the philosophy of Sartre and Camus became known, Wright had named it "personalism."

In the spring of 1937, Richard Wright left Chicago for New York, where he worked as a reporter for the Communist newspaper, The Daily Worker, and participated in activities of the Federal Writers' Project. Shortly before his departure, the Chicago post office had offered him a good job, but Wright had decided to focus his future on his literary career.

In New York he lived in Harlem, where he met a young black man, Ralph Ellison, whose friend and literary adviser he became. Wright then decided to edit a new literary magazine, The New Challenge. He asked Ralph Ellison to write a critique of Waters Edward Turpin's book, These Low Grounds, for his magazine.[28] The first issue of The New Challenge appeared in November 1937.[29] It was to be the last one, because, for lack of money, Richard Wright could not continue its publication. That single issue of the magazine is important because it contains an essay by Wright, "Blueprint for Negro Writing,"[30] which is a program of action in Afro-American literature revealing a profound black revolutionary nationalism. Wright was not only determined to become a writer, but he had also outlined a plan of action for himself from the moment he arrived in New York. That plan, although little understood at the time, was to be followed literally more than thirty years later by LeRoi Jones.

In 1938 Richard Wright began to write Native Son and he went to settle in Brooklyn. He kept company with a number of whites because he knew that their aid would be invaluable to him for his future as a writer. Blacks could not give him the moral and intellectual support he needed to succeed in his chosen career. Still in 1938, he published a collection of four short stories, Uncle Tom's Children: Four Novellas.[31] Those stories, written in Chicago, were generally well received. From that time on, Paul Reynolds was Richard Wright's literary agent. He remained in that capacity until the author's death. Edward Aswell agreed to be his editor. He held that position until his sudden death in November 1958.

American literary circles began to talk about Richard Wright. He even had the pleasant surprise of receiving a letter from Eleanor Roosevelt, congratulating him on his work in Uncle Tom's Children and encouraging him to pursue his literary career. Those compliments arrived at the time when, thanks to a Guggenheim Fellowship, he was finishing Native Son. From the moment of its publication in March 1940, the novel, through its brutal force and its unreserved frankness, made Richard Wright an overnight success. A few months before, in August 1939, he had married a young, white divorcee, Dhimah Rose Meadman. She was a ballet dancer and a member of the Communist Party. Ralph Ellison had been the best man at Richard Wright's wedding.

But after spending a few weeks in Mexico in the spring of 1940, Wright realized the little affection he felt for his wife. She loved being served too much and believed herself superior to those around her. Since he had decided to end an unpleasant and meaningless union, Wright returned to New York alone. On the way, he stopped in Mississippi to visit his father, whom he had not seen since 1915. The stay in Mexico had allowed Wright to enjoy, for the first time in his life, an atmosphere free of prejudice against blacks.

Scarcely one year after his marriage to Dhimah Rose Meadman, Richard Wright obtained his divorce. A few months later, on March 12, 1941, he married Ellen Poplar, whom he had met before his first marriage. The new, white wife, of Polish-Jewish origin, worked for the Communist Party.

A collection of five stories, Uncle Tom's Children: Five Long Stories, had been published in 1940.[32] In addition to the four short stories of Uncle Tom's Children: Four Novellas, the book contained an autobiographical essay and another short story written in Chicago.[33] In 1941, Richard Wright wrote a novel, "Black Hope," which dealt with the economic and social changes encountered by blacks who pass for white. That novel was never published. In October of the same year, he published Twelve Million Black Voices: A Folk History of the Negro in the United States.[34] Richard Wright's text is illustrated with gripping photos by Edwin Rosskam. A play based on Native Son and written in collaboration with Paul Green, Native Son, The Biography of a Young American. A Play in Ten Scenes, also appeared the same year.[35]

On April 15, 1942, the first of Richard Wright's two daughters, Julia, was born in Brooklyn Jewish Hospital. World War II was going full swing, but Wright was not drafted. His family responsibilities and his good reputation as a writer had probably earned him the right not to endure the harsh racial segregation that was rampant in the American armed forces.

Toward the end of 1942 Richard Wright was, more than ever, on bad terms with the Communist Party, which had always mistrusted him because he was an intellectual. Two years earlier, Wright had declared that he had become a Communist out of desperation, and that Bigger Thomas, the hero of Native Son, was not Communist but, above all, American. He even added that he had chosen the title of the novel carefully with the sole aim of giving it a well-defined orientation.[36]

In April 1943, Richard Wright went to Fisk University in Tennessee to lecture. The students of the black university were very much interested in what he had to say about white segregationist laws. Richard Wright made the two-way trip by train and had to suffer the humiliation of racism as long as he was in the South. He could only eat his meals in the dining car hidden behind a curtain. After that trip, Wright firmly decided to finish the book on his childhood and his adolescence. This book was to be published in March 1945 under the title Black Boy: A Record of Childhood and Youth.

By 1944 Richard Wright had severed all his ties with the Communist Party. His affiliation with the Marxist movement had lasted more than twelve years. The excellent article written by Edwin R. Embree in 1944 predicted a brilliant future in literature for him.[37] Black Boy: A Record of Childhood and Youth, dedicated to Ellen and Julia Wright, was the

immediate confirmation of that expectation.[38] This autobiographical work
was a great success.   William Faulkner wrote Wright a warm letter.
Incensed by the blunt but nonetheless true descriptions in the book, the
white South reacted violently in the person of Senator Theodore Bilbo from
Mississippi. A symbol of the white hostile to every black intellectual, the
Senator declared on June 27, 1945, before the U.S. Congress:

> "It is the dirtiest, filthiest, lousiest, most obscene piece of writing that I
> have ever seen in print. I would hate to have a son or daughter of
> mine permitted to read it; it is so filthy and so dirty. But it comes from
> a Negro, and you cannot expect any better from a person of his type."[39]

Although influenced by racial prejudices, that diatribe against Wright had
also been partly caused by his Communist past.

During the summer of that same year, Wright spent a few weeks on
the island of Orleans, near Quebec, Canada. That stay in a foreign land,
like the one in Mexico, put him in contact with a new culture and led him to
take an interest in everything that was not American. Since he had not
been able to buy a farm in Vermont because of white racism and because
he had had a number of problems in New York for the same reason, he
gladly accepted an official invitation from the French government to come
to live for a few months in France in 1946. It was largely due to the
influence of Gertrude Stein, then living in Paris, that Richard Wright
received that invitation.   Their friendship had developed after Wright's
enthusiastic review of Wars I Have Seen in March 1945.[40]

Thus, from May to December 1946, Wright and his family lived in
Paris near the Boulevard Saint-Michel. They were treated as privileged
guests by numerous French admirers. That first trip across the Atlantic was
not without problems. Before even leaving American soil, Richard Wright
had had trouble obtaining his passport. Top-ranking officials in Washington
were suspicious of him, for they knew that once he arrived in France, he
would not hesitate to criticize America openly for its racial policy. The U.S.
embassy in Paris did everything possible to make him fully understand that
he would be well advised not to censure his country too severely.   The
mistrustful attitude of his government did not prevent him, however, from
enjoying   a   completely   new   life-style   in   France   and   from   better
understanding the complexity of human nature.

Before returning to the United States in January 1947, Richard
Wright spent three weeks in England. But no sooner was he back in New
York than he decided to go settle definitively in France. His wife, his
daughter, and he had again suffered racial insults. Wright knew that he had
discovered in Paris the only true face of human freedom and dignity. He
sailed for France in July 1947.

Several months after his return to France, in May 1948, Wright
bought a large apartment located at 14 rue Monsieur le Prince on the Left
Bank. He lived there in the Latin Quarter, near French writers and artists
he had met on his first visit. Since he did not wish to break all ties with his

American past, he enrolled Julia in the American school located near his home. His second daughter, Rachel, was born in the American hospital in Neuilly on January 17, 1949.

Richard Wright's literary production was in slow motion, for his life in exile tended to distract him from his work. In Paris, he helped to create the Société Africaine de Culture and its magazine, Présence Africaine: Revue Culturelle du Monde Noir. That excellent initiative pointed to a new international orientation on Richard Wright's part. Nevertheless, he published "The Man Who Killed a Shadow" in 1949.[41] That short story was the author's only work of fiction to appear since Black Boy: A Record of Childhood and Youth.

From the end of August to the end of September 1949, Richard Wright was, for the last time in his life, on American soil. He had gone back to shoot a few scenes from Native Son in the black ghetto of Chicago under the direction of the Frenchman Pierre Chenal. Since he had not seen the South Side in over twelve years, Wright was horrified by the poverty and the squalor he found there.[42] From October 1949 to July 1950, the writer finished the film in Argentina in order to go to Haiti for a brief stay afterward.

The film was a complete flop, not only because Richard Wright, then forty-one years old, played the role of the twenty-one-year-old hero, but also because many scenes were cut. These cuts corresponded with the anti-Communist climate which prevailed in America. An anti-Communist campaign, orchestrated by Senator Joseph McCarthy from 1950 to 1954, tried desperately to pursue and condemn American citizens who had been affiliated with the Communist Party. Since he felt like a target, Wright deemed it wiser not to return to the United States during that time.

As soon as he was back in Paris, he violently attacked the American influence in France. In an article published in 1951, "American Negroes in France," Richard Wright revealed the serious danger of Americanization the French population faced.[43] He declared that the five hundred or so black Americans then living in France could easily find the same racial attitudes there as in the United States. In his conclusion, Wright speaks of an organization of black Americans, the Franco-American Fellowship, whose essential aim is to better acquaint the French with the Afro-American. He emphasizes also that the defense of individual freedom is the main goal of the organization. A few years later, James Baldwin was to say that Richard Wright had tried in vain to ensure the success of the Franco-American Fellowship. For lack of enthusiasm and understanding, the organization had been short-lived.[44] James Baldwin maintains that black Americans could make good friends among the French on their own. This statement seems reasonable. The desire to see his brothers of color again indicated perhaps that Wright missed his native land.

The Outsider was published in March 1953.[45] Richard Wright had dedicated that novel to his youngest daughter in the following manner: "For Rachel my daughter who was born on alien soil." That dedication shows that Wright was feeling more and more alienated from, and even abandoned by, his fellow countrymen. Although he had been invited to come to New York for the publication of the novel, the only important work published in eight years, the author considered it safer to remain on French soil. He did not want to run the risk of being stopped and even arrested because of his former Communist activities. He did not relax, for all that, his struggle against the virulent racism of the American white. In "The American Problem--Its Negro Phase," an essay written at that time, but made public after his death, Richard Wright declared that the progress made by blacks in America was above all the result of violent denunciations by countries scandalized by the way the American black was still being treated.[46]

Since he was not living in the United States, Richard Wright could judge his country more objectively. He could also evaluate with complete freedom the decisions taken by the government in Washington with regard to blacks. He welcomed with very moderate joy the abolition of school segregation by the U.S. Supreme Court.

Eager to know the world better, Richard Wright accepted with great pleasure Kwame Nkrumah's official invitation to spend a few months in the Gold Coast, a British colony in West Africa. Kwame Nkrumah was the prime minister of that colony, which has become present-day Ghana. Thus, from June 16 to September 2, 1953, Wright had the opportunity to visit the land of his ancestors. Unfortunately, he contracted an amoebic intestinal disease from which he suffered intensely the rest of his life. In 1954, Black Power: A Record of Reactions in a Land of Pathos appeared.[47] This book dealt with Richard Wright's stay in Africa. That same year, a short novel, Savage Holiday, was published but went unnoticed.[48] In the fall of 1954 and in the following spring, Wright traveled for a few weeks in Spain before going to Indonesia, a former Dutch possession, to attend the Bandung Afro-Asian Conference in April 1955.

During the fall of 1955, Wright and his wife bought a little farm near Ailly, Normandy so that they could enjoy the calm and solitude of the country from time to time. The writer had to spend a great deal of time there alone in order to write his books without trouble or interruption. The Color Curtain: A Report on the Bandung Conference appeared in 1956.[49] His book on his travels in Spain, Pagan Spain, was published in 1957.[50] The same year saw the publication of a collection of essays, White Man, Listen![51]

Richard Wright was now constantly being criticized by the American press, which did not like to see a black American denouncing racism in America. In its issue of November 17, 1958, the weekly magazine Time published some compromising statements that Wright had never made.[52] The same year, an affair that had begun two years earlier and was known as the Richard Gibson affair was drawing to a close. Although he was not directly implicated, Richard Wright had had to help a very good friend, Ollie Harrington, who had been falsely accused of anti-French activities by Richard Gibson. Through his writings and his actions, Richard Gibson had divided the black American community in Paris into two camps, mainly concerning the Algerian conflict. The Algerian war was in full swing and foreigners living in France could not criticize the French policy in North Africa without risking expulsion. Richard Wright had always avoided getting himself into such a delicate situation. The Giblson affair brought him into conflict with the black American writer William Gardner Smith. Many friendships were broken as a disastrous result of that affair. The Central Intelligence Agency had apparently taken part in the dispute with the sole aim of silencing and even deporting American blacks who were too critical of the United States. That case made a great impression upon Wright, who had always felt himself a target of the American secret services since moving to Paris.

In autumn of 1958 he published a novel, The Long Dream, dedicated to Paul Reynolds and Edward Aswell.[53] Their encouragement and their advice had greatly helped the author during the writing of the novel, a period dominated by the Gibson affair.

Between March 1958 and February 1959, Richard Wright wrote one novel, Island of Hallucinations, only five episodes of which have been published until now.[54] This novel is a sequel to The Long Dream. It mixes reality with fiction and talks, for the first time, about Richard Wright's experiences as an expatriate. During the summer of 1959, the author sold his Normandy farm and his Paris apartment after having decided to go live in England with his family. Julia had obtained a scholarship from Cambridge University; that was probably one of the reasons that had caused Wright to want to leave France. He bought an apartment in the southwest suburbs of London, enrolled Rachel in the Lycée Français, and waited to obtain the visa that would permit him to settle definitively in Great Britain. But to his great surprise, his visa was refused. Was that one of the deplorable repercussions of Black Power: A Record of Reactions in a Land of Pathos, in which he had criticized the British government for its colonist policy in Africa? Or was it this time because of his provocative attitude toward the white world? No one can say.

Richard Wright returned alone to Paris, where he moved into a small apartment at 4 rue Rigis on the Left Bank. His wife and his two daughters remained in England so that the girls could finish the school year they had begun. According to Ollie Harrington, Wright was then barely liked by the American community in Paris.[55] The black Americans and even the Africans were constantly criticizing him. But since he did not lack friends, the writer spent nearly the whole spring and summer of 1960 at the Moulin d'Andé, on the banks of the Seine River, in Normandy. This property belongs to a French family, makers of the drink Virigoud, who take great interest in men of letters. More sensitive than ever, Wright was depressed by the suicide of a Swedish student, Bente Heeris, with whom he had corresponded for some time. Despite all the efforts made to prevent the girl from committing suicide, Wright learned of her death, which occurred on March 18, 1960. That Swedish girl had read all of Richard Wright's major works and was convinced that racism would never be overcome.

Between the late summer of 1959 and the spring of 1960, the author had become fascinated by Japanese haiku poems. While preserving the form of the line, Richard Wright composed more than four thousand of these poems, whose content he made personal and human. This new interest indicated that he was broadening a vast international education. In August 1960, he granted L'Express an interview and declared he had not the least desire to return to America.[56] He wanted to quash rumors about his wanting to return to his country. Saunders Redding, who had met him by chance in May of that same year, reported that Wright had admitted the failure of his exile as an artist. Redding thought he should perhaps return to the United States in order to make headway as a writer.[57] But Richard Wright had remained in France, where the value of, and the respect for, the individual were more important than anything else.

Julia went to join her father in September 1960. Very attached to her father, she decided to leave Cambridge for Paris, where she could just as easily continue her studies at the Sorbonne as at the British Institute. She is now living in Ghana, where her French husband works for a Ghanaian newspaper. Since she had promised Richard Wright, her father, to become a writer one day, it seems that she has kept her promise, because her writings have begun to appear.[58]

Between 1957 and 1959, Wright had written two radio plays, Man, God Ain't Like That . . . and Man of All Work, for Radio Hamburg. Highly successful, they were published in dialogue form in Eight Men in 1961, along with five short stories and an autobiographical essay by Wright.[59]

In 1960 Richard Wright had accepted an offer to write articles on jazz for the French recording company Barclay. Previously, he had translated and adapted a play by the French playwright Louis Sapin, Papa Bon Dieu, which he had entitled Daddy Goodness.[60] During the summer of that same year, he had started a novel, A Father's Law. But tired and suffering from the amoebiasis contracted in Africa in 1953, Wright entered the hospital on November 25, only to die there suddenly of a heart attack on November 28. On December 3, his body was cremated in Père Lachaise Cemetery.

Thus ended a life lived fully yet still full of promises. Numerous writings by the author, such as certain poems composed in the thirties, some blues, essays, novels, short stories, private diaries, and many letters, are waiting to be published. Moreover, only a few of his haiku poems are known to the public.[61]

NOTES

1. Richard Wright, Black Boy: A Record of Childhood and Youth (New York: Harper & Row, 1966). p. 84. (All other references to this book will correspond to this edition. First published in 1945.)

2. Black Boy p. 42.

3. Black Boy p. 112.

4. That is what Richard Wright says in Black Boy, p. 153. In The Unfinished Quest of Richard Wright (New York: William Morrow and Co., 1973), p. 42, Michel Fabre says that the name had been spelled "Vincent."

5. Richard Wright, "The Voodoo of Hell's Half Acre," Southern Register

(Jackson Mississippi), spring 1924. A short story, now lost, published in three installments. Exact dates of publication unknown.

6. Black Boy p. 184.

7. Henry Louis Mencken, Selected Prejudices (New York: Alfred A. Knopf, 1927) and A Book of Prefaces (New York: D. Appleton and Company, 1926).

8. Gertrude Stein, Three Lives (New York: The Grafton Press, 1909); Stephen Crane, The Red Badge of Courage (New York: D. Appleton and Co., 1926); Fedor M. Dostoevski, The Possessed (New York: The Macmillan Co., 1923).

9. Richard Nathaniel Wright, "Superstition," Abbott's Monthly, April 1931, pp. 45-47, 64-66, 72-73.

10. See Richard Wright, "I Tried to Be a Communist," The Atlantic Monthly, August 1944, p. 64, and the introduction, "Apropos Prepossessions", to Black Power: A Record of Reactions in a Land of Pathos (Westport, Connecticut: Greenwood Press, 1974), p. xi According to what Fabre says in The Unfinished Quest of Richard Wright, p. 103, it would seem that Richard Wright did not become a Communist until the end of 1933.

11. Wright, "I Tried to Be a Communist," p. 62.

12. Only eighteen of these poems have been published to date, all during the thirties.

13. The Works Progress Administration was, during the Great Depression of the 1930's, a U.S. government organization that helped jobless people find work. This organization was created as soon as Franklin Delano Roosevelt became President of the United States in 1933.

14. Richard Wright, Native Son (New York: Harper and Brothers, 1940). (First publication date.)

15. "I Tried to Be a Communist," p. 68.

16. "I Tried to Be a Communist," p. 69.

17. Richard Wright, Lawd Today (New York: Walker and Company, 1963).

18. Richard Wright, "Almos' A Man," Harper's Bazaar, January 1940, pp. 40-41. This part consists of the last two revised chapters of "Tarbaby's Dawn," written between 1934 and 1937 and first entitled "Tarbaby's Sunrise." Richard Wright subjected this part to slight revisions in 1960 before including it in Eight Men (Cleveland and New York: World Publishing Co., 1961) under the title of "The Man Who Was Almost a Man." In The Unfinished Quest of Richard Wright, p. 135, Fabre says that "Tarbaby's Dawn" deals with the childhood and adolescence of a future black boxer. Considering the time in which Richard Wright composed this novel, it is highly likely that the author was impressed by the stunning career of the black American boxer Joe Louis.

19. Richard Wright, "Joe Louis Uncovers Dynamite," New Masses, October 8, 1935, pp. 18-19.

20. Richard Wright, "Big Boy Leaves Home", in Alfred Kreymborg et al., eds., The New Caravan (New York: W. W. Norton and Co., 1936), pp. 124-158.

21. Paul Green, Hymn to the Rising Sun (New York: S. French, 1936).

22. The Federal Writers' Project, a part of the Works Progress Administration, tried to create federal jobs for unemployed writers.

23. Richard Wright, "Ethnographical Aspects of Chicago's Black Belt," New Letters 39 (Fall 1972): 61-68. Published for the first time in New Letters.

24. Richard Wright, "Bibliography on the Negro in Chicago, 1936," New Letters 39 (Fall 1972): 68-75. Published for the first time in New Letters.

25. This is the date given by Richard Wright in "I Tried to Be a Communist," p. 55. In The Unfinished Quest of Richard Wright, p. 138, Fabre says that the year was 1937.

26. So far the numerous biographical details have been largely based on the autobiographical writings of Richard Wright: Black Boy: A Record of Childhood and

Youth, "How Jim Crow Feels," "American Hunger," "The Man Who Went to Chicago," "What You Don't Know Won't Hurt You," and "I Tried to Be a Communist." The rest of this biography is in general based on the writings of Richard Wright, Richard Wright: A Biography (New York: G. P. Putnam's Sons, 1968) by Constance Webb, and The Unfinished Quest of Richard Wright by Fabre (note 4, above).

27. Constance Webb, Richard Wright: A Biography, p. 138.

28. Waters Edward Turpin, These Low Grounds (New York: Harper and Brothers, 1937).

29. The New Challenge: A Literary Quarterly 1 (Fall 1937). Ralph Ellison's review, "Creative and Cultural Lag," is on pp. 90-91.

30. Richard Wright, "Blueprint for Negro Writing," The New Challenge 2 (Fall 1937): 53-65.

31. Richard Wright, Uncle Tom's Children: Four Novellas (New York: Harper and Brothers, 1938). These stories are "Big Boy Leaves Home," "Down by the Riverside," "Long Black Song," and "Fire and Cloud."

32. Richard Wright, Uncle Tom's Children: Five Long Stories (New York: Harper and Brothers, 1940).

33. Richard Wright, "The Ethics of Living Jim Crow: An Autobiographical Sketch," and the story "Bright and Morning Star."

34. Richard Wright, Twelve Million Black Voices: A Folk History of the Negro in the United States (New York: The Viking Press, 1941).

35. Richard Wright and Paul Green, Native Son, The Biography of a Young American. A Play in Ten Scenes (New York: Harper and Brothers, 1941).

36. "Negro Hailed as New Writer," The New York Sun, March 4, 1940, p. 3.

37. Edwin R. Embree, "Native Son," in his 13 Against the Odds (New York: The Viking Press, 1944), p. 45.

38. Richard Wright, Black Boy: A Record of Childhood and Youth (New York: Harper and Brothers, 1945).

39. Congressional Record, 79th Congress, First Session, Wednesday June 27, 1945. In Thomas Knipp, ed., Richard Wright: Letters to Joe C. Brown (Kent, Ohio: Kent University Libraries, 1968), p. 16.

40. Gertrude Stein, Wars I Have Seen (New York: Random House, 1945). Wright's review is entitled "Gertrude Stein's Story Is Drenched in Hitler's Horrors," PM Magazine, March 11, 1945, p. m15.

41. Richard Wright, "The Man Who Killed A Shadow," Zero 1 (Spring 1949) :45-53. (First published in French under the title of "L'Homme qui tua une ombre", Les Lettres Françaises, 4 October 1946, pp. 1, 10).

42. Richard Wright gives his impressions on his stay in Chicago in "The Shame of Chicago," Ebony, December 1951, pp. 24-32.

43. Richard Wright, "American Negroes in France," The Crisis, June-July 1951, pp. 381-383.

44. James Baldwin, "Alas, Poor Richard," in his Nobody Knows My Name (New York: Dell Publishing Co., 1964), pp. 165-166.

45. Richard Wright, The Outsider (New York: Harper and Brothers, 1953).

46. Richard Wright, "The American Problem--Its Negro Phase," New Letters 38 (December 1971): 9-16.

47. Richard Wright, Black Power: A Record of Reactions in a Land of Pathos (New York: Harper and Brothers, 1954).

48. Richard Wright, Savage Holiday (New York: Avon Publications, 1954).

49. Richard Wright, The Color Curtain: A Report on the Bandung Conference (Cleveland and New York: The World Publishing Company, 1956). (First published in French under the title of Bandoeng, 1.500.000.000 hommes (Paris: Calman-Lévy, 1955).

50. Richard Wright, Pagan Spain (New York: Harper and Brothers, 1957).

51. Richard Wright, White Man, Listen! (New York; Doubleday and Co., 1957).

52. "Amid the Alien Corn," Time, November 17, 1958, p. 28.

53. Richard Wright, The Long Dream (New York: Doubleday and Co., 1958).

54. Richard Wright, "Five Episodes," in Soon, One Morning, edited by Herbert Hill (New York: Alfred A. Knopf, 1963), pp. 140-164.

55. Ollie Harrington, "The Last Days of Richard Wright," Ebony, February 1961, pp. 83-94.

56. "Entretien avec Richard Wright," L'Express, August 18, 1960, p. 22.

57. "Reflections on Richard Wright: A Symposium on an Exiled Native Son," in Anger and Beyond edited by Herbert Hill (New York: Harper and Row, 1966), p. 206.

58. Julia Hervi, "The Forget-For-Peace Program," Black World 22 (May 1973): 56-64. A political short story.

59. Richard Wright, Eight Men (Cleveland and New York: World Publishing Co., 1961). These writings appear in the following order: "The Man Who Was Almost a Man," "The Man Who Lived Underground," "Big Black Good Man," "The Man Who Saw the Flood," Man of All Work, Man, God Ain't Like That . . . , "The Man Who Killed a Shadow," and "The Man Who Went to Chicago" (auto-biographical essay). Richard Wright had grouped them in that order in 1960.

60. Louis Sapin, Papa Bon Dieu, a play in five tableaux, L'Avant-Scène, February 15, 1958, pp. 7-32. As Daddy Goodness, it was staged in 1968 at the St. Mark's Playhouse, New York.

61. Eight haiku poems were published in Harrington, "The Last Days of Richard Wright," pp. 92-93. These same poems were published under the title of "Hokku Poems" in American Negro Poetry, edited by Arna Bontemps (New York: Hill and Wang, 1963), pp. 104-105. Four haiku poems were published in Webb, Richard Wright: A Biography, pp. 393-394. Among "Fourteen Haikus," Studies in Black Literature 1 (Fall 1970): 1, only eleven are new. The ten haiku poems under the title of "Haiku," published in Fabre, The Unfinished Quest of Richard Wright, pp. 506, 513, are not new. Only twenty-three haiku poems by Richard Wright are known today.

2

CONDITIONS
IN THE SOUTH

THE HUMAN HELL

During his life, Richard Wright constantly attempted to make the world understand the lot reserved in America for the American black. For the author, the black American bourgeoisie can in no way represent the situation of the black American man of color. Richard Wright knew the special meaning that life had for the black masses from which he descended. His foreword to <u>Twelve Million Black Voices: A Folk History of the Negro in the United States</u> clearly indicates that Wright always worried about the poor and despised black majority, "that vast tragic school that swims below the depths, against the current, silently and heavily, struggling against the waves of vicissitudes that spell a common hate."[1] Wright was a member of that immense black crowd and wanted at all costs to have its history perceived in the purest and truest light possible.

The first two parts of <u>Twelve Million Black Voices</u> deal with Southern blacks. In the first part, "Our Strange Birth," the author speaks in simple but precise terms about the turbulent adventure of the African blacks taken by force to a country where they had to undergo a complete change of life-style.[2] Whence the idea of a metamorphosis or second birth on foreign soil implied by Wright in the title. In that first part, Richard Wright traces the history of black African slavery from its origins to the Civil War. He skillfully brings out the brutality with which the natives were treated when, from the seventeenth to the nineteenth century, they were taken to the New World. The author poignantly describes the long, hard Atlantic crossing to which they were subjected. He does not hide the fact that, for the white slave traders, the lives of the blacks had no human value. Only the profits to be derived from them mattered.

Once they arrived in America, blacks were subjected to hard labor on the Southern plantations. Only death could deliver them from such a nightmare. The poor whites with whom they rubbed shoulders were cleverly brought around to hating them by the landlords. This hate was caused not only by competition at work but also by all kinds of fabricated racial prejudices. Since they wished to reign supreme and they wanted to prevent any alliance between those two oppressed groups, the landlords had deemed it wise, from the beginning, to embitter, the relationship between poor whites and black slaves. Wright calls the landlords the "Lands' Lords." He indicates that, to reassure their troubled consciences, the "Lands' Lords" quoted verses from the Bible to prove the inferiority of blacks.   These verses still exert a great influence over the minds of puritanical whites. The author stresses the attitude of superiority white America has always had towards blacks in order to keep them in ignorance and in slavery

In this first part, Richard Wright shows how the conduct of the Southern landlords became a kind of sacred religion and how it was strictly forbidden for blacks to meddle with the order of things. Thus thousands of blacks were lynched in the name of the Christian God. But the emerging industry of the nineteenth century put an end to that atmosphere. Northern bankers, whom Wright calls "Patrons of the Buildings," had begun to worry about the role of the black slaves in a very imminent industrial future. According to the author, it was above all the industrial inventions of the nineteenth century that led a part of the white American population to challenge black slavery. Wright gives the impression that, without those inventions, the black slave's lot would not have changed. It was out of material necessity and not out of moral duty that America decided to revise its attitude toward blacks. This revision was not painless, since the "Lands' Lords" united and declared their independence in order to maintain cheap labor.

Wright said that if the Civil War lasted for such along time, it was because the North wanted to ensure a lasting future for its industry. The total crushing of Southern institutions was its sole guarantee. The North put an end to the three hundred years of black slavery because the economic future of the United States required it. The author thinks that, up to that point in the history of America, blacks played no important role. Wright implies that the Civil War was essentially a struggle between Northern bankers and Southern landlords. Charles Curtis Munz, in The Nation, rightly comments that such an insinuation simplifies a problem which in reality is very complicated.[3]

Completely stripped of his cultural heritage and all his possessions, the black American found himself, from 1863, free to do what he pleased. In "Inheritors of Slavery," the second part of Twelve Million Black Voices: A Folk History of the Negro in the United States, Richard Wright speaks of the turbulent history of the black American from the end of the Civil War to 1920.[4] This period was troubled because black Americans wanted to do something with their lives and because Southern whites believed them incapable, and opposed all their attempts. This negative attitude had one unfortunate consequence: most Southern blacks went from the condition of slaves to that of day laborers or sharecroppers. The term designating their social situation had perhaps changed, but their living conditions had not evolved. They had even worsened, since the freedom blacks now officially enjoyed jeopardized the social and racial equilibrium of the South. Wright does not conceal the truth on that subject. With his direct and brutal style, he is adept at contrasting the beauty of rural scenes with bloody lynchings. Thus he is able to explain the attitude of the blacks who, ignorant and fearful, remained on the plantations where they had always lived. Wright forcefully emphasizes how sacrosanct the power of the white world was in those days. The white world of the South did not allow its authority to be contested.

To survive in a hostile world, blacks constantly had to try to guess what was going on in the head of the white god in order to avoid incurring his wrath. Every white, whether a landlord or poor, became his mortal enemy as soon as he offended him.

Richard Wright explains that it was to escape this human hell that thousands of blacks, eager to enjoy their new freedom, moved aimlessly from one southern state to another toward the end of the nineteenth century and at the beginning of the twentieth. The author points out that these moves had their origins under slavery when the black family, as a family unit, did not exist. Since Southern whites then had seen in blacks only a source of profits, they had not hesitated to separate parents from their children. The father or the husband had no right to speak and had been, himself, separated from his family. Wright insists on emphasizing this condition of the past. He is convinced that it has contributed to reinforcing the image of the black man as a good for-nothing, unconcerned about his family obligations. This same situation, on the other hand, consigned the black woman to a primordial place within the black family and in American society.

According to the author, in order to survive after 1863, the black man was at the mercy of Southern whites. The role of farmhand which the white man let him play, with the possession of a few acres of land and a mule, was in reality a life contract since the black man was constantly indebted to his white creditor. He was always put in that situation by the white man and by the elements. The cotton that he cultivated made unlimited demands. Thus Wright compares cotton to a despotic and destructive queen because its cultivation rapidly exhausted the already poor lands of the blacks. The work required of black farmers was inhuman and impossible, because at that time they had to produce cotton for the entire world. Abandoned to their own fate, blacks were forced to lead a life of slaves in order to subsist. Before the Civil War, blacks had more or less lived in harmony with whites. After their emancipation, these same whites had decided to make them pay dearly for a war and dreams forever lost.

Rejected by a white world that had never wanted to recognize their human rights, blacks had created for themselves a world apart. Richard Wright explains how black language developed its distinctive character by giving a new meaning to words used by whites. The way those words were pronounced and the accompanying gestures contributed to forming the basis of an Afro-American language. This language was not well understood by whites, even if the words of which it consisted had a precise meaning. This way of speaking went hand in hand with a way of behaving that Southern blacks adopted toward whites, with the sole aim of concealing their true ideas and intentions.   Realizing that blacks lived in a world different from theirs, whites began to mistrust them.   This mistrust caused misunderstanding and often provoked bloody brawls and hideous lynchings. Wright speaks of the Ku Klux Klan and of various means it employed to humiliate blacks, particularly landlords' trick to provoke poor whites to anger toward blacks. The "Lands' Lords" were thus assured by all of respect for their power. The poverty and ignorance of blacks guaranteed the landlords a good economic return.   Whenever this guarantee was lacking, fear gripped them and blacks were the first to suffer from their anger.

Richard Wright says that, despite all these sufferings, blacks always held onto the hope for a better future. This future depended, in large measure, on the decisions taken by the American government. Now, the rigid segregationist laws of the South prevented federal aid from reaching the black man in his poverty. This destitution was made even more severe by the scientific discoveries that replaced cotton. At the beginning of the twentieth century, the invention of farm machinery deprived blacks of work in the fields, and many of them had trouble finding jobs in the South. Wright reveals that the Northern bankers bought large tracts of Southern land because the plantation owners were no longer in a position to exploit them. Industry had taken possession of the South through the intermediary of the Patrons from the North.

Besides the presentation of the state of the South at the beginning of the century, Wright indicates the feelings of anguish experienced by blacks. Unable to flee because they were very attached to their lands, most blacks remained on the spot. Deprived of any protection, blacks sought courage and comfort in their large families. Wright emphasizes, in fact, that the black family, however important it might be, was united and inspired a very special solidarity among its members. It also inspired an obvious veneration of the children for their parents. This state of affairs still exists in families that have remained in the rural areas of the Southern United States and gives significant insight into the present social milieu Black children did not have time to go to school because they helped their parents grow cotton. Hunger was the price paid by families if cotton was not picked on time. Thus, most Southern blacks remained illiterate long after their emancipation. If the children could attend school regularly, they still learned little because the black elementary schoolteachers knew almost nothing. Whites, at that time, discouraged the education of blacks by fair means or foul.   Granted that today the South has officially proceeded to integrate most of its schools, the fact remains that black and white pupils do not try to get to know one another because racism is so well implanted there.

Living continuously in the fear of brutal actions from the white world, blacks had found an escape and comfort in religion. They could thus give vent to their fears and their emotions in the shelter of their churches, and they could try at the same time to give a positive meaning to their wretched life. Far from the hatred of whites, they imagined a life in which human respect and dignity had a definite value. This religious faith permitted thousands of blacks to nourish the hope of a better future.

Before this future could manifest itself, the children decided to leave their parents and set out in search of a new life. This brand-new life was not at all attractive since it consisted in roaming aimlessly in the South. World War I put an end to this wandering by encouraging thousands of blacks to go to work in the factories of the North. Ending here, the second part of his book, Richard Wright does not stress the disastrous consequences this wandering life and the great rush to the North had on black families. Overnight, these families were scattered over the four corners of America. He does not say either that if many black sharecroppers became idle day laborers, the exhausted lands of the South were easy prey for the Patrons from the North who did not hesitate to apply their modern farming methods there. It followed that the black man could no longer come back to his plantation, for it would have been impossible for him to compete with farm machines. The North remained his only salvation.

In the first two parts of this book on the history of the black man in America, the author retraces, in detail and with emotion, the tumultuous adventure of the black American from his African origins to 1920. He accurately describes the way the American man of color was treated by Southern whites. The intimidations, vexations, insults, and brutalities of which he speaks are made even more vivid in an essay written in 1936, "The Ethics of Living Jim Crow: An Autobiographical Sketch."[5] This essay relates some of Wright's adventures in the South during his childhood and adolescence. The "Jim Crow" laws designate the way blacks were supposed to live and conduct themselves in the South. A simple infraction of these taboos can provoke the anger of whites and often cause the violent death of the black man. However young he was, Richard Wright had had to learn what to do or say in order not to anger whites. The anecdotes recounted in his essay, although very personal, are representative of the daily life of blacks in the South.

Thus, it is the role of black parents to see to it that their children behave according to the norms established by Southern whites. According to Richard Wright, the black man is born in an atmosphere in which the racial struggle is constant. He must learn very early to protect himself from a world that tries to control his life by all means imaginable. At the age of ten, when he was living in West Helena, Arkansas, Wright learned his first Jim Crow lesson. At that time, as still today, the railroad track was the line of demarcation between the white and the black community. Wright and his little friends liked to go near the railroad, where they could wage real, pitched battles against one another with smutty refuse. One day the white children who lived on the other side of the tracks provoked them. Assured by their experience and certain of their victory, the little blacks attacked with sooty trash. But their defeat was complete when the little whites responded by throwing pieces of broken bottles. Richard Wright suffered a head injury and had to get three stitches right away. His surprise was all the greater since he did not understand why the little whites had cheated by throwing broken bottles. He had not yet realized that he was a member of a race scorned by whites. That evening, when his mother returned from work and learned what had happened, she gave him such a fierce whipping that he fell sick from it. Although very surprising, this strange display of love is still common among black parents who prefer to take direct responsibility for teaching their children respect for the sacrosanct rules of Jim Crow life. They know that whites do not hesitate to suppress any black whose conduct is dangerous or even suspect.

Although young, Richard Wright was struck by the experience. He forever remembered that he should do everything possible not to provoke whites.

Some six years later, after having grown up within the black community, Wright went to look for work in a white town. Since he had lived far from whites for several years, his conduct had taken a very confident turn. But this conduct did not please his white employers. When he began to work for an optical goods business, he was sure of having a good future, since the boss had recommended him to the other two white workers. After a month, declaring that he had learned nothing, Wright asked his two white colleagues to teach him the trade. Their reaction was so violent that, for fear of being killed, Wright left his job immediately. After having brutalized and accused him of disrespect, the two white workers made it very clear to Wright that he had to content himself with what he had. Not only was he trying to surpass them in social rank, they said; he even took himself for white. Unwittingly, Wright had enraged Southern whites, for whom the black man was not supposed to be human and ambitious. Their anger had been all the greater since their jobs had been threatened by a black man who wanted to learn their trade. Segregation in the South does not allow blacks to learn trades reserved for whites; it demands that whites, first of all, obtain what they desire. The black who does not respect these rules often finds himself out of work and even closely watched by whites who consider him a dangerous individual. It is certain that Richard Wright's fate would have been quickly sealed if he had dared to stand up to the two white workers. That is why he left without giving the boss any explanation.

If the black man cannot fight against southern whites and thus affirm his manhood, it is impossible for him to protect his people from whites. When Wright worked in a clothing store in Jackson, Mississippi, one day he heard the boss and his son beating a black woman who had not paid her bills. When the poor woman, covered with blood, staggered out of the store, a policeman stopped her and locked her up forthwith for drunkenness and for public disturbance of the peace. It all happened without Wright's being able to say or do anything. Any intervention on his part would have cost him his job. The white policeman knew what had happened inside the store. He had apprehended the poor woman with the aim of protecting the white storekeeper's reputation. Whites, whoever they may be, do not hesitate to hide the truth and side with one another when one of their people is in the wrong with a black man. The law is white; it makes sure this is the way things will always be.

Wright, who was a messenger for the store, often went to deliver packages in the white suburbs of Jackson. One scorching hot midsummer day, a bicycle tire burst and he had to walk the rest of the way while pushing his bicycle. Some whites, passing by in a car, offered him a ride into town perched on the running board of their car. He gladly accepted this unexpected aid. But, for having simply said "no" to one of the whites who was offering him some alcohol to drink, Wright received a bottle of whiskey right in the face. He lost his balance and fell with his bicycle into the middle of the road. Before leaving him, the whites, crazed with anger, advised him to learn always to say "Mister" to a white man if he wanted to live long. In that affair, the whites' anger had been all the more intense because the young black man they thought they were doing a favor had not behaved according to the norms of the South. In view of his response given, they must have thought that Wright considered himself their equal or, worse still, was making fun of them.

If the black man must pay attention to what he says to the white man and force himself to be polite, the color of his skin makes him very vulnerable, especially when he is where he is not supposed to be. All his efforts can still fail to convince the white man of his innocence or of his good intention, because mistrust of the white man always works against him. Late one Saturday evening, when he had just finished his deliveries in a white neighborhood, Wright was stopped by some white policemen. He had to allow himself to be searched under the threat of their revolvers. The least resistance would have cost him his life. Disappointed at not having found any weapons on him, the policemen advised him not to venture alone any more into white neighborhoods after nightfall. The sole fact of being black had made Wright suspect and almost guilty of all the crimes imaginable in the eyes of the defenders of the law of the whites.

This tactic is still employed today by the American police which, in the South as well as in the North, wishes to assure itself that blacks remain where they live. The lack of trust and understanding between whites and blacks has always been at the root of sometimes brutal and bloody quarrels. Whites are especially afraid that blacks will suddenly invade their neighborhoods to spread terror and bring destruction there. This fear is due particularly to a guilt feeling experienced by the white man at the sight of the poverty and destitution in which he keeps most blacks.

The only way the white man can accept the black man is to deny him any human significance in order to consider him a savage. But here sexuality plays an important role, for the white man, believing he is sexually inferior to the black man, insists on doing everything to protect the purity of the white woman.   When Wright worked as a bellboy in a white hotel in Jackson, the white prostitutes often had him run errands and were scarcely concerned about their nudity when he entered their rooms. For them, he did not belong to the human race. One day he was called into the room of a white prostitute whom he found in bed with a white man. He had only just arrived when the young white woman got out of her bed stark naked to get some money from her dressing table. The woman naturally caught Wright's attention. But the white man, crazed with anger, ordered him to turn his head away. This reaction had been spontaneous, since in the eyes of whites the sexual desires of blacks are supposed to be bestial and can only defile the white race. The white man had acted with the object of affirming that the white woman belonged to him. Lack of confidence in himself, reinforced by rejudices of all kinds about the black race, had driven him to react violently against a young black man whose only mistake had been to look at the nude body of a white prostitute. If Wright had been white, the prostitute's client would have probably said nothing or would have perhaps yelled a dirty word at the white woman.

White men do not allow black men to go to bed with white women. Often, when such a thing is discovered, white women accuse the black man of having raped them. They thus avoid punishment by white men. The black man does not have that way out. He is either savagely beaten or, as in Richard Wright's time, lynched. In both cases, he has always paid dearly for any contact with the white woman.

If white men can do whatever they please to protect the virtue of white women, black men, on the contrary, can do nothing to defend black women from the sexual assaults of white men. In the eyes of white men, black women are lustful women without virtue. Wright relates that the police forced a black bellhop to marry a black maid under the pretext that he was the father of the child she was expecting. The child that was born had much lighter skin than that of his mother or the black bellhop. The incident did not surprise the amused whites who knew the father was a white man. Constantly enslaved and humiliated by white men, the black woman involuntarily makes her black companion suffer the grave consequences of her situation. The black man is diminished not only by white men but also by his female companion.

White men often make passes at black women, whether black men are with them or not. This attitude shows a total lack of respect on the part of white men toward black women, whom they consider only as sex objects. It would never occur to them to be polite and mannerly to a black woman. One evening, when Wright was coming out of the hotel with a black lady friend, the white night watchman gave the young woman a resounding slap on the posterior. Seeing Wright's amazement, the white man forced him, under threat of a revolver, to declare that he had nothing to say about what he had just seen. Since he knew that the white man had already killed two black men in so-called self-defense, Wright hastened to comply fully with the order. He knew that the white man would not have hesitated to kill him.

The various anecdotes of "The Ethics of Living Jim Crow: An Autobiographical Sketch" give an idea of the dangerous kind of life that the Southern black must lead every day. These are isolated incidents, but they accentuate precise situations in which the black man finds himself as a result of the segregationist policy and the prejudices of Southern whites. After declaring that "the theme of initiation into violence and escape from it is one Wright was obsessed with," Keneth Kinnamon adds: "This important essay is a powerfully compact statement of the theme."[6] These anecdotes have a much more striking effect than those related in Black Boy: A Record of Childhood and Youth. In this autobiographical book, which stops when Wright leaves Memphis for Chicago, the effect of these same anecdotes is attenuated by the author's narrative style.[7]

This is not to say that Black Boy is less convincing than "The Ethics of Living Jim Crow." In Black Boy, Wright describes forcefully and colorfully situations in which Jim Crow laws take pleasure in humiliating the black man and making him suffer. That is what prompted Dan McCall to write: "The villain in Black Boy is the depraved consciousness of the white community which has dwarfed itself into a snarling thing."[8] As soon as he arrived in Memphis, Wright was easily duped by a white and a black who used him to get what they wanted. While walking along the Mississippi, Wright had met a black man his age. Together, they had discovered, as by chance, in the grass bordering the river, a big flask containing alcohol. After finding a white buyer, they had left their find in his car in exchange for a five-dollar bill.

Under the pretext of going to get change for the money to be shared, Wright's friend had entered a store and disappeared. Wright then realized that he had played into the hands of a white man and a black man surprised to meet him near the coveted object. But what especially upset Wright was seeing that a white man could use a black to deceive another black man. In fact, the white does not hesitate to divide blacks in order to achieve his ends. The means used may be extremely varied, since the black man is not supposed to be human. In its excellent critique of Black Boy, Time showed a clear grasp of the problem: "It is the story of a man set apart from his own race by sensitivity and intellect, yet barred forever from the white race by the color of his skin."[9] In any case, it is clear that the black man can be easily humiliated by people of his own race without whites' being directly responsible for it. Howard Mumford Jones said concerning Wright: "His family and his friends do not treat him wisely because they do not know any better, and they do not know any better because they are forever cut off from graciousness, from culture, from universalism."[10] This remark may be applied just as easily to the mass of Southern blacks.

Shortly after his experience with the flask of alcohol, Wright learned to fear his race. He was working then for an optical goods company in Memphis. This small industrial establishment employed a dozen whites, the majority of whom hated blacks and did everything they could to humiliate them. Shortly, the black elevator operator in the building, gave them every reason to believe in the stupidity of the black race, for he let them kick him in the behind for a few cents. It mattered little what blacks thought, including Richard Wright, since his silly tricks brought him in some money. Now, his behavior deeply hurt the blacks around him and contributed to reinforcing the image of the comical and simple-minded black in the eyes of whites.

Many times Wright had asked Shorty to stop his degrading clowning for he knew he was intelligent. Shorty had ignored his pleas and continued to behave as in the past. As soon as he was in the presence of whites, the black man would adopt an attitude that assured him of both protection from whites and money. This dual personality, of which he was fully aware, permitted him to live safely in a hostile world.

Not content to make fun constantly of blacks, whites try to sow discord among them. As they do not recognize any human value in blacks, whites are happy when blacks destroy one another. Or at least such scenes are entertaining and very much appreciated. Wright's white foreman at the optical goods store in Memphis tried to provoke a knife fight between Wright and another black man, Harrison. Not having succeeded, he ended up persuading the two black men to fight in a boxing match by promising them five dollars a piece. The fight took place on a Saturday afternoon in the presence of whites eager to see two black men killing each other. After five long rounds, Wright and Harrison, their bodies bruised from blows, covered with blood, and exhausted from fatigue, were separated by the whites, beside themselves with joy. Before the fight, Wright and Harrison had promised each other to pretend to fight. They had not been able to keep their promise because, knowing nothing about boxing, they had been forced to defend themselves fiercely against the awkward and painful blows. Speaking of Wright, R.L. Duffus said: "He did not feel himself inferior, yet in order to survive he had to act the part of an inferior."[11] The white world had thus destroyed the little self-esteem that Wright and Harrison hoped to save.

The life of an inferior being, imposed on the Southern black by whites, gives him clearer insight into the world of which he is not a part, because he is observing it from the outside. Rejected by a society he hates, the black tries to understand it in its smallest details. Richard Wright explains that the white man at the optical goods establishment in Memphis who had lent him his library card was scorned by the other white workers because he was Catholic. He rightly says this white man understood blacks and felt pity for them because of his own situation. Although of different races, Richard Wright and that white man, Mr. Falk, were linked by a silent friendship in a hostile world.

If this Mr. Falk suffered because of his religion, Wright suffered because of his race and even had to lead a life completely unknown to the white world. For the black man to reveal his true feelings and his true attitudes to the white world is to commit suicide. In order to obtain the books he wanted to read, Wright had to play the white man's game by passing for a simple-minded black man: "Dear madam: Will you please let this nigger boy have some books by H L Mencken?" he had written so that the librarian, thinking that Mr. Falk had written the note would not suspect his intention.[12]

If Wright took refuge in reading to escape the world that oppressed him, most blacks often prefer to practice religion or give themselves over to sexual debauchery, alcohol, or drugs. Those are evasions used to flee reality. Whites approve of them since they do not threaten their world directly. On the contrary, whites are then assured that blacks are with their own kind. They do not wish for the white race and the black race to have anything in common. When he worked for the optical goods company in Memphis, Wright had quickly realized that it was impossible for him to talk about anything whatsoever with whites, except sex and religion. Otherwise, he would have caused trouble for himself:

> Among the topics that southern white men did not like to discuss with Negroes were the following: American white women; The Ku Klux Klan; France, and how Negro soldiers fared while there; French-women; Jack Johnson; the entire northern part of the United States; the Civil War; Abraham Lincoln; U.S Grant; General Sherman; Catholics; the Pope; Jews; the Republican party; slavery; social equality; Communism; Socialism; the 13th, 14th and 15th Amendments to the Constitution; or any topic calling for positive knowledge or manly self-esteem on the part of the Negro.[13]

One can understand that, in such a situation, the Southern black looks for a way out that will permit him to live the semblance of a normal life. That is why thousands of blacks left the South for the North during the twenties.

Before leaving, the Southern black had to get used to the idea of going to live in another white world. For him, all whites were dangerous. If he had already come across Northern whites in the South, he knew that the atmosphere of the North must have been different from that of the South. As accustomed as he was to Southern whites, the black man did not know how to behave with a white from the North. That is what happened to Wright when he suddenly left the optical goods firm in Jackson to avert a racial confrontation with two white colleagues. The boss, Mr. Crane, a Northern white, had wished to know the whole truth about the incident. Knowing that Mr. Crane was ready to punish the two white workers, Wright had found it wiser to say nothing. Never would a Southern white in Mr. Crane's position have thought of doing such a thing. If he had said anything whatsoever, Wright would probably have been killed by the two white men, as he knew perfectly well. Those are experiences similar to the ones that permit the Southern black to realize that Northern whites are different from those of the South. Southern Jim Crow laws require that blacks should always please whites. Any violation of this principle is considered a dangerous act. It was particularly the mystery surrounding this new kind of white from the North that prompted a great number of Southern blacks to leave for the North.

The different adventures of which Wright speaks in Black Boy: A Record of Childhood and Youth are personal experiences. They are the result of factors unfavorable to the Southern black, since the actions of whites have constantly succeeded in disorganizing his family life, in depriving him of a good education and making him live in poverty. One can understand why Lionel Trilling wrote: "Black Boy is an angry book. But the amount of anger that Mr. Wright feels is in proportion not only to the social situation he is dealing with; it is also in proportion to the author's desire to live a reasonable and effective life."[14] This book is laden with emotion and bitterness because Wright possessed, from the time he was very young, special intellectual qualities. Moreover, he was an excellent observer. It was the white world that, in its blind refusal to recognize those qualities, forced him to trust only himself and develop an unrelenting aggressiveness toward and against everything that was white. The main factor that caused Wright to write in such a manner was the memory of the fear he had experienced in the South. Ralph K. White said that "his hostility is rooted in anxiety his rage is rooted in fear," and this idea has also been stressed by such critics as Sinclair Lewis, George Mayberry, and Orville Prescott.[15] According to Wright, the black world as well as the white was incapable of understanding him and distrusted him. Repulsed by reality, Wright had to live in an isolated world all his own.

This isolation has led many critics, like David Littlejohn, to say, justifiably, that Wright had never understood blacks and whites well.[16] Yet they fail to explain the reason Wright was in such a situation. <u>Black Boy: A Record of Childhood and Youth</u> reveals that Wright's childhood and adolescence consisted of constant moving; the young boy never had a fixed address. The psychological instability that ensued is probably the reason that Wright was never able to get to know people of his race and whites. However, these critics' remarks cannot question the human value and the great literary importance of <u>Black Boy: A Record of Childhood and Youth</u>.

This book reveals the kind of life the Southern black has to lead. The author's aim was simply to confront America with the problem that it has always avoided, since it wanted to ignore its very existence. In order to make Wright's intention better understood, Ralph Ellison said, "He has converted the American Negro impulse toward self-annihilation and 'going underground' into a will to confront the world, evaluate his experience honestly and throw his findings unabashedly into the guilty conscience of America."[17] The fact that America had done everything to ignore its problem ends up being known by all. This bad deed still surprises the entire world.

One must not think, after a hasty reading of <u>Black Boy: A Record of Childhood and Youth,</u> that black Americans belong to a mysterious world apart. Whether they like it or not, black and white Americans constitute the same American family. Ralph Ellison understood and expressed the matter well when he stated, "Wright knows perfectly well that Negro life is a by-product of Western civilization, and that in it, if only one possesses the humanity and humility to see, are to be discovered all those impulses, tendencies, life and cultural forms to be found elsewhere in Western society."[18] Although he is an integral part of the Western world and American society, the black American is without any means of defense against the numerous threats that the majority of his white fellow countrymen carry out to silence him and keep him in slavery. One can understand why, at the end of his book, Wright exclaims: "But in what other ways had the South allowed me to be natural, to be real, to be myself, except in rejection, rebellion, and aggression?"[19] This heart-rending cry of despair and of anger is understandable because <u>Black Boy</u> is the tragic drama of a sensitive and tortured soul in search of a release. Wright found that release by leaving the South.

Blacks who have remained in the South must accept their condition if they do not wish to be annihilated by whites. In 1936 and 1937, Wright wrote one short story, "Silt."[20] The title evokes that thick, rich mud, alluvium, which every river leaves behind it after flooding waterside lands. In this short story, we are placed in the presence of a poor black sharecropper, Tom, all of whose possessions are destroyed by floods from the Mississippi. His barn and his hen-house have disappeared. All he has left is a cow. His little cabin has been damaged by the devastating waters and everything is covered with a thick layer of mud. His wife and little daughter have trouble recognizing their former home and do all they can to recover the few belongings spared by the disaster. Discouraged by such desolation, Tom decides simply to go find his white boss, Burgess, whom he owes nine hundred dollars. Since he is already in debt, Tom thinks he cannot manage on his own. He could run away, but his wife encourages him not to do such a thing. Crushed and defeated by the elements, Tom allows himself to be easily enslaved by the white world. His total submission to the omnipotence of whites continues as in the past. Without the priceless help of the white man, he says, how could he get himself a horse to pull the plow, food for his family and seeds for sowing time.

Here we have the typical image of the simple, unenlightened black man, that most American whites still like to see, and for good reason. Tom plays the role of Uncle Tom. When he makes the decision to go see Burgess, he is convinced that he has no choice and that he has no other way out except contracting more debts. Burgess's sudden arrival imposes the implacable will of the white world on the life of this poor black family. Tom leaves with his white boss to go buy some food on credit. This short narrative is the simple story of the Southern black sharecropper, who must, aimlessly, start his wretched life in an ungrateful, inhuman world over and over again. James Baldwin said about him: "There is nothing funny about 'The Man Who Saw the Flood,' which is as spare and moving an account as that delivered by Bessie Smith in 'Backwater Blues'."[21] It is precisely this type of experience that has enabled blues to give the Southern black man's life a deep meaning.

If Tom does nothing to change his condition, Dave Saunders, in "The Man Who Was Almost A Man,"[22] does not hesitate to go into action in order to escape the environment that is oppressing him. This narrative is the story of a seventeen-year-old black man, who, stifled by the atmosphere of the South, decides to leave for the North. The action takes place at the end of a long summer during which young Dave Saunders has worked without spite on the estate of a white man, Jim Hawkins. His work has consisted of plowing the fields. But the young black man is not happy because he knows that nobody takes him seriously because of his age.

The blacks with whom he works as well as his parents treat him like a little child. His parents do not even let him have part of the money he has earned by the sweat of his brow.

Determined to assert his personality, young Dave decides one evening to buy a pistol. He thinks the possession of a firearm will make him respected by all. He succeeds in extracting the necessary money from his mother by using more or less valid arguments. He knows that his father, Bob, would be violently opposed to the acquisition of a weapon, for he is the very type of Southern black who is submissive to the laws of whites. Here Wright emphasizes the fact that any possession of a firearm by a Southern black is already a challenge to the omnipotence of the white world. Dave Saunders merely sees in the pistol the mark of his personality that everyone refuses to recognize. If his intention is simple, it is also understandable, for he wishes to assert himself with regard to all.

Just a few hours after buying the pistol, Dave Saunders cannot prevent himself from firing a shot. He is then in the fields, at the edge of a forest, far from everyone. His only witness is Jenny, the old mare hitched to the plow. But, since he does not know how to hold his weapon properly, the young black man mortally wounds the mare, which belongs to Jim Hawkins. Although this is an accident, it turns out that Dave has unwittingly taken revenge on the white man. Later, unsuccessful in convincing his parents and the whites that the mare is dead because she fell on the plow share, the young black man finds himself in an uncomfortable situation. Not only does he know his father is going to beat him, but also Jim Hawkins tells him he will have to work for him free for two years in order to pay the price of the slaughtered animal.

Since he no longer wishes to suffer such insults, the young black man decides to run away. In the middle of the night, he leaps into a train bound for Chicago. Dave Saunders thus leaves an infernal situation that could have cost him his freedom and his dignity as a man. The pistol he has on him is all he takes. Wright seems to suggest that this firearm is the key to a new life in which oppression and tyranny have no place. If James Baldwin said that "The Man Who Was Almost a Man" possessed: "a dry, savage, folkloric humor," he also emphasized that this short story and "The Man Who Saw the Flood" "made me think of human loss and helplessness."[23] The sudden flight of Dave Saunders towards the North shows that this is the only means at the Southern black's disposal in order to extricate himself from an environment that has always wanted to possess him body and soul.

DESTRUCTIVE REALITY

If the Southern black takes to his heels in order to escape a humiliating situation, it is because whites watch him all the time and do not permit him to show any initiative whatsoever. All actions or words running counter to the views of the white world are immediately repressed by force, going as far as destruction. The Southern black man lives constantly in fear. His life and his belongings may be destroyed at any minute as the result of a fit of anger on the part of whites. He leads an existence whose future is always uncertain. It is not surprising that, crushed by an environment that scorns and hates him, the black man revolts, sometimes violently, in order to assert his existence. Although such rebellions are rapidly quelled by the white world, the black man experiences, in spite of everything, the satisfaction of having disturbed the social equilibrium of the South nonetheless, if only for a few minutes in a determined place. That is important because he is becoming more and more aware of it.

The five stories of Uncle Tom's Children: Five Long Stories reveal a new black man to white America.[24] As the title indicates, the individuals of whom Richard Wright speaks are the children of Uncle Tom; they belong to a new generation in the South that no longer wishes to be enslaved by the white world. The black man we discover there is not passive and inactive like Tom in "The Man Who Saw the Flood"; he goes into action. Keneth Kinnamon said: "Violent conflict, both physical and psychic, between the races is Wright's special subject, and in Uncle Tom's Children this subject is presented with an immense dramatic immediacy."[25] In these five stories, Wright permits his characters to act in several ways. In the first three, "Big Boy Leaves Home," "Down by the Riverside," and "Long Black Song," the heroes react with rage. In the fourth, "Fire and Cloud," the main character compels recognition because of his religious faith, while in the fifth, "Bright and Morning Star," the hero stands out because of his patience and his political ideology.[26] The human qualities that one finds in the last two stories present a striking contrast to the violence of the first three. We have here some events Wright witnessed during his youth and which bring to light the hard and turbulent life of the Southern black. This life is full of dangers, yet made up of hopes and disappointments too.

In "Big Boy Leaves Home," Wright introduces certain autobiographical elements having to do with his Mississippi childhood. Although written in 1935, this story recreates with precision the atmosphere in which Wright grew up. In the beginning, we are confronted with four young blacks who are playing hooky from school. The afternoon is hot and they are having fun in the country. Their songs and their wild races are directly inspired by the experiences of the author, who, when he lived in Jackson, loved to caper about in nature with his little friends. He had become the leader of a gang, the Dick Wright Clan. In "Big Boy Leaves Home," one can easily identify young Wright in the person of the hero, Big Boy, who is the undisputed leader of the little gang. The joyful frolics of the four blacks take them to the edge of a stream located on property belonging to a dreadful white man, Harvey. Unable to resist the temptation, the four friends take off their clothes and dive stark naked into the cool water.[27] A few minutes later, they are surprised by the arrival of a young white woman, Bertha, who, shocked to see four blacks completely nude, begins to scream with terror. As she finds herself beside the little black boys' clothes, she is all the more horrified when Big Boy and Bobo, another one of the boys, approach her in order to recover their garments. The other two black boys, Buck and Lester, do not have the time to join them because they are shot down. Deeply distressed and not knowing what to do, the young woman had called her fiancé, Jim, Harvey's son. Realizing that the white man also wants to kill them, Big Boy and Bobo rush at him, grab hold of his weapon and, terrified by his threats, kill him point-blank before fleeing as fast as their legs can carry them.

Those senseless murders have their origins in the prejudices of Southern whites. Why, otherwise, pitilessly kill innocent victims whose only crime is to swim in a forbidden place? Jim Harvey kills Buck and Lester for two precise reasons, which, in his eyes, justify the legal aspect of this massacre. First of all, the nudity of the four blacks offends Bertha; then the sacrosanct virtue of the white woman is endangered by the proximity of those blacks. The presence of a white woman alone with blacks, unable to hide their sex from her eyes, creates a situation of which Southern whites have always been afraid because of the dangers it represents. In fact, whites do not tolerate white women being touched by black men, let alone their being forced to have sexual relations with them. That is why Jim Harvey, who rushed to his fiancée's aid, thinking she risks being raped, shoots Buck and Lester in cold blood. He probably would have killed Big Boy and Bobo if he had not been cut down himself. Big Boy and Bobo fight him merely to protect their lives. They know that if they do not succeed in killing the white man, they will suffer the same fate as Buck and Lester.

The four blacks attacked by Jim Harvey are only children. But because of the color of their skin, the white man does not hesitate to shoot them. He could have thought he was dealing with young adolescents taking advantage of a beautiful hot day. It is the prejudices of Southern whites that suddenly create an infernal situation for Big Boy and Bobo. This new situation has disastrous consequences on these two young blacks' lives, which up until then has been peaceful. Furthermore, the black community of their city must incur the rage and violence of whites who want to avenge the death of one of their people.

As soon as he is back home, Big Boy tells his parents everything. The scene described here by Wright is very important because it emphasizes the lack of respect, indeed, the hate, that blacks feel for whites. Big Boy's father does not reproach his son for having killed a white man. Wright's aim is to show that, in the South, blacks and whites live side by side but do not consider one another as human groups capable of cooperating and appreciating one another. If, for whites, blacks are inferior and limited beings, for blacks, whites are hideous and monstrous beasts. Saunders Redding fully understood the role played by Big Boy in Wright's work as a whole when he wrote:

> . . . in Big Boy . . . he has already created the prototype of all his heroes, who were ever to be hungry, bitter, vengeful, violently hurting themselves against the walls that barred them from a life that they knew was a better life than theirs, belonging to people no better than

themselves.[28]

This story, in fact, announced the attitude that Wright was to have all his life toward the white world

But if Big Boy is scolded for having played hooky from school, his father asks his assurances that he has not touched the white woman. So it seems that Bertha's presence and the black children's attitude towards her are more important to the blacks than the murder of Jim Harvey. The blacks attach a great deal of importance to respect for the white woman, who, in many cases, is at the root of their misfortunes. They know the leading role played by the white woman in white society, which venerates her like an idol and fiercely defends her from black men.

Since he must make a decision quickly, Big Boy's father consults his friends. He wants their advice, for they all belong to the same religious sect and thus form one big united family. After a few discussions, it is decided that early the next morning, Big Boy will board a truck, driven by the son of one of them, to go to Chicago. This type of impromptu and secret meeting is typical of the South. In that part of the United States, religion plays a primordial role in the life of blacks, harassed and oppressed by the white race. It is often under the shelter of religion that blacks are able to support one another in order to fight against the white world. Big Boy is lucky to profit from the experience and wisdom of his elders. Predicting the whites' reaction, they make him leave his parents' house as quickly as possible. They advise him to go hide in a disused furnace located near the road where the truck is to pass.

Big Boy has to kill a snake before slipping into his temporary refuge. It seems that the world around him has suddenly formed a league against him and wishes his death. The black adolescent's earthly paradise is annihilated by the appearance of a woman and the savage attack of a serpent. Wright probably wanted to use these biblical symbols to show that his hero's innocence is confronted by a savage and cruel reality. Big Boy witnesses, powerless, the monstrous lynching of his friend Bob. The latter, in his attempt to come and join him, has been intercepted by whites thirsty for vengeance. The calm and pleasant life enjoyed by Big Boy in the South until then becomes an unbearable nightmare, and he hears a white man say that fire has been set to his parents' house by way of reprisal. To avoid discovery, Big Boy has to strangle a dog, which had sensed his presence and jumped into his hideout. As night has fallen and it is raining, the whites stop their search. The author establishes a very literary relationship between the changes occurring in the elements and those noted in Big Boy's life. This relationship brings out and clarifies the state of mind of the young man, forced to spend the rest of the night in his hole, which has been transformed into a filthy mess. Early the next morning, the young black man boards the truck that takes him to a new life in the North. Unlike Dave Saunders in "The Man Who Was Almost a Man," the hero of "Big Boy Leaves Home" knows that he has no choice: if he wants to live, he must leave the South right away. Violence and flight are closely linked here; these two elements show how narrowly Wright's hero escapes a brutal death.

Southern whites take it out on all blacks, no matter who they are. If in "Big Boy Leaves Home" we are dealing with an adolescent, in "Down by the Riverside" the hero is the father of a family who is killed in cold blood by whites for having tried to save the life of his pregnant wife. This story, written in 1936, accurately recreates, indeed, a situation aimed at destroying a black man. The action takes place during devastating floods from the Mississippi. Blacks as well as whites are affected by this natural disaster. But, the first ones to suffer the grave consequences of such an upheaval are blacks. In addition to ensuring the protection of their families, they are forced by whites to combat the rising waters and give assistance to isolated white families. This is the case with Mann, who must not only struggle relentlessly against nature, but also face the hostility of the white world.

Since his wife, Lulu, is about to have a child and is suffering enormously, Mann is taking her to the hospital in a small white boat stolen by his brother-in-law. This frail craft belongs to a white man, Henry Heartfield, well known for his deep hatred of blacks. Mann, whose cabin is about to be engulfed in the waters, does not hesitate to brave the dangerous waves hoping to save his wife's life. He promises himself to return the boat to its owner as soon as he has left Lulu at the hospital. On the way, he has to kill Heartfield, who, having recognized his little white boat, opened sustained fire on its occupants. Heartfield and his family, for lack of a boat, had not been able to leave their house and had remained prisoners of the waters. Utterly distressed by this murder, committed in self-defense, Mann reaches the hospital too late; his wife is already dead. He has lost his wife and the child she was carrying.

At the hospital, whites hold them in low esteem, with no compassion whatsoever. Mann is a black man, thus half human, half animal. Keneth Kinnamon said on this subject: "Racial prejudice emerges constantly in the story when the two races meet or think of each other. Communication between the races is thus difficult or impossible because whites simply will not listen to blacks, preferring instead to consign them automatically to a category of subhuman stereotypes."[29]

There is no human relationship between blacks and whites. Mann is requisitioned by the whites to fight the waves and particularly to help transport white families to the hills close by. He is fated to be sent to search for Henry Heartfield's wife and two children in a motorboat. Recognized by them, he is summarily judged and condemned to be shot.

Although Mann's second encounter with the Heartfield family is surprising, it is clear that Wright wanted to show the omnipotent influence exercised by whites over blacks. No matter what he does and wherever he may be, the black man is constantly at the mercy of whites. The little white boat, which turns up at the beginning of the short story, predicts already an uncertain and dangerous future for Mann and his family. The color of the craft indicates its origin and its ownership. It is white and the world it belongs to is white. It works towards destroying all the hopes and good intentions of a black man who ends up being charged with theft and murder by the whites. Mann is deeply religious and aware of his family and social responsibilities. But the environment in which he lives refuses to recognize these qualities in him and treats him like an inferior and dangerous being. Kinnamon emphasizes that "'Down by the Riverside' thus demonstrates the failure of both religious faith and pragmatic individualism in coping with white oppression."[30] The white general who condemns him to death does not consider the risk Mann took in going to give assistance to Mrs. Heartfield and her two children. The white world rejects every human aspect of the behavior of a black man exhausted by fatigue and overcome with grief. Mann's physical condition and his state of mind reflect the tearing of the elements, which, in their violence, do not know where they are going or when they will stop. As in "Big Boy Leaves Home," the author establishes, here too, a comparison between the unleashed elements and Mann's helplessness and his vein of feeling.

If Mann succeeds in braving nature in order to take his wife to the hospital, he is defeated by the implacable attitude of the whites. In one sense, this short story marks a distinct evolution in the Southern black's condition in comparison to "Big Boy Leaves Home." Big Boy flees whereas Mann accepts his destiny after confronting and conquering the unbridled elements of nature. He showed that he could do something that whites considered impossible. His name, Mann, is symbolic. Whether they like it or not, the whites confer the title "man" on him each time they call him by his name.

Far from letting the whites determine the time of his execution, Mann chooses the moment of his death by starting to run with all his might. He is immediately riddled with bullets. Fully aware of the consequences of his act, Mann commits it with complete freedom. Master of his fate, he says to himself: "Gawd! they were going to kill him, Yes, now, he would die! He would die before he would let them kill him. Ahll die fo they kill me! Ahll die."[31] Wright's interpretation is existentialist. In deciding on the time of his own death, the black man acquires a manly quality that whites have always refused him. He does not give whites the almost sadistic pleasure of playing with his life as they please.

The same theme is repeated in "Long Black Song," with the difference that the hero, Silas, kills a few whites before perishing in the flames of his cabin. This story, written in 1936, shows that the black man can be humiliated by his own race. It is Silas's conduct that leads his young wife, Sarah, to be unfaithful to him with a white transient. Wright presents in the person of his hero a black man who, in order to compete with whites, is forced to neglect his wife. Thus, Sarah's infidelity will be partly justified.

The action takes place in the summer. Sarah is alone in her cabin with her baby. Silas has been away for a week already selling his cotton to the whites. The image of Sarah presented by the author is that of a being influenced by the regular movement of nature. This black woman has always known the country and the graceful change of the seasons. She is dreamy and her simple soul is inclined to give free rein to her desires. When the action begins, the sun has just set. Sarah is thinking about a certain Tom, whom she always loved, when she is suddenly diverted from her daydreaming by the arrival of a young white traveling salesman, who wants to sell her a record player. After learning she is alone, he seduces her. Before leaving, he tells her he will come back early the next morning to receive payment for the phonograph.

Since she has always lived in the country, Sarah is impressed by the record player the white man wants to sell her. This appliance is something she has never seen and which arouses her curiosity. The white salesman appears to her like a being from another world, and the attention he pays her surprises her because he is white. This would explain the slight resistance she offers to his advances. Here Wright wishes to emphasize the great cultural difference which exists between a poor and simple-minded black woman living in the country and a young white man from a modern urban environment. In the story Wright brings out the solation and ignorance of a young black woman, who, outside her rural experience, knows nothing about the world. She has always led a life of leisure and the men she has met have known how to arouse her natural instincts, which would explain her pronounced taste for sex and also the way she yields to the white salesman. Keneth Kinnamon believes that Sarah's conduct gives "Long Black Song" a distinct aspect. He remarks:

> Sarah is unlike the protagonist of the other stories in Uncle Tom's Children: she does not participate directly in interracial violence. Indeed, she not only participates in interracial sexual intercourse, but she also has vague notions of interracial amity within a harmonious natural order.[32]

According to Kinnamon, it would seem that the future of race relations in the United States would depend greatly on the role played by the black woman. Malcolm Cowley, however, does not like "Long Black Song" precisely because of the way Richard Wright describes, in a colorful and bombastic style, the scene in which the young white man seduces Sarah.[33]

Considering these two contrasting remarks, one can say that the conduct of a character such as Sarah could, in the long run, improve race relations between blacks and whites. But even then the racial climate would have to be free of today's hatred and violence. Moreover, the black race and the white race should, above all, learn to respect each other if they wish to guarantee their harmony a lasting future.

A few hours after the white man's departure, Silas arrives. Although it is the middle of the night, he is proud to inform his wife that he has indeed sold his cotton and has even bought four acres of land. He shows Sarah the cloth and the shoes he has bought her. But he is not long in discovering what has happened during his absence. In his rage, he breaks the record player and beats Sarah with a whip. Escaping the blows, she takes her baby and goes to hide in the countryside. Early the next morning, the white traveling salesman comes back with a male friend to get paid. He is shot down in cold blood by Silas. His friend flees and goes to inform the whites in the vicinity.

Since she has witnessed the scene, Sarah goes to find her husband in order to try to convince him to take flight. Instead of treating her rudely, he makes it clear to her that he is determined to stay where he is and face the whites. He has realized that his wife is not guilty of adultery with the white man. He now knows that the white world controls blacks and is at the origin of all the ills that afflict him. That is why Edwin Burgum says, "His hatred turns away from his wife, whose offense he now sees has been imposed upon her by the social system he had accepted and expected to profit by."[34] Silas is convinced he must show his anger and take revenge on the white world. His firmness and determination prevent Sarah from further pleading, and she returns to the country. Silas awaits, like a worthy and resigned man, the inevitable consequences of the murder he has just committed. Through that determination he finally enjoys free choice, which the white world has always forbidden him. He can give his death a deep sense of human dignity.

When the whites arrive, he exchanges gunfire with them and succeeds in killing one of them before fire is set to his cabin. Instead of fleeing the flames and risking a lynching, Silas prefers to stay home and be burnt alive. He does not allow whites to satisfy their cruelty. By choosing his death, the hero shows the whites that every black man is capable of freely choosing his fate. Although this death is an end in itself, it indicates that the black man can refuse whites what he wishes.

If the first three stories of Uncle Tom's Children are marked by extreme violence, "Fire and Cloud" points to a new phase in the evolution of the Southern black's condition. Big Boy, Mann, and Silas are plunged into tragedy because, to begin with, they have committed an error. The first one is caught on private property. The second uses a stolen boat. The third neglects his wife. In "Fire and Cloud" the hero has not sinned. His innocence contributes greatly to the total success achieved over the whites. This short story, written in 1936, shows that the black man can make whites respect him by placing his confidence in his brothers of color and in religion.

"Fire and Cloud" is the eventful story of a Southern black pastor, Dan Taylor, in search of food for his faithful. The action takes place in the early thirties, a time when America was undergoing a serious crisis. Dan Taylor has done everything to help the five hundred or so blacks of whom he is in charge. But the office of public welfare and the municipal authorities have categorically rejected his urgent requests. If the members of his congregation suffer from lack of food, Dan Taylor also knows that more than three thousand poor whites are in the same situation. Not understanding why they do not want to listen to him, he does not know what to think. The Communists want him to encourage his members to join the poor whites in demonstrating against the white city officials. But Dan Taylor is a religious man to whom violence makes no sense. He understands, however, that his members are desperate and ready to do anything to obtain something to live on.

He realizes the extreme seriousness of the situation when the mayor, the chief of police, and the director of an anti-Communist organization come to his home to assure themselves that the blacks are not going to demonstrate.   Or at least, they demand that he ask his church members not to do anything. Dan Taylor does not give them complete satisfaction, for he knows that blacks will not be able to tolerate this situation very long. As he is the spokesman for the black community, Dan Taylor is aware of his heavy social responsibilities.   He does not intend to play the role of Uncle Tom in a situation on which hundreds of black lives depend. He is sure that the presence of the whites in his house is partly due to Deacon Smith. Knowing that some Communists have seen Dan Taylor, this deacon openly criticizes the pastor before the assembly of the elders. His aim is to have Dan Taylor relieved of his religious duties. Deacon Smith, in fact, is afraid of violence and any confrontation with the white world. That is why he warned the white city officials that the blacks were planning to go into action. In so doing, he plays the role of Uncle Tom and has become a Judas by betraying his religious leader.

Shortly after his meeting with the mayor, Dan Taylor is abducted by whites, who take him to the countryside, insult him, and savagely beat him with a whip. If words do not succeed in convincing the black pastor, the mayor hopes to make him change his mind through violence.   But the baptism of fire and blood that Dan Taylor receives at the hands of his white torturers succeeds only in making him better understand the strength and the wisdom of the soul.   Wanting then to use the power of the black masses, Dan Taylor does not hesitate to lead his church members towards city hall.   On the way, the poor whites swell the ranks of the black demonstrators. A while later, the mayor, both sheepish and shameful, comes to Dan Taylor to ask him to stop the demonstration and promises him the food desired.

The success achieved by Dan Taylor is due especially to his religious faith and the confidence he has in his people.   When he exclaims, "Freedom belongs to the strong!", the black pastor shows that he has finally understood that the black man can play an important role in American society.[35] This cry, full of joy and pride, indicates that the black man is resolved no longer to give in to the white world's demands. If Dan Taylor succeeds in getting what he wants through peaceful means, he has, nevertheless, turned a religious duty into a political one. It is after having been brutally beaten by whites that he can identify God in oppressed and persecuted people. The decision to demonstrate will have a religious as well as a social meaning.

Although the union of blacks and whites is, in reality, very unlikely, Wright wished to show in "Fire and Cloud" that it is because of the black pastor's action that the poor people of the city, without distinction of race, can finally obtain satisfaction. It is through this demonstration that the blacks succeed in making the white city officials bend. Proof that blacks can change American politics through strong and united pressure is a direct result of Dan Taylor's action, born of a racial conflict and an economic necessity. To attain this goal, Wright does not advocate violence, but rather a religious union among blacks. According to the author, the success achieved by blacks has nothing to do with the Communist Party. It is religion that plays the important role and Keneth Kinnamon is wrong to say that Dan Taylor "moves from religious resignation to social action. As always in Wright, the futility of religion is emphasized in 'Fire and Cloud'."[36] On the contrary, Wright wishes to stress in the short story the primordial role of religion, which it has always enabled blacks to give a perfectly meaningless life a positive meaning.

If the white forces of order had received orders to resist the demonstrators, it is likely that Dan Taylor would have encouraged his members to stand up to the enemies. The aim of the decision to march on city hall is to show that blacks want to make their presence felt with calm and dignity. Jimmy, the black pastor's son, is the opposite of his father and thus ready to move directly to violent action. He is dissuaded from doing anything at all by his father who knows that nothing positive can be born of anger. Jimmy is the perfect type of the young black militant of the sixties, who, by word and deed, succeeded in making it clear to white America that the order of things must change at all costs. In his description of Dan Taylor and of Jimmy, Wright presented two types of blacks who were going to change America's way of living and thinking in the years to come. In fact, during the sixties, Martin Luther King's conduct closely resembled Dan Taylor's whereas Edridge Cleaver and H. Rap Brown played the role that Wright assigned to Jimmy.

This awareness of the social and political role of the black man in "Fire and Cloud" marks a decisive evolution in the first four stories of Uncle Tom's Children. Big Boy, Mann, Silas, and finally Dan Taylor find themselves more and more involved in their social struggle as Richard Wright presents them. Each stands out more victorious than his predecessor because he acts in a group and not in isolation. If the flight of Big Boy is a victory in itself, the total success achieved by Dan Taylor has positive results on a Southern black community.

Although closely resembling "Fire and Cloud," the fifth story of Uncle Tom's Children, "Bright and Morning Star," does not have the same deep religious faith. Wright tries to infuse into it a Communist influence, in which, deep down, he does not believe. This story, written in 1937, tells of a black woman, Sue, who became a Communist out of love for her two sons. The older son, Sug, is already in prison for his Marxist activities. Johnny-Boy, the youngest son, still free, has become the leader of a Communist unit. The action takes place in the South, near Memphis. The activities of the characters are constantly menaced.

In this short story, Wright's aim is to show that it is possible to devote oneself to Communist activities in the South if one observes a certain caution. But the way the short story ends emphasizes that it is the racial aspect of the question, not the Marxist ideology, that helps to save several people from a certain death. Blinded by Communism, to which he is totally converted, Johnny-Boy refuses to make the distinction between white Communists and black Communists. He only wants to see poor and rich people. His mother, made wiser by the years, distrusts whites and has confidence only in blacks. She feels, however, a certain affection for Reva, a young white female friend of Johnny-Boy's, who is trustworthy and honest. It is, however, Reva who, because of her blurred character, does not succeed in convincing the reader of a total fusion of black and white Communists.

Fate wills that the sheriff should learn of the next meeting of Johnny-Boy's Communist friends at Reva's father's house. Warned in his turn, Johnny-Boy eaves in the middle of the night to inform his friends that the meeting will not take place. Shortly after his departure, the sheriff and his men burst in on Sue and demand that she give them the names of the members of the Communist unit. As she refuses to tell them anything, the old woman is beaten by the sheriff, then knocked out by a blow right in the face. When she regains consciousness, she finds beside her a white man who has recently become a Communist, Booker, whom she has always mistrusted. He informs her that Johnny-Boy has been apprehended by the sheriff and persuades her to give him the names of the Communist friends that must be warned. Shortly after his departure, Reva comes to tell Sue that Booker is a sneak who is not to be trusted. Realizing the dangers facing the Communists whose names she has given Booker, the old black woman takes a woolen cloth, hides a pistol in it, and goes to find the sheriff. As she knows the countryside well, she takes a shortcut and reaches the sheriff before Booker. She explains to the sheriff's men that the cloth will serve as a shroud for Johnny-Boy, for she is convinced he will not talk and his death is certain. She witnesses the torture of Johnny-Boy in order to wait for Booker's arrival. As soon as the latter appears, she kills him with a bullet to the head, thus preventing him from naming the Communists she has pointed out to him. Crazed with anger, the whites finish off her son before her eyes, only to savagely kill her next.

It is the mistrust that Sue has always felt towards whites that causes her to doubt Booker's intentions. This doubt is confirmed by Reva. Sue says nothing to the young white woman and acts right away. She is determined and, like Silas of "Long Black Song," carries a choice freely made to the point of heroism. From the moment the two sons had begun to become interested in Communism, Sue had lived in danger. She had become accustomed to the idea that, sooner or later, she would lose them. After accepting her lot, the old black woman follows her destiny while giving it a quasi-religious devotion. Her decision to kill Booker, after learning he is a spy, closely resembles the very biblical social mission of Dan Taylor in "Fire and Cloud." Although Wright did not consciously feel this way, it is rather the interests of the black race that drive Sue to act and save black and not white lives. This is what led Constance Webb to say, "in the crisis of her life, she turns away from Communism to her Negro experience to find the deep resources of power, defiance and endurance which lift her above the Communists, heroic as they are."[37] Richard Wright does not succeed in convincing the reader that Marxism can offer a positive solution to the race problem in America. As he was black, the author could not, it seems, totally detach himself from race. This would explain why the spy is a white and not a black man.   This would also explain the fall of Johnny-Boy, who has always blindly placed his confidence in all his white friends.

In the person of Sue, Wright presents a soul in which religious faith partly makes room for a Communist vision. This is because the author was a Communist at the time he wrote "Bright and Morning Star." But the racial element essentially motivates the story for Wright had himself witnessed the same scenes described.   The theme of the black woman who hides a firearm in a woolen cloth in order to kill some whites is explained in detail in Black Boy.[38] The commitment Sue makes to Communism resembles in no way that which Dan Taylor makes to his religious and social responsibilities. "Bright and Morning Star" must be seen as a story whose principal aim, clumsily pursued, is to propagate the Communist ideology.

The five stories of Uncle Tom's Children form a homogeneous whole in which the Southern black's condition evolves slowly in a necessary order. If one compares the first to the last of the five short stories, there is an enormous difference between the little black boy in flight and the black Communist leader who is aware of his responsibilities. The aim of the successive changes in the Southern black's personality throughout five stories is to show that Uncle Tom's era is forever past, and that the future belongs henceforth to children in love with liberty and social equality. If Hugh Morris Gloster said, "The horror and tragedy suffered by Negroes in the narratives seem unnecessary in the light of the trivial incidents which cause them," one must add these five short stories, very realistic, describe precisely the life of Southern blacks.[39] Richard Wright chose his words so as to depict as simply as possible memories that were dear to him. While showing that the Southern black was capable of displaying both courage and humanity in a hostile environment, Wright assigned to himself the mission of reporting, as faithfully as possible, real-life events he had witnessed.

NOTES

1. Richard Wright, "Foreword," in his Twelve Million Black Voices: A Folk History of the Negro in the United States (New York: The Viking Press, 1941), p. 5.

2. Richard Wright, "Our Strange Birth," in Twelve Million Black Voices: A Folk History of the Negro in the United States, pp 9-27.

3. Charles Curtis Munz, "The New Negro," The Nation, December 13, 1941, p 620.

4. Richard Wright, "Inheritors of Slavery," in Twelve Million Black Voices: A Folk History of the Negro in the United States, pp 29-89.

5. Richard Wright, "The Ethics of Living Jim Cow: An Autobiographical Sketch," in American Stuff, an (anthology of the Federal Writers' Project) (New York: The Viking Press, 1937), pp 39-52 Also published in Richard Wright, Uncle Tom's

Children: Five Long Stories (New York: Harper and Brothers, 1940) All the other references to Uncle Tom's Children: Five Long Stories will concern the Harper and Row edition of 1965.

6. Keneth Kinnamon, The Emergence of Richard Wright: A Study in Literature mand Society (Urbana University of Illinois Press, 1972), p 85.

7. Richard Wright, Black Boy: A Record of Childhood and Youth (New York: Harper and Row, 1966) All the other references to this book will be to this edition Published for the first time in 1945.

8. Dan McCall, The Example of Richard Wright (New York: Harcourt, Brace and World, 1969), p 128.

9. "Black Boyhood," Time, March 5, 1945, p 96.

10. Howard Mumford Jones, "Up from Slavery: Richard Wright's Story," The Saturday Review of Literature, March 3, 1945, p 9.

11. R. L. Duffus, "Deep-South Memoir," The New York Times Book Review, March 4, 1945, p 3.

12. Richard Wright, Black Boy: A Record of Childhood and Youth, p 270.

13. Black Boy, pp 252-253.

14. Lionel Trilling, "A Tragic Situation," The Nation, April 7, 1945, p. 390.

15. Ralph K. White, "Black Boy: A Value-Analysis," Journal of Abnormal and Social Psychology 42 (October 1947): 451. Sinclair Lewis, "Gentlemen, This is Revolution," in Sinclair Lewis Reader, edited by Harry E. Maule and Milville H. Cane (New York: Random House, 1953), p. 149. George Mayberry, "What Man has Made of Man," The New Republic, March 12, 1945, p. 365. Orville Prescott, "Books of the Times," The New York Times, February 28, 1945, p. 21.

16. David Littlejohn, "Wright," in his Black on White (New York: Grossman Publishers, 1966), p. 109.

17. Ralph Ellison, "Richard Wright's Blues," in his Shadow and Act (Toronto: The New American Library of Canada, 1966), p. 104.

18. Ellison, "Richard Wright's Blues," p. 103.

19. Richard Wright, Black Boy, pp. 283-284.

20. Richard Wright, "Silt," New Masses, August 24, 1937, pp. 19-20. Published in Eight Men (Cleveland and New York: World Publishing Co., 1961) under the title of "The Man Who Saw the Flood."

21. James Baldwin, "Eight Men," in his Nobody Knows My Name (New York: Dell Publishing Co., 1964), p. 148.

22. Richard Wright, "The Man Who Was Almost a Man," in his Eight Men (Cleveland and New York: World Publishing Co., 1961).

23. James Baldwin, Nobody Knows My Name, p. 148.

24. Richard Wright, Uncle Tom's Children: Five Long Stories.

25. Keneth Kinnamon, The Emergence of Richard Wright, p. 109.

26. Richard Wright, "Big Boy Leaves Home," published for the first time in Alfred Kreymborg et al., eds. The New Caravan (New York: W W Norton and Co., 1936), pp. 124-158; "Down by the Riverside," published for the first time in Uncle Tom's Children: Four Novellas (New York: Harper and Brothers, 1938); "Long Black Song," published for the first time in Uncle Tom's Children: Four Novellas; "Fire and Cloud," published for the first time in Story, March 1938, pp. 9-41 (Richard Wright had the honor of receiving the Story magazine prize for this short story in December 1937); "Bright and Morning Star," published for the first time in New Masses, May 10,1938, pp. 97-99, 116-124.

27. This water hole was probably inspired by Rock Bottom Creek, a small stream near Jackson, Mississippi, where Wright often went to bathe.

28. Saunders Redding, "The Alien Land of Richard Wright," in Five Black Writers, edited by Donald B Gibson (New York: New York University Press, 1970), p.6.

29. Kinnamon, The Emergence of Richard Wright, p. 91.

30. Kinnamon, The Emergence of Richard Wright, p. 93.

31. Wright, "Down by the Riverside," in his Uncle Tom's Children, p. 102.

32. Kinnamon, The Emergence of Richard Wright, p. 95.

33. Malcolm Cowley, "Long Black Song", The New Republic, April 6, 1938, p. 280.

34. Edwin Berry Burgum, "The Art of Richard Wright's Short Stories," in Five Black Writers, p. 45.

35. Richard Wright, "Fire and Cloud," in his Uncle Tom's Children p. 180.

36. Kinnamon, The Emergence of Richard Wright, p. 105.

37. Constance Webb, "What Next for Richard Wright?", Phylon 10 (Second Quarter, 1949): p. 161.

38. Richard Wright, Black Boy: A Record of Childhood and Youth, pp. 83-84.

39. Hugh Morris Gloster, "Richard Wright," in his Negro Voices in American Fiction (Chapel Hill: University of North Carolina Press, 1948), p. 227.

3

CONDITIONS
IN THE NORTH

UNCERTAINTY

Like Dave Saunders in "The Man Who Was Almost a Man," the black man cannot always endure the reality of the South and decides to leave for the North.[1] In the third part of <u>Twelve Million Black Voices: A Folk History of the Negro in the United States,</u> Richard Wright speaks of the life led by the Southern black as soon as he arrives in the North.[2] This section, "Death on the City Pavements," traces the life of the Northern black from his beginnings to 1940.[3] Since the conditions he describes there have scarcely changed, Wright's remarks still apply today to a society that refuses to treat the black man as a human being.

The mass exodus of blacks to the North began in 1920. That is the date chosen by Wright to situate the new life of the Southern black in the Northern cities. Far from finding an earthly paradise, the Southern black must face a world that treats him with the utmost indifference. Left to his own devices, the black man does not know how to organize himself, for he has not been prepared for this type of life.

From foreign immigrants whom he does not understand because of their accent, to the poor whites who compete with him at work, the black man finds it difficult to adapt to a life he never would have suspected if he had stayed in his native South. But since he must earn a living, he must accept any job whatsoever, however degrading it may be. He is obliged to live in a ghetto, along with his fellowmen, in order not to disturb by his presence whites who want nothing to do with him. If chance decrees that he meet whites, he quickly realizes that the color of his skin forbids him from enjoying the progress that the white American majority does. Shut up in the ghetto and constantly at the mercy of his job, required to subsist, the black man quickly finds himself under the all-powerful domination of the Patrons of the North who take advantage of him unabashedly. The only jobs he finds are for laborers and domestics. Extremely high rents permit him only to live in a small room, a kitchenette, which he has to share with several other persons. Given this situation, it is not surprising that violence and vice are so often a part of the daily lives of inhabitants of the black ghetto.

The two million or so blacks who swelled the ghettos of the North during the twenties realized the necessity of organizing themselves in order to protect their interests. But since it was forbidden for them to belong to trade unions because of the color of their skin, anger often drove them to revolt against the whites. Always the last to be hired and the first to be fired, blacks could often formulate their demands only in rage. Wright sheds light on their situation, impossible because they were no longer in a position to pay high rent and feed their large families without a stable job. The blacks knew that the ghettos in which they lived had no important status in the municipal affairs of their city, judging from the dirtiness and illness that reigned there like absolute rulers. Such situations had serious consequences, since they discouraged many black men who were forced to abandon their families. They thus left wives and children without resources.

In this part, Wright brings out the inhumane way the Patrons of the North used blacks when, for example, they asked them to replace striking white workers. The blacks knew that the whites would never forgive them for accepting such offers; but the need to provide for their families made them accept the jobs proposed while running the risk of reprisals from white workers. The author emphasizes that the social situation will worsen in the early thirties, a consequence of the Depression in America. When Wright says that the jobs of black domestics were then taken by whites, he shows the poverty the Northern black masses experienced during that critical period. But the author manages to make us feel that the black church and faith in God will succeed in saving millions of souls ready to give up all hope. He points out that the black church has always played an important role among Northern blacks. Penned up in their ghetto, they find comfort in the religious words of their pastors.

Toward the end of the third part of Twelve Million Black Voices, Wright says that the relative freedom in the North enabled ghetto blacks to express their sorrows and their hopes in blues and jazz. According to Wright, these two modes of musical expression are typically Afro-American and reflect the sufferings of a tortured soul on the lookout for a just and equitable future. The author is correct in adding that from this trying experience also emerged a language that, little by little, influenced the American language. Today, more than ever, black music and the black dialect influence American life and show the degree to which blacks are an integral part of a society that does not, however, want them.

When Twelve Million Black Voices was published, President Franklin Delano Roosevelt had already done a great deal to improve the lot of black Americans. But Wright says not one word about it in his book. William Shands Meacham declared in The New York Times Book Review that Wright had been wrong not to recognize the Roosevelt administration's efforts: the photos that illustrated the text of his book came from the archives of the Farm Security Administration and proved indeed that Washington was following the black American's situation very closely.[4] Wright's aim was to denounce the implacably blind attitude of whites toward blacks.

Aware of the blacks' situation in the Northern ghettos, Wright wrote, between 1931 and 1937, a novel about the monotonous and aimless life of a black Chicago post office worker. This novel, Lawd Today, takes place on February 12, Abraham Lincoln's birthday.[5] The hero's name is Jake Jackson. The action takes place during the thirties and is divided into three parts. The first part, "Commonplace," shows the way Jackson spends the morning before going to work. The second part, "Squirrel Cage," describes the conditions in which the hero is obliged to work. The third part, "Rats Alley," shows how Jake Jackson tries to free himself from his frustration once he is out of the post office. Wright did not pick the date February 12 by chance. By choosing the birthday of the great emancipator of blacks, he ironically shows how little freedom the black hero of his novel enjoys. Wright contrasts the promises of the past with the destitution of the present. As the action progresses, the learned words of a University of Chicago professor continuously laud the greatness of Abraham Lincoln. The whole day long Jake Jackson hears these praises on the radio. They show the reader that reality is unpleasant.

In this novel, Wright uses Jake Jackson to talk about his experiences. Since he worked at the Chicago post office, he gives an accurate idea of the type of work Jake Jackson has to accomplish. The various scenes described are drawn directly from the Chicago of the thirties, which the author knew so well. The novel is written in the third person singular and allows Wright to present his character objectively.

At the beginning of the first part of Lawd Today, we discover Jake Jackson at home in the morning. As he is employed at the post office, he can lead a comfortable life on the South Side free of destitution. The life-style that he can afford enables him to belong to the black middle class. Just before waking up, Jake Jackson has a disturbing dream in which he sees himself climbing some unending stairs. This nightmare seems to illustrate his hard life without prospects. To a certain extent, the dismal life of the hero strangely evokes the useless and absurd labor of Sisyphus condemned by the gods forever to roll a rock to the top of a mountain, from which the stone falls back from its own weight.

For lack of a choice, Jack Jackson must lead an aimless life. He, nevertheless feels a certain joy, indeed a deep personal satisfaction, in living a life for which he alone is responsible. At the end of the novel, after having been thrown out of a disreputable house, he exclaims, despite his anger: "But when I was flying, I was a flying fool."[6] Long before existentialism appeared in literature, Wright had already set forth its broad lines. Albert Camus declares in Le Mythe de Sisyphe, "Happiness and the absurd are two sons of the same earth. They are inseparable."[7] He also adds, "All the silent joy of Sisyphus is there. His destiny belongs to him. His rock is his own."[8] In other words, any human being wishing to be happy must accept himself entirely with complete freedom. That is the case of Jake Jackson, who finds, nevertheless, a certain joy in the hell of his life. Jean-Paul Sartre writes, in L'Existentialisme est un humanisme:

We want freedom for freedom's sake and through each particular circumstance. And in wanting freedom, we discover that it depends entirely on the freedom of others, and that the freedom of others depends on ours.[9]

Jake can thus give his life a positive meaning; those around him lead the same type of life as he.

Jake does not get along with his wife, Lil. He forced her to have an abortion. He is deprived of any sexual satisfaction with her, for she is suffering greatly from the aftereffects of her operation. She has found consolation and refuge in religion and constantly arouses the anger of her husband, who despises and beats her for the slightest reason. Selfishness drives Jake Jackson to refuse his wife any money. As he is a native of Mississippi, Jake probably wishes to take full advantage of what the North cares to offer him. That is why he insists on keeping all his money and refuses to have a child.

Since he works at the post office from noon until late evening, Jake Jackson spends the morning wandering about the streets in his neighborhood. He hates his wife's presence and does everything to be with her as infrequently as possible. He prefers three good friends from the post office, Bob, Al, and Slim, whom he frequently meets in the morning to play cards and discuss the day's events. They like to get together to talk about their misfortunes, which helps them to endure them. Bob has a venereal disease. He also has to give a portion of his meager salary to his former wife and his children because he is divorced. Slim suffers from an acute case of pneumonia. Only Al seems to be spared. He likes to eat well and is good at telling his friends amusing stories.

The morning that Wright has his hero spend seems to be typical of life in the black ghetto. Jake Jackson is going to try his luck at a lottery in order to win some money. This game is founded on the dreams of the individual. As each dream has a number, the winning number is determined by drawing lots. This type of game is played frequently in Northern ghettos where the hope for a better world is only a dream. The dream on which Jake Jackson stakes his money is the one in which he has seen himself climbing some unending stairs. But as in his dream, Jake does not win; he loses his money. This dream has an important symbolic significance in the novel. In a General Introduction to Psychoanalysis, Sigmund Freud declares that "the act of mounting ladders, steep places or stairs is indubitably symbolic of sexual intercourse."[10] Wright's intention is clear; he wants to emphasize his hero's sexual frustration.

Richard Wright succeeds in indicating the exact year of the action of the novel by presenting the chance meeting of Jake Jackson with a jobless and penniless friend, Streamline. It is the thirties, a period when thousands of American blacks and whites could not find work. Although he is a simple postal employee, Jake Jackson knows that he is envied by those who have nothing. He treats Streamline with the greatest disdain and refuses to lend him the least amount of money. According to their conversation about the black boxer, Joe Louis, the action of the novel takes place February 12, 1937. They are talking about the defeat inflicted on Joe Louis by the German Max Schmeling. This fight took place on June 19, 1936, and Wright completed the revision of Lawd Today in the spring of 1937.

If Jake Jackson admires Joe Louis and wants him to take his revenge on Max Schmeling, it is because he hates the white world and he wants a black man to triumph over a white one.[11] But the hero of the novel knows that he can do nothing alone, and that blacks need to organize themselves before making their demands known. His barber, Doc Higgins, represents in his eyes the black man who knows how to win the respect of all by using blacks and whites. The great influence this barber exerts is due to the politics of the municipality of Chicago, and to money. Doc Higgins achieved his status by playing the white man's game. Jake Jackson knows that blacks need whites, and that any other attitude would be dangerous. At Doc Higgins's place, he comes across an individual, Duke, who says he is a Communist ready to overthrow the American government in order to establish justice and equality in America. If Jake Jackson and Doc Higgins take Duke for a madman, it is disturbing to find again thirty years later the same type of individual in the person of Eldridge Cleaver, who skillfully denounced the hypocrisy and the prejudices of white American society against blacks in Soul on Ice.[12] There has always been in America people who believe that only a radical change of political regime could improve the lot of black people. That is not the opinion of Wright, who lets his hero take sides.   When Jake Jackson attends a big parade sponsored by a back-to-Africa group, he thinks that the leaders of that movement are as crazy as Duke.   This nationalist movement is the Universal Negro Improvement Association, very well known in America during the thirties.

In rejecting both exile and violence in order to improve his lot, Jake Jackson shows that he prefers to go on leading the type of life he has always known. He is neither a nationalist nor a Communist, but only a man of the people. This is what led Staughton Lynd to say, "In Lawd Today, Wright looks for answers not in Marxism but in the collective experience of his people."[13] Although a Communist at the time he wrote the novel, Wright wanted at first to describe the life of a ghetto black man without cluttering it with Marxist ideas.

Jake Jackson's life consists of the day's events and what America is willing to give him. He is intrigued by a black man, Father Divine, whom millions of Americans, white and black, took for God during the twenties. This black man, a native of Georgia whose real name was George Baker, had founded an organization that gave aid and support to jobless people. The miracles and the healings attributed to him were sufficient to capture the attention of a mind as simple as Jake Jackson's. The hero of Lawd Today is not very intelligent and can be easily impressed. On a street corner, he listens attentively to a quack who is cleverly praising the wonders of his drugs before an ignorant and naive public.

In the first part of the novel, Wright gives as many details as possible concerning the reality and the would surrounding his hero. His descriptions, often long, have a tendency to blur some scenes that are nonetheless interesting. The description of the lottery and that of Jake's bridge game with three friends include too many details. But this flaw is balanced by the lively way Wright describes some scenes that are full of life. The repartee between Al and Jake, called the Dirty Dozens by American blacks, would have no appeal to the uninformed reader without the direct intervention of Wright, who knows how to give these typically Afro-American replies a human and personal meaning.

The second part of Lawd Today shows the way Jake Jackson is obliged to work at the main post office in Chicago. This building still stands at the corner of Clark Street and Jackson Boulevard, but the working conditions are no longer today what they were at that time. In order to recreate the tense and unpleasant atmosphere which reigns at the post office, Wright addresses himself directly to the readers. He describes a virtual prison in which the postal employees are reduced to playing the humble role of convicts stripped of all freedom. As Jake's job and his friends' consist in sorting the mail, Wright succeeds in showing how this toil stifles all intellectual curiosity in the individual and the very desire to want to create a particular identity for himself. The managerial staff is made up of whites who do everything to make the black employees unhappy. The hell in which Jake Jackson is obliged to work prevents him from going to the toilet too often, for fear of losing points. The accumulation of many points could cost him his job. It is forbidden for him to smoke and he has only half an hour to eat his meal and relax. Finally, he must pay close attention to what he says and what he does, for he is constantly watched.

In view of this situation at work, it is not surprising that Jake Jackson devotes himself entirely to his work and tries, at the same time, to forget his pride. He knows he has no future and that his life depends on the goodwill of whites. The bitterness he feels is great: he realizes that the color of his skin prevents him from nourishing the same hopes as his white colleagues. He knows that the post office is not an end in itself for many white employees, who take courses at the University of Chicago in order to improve their condition. He also knows that American society is essentially white and that whites always have priority over blacks. Despairing of everything, Jake Jackson gives himself over to sexual debauchery and violence during his off hours. But since the money earned is not sufficient to lead such a life, he has to borrow small sums from his employers. His debts pile up and enslave him to a job he hates but cannot do without.

Jake and his friends take turns paying for their vile and costly pleasures. In Lawd Today, Wright shows the way Jake conducts himself with his white bosses in order to borrow the money he needs to offer his friends a pleasant evening. But after learning that his wife has come to complain about the blows she received that very morning, Jake Jackson sees himself about to lose his job. The quick intervention of Doc Higgins saves him from an unfortunate situation and allows him to borrow the desired sum. He must, however, humiliate himself and swallow his pride before the whites who despise him. They decide not to fire him because they know that they are going to be paid. It is not because they feel pity for him. The payment will be made through the intermediary of Doc Higgins, to whom Jake will hand over the money.

In this part, Wright's main goal is to show that all those around his hero want to take advantage of him. His wife, Lil, refuses to leave him and is determined to live at his expense as long as he has a job. She avenges herself for the abortion that he forced her to have and which left her almost crippled. They only way Jake could get rid of her would be to stop working. Doc Higgins and Jake's white bosses take advantage of the family situation and the hero's violent temperament to extract as much money as possible from him. The only result of the blackmail to which he is subjected is to make him hate himself, his wife, his race, and whites. The only human beings with whom Jake Jackson can still communicate are his three friends. The very vague conversation they have at work reflects the monotony of the atmosphere and their isolation.

The third part of Lawd Today is the end of a long day filled with bitterness and frustration. Jake and his friends go to a disreputable house, where Jake gets all his money stolen. Convinced that the theft had been prepared in advance, Jake gives vent to his anger. Knocked out, then thrown into the street, he is left alone in the freezing cold night. His friends, exhausted with fatigue, leave him and return home. Crazed with rage, Jake goes back home, where he beats his wife and accuses her of all the ills that afflict him. As at the beginning of the novel, the last scene described by Wright is filled with hate and violence. The lack of sexual satisfaction is its direct cause. The blows that Jake gives his wife replace the love he cannot give her. Sexual frustration seems to be the main theme of Lawd Today.

In this novel, Wright's main goal is to criticize American materialism, which divides blacks and often destroys their personality. This criticism is what led Nick Aaron Ford to say that Lawd Today "contains practically every offensive Negro stereotype known to American literature." Moreover, he strongly doubts that the novel is Richard Wright's because it is poorly written.[14] The idea just mentioned has also been advanced by Granville Hicks.[15] One must remember here that Wright had written this novel in Chicago, and that it was published thirty years later without the author's being able to revise it. Lawd Today reflects the awkward style of a writer in the throes of his development.

Lawd Today clearly indicates that the black American bourgeoisie needs to become aware of its power with the aid of politics and education. The scenes described in the novel date perhaps to the thirties, but the condition of the ghetto black has not changed. Contrary to opinions expressed by Time and Library Journal, Lawd Today does not belong to the past, but precisely reflects a situation that still afflicts the ghetto black.[16]

Deprived of every means of improving his condition, the black American is often reduced to living on the fringes of American society. To illustrate this idea, Wright wrote a short novel in the fall of 1941. Of the three sections of this novel, only the third was published, in 1944, under the title "The Man Who Lived Underground."[17] Two short parts of this section had been published in 1942 under the same title.[18] The subject of this short story had been inspired by an article Wright had read in the August 1941 issue of True Detective. This article, "The Crime Hollywood Couldn't Believe," spoke of a twenty-three-year-old white man, Herbert C. Wright, who, for lack of money and a job, had lived in the sewers of Los Angeles for over a year.[19] Thanks to the discovery of a completely new underground life, he had found the way to enter all the stores he wished in order to get everything he needed free of charge. A close surveillance of the stores thus frequented had enabled the police to apprehend him. Wright had been intrigued by this adventure in which the hero was looking for his place within a society that was rejecting him. He had understood that through his actions, Herbert C. Wright had left in search of himself.[20]

The 1944 story presents a black man forced to hide himself in the gutters of a city because of a murder he has not committed, for which he does not want to be made responsible. The underground world in which he lives for some time makes him understand that man, whatever he may be, is fundamentally guilty. The discovery of this human guilt enables the hero to come out of his subterranean refuge in order to give himself up to the police. But great is his surprise when he learns that the author of the murder of which they wanted to accuse him has been arrested. Convinced of man's guilt, he insists that the police go down into the gutters with him in order to discover his underground world. Taken for a madman, he is coldly killed in a sewer hole.

The long subterranean pilgrimage which transforms the hero's personality follows a precise evolution in Wright's thought. The author wishes to show that the position occupied by his protagonist is never stable. If he escapes his racial condition by living in an underground world, the hero is guilty of abandoning the social system of which he has always been a part. Furthermore, if his underground life enables him to become a human being, the sewers, cellars, and basements into which he wanders cannot be a part of a healthful human environment. The life the hero of this short story must lead seems to be the symbol of the black man's life. The hero discovers his new identity because of experiences provoked by the color of his skin and a forced isolation.

After having observed some blacks in a church and some people at the movies, the hero of "The Man Who Lived Underground" concludes that man is guilty if he is not satisfied with his lot and constantly seeks happiness in religious escape or diversion. As he has taken a liking to his new underground life, the hero steals what he needs to settle into his new domain. He visits successively an embalming establishment, a jewelry store, a radio shop, and a grocery store. The objects he appropriates for himself represent his unlimited powers. His sole aim is to show that he can do what he wishes in a world without constraints. His numerous acquisitions belong to his underground world. They would have no meaning for him elsewhere. From the grocery store's chopper to the jewelry store's diamonds, the hero sees in these objects only tangible proof of his new-found power. This is why, once back in his hideout, he tells himself that everything is permitted. He makes this remark out loud, after playing like a child with the watches, rings, money and diamonds stolen from the safe in the jewelry store. He sticks bank notes on the walls of his cave and just about everywhere he hammers in nails on which he hangs the watches and the rings. He scatters the diamonds on the ground in his hideout and tramples them underfoot.

The hero's attitude is all the more interesting since Wright reveals his name only by chance. Wright wishes to make it clear that his hero's situation is universal. This black man's condition is not only symbolic of all black Americans, but also of every oppressed person. Wright's aim is to show that man can, when he wishes to, lead the kind of life he desires. The hero's color makes the matter easy, for, blinded by racial prejudices, whites cannot know him. He can do whatever he wishes by hiding behind the pigmentation of his skin. The underground life he leads allows him to give free rein to the feelings of the human species that he represents. While he is learning to type on a stolen typewriter, the hero tries in vain to remember his name.   A little earlier, when he had emerged from his underground world to work his way into the jewelry store, where he found the typewriter, he had easily remembered that his name was Fred Daniels. Wright thus succeeds in showing that his hero's condition is human and without any precise identity when the action takes place in the underground world.

Wright does not hide the fact, however, that even outside of his subterranean universe, Fred Daniels remains unknown to those who meet him by chance. If this situation is partly due to the color of his skin, it is also due to human indifference. When he strolls down the corridors of the cinema, the hero is shown the toilets by a worker accustomed to a monotonous job. When he comes out of the grocery store to get a breath of cool air, Fred Daniels is surprised by the sudden arrival of two white men who, mistaking him for a traveling salesman, buy a pound of grapes and leave. Neither the movie theater usher nor the two white men can suspect the fantastic world the hero has created for himself underground. For them, Fred Daniels is a being whom society permits to play only certain well-defined roles. The hero's underground world is very different from that he has left behind him. Everything is new there, including the notion of time, which has no value. Thus Fred Daniels assembles the stolen watches while caring little about the exact time.

The main attraction of "The Man Who Lived Underground" is the alternation of the story between the mysterious and the ordinary. The mysterious comes from Fred Daniels's underground world, whereas the ordinary is due above all to the consequences of his action.   These consequences are ordinary for him, but intriguing for others. Wright wishes to show that his hero's power is almost divine. The author's primary aim is to show that every human being is imperfect. The thefts committed by Fred Daniels enable him to understand here again that man, whether he likes it or not, is guilty by nature. A young radio shop worker is beaten by his boss and accused of having stolen the radio taken by Fred Daniels. Trembling with fear because she saw the hero, the secretary at the jewelry store is taken for a madwoman by her bosses after she told them she saw a black man. The night watchman at the jewelry store commits suicide because all those around him are convinced of his guilt after the disappearance of the contents of the safe. Since he cannot understand this crime, the night watchman ends his days by firing a bullet into his head. This suicide will be considered definite proof of guilt by the police. Wright wishes to emphasize that, dead or alive, the night guard has no hope of proving his innocence.

If Fred Daniels's invisible behavior causes acts of brutality and a suicide, it also permits him to observe the world he has left and to judge it. In The Art of Richard Wright, Edward Margolies rightly says that:

> He comes to understand that neither world in which he dwells is the real world of the human heart -- and that the surface world which hums above him in the streets of the city is senseless and meaningless -- a kind of unreality which men project to hide from themselves the awful blackness of their souls.[21]

Aware of the culpability of the human species, he knows that sooner or later the individual must give an account of his life's deeds. After having seen someone steal money from the safe, Fred Daniels is convinced that the author of the theft will pay for his deed in the future in one way or another.

Driven by a deep feeling of human guilt, Fred Daniels goes to find the police. He wants to prove his guilt and try to explain its cause. By acting in this manner, he hopes that all of humanity will realize this original sin and will improve the human condition. But he comes up against the lack of understanding of the policemen, who decide to kill him because they feel he would endanger the order of things. Robert Bone explains well Fred Daniels's conduct with the representatives of the forces of law and order:

> He wants to share his vision with the whites, disclose his underground reality, make his darkness visible. But words fail him; it is an incommunicable vision.[22]

The one who kills him is named Lawson. His name is symbolic since he is supposed to protect society by making people respect the law. "The Man Who Lived Underground" is an existentialist parable because the hero acquires his identity from his relationships with others. In L'Existentialisme est un humanisme, Jean-Paul Sartre says that man:

> ". . . realizes that he can be nothing . . . unless others recognize him as such. In order to obtain any truth about myself, I must go through the other [man]. The other [man] is indispensable for my existence, as well as, moreover, for my self-knowledge."[23]

Before Sartre and Camus, Wright had touched on their philosophy in this short story. In it he had tried to define the individual's position within modern society. Fred Daniels is the symbol of the individual alone and anonymous in a materialistic and unfeeling society.

It is likely that the writing of this short story was also influenced by Feodor Dostoyevski's Notes from Underground.[24] The fundamental difference between those two works lies in the heroes, their conduct, and the world in which they live. Dostoevski's hero hates people and lives of his own free will in a secret spiritual world. Fred Daniels, on the other hand, was rejected by men and does not understand the reason. His nether world is real since it consists of sewers. The hero's attitude in "The Man Who Lived Underground" offers much hope to the world ever in search of peace and happiness. Dostoevski's hero, condemned to total isolation by his lack of human love, has no desire to improve humanity's lot.

The two short fragments of "The Man Who Lived Underground" published under the same title in 1942, cover the period of time the hero spent in his underground hideaway with his loot. The order in which he conducts his various activities is not the same as in the 1944 version. But everything is there; Wright even introduces an episode that does not appear in the 1944 version and in which the hero escapes drowning in the waters of the sewers. This incident gives the short narrative a very unusual aspect, especially since neither the hero's name nor color is mentioned. Because of its brevity, the 1942 two-part short story is much more symbolic of man's life than the 1944 version.

FEAR

Fear has always played an important role in Richard Wright's work. That is true at the beginning of his literary career. When he wrote "Superstition" in 1930, Wright revealed a personality harassed by anguish and haunted by horror.[25] This short story may be considered as Richard Wright's first work since those written previously have left no traces of their existence. "Superstition" reflects the sensitive soul of young Wright, who was then only twenty-two. This short story was the fruit of his numerous readings and his own experiences. Since he had experienced terror in the South, Wright had been better able to understand certain of his favorite writers, Edgar Allan Poe in particular. The latter had known great fear in real life and had taken refuge in a world of dreams and strange illusions. Strongly attracted to Poe, Wright had read his tales avidly and had ended up trying to imitate him by writing "Superstition."

The manner in which Richard Wright wrote "Superstition" demonstrates his desire to follow Poe's technique as closely as possible. He succeeded well, for the three essential qualities of Poe's story appear in "Superstition." Thus the brevity, unity, and intensity of the action make it possible for "Superstition" to describe an atmosphere full of mystery and anguish. The subtitle summarizes the entire story precisely.[26] This subtitle closely resembles the first sentence of every Poe tale, whose essential function is to embody the main idea of the story. That is why, in his article "Black Cat and White Cat: Richard Wright's Debt to Edgar Allan Poe," Michel Fabre stresses that in this story "Wright owes much to Poe's technique of describing the setting in order to suggest an eerie, dreary atmosphere."[27] The mysterious and natural combine to give a bizarre as well as a disturbing impression. "Superstition" is a story told by a black businessman, Fently Burrow. During two business trips, at one-year intervals, to the same city he is witness to the strange effects of a family reunion on the people with whom he lived. The action each time takes place a few weeks before Christmas. During his first stay, Fently Burrow meets the youngest daughter of the family, Lillian Lancaster, who tells him every family reunion is followed by a death. She declares to him that some neighbors have been afflicted by sudden and mysterious deaths during family reunions. At that moment, the rest of the family arrives unexpectedly, and Lillian dies of pneumonia the same day. A year later, Fently Burrow witnesses the sudden death of his hostess, Mrs. Lancaster, struck down by a heart attack after her children's arrival.

The supernatural in this short story is found in the mysterious death of the daughter and mother. Lillian's paleness and the secret surrounding her create a strange atmosphere reminiscent of Poe. The fall of Lillian's portrait from the moment of Fently Burrow's arrival, during his second visit, appears to add a disquieting note. The members of the Lancaster family seem unable to free themselves from the superstition that afflicts them. They are as if crushed by an all-powerful magic spell.

The supernatural in "Superstition" is to a certain extent explained by the natural aspects of the short story. Shortly before her death, Lillian is seized by coughing fits and is spitting out blood. Her feverish face and her emaciated body seem to indicate that she is suffering from tuberculosis. Wright says that mother and daughter resemble each other closely. It is perhaps not surprising that, because of her old age and her fragile constitution, Mrs. Lancaster dies suddenly when she relives the circumstances that had surrounded her daughter's death a year earlier. In spite of that, Wright succeeds in making one feel the unexplainable influence of fate on the lives of the Lancasters. He often does so awkwardly by repeating the same word or the same idea. But the anguish is the dominant feeling in this story of Gothic inspiration.

The technique Wright uses to develop his subject is simple. It is through Fently Burrow that Wright is able to express his ideas. Already in this short story, one sees that the author has a tendency to want to explain what he is describing in excessive detail. This is a characteristic that has always dominated his work. Thus the narrator of the story announces Lillian's death in advance. This passing is also predicted by the girl at the beginning of the story. The reader is warned in advance that fate can also strike the Lancaster family. This naïve way of approaching the subject shows that Wright was far from mastering his literary technique and achieving his mental maturity. This is why Keneth Kinnamon said, "As literature 'Superstition' is an unqualified failure, with stereotyped characters, contrived action, and stilted diction."[28] Wright had written "Superstition" for the black masses whom he wanted to impress.

One must recognize that the characters and the situation in "Superstition" could have just as easily been white. It is even strange that at the beginning of his novel, Wright presents three black businessmen who, after a good meal, take turns telling one another mysterious stories in the living room of an opulent-looking apartment. His reason for describing such a scene may be that he wanted to make his story intriguing from the beginning. He knew that his readers were in great economic difficulties in America and that the situation would seem unlikely, if not unbelievable. Like Poe, Wright was seeking evasion in a work that reflected in no way the wretched conditions in which he lived at that time.

If Richard Wright says that Fently Burrow is living with the inhabitant, it is probably to avoid referring to the racial reality. The reason he gives is that the hotels of the city are crowded with participants at a congress. Wright could have also stated that there were no black hotels in the city, and that the white hotels refused to admit blacks. Racial segregation, which was rampant at the time the short story was published, would have given the work a much more authentic character. "Superstition" is the only work in which Wright talks about blacks without alluding to segregation. Here the author attempts to describe an atmosphere void of any social and human context. A few years after the publication of his story, Wright was to disown it publicly. He even went so far as to stop using his middle name, Nathaniel, in his subsequent works -- so much he had his heart set on not being recognized as the author of that particular story. But the faithfulness with which Wright had imitated Poe showed that he knew how to appreciate a literary genre which was going to enable him to convey his ideas in the years to come.

Nearly ten years later, he was to dedicate a novel in the following manner: "To my mother who, when I was a child at her knee, taught me to revere the fanciful and the imaginative." This novel was Native Son.[29] Poe's influence is strongly felt in this powerful, imaginative work. It is the story of Bigger Thomas, a twenty-year-old black man from the black ghetto of Chicago, who kills a white woman, accidentally. Next he is hunted down, apprehended, and condemned to death by the whites. The novel, constantly plunged into an atmosphere cf anguish and fear, is divided into three books entitled respectively "Fear," "Flight," and "Fate." Poe's imprint is found from the beginning of the work, when the Thomas family is awakened with a start by the strident ringing of an alarm clock. A few minutes later, Bigger's mother and his sister, Vera, are paralyzed with fright at the sight of a huge rat that makes its appearance in their dilapidated kitchenette. This rat gives Bigger a fierce fight when it realizes it cannot escape. Bigger and his brother, Buddy, finally kill it by dealing crushing blows to its head with shoes. This gory scene foreshadows the tragic end of Bigger, who, like the animal he has just killed, will be seized by whites despite all the efforts undertaken to escape them. It is especially this scene which, through its symbolism and its importance, makes Native Son a work strongly influenced by Poe. It contains the main idea of the novel.

Poe's mark is evident when Wright's hero is constantly dominated and watched by the white world. No sooner has he arrived at the home of his white employers than the young black man is struck by Mrs. Dalton's white hair, white face, white clothes, and white eyes. She is blind and looks like a ghost that noiselessly dodges in and out everywhere. It is her unexpected presence, late in the night, that will drive Bigger to smother Mary Dalton with a pillow so that she will not reveal his presence in the white girl's room. Kate, the Daltons' white cat, like the finger of accusation of the white world's justice, seems to pursue Bigger in his reprehensible acts. It makes a brief appearance while the young black man is carrying the girl's body to the basement of the house, where the furnace is located. It appears again when Bigger is stuffing Mary's corpse into the furnace with all his might. Finally, it leaps up on the young black man's shoulders while newsmen are taking photos in the basement and shortly before Mr. Dalton reports having received a note announcing that his daughter had been kidnapped. Like a mute witness, the white cat is constantly by the side of Bigger Thomas, whom it seems to want to denounce. Its presence is important to Richard Wright, for it is the symbol of fear often used by Poe in his strange tales.

Not content with presenting disturbing situations, Wright creates scenes of Gothic inspiration in which his rich imagination equals Poe's. When Bigger severs Mary Dalton's head, his aim is simply to destroy all proof of his murderous act, but such a scene, illuminated by the flames from the furnace and dominated by the presence of the white cat, has extraordinary effects. The scene describing the brutal and bloody murder of Bessie Mears, Bigger's girlfriend, has the same effects. Bigger works away furiously with a brick at crushing Bessie's head until she is nothing more than a formless mass swimming in a pool of blood. The action takes place at night, in an abandoned building, while a snowstorm rages outside.

Snow plays a very important role in the novel, since its color indicates symbolically that the white world is omnipresent. Snow begins to fall after Bigger Thomas has incinerated Mary Dalton's body late on Saturday evening, and it stops snowing early on Monday morning after the death of Bessie Mears. In the space of about twenty-four hours, Bigger Thomas commits two murders. The snow that fell relentlessly on Chicago seems to represent the white world's conscience, horrified by the savage deeds of the young black man. After the hero's capture, this snow will remain tenaciously on the ground until the end of the novel. Its mute role closely resembles that of the Dalton's cat, determined to denounce the guilty black man and see him punished. If the symbolic role of the white cat is recognizable during its numerous quick appearances, the no less symbolic role of the snow is heightened by the snowstorm that paralyzes Chicago for more than twenty-four hours. The author emphasizes this idea by repeating the word "snow" more than one hundred times in his novel. The symbolic use of the snow enables Wright to highlight a situation bearing Poe's mark.

But in this novel, Poe's influence is not limited to the inspiration of scenes rich in imagination. It is also found in Wright's somber and disquieting style when he depicts the black ghetto at night[30] and when Boris Max, Bigger Thomas's lawyer, makes his speech for the defense.[31]

This is not to suggest that Native Son owes its success solely to Poe's influence. It is above all the diligent work of Wright, entirely devoted to his own novel, that made this work a resounding literary success. Ralph Ellison was to declare: "This work possesses an artistry, penetration of thought, and sheer emotional power that places it in the front rank of American fiction."[32] Two major factors enabled the author to complete his work successfully. The first is historical and the second is personal.

From the historical viewpoint it was the Robert Nixon case that exerted a great influence on the author when he had already started the novel. On May 27, 1938, two young black men from Chicago, Robert Nixon and Earl Johnson, had been arrested for the murder of a white woman, Mrs. Florence Johnson, mother of two children. She had been savagely beaten to death with a brick. Since the African features were much more pronounced in Robert Nixon than in Earl Hicks, the public's attention quickly focused on Nixon. He represented in the eyes of whites the human beast par excellence. In its editorials and its numerous articles, The Chicago Daily Tribune undertook to convince the white population that Mrs. Florence Johnson had been raped before being murdered. That was never proved beyond question or doubt. In any case, this newspaper did not hesitate to launch a violent campaign against Robert Nixon, calling for him alone to be executed. The young black man, then eighteen years old, was quickly judged, condemned to death, and executed in the electric chair on June 16, 1939.

Very interested in this case, Richard Wright went to Chicago to attend the young black man's trial and to immerse himself in an atmosphere he needed in order to finish his novel. This is where the personal factor comes into play for, like Robert Nixon, Wright had been born and raised in the South before coming to live in Chicago. But the Nixon case resembles above all that of Bigger Thomas.

Native Son comprises, however, numerous autobiographical elements. Much like Richard Wright shortly after his arrival in Chicago, Bigger Thomas lives in a wretched kitchenette with his mother, brother, and sister. To make the comparison more exact, one could replace Bigger's sister with Wright's Aunt Maggie. These people live in the poverty of the South Side. They are all originally from Jackson, Mississippi, and have been in the North for only five years. Bigger assumes the role of head of the family since his father was killed in the South during a race riot. He has no job and lives from what the office of public assistance cares to give him. The young black man is devoured by hatred of the world around him. He hates whites because they oppress him, and he hates blacks because he realizes their total powerlessness in the face of white oppressors. He knows that his mother must pay eight dollars a week to enable her family to live in a slum crawling with rats and roaches. He also knows this rent is collected by a real estate agency, The South Side Real Estate Company, which belongs to Mr. Dalton.[33] Since he understands that whites do not hesitate to take advantage of blacks at the slightest opportunity, Bigger Thomas tries to act in a similar fashion by stealing from whites.

These larcenies earned him confinement in a house of correction for some time. But the young black man does not consider himself guilty, for in his eyes, only whites are at fault. Bigger knows that his mother's religion, Bessie Mears's alcohol and sexual debauchery are only evasions of the reality of the white world. He understands, along with the members of his gang, Jack, G.H., and Gus, that the white world is closed to them because of the color of their skin. These four boys refuse to submit entirely to the white world. They still nurture the hope that, maybe one day, they too will be able to be a member of the society that is oppressing them. But their dreams are constantly transformed into a bitter reality. They know that they will not be able to learn to pilot an airplane because of the segregation that is rampant in the American armed forces. They have no right to the world around them and they realize they cannot exercise any control over the prejudices of which they are the object. The rage that often erupts in them has some negative effects, for it always backfires on them or their fellowmen. In order to hide his fear of committing a theft in the store of the Jew, Blum, Bigger beats and insults Gus. Then he slashes the green carpet of a pool table in a pool hall whose owner, Doc, is black. It is the first time that Bigger and his friends attempt to commit an armed robbery in broad daylight. But to dare such an act against a white man presents, in their eyes, a great danger. They know that the white police do everything necessary to guarantee the protection of white establishments in the black ghetto. They also know that the police are scarcely concerned about what may happen to black establishments.

Bigger looses his fury on Gus and the pool table because he knows that the office of public assistance found him a job as chauffeur for the Daltons. He does not want to lose a sure thing, the job, by embarking on an uncertain adventure, the immersion in a white-dominated environment. His anger is directed against his own race and plays into the hands of whites, always delighted to see blacks killing one another. Bigger understands that he is part of a world that controls him totally. The only way he can assert his individuality is by denying the values of this world, even if blacks are a part of it. When he is in prison, Bigger smashes the face of the black minister, the Reverend Hammond, by violently closing the door of his cell. A while back, the preacher had given him a little cross. While coming out of the Daltons' house, where the police had taken him for the reenactment of the crime, Bigger had seen an immense cross in flames on the other side of the street. Realizing that the cross had been planted there by the Ku Klux Klan, the young black man had concluded that Christianity was at the root of all the ills afflicting his race: "It is not religion but hypocrisy accompanying Christianity that he is disavowing," says Russell Carl Brignano.[34] That is why Bigger looses his fury on the black preacher as soon as he sees him again.

Richard Wright wanted to make Bigger the symbol of the Northern ghetto black man, who is aware of his deplorable life. The author is very attached to his hero because he gives him ideas and attitudes that he encountered himself on the South Side of Chicago for nearly ten years. Bigger Thomas represents the oppressed Northern black man who hates his race and who hates himself because he is unable to do anything whatsoever to improve his people's lot. But Bigger Thomas is different from Richard Wright, lacking his intelligence and his wisdom. He has always lived in terror and oppression. A stock of general knowledge is totally meaningless to him.

Although the personality of the hero of Native Son suits his human condition perfectly, the novel lacks balance. In Book Three, the author explains the acts, the ideas, and the feelings of his hero through the intermediary of his lawyer. If Book One describes, in detail and with precision, the social conditions which led to Bigger's act, and if Book Two shows that Bigger freely accepts his act, Book Three, on the other hand, loses some of its naturalness because of Boris Max's intervention. In Book One and Two, the black hero is constantly doing battle with the world that is oppressing him. In Book Three, he does not seem capable of doing anything whatsoever without the aid of the white lawyer, who is both Jewish and Communist. The new direction taken by Book Three is due to the author's Communism at the time of the novel's composition. For the Richard Wright of 1940, only the Communist ideology could help the black American better understand his situation and try to improve it. That is why Book Three of Native Son is so different in its approach and in its content. Wright's imagination makes room in it for Marxist ideas.

Despite the author's militant Communism in Book Three of the novel, Native Son is, first of all, a work which deals with an American. He is neither a foreigner nor an immigrant but a native son. The whites around him refuse, however, to grant him any citizenship rights and force him to live on the fringe of society. The whites who tolerate his presence do so out of pity for his race and not for him. The black man as an individual is not entitled to any place. When Mary Dalton and her friend, Jan Erlone, try to win Bigger Thomas's confidence, the color of his skin prevents them from realizing that they are in the presence of a human being. The fact that Jan Erlone is a Communist, and that Mary Dalton sympathizes with the ideas of the Communist Party, emphasizes that even a Marxist can be blinded by the black man's color. Edwin Berry Burgum also pointed out that the social equality desired by the two whites is transformed into an act of racial arrogance in Bigger's eyes.[35] Wright especially wanted to have the black man's humanity recognized. The frankness of his novel is a direct criticism of Communism. John Milton Hughes stressed that "Moral indignation and the philosophical concepts underlying American democracy inspired Native Son and not Communism."[36] That is why the American Communist Party hesitated a long time before approving Native Son. The author wanted simply to give his point of view as a black man in the novel. A few years before the publication of Native Son, Wright had wondered quite frankly:

"What did seem important was: Could a Negro ever live halfway like a human being in this goddamn country?"[37] Whether whites were liberals or Communists, Wright knew that the color of his skin was a barrier that they had to learn to get over. That is why, suspicious of the Communist ideology, he had said, "I wanted to be a Communist, but my kind of Communist. I wanted to shape people's feelings, awaken their hearts."[38] He was speaking of the black masses whose sufferings and misfortunes he wanted to explain in Native Son.

If Mary Dalton and Jan Erlone are blinded by the color of Bigger's skin, the black hero is also blinded by the color of the two whites. He does not understand why two white strangers suddenly want to become his friends. He concludes that they want to make trouble for him. As soon as he runs into Mary in Mr. Dalton's office, Bigger has a strong feeling she is not to be trusted, especially after she asked whether he belonged to a trade union. This unexpected question surprises him very much, for he knows that such an affiliation would not be tolerated by Mr. Dalton. The young white woman's casual attitude makes him feel that he runs the risk of losing his new job if he does not pay attention to her. He does not understand that Mary's intentions are sincere and honest. The distance separating the young woman and the young black man makes those intentions dangerous.

The same goes for Jan Erlone, whom Bigger considers a fearsome individual after their first chance meeting. The idea that the young black man has about Communists is naïve. He imagines that Jan Erlone is an anarchist who is only seeking to create chaos in the order of things. A few hours before meeting Jan, Bigger and his friend Jack had seen a film, The Gay Woman. In this film, a disheveled and troubled man had tried to commit a bomb attack. Since he was a Communist, Bigger and Jack had concluded that Communists were fanatics prone to violence and destruction. This is the only concept, narrow and simplistic, that Bigger has of Communists. It is not surprising that he feels great fear when, that same evening, he is introduced to a real Communist. This fright is all the greater since he was not expecting to make such an acquaintance. Mr. Dalton had asked him to drive his daughter to the university. On the way, Mary tells him that she is not going to the university and that the outing is just an excuse to meet a friend on the sly. Surprised by such a change of plans, Bigger accepts the situation, telling himself his duty is to obey orders given. As Dalton's chauffeur, he has to do what he is asked, even if this task requires that he take Mary and her friend to a black Chicago restaurant, Ernie's Kitchen Shack.

However, he has not anticipated that the young white woman and Jan Erlone want to invite him to dinner with them. Not knowing what to do, Bigger refuses at first. But Mary Dalton's tears leave him no choice. The young black, with the two whites, reluctantly enters the black restaurant that he knows well. By asking Bigger to join them, Mary Dalton and Jan Erlone simply want to show their sincere friendship. But for the young black man, this invitation is a great humiliation: he cannot explain the presence of the two whites to his black friends. Bigger feels he has betrayed his race by accompanying whites into a black establishment. Dalton, the name that Wright has chosen for the young white woman's family, evokes John Dalton, the English chemist and physicist who had color blindness and after whom "Daltonism," or color blindness, is named. Here "Dalton" is symbolic of the total blindness of these whites in the face of the ghetto black's wounded humanity. Bigger Thomas' pride is ignored by Mary Dalton. She cannot perceive that her new chauffeur may have a personality as pronounced and as respectable as hers. A few hours later, under the influence of the alcohol he has consumed, Bigger makes so bold as to help Mary Dalton back to her room. As she is drunk, the young white woman is incapable of standing up. After having reached the girl's bedside, Bigger is about to make love to her when Mrs. Dalton arrives unexpectedly.

If the young black man kills Mary accidentally, he is nevertheless happy to have ended the life of a person who tormented him. The punishment he wanted to inflict on the young white woman, by having sexual relations with her, is involuntarily transformed into murder. Bigger knows that being discovered in a white woman's bedroom is both a compromising and a dangerous situation for a black man. He reduces Mary to silence with the aim of protecting himself. After realizing he has killed her, he burns the girl's body in order to destroy all evidence of his crime. As he is a black man, he knows that the whites will never understand the motives for his act; they will accuse him of having raped Mary Dalton before savagely killing her. It is through fear of this idea that he incinerates the girl's body.

The same desire for vengeance makes him turn against Jan Erlone, whom he manages to get incarcerated for some time. It is the false information given to the police by Bigger that leads to the arrest and then imprisonment of Mary Dalton's Communist friend. Not content with deceiving Jan Erlone, the young black man scoffs at society. He writes a note saying that Mary has been kidnapped, and that she will be released in return for the sum of ten thousand dollars. The way Bigger signs this note directly implicates the Communists. While going about his daily business, he enjoys observing the effects of his actions on the Daltons and on the police. He knows that the color of his skin protects him, for the whites would not suspect a black man of organizing such secret maneuvers. Bigger fully enjoys the powers he can exercise over a society that has always oppressed him. His vengeance is total.

For the young black man, such actions are possible because he has killed Mary Dalton. Without that accidental murder, he would never have been able to capitalize on his almost unlimited power. M. E. Grenander rightly comments: "Although Mary's murder was accidental, he draws strength from it. Justifying it as an existential choice affirming his own personality."[39] He knows, nonetheless, that the game he is playing cannot last for long, even if he has easily duped the private detective, Britten, by playing the role of the docile and stupid black. Bigger will never feel any remorse. Mary Dalton's accidental death has allowed him to enjoy for a while a freedom up until then unknown. That is why Keneth Kinnamon wrote: "Bigger can attain a sense of life only by inflicting death."[40] Mary's death has a positive, humanitarian influence on Bigger, since he accepts the consequences of his act and decides to face the white world's challenge.

The young black man's actions have disastrous repercussions on blacks in Chicago. From the moment he is arrested until his death, these blacks are mistreated by whites and lose their jobs. Numerous Communists are imprisoned by the police when they are suspected of having abducted Mary Dalton. Wright aims to show that the hero makes his discoveries at the expense of those individuals who could help him. Wright indicates clearly that the individual, whatever he may be, is never alone in his actions and must take into account those around him. To say that Bigger Thomas is selfish would be exaggerated, for he could not predict what would happen. The events that shake Chicago up after the discovery of Mary Dalton's murder are due to the blind racism of white American society, which refuses the black world. Hugh Morris Gloster has commented:

> The all-pervading thought of Native Son is that a prejudicial and capitalistic order, rather than any intrinsic human deficiency, is the cause of the frustration and rebellion of underprivileged Negro youth of America."[41]

American capitalism is directly indicted here since it has always profited from prejudices engendered by racism.

The action of the novel unfolds in about two weeks. Its principal aim is to show the rapidity with which a black man is judged and condemned to death in America. In order to create a gloomy atmosphere, the author has set the action in the middle of winter. Native Son begins around mid-February and ends in early March, only a few hours before Bigger's death. Social and especially political reasons contribute to the haste with which the young black man is condemned to the electric chair. First of all, the Chicago white population wants him to be punished as soon as possible so that blacks on the South Side will not repeat his act on a larger scale. Then, the attorney general of the state of Illinois, David A. Buckley, is eager to close the Thomas case without delay, for important elections are going to be held in April. Buckley wants at all costs to please the white masses, whose votes are very important for his reelection. The manner in which Wright describes the social and racial atmosphere of the novel suggests that the action takes place during the Great Depression in the thirties.

· The best part of the work, Books One and Two, owes its appeal and its force to the thrilling way the author develops his subject. The action takes place in the space of sixty hours. From the rude awakening of the Thomas family on Saturday morning to Bigger's capture late Monday evening, Wright powerfully describes a person that hates his environment and revolts against it. The author's great imagination enables him to use to the hilt each hour of those two and a half days and to describe skillfully the causes and the consequences of the young black man's act. Bigger spends Saturday morning with his gang and goes to the movies in the early afternoon. He goes to Mr. Dalton's house in the late afternoon and begins his duties as chauffeur that same evening, when he is supposed to drive Mary to the university. The girl's murder takes place on Sunday around three o'clock in the morning, and Bigger reaches the South Side again an hour later. He comes back into the Daltons' sumptuous dwelling on Sunday morning around nine o'clock. As if nothing had happened, he takes Mary's trunk to the train station, for the girl was supposed to take the train that very morning for Detroit. Back at the Daltons' he convinces everyone that Jan is implicated in the girl's mysterious disappearance. Given the rest of the day off, Bigger goes to meet Bessie Mears.

He comes back to the Daltons' in the afternoon. But he realizes that he must make people believe that Mary was kidnapped by the Communists, for the Daltons' private detective is too suspicious of him. He goes back to his girlfriend's house to write the note demanding Mary's ransom and comes back almost immediately to the Daltons' to slip it under the front door. A few moments later Mr. and Mrs. Dalton announce to the journalists that their daughter has been kidnapped. Shortly afterward, one of the newsmen discovers some human bones and an earring belonging to Mary in the ash pan of the furnace. Bigger takes flight immediately and goes to meet Bessie. He forces her to come hide with him in an abandoned building. It is Sunday evening. When day breaks, the young black woman will be dead. All day Monday, Bigger will attempt to escape the immense efforts undertaken by the Chicago forces of law and order to capture him. But he will be apprehended in the evening after a wild chase on the roofs of the black ghetto.

Book Three of Native Son does not have the dramatic intensity of the first two books. Wright's Communist ideology takes up too much room and therefore the action no longer has the natural fire of Books One and Two. This action takes a very political Marxist form. Wright describes Communism from three points of view: that of Boris Max, his own, and Bigger's. According to Boris Max, Communist ideology must enable the individual to acquire great human dignity, whatever the color of his skin may be. This extremely utopian stand was that of the white American Communist leaders during Richard Wright's time. But for the author, this attitude denied the individual's historical and racial past; Wright especially wanted to be accepted as a black man. In the course of his excessively long search for the defense, Boris Max first highlights the tortured life of a man who has never known the meaning of life because of the color of his skin.[42] That is why the Jewish lawyer asks that the young black man not be condemned to death, but rather to life in prison. According to Boris Max, the condemnation would give Bigger an understanding of human goodness and would enable him to know himself better. M.E. Grenander thinks that Boris Max does not see Bigger as an individual but rather as a mere representative of the twelve million blacks who lived in America at the time of the publication of Native Son.[43] The white Communist lawyer thus denies the young black man any personality. Any other attitude would have given

Bigger's action a black nationalist aspect, something that Communism does not try to encourage.

Wright expresses his Communist point of view as a black man through the intermediary of Jan Erlone. When Jan comes to visit him in prison, Bigger is struck by the frankness with which the young white man admits his blindness to him and offers help by introducing him to Boris Max. The humility with which Jan Erlone speaks is sure to arouse in Bigger's soul feelings until then unknown. Kinnamon points out: "If Jan's good will is expressed in a bumbling and insensitive manner in his initial approach to Bigger, he more than compensates for this mistake by his heroic support of Bigger after Mary's death."[44] The young black expected to find hate and rage in a person that he had caused to be imprisoned by his lies after killing the one he loved. Bigger understands that Jan Erlone, through his sufferings, has managed to recognize and accept his own mistakes. The young black man realizes that, like his own, the young man's sufferings have also enabled him to see better and to better judge the environment in which he lives. Erlone, the family name, chosen by Wright for the young white man, suggests isolation. It is the solitude surrounding Jan and Bigger which, in the raging storm, will bring them closer and make them true friends. Here Wright identifies entirely with Bigger. Wright shows Communism as he sees it and accepts it by describing the development of an interracial friendship between two young people belonging to the proletarian class.

A few days before his death, Bigger has complete faith in Jan Erlone and Boris Max. They are the only human beings he will ever be truly able to know. Although he knows nothing about Communism, the young black man realizes that these two whites understand and want to help him. He knows that their feelings are sincere since they attach great importance to his life. Bigger is no longer frightened by their membership in the Communist Party. He knows that they have accepted him as he is and that they have even helped him to discover his dignity as a man. Bigger is not only an individual, but a symbol of revolutionary black nationalism. Even if he understood it, the Marxist ideology would be of no use to him. It was probably Bigger's nationalist attitude that also made the American Communist Party hesitate in pronouncing itself in favor of Native Son.

The Attorney General of the State of Illinois, on the other hand, does everything possible to make Bigger's condemnation to death certain. He makes more than sixty witnesses appear before the judge in order to prove that the young black man is not insane but a monstrous beast that must be killed. The law officer in charge of investigating the circumstances of Mary Dalton's death uses Bessie Mears's body to show the savagery with which Bigger attacked the young white woman before burning her. The whites believe that the black man incinerated Mary Dalton in order to hide all evidence of rape. The body of Bigger's black girlfriend only serves to illustrate a murder about which no one is sure. Nobody feels compassion for the sad lot of Bessie Mears, whom Bigger never loved and whom he kills to protect himself from the white world. Even if he pleads not guilty, Bigger is condemned to death by the white judge.

The vague fashion in which Wright describes the white characters in his novel is essentially intended to bring out the destitution and poverty of the black world. The author can also highlight the distance that separates the black world from the white. These two worlds do not know each other and wish to make no effort in this direction. By writing a realistic and even naturalistic novel, Wright was trying to shock the white liberals of the time while denouncing American racism. If Mr. Dalton aids in financing the activities of the National Association for the Advancement of Colored People and gives ping-pong tables to the South Side Boys' Club, he is nevertheless ignorant of the reality of the black world. Only Bigger's violence will make him understand the enormity of his mistake. He will realize that his commitment must be deeper and personal. Making the most of his violent attack on liberal whites, Wright also mercilessly criticizes the black American bourgeoisie. Bigger knows that these blacks consider him a disgrace to the black race. In their eyes, he has behaved like the human beast that whites see in every black. The hero of the novel scorns the lies and the hopes of the black bourgeoisie ready to do everything to please whites and to be accepted by them. He will tell Boris Max that he expects no help from those blacks.

Once in prison and as soon as his crime is known, Bigger cannot help but feel great pride at the thought of having acted in the name of all oppressed blacks. He is surprised, even disappointed, when his mother, his sister, his brother, and the friends in his set come to visit him and exhibit a sad look full of pity whereas he is convinced his action has affirmed a black presence within the American society. As he realizes that his country is finally granting him social and human importance, Bigger Thomas would like all blacks to be thrilled about his act. He knows that he has dared to do what every black has always wished to carry out against the white oppressor.

If Book Three of the novel lacks the dramatic intensity of the first two books, it nonetheless enables Wright to describe the action in a period of time that lends itself to his ideas. From the moment of his arrest, Bigger is caught up in the gears of a racist justice that wants only his death. Wright accurately depicts the important moments of this legal action: a mere eleven days elapse between the young black man's arrest and his condemnation to death, set for Friday, March 3. Three days after his capture, on Thursday afternoon, Bigger attends the judicial inquiry. He is then taken to the Daltons' for a recreation of the crime and is finally locked away in the Chicago Central Prison. The next day his indictment takes place. It is decided that his trial is to open three days later. The trial takes place at the Criminal Court of Chicago. After three days, Bigger Thomas is condemned to die in the electric chair. A few days later, the young black man will no longer be of this world.

In order to plunge Book Three into an atmosphere as real as that of the first two books, Wright shows the extent to which a single black man can affect the lives of millions of whites. Since he fears serious social problems, the mayor of Chicago encourages the police to step up their vigilance. During Bigger's trial the governor of Illinois calls on the help of two regiments of reservists to guard the court and the Central Prison. The young black man's trial takes place in an extremely tense political and social atmosphere. Bigger appears as a social symbol void of any human conscience. He represents modern man. Margaret Just Butcher thinks that Communism is uncalled for and that it hampers the development of the novel.   This black American woman finds it unpleasant that Wright's Marxism denounces the wrongs of American society.[45] Numerous American critics feel, like her, that Wright could have attained the same goal without using Communist ideology. But in 1940, Marxist ideology was practically the only means by which the American black could express his thoughts and his desires.

Wright thus enables Bigger Thomas to confront, alone, a society that denies him human value. This young black man goes into action to attract the attention of those around him and to prove his existence to eyes until then blind. Bigger Thomas's conduct shows that, for the first time in his works known in 1940, Wright had clearly formulated certain fundamental elements of existentialism.[46] In Richard Wright, Robert Bone underlines the fact that, "Having rejected Christianity and Communism, Bigger finds the strength to die in the courageous acceptance of his existential self."[47] When he says, "What I killed for, I am," The hero of Native Son is, in his own way, an existentialist.[48] In his philosophical essay L'Existentialisme est un humanisme, Jean-Paul Sartre says, "Man is constantly outside of himself; it is by projecting himself and by losing himself outside of himself that he makes man exist and, on the other hand, it is by pursuing transcendent goals that he can exist."[49] Bigger's symbolic action is taken in the name of the twelve million blacks who were living in America in 1940. To use Sartre's terms, Bigger projects himself, loses himself outside of himself, in order to establish the human value of the man of color. Thanks to his act and especially to the privileged position he holds in the eyes of the oppressed blacks, the hero of Native Son becomes the symbol and the hope of a race that has never ceased to struggle. The essential aim of this struggle has always been to create a human identity respected by all ethnic and racial groups who form the framework of American society. Bigger becomes the center of a question that preoccupies black America.

One should not think that Bigger's action is that of the ordinary black. It is that of the young black man who has become aware of his freedom and of his acts. He acts with the sole aim of creating an identity for himself. He knows that he will be what he does. The future of his life will depend on the way he conducts himself. It is only through his action that the young black man shows his brothers of color the road to follow.

Even after having learned of his condemnation to death, Bigger has the profound feeling of having accomplished something important for himself and his race. Wright accentuates the isolation and lack of understanding surrounding his act and the hero himself: Bigger only trusts himself. Here

Wright explains an idea later developed by Sartre, who says, "Man must find himself again himself and convince himself that nothing can save him from himself."[50] Man is always alone and can count on no one. Blacks and whites in Chicago reject Bigger's act and do not understand its symbolic significance.

The accidental murder committed by Bigger Thomas strangely resembles what happens to the man of whom Albert Camus speaks in L'Étranger.[51] Meursault becomes a murderer because of a beach, an Arab, some sunlight, and a revolver. He kills the Arab following a combination of fortuitous circumstances. Bigger Thomas smothers Mary Dalton by instinct, to avoid being discovered in the room of a white woman. Panic-stricken, he can no longer control his acts.

There is, however, a fundamental difference between Meursault and Bigger. Each of them adopts a different attitude towards the world after the crime. The young Frenchman shows only indifference towards everything around him. The young American becomes aware of his human value after having accepted the consequences of his act. Meursault invites one to think of the world in terms of absurdity, life in terms of despair, whereas Bigger gives life a positive meaning.

A few days after the publication of Native Son, Wright drafted the text of a lecture he gave at the Schomburg Collection in Harlem. The black audience permitted him to express freely his views on the manner in which he had conceived the novel. That essay "How 'Bigger' Was Born" gives Native Son a complex meaning.[52] If in it Wright relates certain events of his youth which influenced the composition of the novel, he wishes above all to show that there is a close relationship between real life and the imaginative work. Disappointed after seeing some bankers' daughters weeping on the pages of Uncle Tom's Children: Four Novellas, Wright had decided to reveal the reality of the black world.[53] His aim was to make that reality as harsh and as violent as possible so as to prevent any person from getting over the plight of blacks by shedding some comforting tears. Native Son was the result.

Many years passed between the moment Wright became aware of Bigger's existence and the day he began to write the novel. It was the freedom of the North that enabled Wright to accept and analyze feelings until then repressed. His association with white writers in Chicago was very helpful to him in his literary career. He does not try to hide the fact that:

> This association with white writers was the life preserver of my hope to depict Negro life in fiction, for my race possessed no fictional works dealing with such problems, had no background in such sharp and critical testing of experience, no novels that went with a deep and fearless will down to the dark roots of life.[54]

The Communist ideology enabled him to see that Bigger Thomas's condition was not peculiar to blacks, but universal and human. In "I Tried to Be a Communist," when he wondered "Why was I a suspected man because I wanted to reveal the vast physical and spiritual ravages of Negro life, the profundity latent in these rejected people?", he knew that his black Communist friends did not understand him.[55]

In this essay, Wright emphasizes that the black masses represented by Bigger can, if the case arises, subscribe to Fascism or to Communism if their social conditions do not improve. The author makes "How 'Bigger' Was Born" an expert psychological analysis of oppression by showing how man can be skillfully manipulated and kept in utter ignorance. Thanks to numerous examples given and to the manner in which he presents them, Wright demonstrates that literary techniques may be adapted to social and political protest. He wishes to stress that the hero of the novel is nothing but the product of an unbalanced society whose sole aim is the destruction of the black man.

The main appeal of Native Son was due largely to Bigger's violence. That was the only way to attract the white world's attention to the wretched living conditions of the American black. The play Native Son, which Wright wrote in the summer of 1940, does not follow the novel closely.[56] It even betrays its main idea. This is perhaps due to the influence of the white playwright, a native of the south, with whom Wright composed the play. Bigger's black playwright girlfriend is killed by a bullet fired by whites and Scene 10 is very different from the end of the novel. In that scene, Bigger is presented as a raving madman. The presence of a priest wearing a white surplice and reciting religious words make him almost unrecognizable. The lack of violence makes the play inferior to the novel. That is what numerous critics have also said, particularly Joseph Wood Krutch in The Nation.[57] In his novel, Wright's aim is to show that violence was the only means by which Bigger could create himself, discover himself, and accept himself. It is true that a play cannot bring back in all its details the atmosphere of a novel as poignant as Native Son, but the moral that emerges from the play is heavily stamped with Christianity and has nothing to do with the human and social message of the novel.[58]

ACTION

Forced to lead an uncertain life because of fear of the white world, the American black often decides to do all he can to change his lot. In the fourth part of Twelve Million Black Voices: A Folk History of the Negro in the United States, Wright speaks of the means used by blacks to improve their living conditions. That section, "Men in the Making," stresses that the Depression of the thirties enabled the black man to gain an awareness of his social, political, and economic role.[59] Since then, he has been a member of trade unions that have guaranteed him the same protection as whites. He can also fight injustice done to him by getting organized with whites. Here the author is referring indirectly to the Communist influence. He shows the positive aspect of such actions when he talks about the Scottsboro case, which lasted from 1931 to 1937. Originally, eight of the nine black men falsely accused of the rape of two white women were condemned to death by the State of Alabama. Their fate was changed thanks to the direct intervention of the U.S. Supreme Court. Such a result had been made possible only by the union of all blacks aware of their future and determined to indict American racism. Wright wished to make it clear that black Americans have no other country but America and that they intend to be an integral part of it. He explains that it is not surprising that, often, certain blacks, despairing of everything, dream of an independent black state within America or, even now, of a return to Africa. He indeed makes one feel that, within the space of three hundred years, the black American had to progress from the stage of a simple African native to that of a citizen of the most advanced nation in the world. The author stresses that such an experience was painful and difficult for the American black, who was forced to assimilate in relatively little time a civilization that whites had taken more than two thousand years to develop.

Wright explains that the blindness and the prejudices of the white world often lead the black man to the destruction of everything around him in order to make himself heard. The author is alluding to the riots that tore Harlem apart in 1935. But these remarks may also apply just as well to the riots that rocked America in the sixties. Wright's message is clear: the black man will not be satisfied until America has accepted him. Although he denounces the negative and bloody aspect of these urban revolts, Wright does not condemn them entirely. That is what led The Nation, The New Republic, and The New York Times to declare, shortly after its publication, that Twelve Million Black Voices: A Folk History of the United States was filled with anger because the author wanted to see the black man occupy the position he deserved within American society.[60] The five decades that have passed since the publication of that book have shown that violence was, for the black man, the most effective means of reminding America that he was discontented with his lot. His goal is to be treated like a full citizen. "Men in the Making," in which the struggle of the urban proletariat is exposed, highlights Wright's socialist visions and the book's Marxist tendencies. However, if Samuel Sillen wrote a highly favorable review of Wright's book in New Masses, he made sure to note that "Men in the Making" did not deal enough with the black worker and his future in a Communist context.[61] This occurred because Richard Wright was a Marxist in his own way, and he had already decided to break with the Communist Party at the time of the writing of the book.

Wright was above all proud of his race. Two weeks after the victory of the black boxer Joe Louis over the white boxer Max Baer, he published an article, "Joe Louis Uncovers Dynamite."[62] In the report, the author analyzed the effects of this victory on the inhabitants of the black ghetto in Chicago. This match, which pitted two Americans against each other in New York's Yankee Stadium, took on great importance for America. Not only did it open the door to the world's championship, but, above all, each of the two fighters represented his race. As soon as Joe Louis got the better of Max Baer in the fourth round in the evening of September 24,

1935, the Chicago South Side exploded with joy. No sooner had the radio announced that a black man had beaten a white man than thousands of blacks descended into the streets of the ghetto to celebrate the event. In his article, Wright emphasizes that Joe Louis's victory proved to America that blacks were not inferior to whites. The author also stresses that the enthusiasm of Chicago blacks surprised whites, who did not suspect them of having such reactions. Chicago officials did not know what to do for several hours to contain the delirium of blacks, filled with pride and anger, who suddenly felt superior to the white race. The black policemen sent to reestablish order did not use violence. They knew that the slightest provocation could trigger a dangerous and destructive reaction on the part of their brothers of color. This feeling of racial superiority made it clear to Wright that such an outburst of black nationalism had to be exploited in order to fight against the racism of Northern industrialists and the big landowners of the South. In this report, the author emphasizes that often the symbolic victory of a single individual is sufficient to make his fellowmen identify with him. In beating Max Baer, Joe Louis enabled black America to take revenge on white America.

The vast majority of American blacks consider themselves, first of all, as Americans. If the bout between Joe Louis and Max Baer had racial repercussions, the one that matched Joe Louis and Max Schmeling was viewed differently by blacks. Although white, Schmeling was, above all, a Nazi in the eyes of black America. On the evening of June 19, 1936, Joe Louis was defeated in the fourth round. The victory of a German over an American had shown that Fascism could triumph over democracy. It was in those terms that Wright wrote an article, "High Tide in Harlem," in which he spoke of the stunning victory of Joe Louis over Max Schmeling.[63] This second fight was important on more than one account. Not only did the American black have to try to regain the title of world heavyweight boxing champion, but he also had to prove that he could beat Max Schmeling. That fight took place on the evening of June 22, 1938, at Yankee Stadium, where Joe Louis beat the German with a knockout in the first round.

In "High Tide in Harlem," Wright speaks of the reaction of the inhabitants of Harlem to the announcement of Joe Louis's victory. For those blacks, the American boxer had to prove that the black race was not inferior to the other races, and that the Aryan race could not claim to be superior to all the races. The author skillfully shows that, for this fight, Joe Louis was not only the symbol of his race, but also the symbol of freedom; he was the representative of the free world. The undisputed victory of Joe Louis over Schmeling made ghetto blacks aware that their race could aid in making the egalitarian and free democracy of America respected. If the thousands of blacks who entered the streets of the South Side, after Joe Louis's victory over Max Baer in 1935, had frightened Chicago whites, the thousands of blacks who descended into the streets of Harlem in 1938 had, on the contrary, encouraged whites in New York to share their joy.

In these two articles, Wright shows that, thanks to racial pride on one hand and to proletarian democracy on the other, blacks can discover their deep humanity. But the author's Communist ideology does not allow these two articles to reflect daily reality. At the time of the writing of these articles, Wright knew very well that America was a racist country and that only a social revolution could bring about pronounced improvement of the American black's lot. That is perhaps what he was hoping when he wrote his Marxist poems.

The revolutionary spirit of the first six poems, published in 1934, shows that Wright firmly believed in the Communist cause. Each of these poems touches on one aspect of the social struggle then led by the author. They are addressed directly to the common people with whom Wright wished to share his new proletarian views. "A Red Love Note" condemns capitalist institutions in the form of a love letter addressed to an insolvent debtor.[64] In this poem, the author highlights the errors of capitalism by using legal jargon.

In "Rest for the Weary," Wright announces the impending end of capitalism and the imminent victory of Communism.[65] In "Strength," he says that the union of the workers will constitute their strength against capitalism, which they will have no trouble destroying.[66] In "Child of the Dead and Forgotten Gods," the author shows the total ineffectiveness of the liberal ideology.[67] Furthermore, in "Everywhere Burning Waters Rise," Wright indicates that the discontent of the oppressed will be transformed into a violent revolt that will provoke the total destruction of capitalism.[68]

The last of the six poems, "I Have Seen Black Hands," is the only one to speak of the American racial problem by recounting the stages of the Afro-American experience.[69] As it is directly inspired by the author's experiences, it gains a great deal in natural beauty. His Marxist interpretation, although secondary, constitutes its originality. This poem brings out Wright's desire to do and say what he wishes. "Rest for the Weary" and "Child of the Dead and Forgotten Gods" encompass a more poetic message than "A Red Love Note," "Strength," or "Everywhere Burning Waters Rise" because Wright says in the last three poems especially what he thinks without forcing himself to follow the rigid thought of Marxism.

Wright's passion for Communism is evident in these six poems. But it is clear that the author does not want to sacrifice his sensitive soul and his human experiences for the Communist ideology. This dichotomy in the author's attitude is found again in a more pronounced way in the rest of his Marxist poems. Of the seven poems published in 1935, two deal with lynching. In "Obsession," Wright makes a quick sketch of a lynching, whereas in "Between the World and Me" he gives a complete description.[70] "Obsession" is filled with emotion and has nothing to do with the author's Marxism. The same is true of "Between the World and Me," in which the author identifies with the victim in order to relive the lynching. These two poems bring out the human suffering endured by the Southern black. This suffering is caused by conditions which require only enslavement of the blacks and which have already been evoked in "I Have Seen Black Hands."[71] Among the five other poems published in 1936, "Ah Feels It in

Mah Bones" has the distinctive feature of being written in black dialect.[72] This poem places special emphasis on the wretched living conditions of a penniless black man who feels that some social upheavals are going to take place. The title of this poem, repeated as a refrain at the end of each verse, allows Wright to give the poem the form of a blues. This form is very common in the author's Marxist poems.

The four other poems published in 1935 are Communist propaganda and reveal a Wright totally devoted to the Marxist cause. "Rise and Live" speaks of oppression but in its form closely resembles a blues.[73] "I Am a Red Slogan" comprises twelve slogans supposedly leading to the final victory of Communism.[74] "Red Leaves of Red Books" declares that Marxist works must serve as Bibles for the masses thirsty for social equality.[75] In this poem, the author reveals his desire to learn when he encourages an entire people to educate itself. In "Spread Your Sunrise!" finally, Wright greets the progress of socialism in the United States.[76]

The three poems published in 1936 seem to show that the author was trying to convince himself of the final victory of Communism. "Transcontinental," Wright's longest and probably most ambitious poem, takes the reader on a trip through socialist America.[77] The trip is taken in a car taken from the rich during the revolution. In the course of this long journey, Southern black sharecroppers, Indians from the Western reservations and even vagrants have the right to speak. In other words, the oppressed minorities take their revenge on a society that has always ignored their rights. The aim of this long poem is to demand that justice be fair and equitable to all. But a certain bitterness emerges from the work and seems to indicate that Wright was disappointed either by his own experiences with capitalism or by the uncertain future of Communism in America.

"Hearst Headline Blues" seems to show that the author was not sure of his country.[78] This poem is an ironic criticism of the illusory solutions discussed by the American government in order to resolve the economic and social crisis of the thirties. Each line represents the title of an article published in the newspapers of William Randolph Hearst. In "Old Habit and New Love," on the other hand, Wright seems to have found peace of mind because he assigns to himself the sole aim of making the worker happy by finding him a job he likes.[79] This poem represents no political tendency and reflects the soul of the author in search of peace in a simple world. Although it looks utopian, this poem seems to reflect the author's personal attitude towards life. "Old Habit and New Love" is the compromise that enables the individual to accept himself after he has realized the profound meaning of life. Here Wright wishes to show that everything depends on the individual who becomes what he wants to be. This attitude is found again in "We of the Streets," the only poem published in 1937, with the unique difference that, here, the author praises the strength of the urban proletariat.[80] This poem stands out especially because of the way Wright celebrates the simple life of the poor in the ghetto.

Wright's intense desire to be himself, that is to say, black, before being a Communist was the main reason he was never entirely converted to the Marxist ideology. This will to be first of all a member of the black race led him to write "Red Clay Blues" in 1939.[81] This poem, written in collaboration with Langston Hughes, has a completely blues rhythm and evokes the nostalgia of the ghetto black for his native South. "Red Clay Blues" speaks of the disenchantment of the black who realizes that the North is not the promised land glorified so much by Southern blacks. This disillusionment reflects perhaps that of Wright in regard to the Communist Party and explains his great interest in black culture.[82] Speaking of Richard Wright's Marxist poetry, Keneth Kinnamon declared: "Through this poetry he hoped to humanize Communist propaganda, to effect a rapprochement between Communist intellectuals and the masses, to interpret each to the other."[83] Wright wanted, in the first place, to use all the means possible to make the feelings of the black masses known. Communism was only one means to arrive at his ends.

Aware and proud of his origins, Wright wrote in 1941 a blues, "King Joe," in honor of the black boxer Joe Louis, who was still heavyweight champion.[84] This composition has the classic form of the blues. Each verse ends on the exploits of the boxer. This blues uses objects and animals from black folklore to celebrate a man who gave blacks victory and superiority over the white race. Wright turns the blues into a song of battle and vengeance, whereas this form of black protest usually wishes to express hope for a better future. Closely resembling "Joe Louis Uncovers Dynamite" and "High Tide in Harlem" in the racial pride that emerges from its stanzas, this blues shows, however, that Wright knew how to accentuate the qualities of his race without going through Marxism.[85]

This awareness of the power of black culture had enabled Wright, as early as 1937, to write a declaration of literary independence for the black American writer. This essay, "Blueprint for Negro Writing," aimed essentially to say there was a close relationship between the black writer's technique and the content of his work.[86] According to Wright, a work is good only if the author is sincere and if the work itself represents a certain artistic unity. Only the total commitment of the author to his work enables him to create a true work of art. In this essay, Wright pitilessly attacks the traditional tendencies of black American literature which create either artificial and light works or works imitating the style and manners of whites. In both cases, the life of the black masses has no right to any place. This essay forms such a striking contrast to Wright's Communist poems that Keneth Kinnamon thinks: "In some respects, indeed, the essay may be considered an implicit criticism of his earliest poetry."[87] Thus Wright says that the lives of these millions of blacks are a part of a culture different from that of whites, since it was forged in suffering. According to him, this Afro-American culture is the product of two important elements: the black church and black folklore. Wright suggests that the black writer should study that culture in order to give his work new goals. He stresses that, thanks to its oral and popular tradition, black folklore is an inexhaustible source of materials and ideas for the black artist.[88]

It is by turning to his own culture that the black writer can validly establish a black nationalism of which he must be proud. Wright's Communism at the time of the writing of this essay makes him say that the black writer's Marxist vision must aid him in better understanding his culture. But Wright hastens to add that the Communist ideology is only a point of departure, and that the rest of the work depends upon the artist. If the black artist must describe the complex simplicity of Afro-American life, it must also reveal the social, economic, and political aspects of that culture. Great love of freedom of expression causes Wright to say the black writer can utilize any technique or literary form to serve his needs and draw from the sources of Afro-American culture. Wright adds that it is only after having fully understood the history of his race that the black writer will be able to find themes for his works. He also says that the black artist's work must be beneficial to the black community and destroy all internal rivalries and jealousies. Wright encourages a close and fraternal union among blacks. He makes it clear, however, that the black artist must devote himself entirely to his work and cannot be bothered by excessively rigid opinions or views. Wright recommends great autonomy for the black writer, whose main role is to accentuate the complexity and the individuality of Afro-American culture.

Wright's aim in this essay is to appeal directly to the black masses and to give them a precise meaning. In The Crisis of the Negro Intellectual, Harold Cruse criticizes Wright's approach because it was influenced by Communism. Harold Cruse feels that Wright should have addressed black intellectuals first, for he says: "It was the Negro intelligentsia who had no goals, hence how could they impart any to the Negro masses?"[89] Because of the Marxist ideology with which he was imbued, Wright had perhaps not realized that the black masses could have headed the proletarian revolution if they had been guided by a few well-informed and determined blacks. That is why American Communist leaders, who are all white, fiercely opposed all black nationalism. They were afraid of an awakening of the black masses.

"Blueprint for Negro Writing" is Wright's most complete and most coherent description of the black American writer's role. It was the first time the author had formulated a program that accentuated popular black ethnic traditions. He was to follow the main lines of this program for the rest of his literary career.

Thus, in 1946, he wrote a story that explored blacks' blurred and muddled picture of reality in the white world. This story, "The Man Who Killed A Shadow," intended to show that it is often impossible for the black man to separate life from the dream or the real act from the imaginary act.[90] The subject of this story had been inspired by an incident related by Charles H. Houston, then a very famous lawyer for the National Association for the Advancement of Colored People. If, in "The Man Who Lived Underground," Wright had spoken of the invisibility of the black man, he wanted in "The Man Who Killed A Shadow" to emphasize the feeling of nonexistence that the black experienced in the presence of the white world.

This short story tells of a black man, Saul Saunders, who kills a white librarian in order to silence the screams she lets out which arouse feelings of fear in him. He kills her simply to make her shut up. Like Bigger Thomas, he commits this murder by instinct, unwittingly, with the sole aim of controlling the terror incited by the young woman's screams.

Saul Saunders had a stable childhood and adolescence. Since his parents died when he was very young, he had had to live with his grandmother, who moved constantly. This life had always been lived within the black communities of the South. But Saul Saunders quickly learned to be on his guard in the presence of whites. He does not understand them. Numerous experiences have taught him that whites do not see him the way he sees himself. When he begins to work as a janitor at the Library of Congress, he notices that the white librarian is constantly watching him. One day she orders him to come clean under her desk, with the sole aim of showing him her underwear. Offended, Saul Saunders slaps her. The hysterical screams of the young woman makes him commit a crime.

Saul Saunders's act is provoked by the racist attitude of the unmarried librarian. Apparently deprived of any sex life, she takes revenge on a black man. The tension coming from racial prejudices and repressed sexual desires drives the white woman to offend the pride of a young man whose skin is black. The way Wright describes the young woman's murder is both prosaic and extraordinary. It is prosaic because Saul Saunders had been preparing to confront this type of situation for a long time, and extraordinary because the murder is violent and bloody. Wright's style permits the reader to share Saul Saunders's detached and almost dreamy state of mind before, during, and after the murder. To a certain extent, the hero of this story closely resembles that of L'Étranger.

Saul Saunders's attitude towards the white world is constantly filled with fear. Saul Saunders is a black man who takes to drinking to escape the hard life that the shadows of the white world make him lead. He tries to commit suicide when he is arrested and when he understands he no longer has any future.

The total lack of understanding that separates blacks from whites is highlighted when Saul Saunders is charged with murder: the whites do not understand why his crime was not accompanied by rape. Blinded by their ludicrous ideas about the sexual prowess of the black man, white Americans firmly believe that the black American man lives only to savagely violate the white woman. Speaking of Saul Saunders, Edward Margolies emphasizes: "Like the underground man he lives on a plane of fear, guilt, and dread . . . the Negro man and the white woman are not only shadows to one another, but shadows to themselves."[91] The white world will be able to know the black world only by listening to it with patience and by trying to understand its actions better. This attitude will also enable the white world to know itself better.

NOTES

1. Richard Wright, "The Man Who Was Almost a Man," in his Eight Men (Cleveland and New York: World Publishing Co., 1961).

2. Richard Wright, Twelve Million Black Voices: A Folk History of the Negro in The United States (New York: The Viking Press, 1941).

3. Richard Wright, "Death on the City Pavements," in his Twelve Million Black Voices, pp. 91-139.

4. William Shands Meacham, "The Bitter Saga of the Negro," The New York Times Book Review, November 23, 1941, p. 11.

5. Richard Wright, Lawd Today (New York: Walker and Co., 1963). All other references to Lawd Today will be to the Avon Books edition of 1969.

6. Wright, Lawd Today, p. 219.

7. Albert Camus, Le Mythe de Sisyphe (Paris: Éditions Gallimard, 1966), p. 165.

8. Camus, Le Mythe de Sisyphe, p. 165.

9. Jean-Paul Sartre, L'Existentialisme est un humanisme (Paris: les éditions Nagel, 1967), p. 83.

10. Sigmund Freud, A General Introduction to Psychoanalysis (New York: Washington Square Press, 1961), p. 165.

11. Joe Louis did so in the evening of June 22, 1938, when he beat Max Schmeling by a first-round knockout in Yankee Stadium in New York.

12. Eldridge Cleaver, Soul on Ice (New York: Dell Publishing Co., 1968).

13. Staughton Lynd, "The New Negro Radicalism", Commentary 36 (September 1963): 255.

14. Nick Aaron Ford, "The Fire Next Time?", Phylon 25 (Second Quarter, Summer 1964): 130.

15. Granville Hicks, "Dreiser to Farrell to Wright," Saturday Review, March 30, 1963, p. 37.

16. "Native Sons," Time, April 5, 1963, p. 106; Louise Giles, "Lawd Today," Library Journal, April 1, 1963, p. 1549.

17. Richard Wright, "The Man Who Lived Underground," in Cross Section, edited by Edwin Seaver (New York: L. B. Fischer Publishing Corporation, 1944), pp. 58-102. Published under the same title in Eight Men.

18. Richard Wright, "The Man Who Lived Underground," Accent: A Quarterly of New Literature 2 (Spring 1942): 170-176.

19. Hal Fletcher, "The Crime Hollywood Couldn't Believe," True Detective, August 1941, pp. 42-47, 107-109.

20. The adventures of Richard Wright in Michael Reese Hospital in Chicago in early 1933 must have also influenced the writing of this short story, for the author had then realized the invisible power of the black over white America.

21. Edward Margolies, The Art of Richard Wright (Carbondale Southern Illinois University Press, 1969), p. 77.

22. Robert Bone, Richard Wright (Minneapolis: University of Minnesota Press, 1969), p. 30.

23. Jean-Paul Sartre, L'Existentialisme est un humanisme, pp. 66-67.

24. Fedor M. Dostoevski, Notes From Underground, in Short Novels of the Masters, edited by Charles Neider (New York: Rinehart and Co., 1948), pp. 125-219.

25. Richard Wright, "Superstition," Abbott's Monthly, April 1931, pp. 45-47, 64-66, 72-73.

26. "Each Year The Family Held A Reunion-Each Year Death Claimed Its Toll-Was It Superstition-Or Was It-Fate?-", "Superstition," p. 45.

27. Michel Fabre, "Black Cat and White Cat: Richard Wright's Debt to Edgar Allan Poe," Poe Studies 4 (December 1971): 17.

28. Keneth Kinnamon, The Emergence of Richard Wright: A Study in Literature

and Society (Urbana: University of Illinois Press, 1972), p. 48.

29. Richard Wright, Native Son (New York: Harper and Brothers, 1940). All the other references to Native Son will correspond to the Harper and Row edition of 1966).

30. As in the following passage: "There were many empty buildings with black windows, like blind eyes, buildings like skeletons standing with snow on their bones in the winter winds." Native Son, p. 163.

31. Especially when he declares: "But, Your Honor, I say: 'Stop! Let us look at what we are doing!' For the corpse is not dead! It still lives! It has made itself a home in the wild forest of our great cities, amid the rank and choking vegetation of slums! It has forgotten our language! In order to live it has sharpened its claws! It has grown hard and calloused! It has developed a capacity for hate and fury which we cannot understand! Its movements are unpredictable! By night it creeps from its lair and steals toward the settlements of civilization! And at the sight of a kind face it does not lie down upon its back and kick up its heels playfully to be tickled and stroked. No; it leaps to kill!" Native Son, pp. 361-362.

32. Ralph Ellison, "Recent Negro Fiction," New Masses 5 (August 1941): 22.

33. More than two years before the publication of Native Son, Richard Wright had severely criticized the white owners of apartment buildings in Harlem because the black tenants had to pay them exorbitant rent. See Richard Wright's article "Gouging, Landlord Discrimination Against Negroes Bared at Hearing," Daily Worker, December 15, 1937, p. 6.

34. Russell Carl Brignano, Richard Wright: An Introduction to the Man and His Works (Pittsburgh: University of Pittsburgh Press, 1970), p. 147.

35. Edwin Berry Burgum, "The Promise of Democracy in Richard Wright's Native Son," in The Novel and the World's Dilemma (New York: Oxford University Press, 1947), p. 229.

36. John Milton Hughes, "Portrayals of Bitterness," in The Negro Novelist (New York: Citadel Press, 1953), p. 49.

37. Richard Wright, "I Tried to Be a Communist," The Atlantic Monthly, August 1944, p. 70.

38. Wright, "I Tried to Be a Communist," p. 50.

39. M. E. Grenander, "Criminal Responsibility in Native Son and Knock on Any Door," American Literature 49 (May 1977): 225.

40. Keneth Kinnamon, The Emergence of Richard Wright, p. 141.

41. Hugh Morris Gloster, "Richard Wright," in his Negro Voices in American Fiction (Chapel Hill: University of North Carolina Press, 1948), p. 232.

42. Wright, Native Son, pp. 353-370.

43. Grenander, "Criminal Responsibility in Native Son and Knock on Any Door," p. 26.

44. Keneth Kinnamon, The Emergence of Richard Wright, p. 134.

45. Margaret Just Butcher, The Negro in American Culture (New York: Alfred A. Knopf, 1957), p. 178.

46. Although written between 1931 and 1937, Lawd Today was not published until 1963. Richard Wright had also touched on existentialist philosophy in "Down by the Riverside" and "Long Black Song," short stories written in 1936 and published in 1938. These two stories announced Wright's distinct vision.

47. Robert Bone, Richard Wright, p. 22.

48. Richard Wright, Native Son, pp. 391-392.

49. Jean-Paul Sartre, L'Existentialisme est un humanisme, pp. 92-93.

50. Sartre, L'Existentialisme est un humanisme, p. 95.

51. Albert Camus, L'Étranger (Paris: Librairie Gallimard, 1957).

52. Richard Wright, "How 'Bigger' Was Born," appeared for the first time with a few deletions in The Saturday Review of Literature 22 (June 1, 1940): 3-4, 17-20.

Text published in its entirety in July 1940 by Harper and Brothers in the form of a little book of thirty-nine pages bearing the same title. (This same text is included at the beginning of Native Son, p. vii-xxxiv.)

53. Richard Wright, Uncle Tom's Children: Four Novellas (New York: Harper and Brothers, 1938).

54. Richard Wright, "How 'Bigger' Was Born," in Native Son, p. xvi.

55. Richard Wright, "I Tried to Be a Communist," The Atlantic Monthly, August 1944, p. 67.

56. Richard Wright and Paul Green, Native Son, The Biography of a Young American. A Play in Ten Scenes (New York: Harper and Brothers, 1941).

57. Joseph Wood Krutch, "Minority Report," The Nation, April 5, 1941, p. 417.

58. Richard Wright had chosen Orson Welles and John Houseman to stage this play. During the production and rehearsals, the content of the play in general and the last scene in particular were modified. Wright had even rewritten his play with Houseman, who wanted to be closer to the spirit of the novel. That is probably the reason the theatrical adaptation of Native Son achieved enormous success in the United States from March 1941 to January 1943.

59. Richard Wright, "Men in the Making," in his Twelve Million Black Voices, pp. 141-147.

60. Charles Curtis Munz, "The New Negro", The Nation, December 13, 1941, p. 620; "12 Million Black Voices," The New Republic, January 5, 1942, p. 29; Ralph Thompson, "Books of the Times," The New York Times, November 18, 1941, p. 29.

61. Samuel Sillen, "12 Million Black Voices," New Masses, November 25, 1941, pp. 22-24.

62. Richard Wright, "Joe Louis Uncovers Dynamite," New Masses, October 8, 1935, pp. 18-19.

63. Richard Wright, "High Tide in Harlem," New Masses, July 5, 1938, pp. 18-20.

64. Richard Wright, "A Red Love Note", Left Front 3 (January-February 1934): 3.

65. Richard Wright, "Rest for the Weary," Left Front 3 (January-February 1934): 3.

66. Richard Wright, "Strength," The Anvil 5 (March-April 1934): p. 20.

67. Richard Wright, "Child of the Dead and Forgotten Gods," The Anvil 4 (March-April 1934): p. 30.

68. Richard Wright, "Everywhere Burning Waters Rise," Left Front 4 (May-June 1934): 9.

69. Richard Wright, "I Have Seen Black Hands," New Masses, June 26, 1934, p. 16.

70. Richard Wright, "Obsession", Midland Left 2 (February 1935): 14, and "Between the World and Me," Partisan Review 2 (July-August 1935): 18-19.

71. In this poem, Wright briefly mentions lynching.

72. Richard Wright, "Ah Feels It in Mah Bones," International Literature 4 (April 1935): 80.

73. Richard Wright, "Rise and Live," Midland Left 2 (February 1935): 13-14.

74. Richard Wright, "I Am a Red Slogan," International Literature 4 (April 1935): 35.

75. Richard Wright, "Red Leaves of Red Books," New Masses, April 30, 1935, p. 6.

76. Richard Wright, "Spread Your Sunrise!", New Masses, July 2, 1935, p. 26.

77. Richard Wright, "Transcontinental," International Literature 5 (January 1936): 52-57.

78. Richard Wright, "Hearst Headline Blues," New Masses, May 12, 1936, p.

14.

79. Richard Wright, "Old Habit and New Love," New Masses, December 15, 1936, p. 29.

80. Richard Wright, "We of the Streets," New Masses, April 13, 1937, p. 14.

81. Richard Wright and Langston Hughes, "Red Clay Blues," New Masses, August 1, 1939, p. 14.

82. Josh White, the famous black American folk singer, included this poem in his repertory of songs in 1941 after Wright and Hughes had requested it.

83. Kinnamon, The Emergence of Richard Wright, p. 53.

84. Richard Wright, "King Joe" ("Joe Louis Blues"), New York Amsterdam Star News, October 18, 1941, p. 16. Also published in New Letters 38 (December 1971): 42-45.

85. "King Joe" was recorded on Okeh record no. 6475 in October 1941. The music is played by Count Basie's orchestra and the words are sung by Paul Robeson.

86. Richard Wright, "Blueprint for Negro Writing," The New Challenge 2 (Fall 1937): 53-65.

87. Kinnamon, The Emergence of Richard Wright, p. 71.

88. Richard Wright had emphasized this idea in an article which had appeared three months before the publication of "Blueprint for Negro Writing." See "Huddie Led better, Famous Negro Folk Artist, Sings the Songs of Scottsboro and His People," Daily Worker, August 12, 1937, p. 7.

89. Harold Cruse, "Richard Wright," in his The Crisis of the Negro Intellectual (New York: William Morrow and Co., 1967), p. 182.

90. Richard Wright, "The Man Who Killed a Shadow," Zero 1 (Spring 1949): 45-53. Published under the same title in Eight Men.

91. Edward Margolies, The Art of Richard Wright, p. 82.

4

FLIGHT

ANGUISH

Incapable of tolerating his country's racist attitude, the American black seeks all the means possible to lead a normal life. During the thirties, the Marxist ideology attracted thousands of blacks who believed to have found in it the solution to their problem. But the vast majority of them quickly realized that the Communist Party wanted simply to use them. Richard Wright's great disillusionment manifested itself in a novel in which he denounced an ideology thirsting after power and prepared to do anything to achieve its ends. This novel, The Outsider, showed the extent to which the author's thought had changed since the publication of Native Son.[1] Thanks to Sartre and Camus' existentialism, Wright had been able to detach himself completely from an environment and an ideology which sought only the total submission of the individual.

The author had started to write The Outsider as early as 1946. He revised and published the novel in three months during 1952. The lot reserved for the hero of the novel by the Communist Party had probably been inspired by the brutal death of one of his very good friends, Hank Johnson, assassinated on orders from the American Communist Party in 1945. The action of the novel is set in 1950, from early February to mid-March. It takes place first on Chicago's South Side then in Harlem and Greenwich Village.

The Outsider is above all a novel of philosophical and existentialist ideas. It is also both a racial and political melodrama. The hero, Cross Damon, is a twenty-six-year-old black intellectual in love with freedom, whereas he lives in an environment of oppression where his actions are controlled. The five books that comprise the novel follow the evolution of a person in search of total independence. A terrible Chicago subway accident leaves Cross Damon mistaken for dead. He takes advantage of this accident to go to New York and create a new identity for himself. If his work as a post office employee and his troubles with his wife and his mistress had humiliated him in Chicago, he is the object of great curiosity on the part of members of the Communist Party as soon as he arrives in New York. No matter where he is, he cannot live independently of all. This novel is an auto-biographical work since it reflects Wright's personal experiences. The unfolding of the action is comparable to that of the author's career. Books One and Two, "Dread" and "Dream," describe the atmosphere of the black ghetto in Chicago and the hard life that Cross Damon must lead there. From the moment he arrives in New York, the hero, aware of his racial origins, goes to Harlem to seek a new black identity. Books Three and Four, "Descent" and "Despair," describe Cross Damon grappling with Communist ideology. Book Five, "Decision," shows the hero living alone on the fringes of a society that does not understand him and distrusts him.

Flight enables Cross Damon to attempt a new life. It also allows him to enjoy unlimited freedom. The resultant feeling is that of an existential anguish in face of the vast number of choices offered to him. Kierkegaard's influence on Wright is evident here. Cross must make his choice in utter silence. The anguish that possesses him is even deeper than Kierkegaard's because, for the hero, God has no right to any place in life. Similar to Nietzsche, Cross Damon is a nihilist; he no longer wants to believe in what is. In L'Homme révolté, Albert Camus says, "In this world rid of God and His moral idols, man is now alone and without a master."[2] That is Cross Damon's situation. If existentialism is the main and declared theme of The Outsider, it was not the first time that Richard Wright had been influenced by it. One sees it in Lawd Today, Native Son, and "The Man Who Lived Underground."[3] The Outsider, therefore, expressed in clear terms a philosophy that the author had known for a long time.

The action described in Book One takes place in Chicago; human and real, it closely resembles Lawd Today because of the kind of life the hero must lead in a hopeless ghetto. Cross's three friends, Joe, Pink, and Booker, live a life void of meaning and strictly programmed by their work at the post office. This book reflects a concrete reality. The four other books of the novel, on the other hand, are influenced by the hero's ideology. This ideology cannot replace the environment depicted by Wright in Book One. The action described in those four books has no continuity and breathes life into only the important episodes of Cross's life after his departure from Chicago. It is easy to follow step by step the hero's actions in Book One, whereas that is practically impossible in the following four books.

Book One begins on Friday, February 4, at four o'clock in the morning, when Cross and his friends leave the post office. It ends when the hero takes the train for New York at six o'clock in the evening on Monday, February 7. Within the space of eighty-six hours, Cross will have had a drink with his friends, seen his mother, his mistress, his wife and then borrowed eight hundred dollars from the post office for his wife. He will also have heard on the radio of his wife's death after the subway accident, spent three nights in a hotel, had an affair with a white prostitute, attended his own burial on the sly, and killed his friend Joe. In addition, he will have used three aliases to cover his tracks.

The action which takes place from February 8 to mid-March lacks reality and a human atmosphere. Certain dates are contradictory. Their aim is perhaps to show that here time has no importance. However, the environment in which Cross Damon evolves is very different from that of the

South Side since he is dealing with the prosecutor of the city of New York, Ely Houston, and the Communist Party. From the beginning of Book Two, Richard Wright wishes to give his novel a completely new orientation when Cross Damon says to Ely Houston, whom he met by chance on the train: "Maybe man is nothing in particular."[4] This existentialist statement closely resembles that of Sartre, who calls man a useless passion. Cross Damon wishes to be free and makes every effort to protect his freedom. That is why he uses two other aliases, kills a Fascist and two Communists in Greenwich Village. He is, finally, the cause of a white woman's suicide in Harlem.

In the composition of the novel, Wright skillfully shows that his hero is an integral part of the world that created him and that he cannot escape. Like the hero's name, each title of the five books of The Outsider begins with the letter "D." This highlights the close relationship between Damon and a reality that possesses him completely. The isolation Cross experiences after his departure from Chicago is only due to the personal desire not to become attached to anything. His loneliness will become a hell to which only death can put an end.

Thanks to his privileged position within a society constantly controlled by laws, the young black intellectual can do whatever he wishes. His three murders in New York, and even that of Joe in Chicago, result from such an attitude. That is what led Donald B. Gilson to say that, in this work, "murder becomes a legal and philosophical problem, but not a moral one."[5] Cross Damon becomes almost a god, free to act as he pleases, as soon as he understands that he is supposed to be dead. He kills Joe more through desire not to be discovered than out of vengeance upon a heartless society. The color of his skin plays only a secondary role in the other three murders, since he does not tolerate Fascist or Communist tyranny. Robert Bone comments: "Wright's hero has discarded all tradition, and with it all restraint. He is a symbol of modern, industrial, and post-Christian man."[6] The three whites killed in New York are, like him, near-gods who want to obtain freedom and power at the expense of the individual and society.

Before the subway accident, Cross Damon is condemned to lead a life of woes and sufferings. He is separated from his wife, Gladys, and the three young sons he must support on the little money he earns. His wife has taken all the necessary steps to appropriate his belongings, since she knows he has a mistress, Dot, who is expecting a child. Dot, not yet sixteen years old, refuses to have an abortion. Moreover, she threatens to accuse Cross of rape and corruption of a minor if he does not marry her. As Gladys refuses to divorce him, Cross cannot marry Dot. Gladys has even gone to see the postmaster to reveal the truth about Dot. The subway accident delivers Cross from an inextricable situation and gives him the chance to create a new life for himself.

Although free of all obstacles, Cross Damon is still forced to live on the fringes of society because of the color of his skin. This situation enables him to observe and understand better the environment he is rejecting. The same holds true for Ely Houston, since he is deformed and hunchbacked. From their first meeting, Cross Damon and the prosecutor for the city of New York have a long intellectual conversation. Intrigued by the hero's ideas, the magistrate gives him his business card. Although not intimately acquainted, these two people belong to the same species. They are suspicious of each other, for each one is powerful in his own way. Ely Houston says to Cross Damon:

> My deformity made me free; it put me outside and made me feel as an outsider. It wasn't pleasant; hell, no. At first I felt inferior. But now I have to struggle with myself to keep from feeling superior to the people I meet . . . . Doc you understand what I mean?[7]

Living well away from society, Ely Houston understands human actions and their motivations better than anyone. This rare quality enables him to solve the most complicated crimes and punish the guilty according to the rules dictated by the law.   Seeing that the hunchbacked magistrate suspects something about him, Cross Damon is not comfortable when he lies about his past and introduces himself under an alias. The arrival in New York puts an end to a mental torture that Cross Damon had difficulty enduring. He knows that Ely Houston is his worst enemy and that he is well advised not to deal with him in the future. To protect himself better, he goes to get lost in the anonymity of Harlem.

Bob Hunter, a black waiter he met on the train and a resident of Harlem, induces Cross, a few weeks after his arrival in New York, to allow Communists interested in him to contact him. Bob Hunter, in fact, works for the Communist Party by organizing Marxist groups within the black dining car waiters' union. The very evening of the day he saw Bob Hunter again, Cross is invited to dinner at his house in order to meet an influential member, Gil Blount, of the Central Committee of the Communist Party. Gil Blount asks the hero to come live with him in Greenwich Village from the next morning onward. The aim of this invitation is for Blount to get to know Cross Damon better and also to challenge Langley Herndon, the white owner of the apartment building in which he lives. Since Herndon refuses to admit blacks into his building, the Communist Party thinks it is time to put an end to such an attitude. Shortly after his arrival at Blount's apartment, the hero witnesses a merciless brawl between the Communist and the Fascist. Realizing that he has before his eyes two demi-gods who want to control the world, Cross Damon kills them by smashing their skulls with a table leg. The double murder takes place in Langley Herndon's apartment. Cross Damon is careful not to leave any trace that might incriminate him.

Some time before, he had witnessed the humiliation of Bob Hunter, to whom Gil Blount had refused his aid. Since he had not strictly followed the Party's orders, Bob Hunter had been expelled from it and denounced to the American immigration officials to boot. A native of the island of Trinidad living in the United States illegally, he knew he was going to be deported. Only Gil Blount could have arranged things. Cross Damon had also read on the sly the personal diary of Eva, Gil Blount's wife. He had learned that Gil had married the young woman not for love, but because she was a famous painter and because the Party needed her renown. Since he understood that the Marxist organization did not consider the individual's feelings in order to attain its ends, Cross had not hesitated to eliminate one of its representatives by way of reprisal.

The day after Gil Blount and Langley Herndon's deaths, Cross Damon goes to find Jack Hilton,the person responsible for the expulsion of Bob Hunter. He kills him in cold blood with a bullet in the head. By doing away with Hilton, Cross avenges Bob Hunter. He ends, at the same time, the life of a person who wants to play god. On the same occasion, he protects his freedom by recovering, from Hilton's room, the handkerchief he had used to wipe the blood and his fingerprints after the murder of Langley Herdon and Gil Blount. Thus he has just obtained proof that the Communist leader had constantly distrusted him, and that, if he had not denounced him to the police, it was in order to subject him to his all-powerful will in the near future. If he had not killed Hilton, he would probably have suffered a fate similar to Bob Hunter's. Unless the Marxist organization, which could have easily denounced him to the police by using the handkerchief as convicting evidence, made it clear to him that henceforth he depended completely on the Party. The freedom so dear to the hero would have been destroyed, even if the Communists had been able to find nothing concerning his enigmatic past.

Ely Houston makes an appearance the day after the death of Gil Blount and Langley Herndon. At first surprised to see Cross Damon implicated in a political affair, he is quick to suspect something. These suspicions become more urgent after Hilton's death. Although possessing no proof that could incriminate Cross Damon, Ely Houston does everything he can to make him confess his crimes. These two minor divinities insult each other in a ruthless psychological duel. It is after having asked the Chicago police to send him the list of books found in Cross Damon's room that Ely Houston is convinced of his guilt. He tells him: "Your Nietzsche, your Hegel, your Jaspers, your Heidegger, your Hussel, your Kierkegaard, and your Dostoyevsky were the clues."[8] Those authors help Houston better understand Damon's behavior.

As he is sure he is dealing with the Chicago postal worker that everyone believes dead, the hunchbacked magistrate suddenly brings Cross Damon face to face with Finch, the white post office worker who had lent him eight hundred dollars. The hero shows no surprise and pretends to know nothing. Houston tells him next that his mother died of a heart attack when she learned he was still alive. Despite his sincere attachment to his mother, Cross Damon remains impassive at the announcement of that news. By acting in this way, he repudiates a person he had always mistrusted, religion, and total submission to the white world. Finally, Cross displays an icy coldness when Ely Houston has Gladys and her three sons appear. Since he has not succeeded in making the hero say anything whatsoever, the magistrate lets him go free.

Both Cross Damon and Ely Houston play their roles of lesser gods to perfection. The first, knowing no one can accuse him of a homicide without proof, acts like a person free of all moral conventions. The second, thanks to his intimate knowledge of human nature, knows what means to employ to achieve his ends. The manner in which Cross foils Houston's clever maneuvers can only incite the magistrate to persist unrelentingly. These two people also learn to know and respect each other.

In his relations with Houston, Cross wishes to protect the anonymity of his identity. With the Communists, on the other hand, he is aware that the Party wants to own him body and soul and deprive him of all freedom. The totalitarianism of the Marxist ideology threatens his actions and his ideas. That is why he does not hesitate in destroying its spokesmen. The authoritarianism of such a philosophy goes against his nature, his love for freedom. Cross tries to create a world all his own with the sole aim of being free, without ties.

This selfishness clashes with the love the hero feels for Eva Blount. He knows that this young woman's sensitivity has been disturbed by the blind and tyrannical attitude of the Communist Party. The secrets she shared with him after Gil Blount's death reveal to Cross that she knew the Communists wanted to use him against the Fascist Herndon only because he was black. Their common fate draws them closer and a deep love is born of their relationship. Eva gives herself to a man whom she trusts completely. Touched by the young woman's attitude, the hero is unable to tell her anything whatsoever about his past and present activities. It is after the Communists have revealed to her the whole truth about Cross that Eva commits suicide by jumping out of a window in Bob Hunter's apartment. Her delicate nature forbade her from living with a monster whose name and acts evoke the devil. Eva Blount is Cross's first true love. He finds in her all the qualities required of an ideal companion. Her femininity and her intelligence form a striking contrast with Gladys and Dot, who caused Cross only problems. Eva Blount is presented as a positive person, Gladys and Dot as negative.[9]

A few hours before Eva's suicide, Cross had spoken to Blimin, a Communist Party theorist and a member of the Committee General.[10] In the course of his long speech, which is a violent diatribe against all totalitarian power, the hero had cleverly succeeded in proving his intelligence. Blimin had realized that he was not only dealing with a black man, but also a dangerous person for Communism. Since they have no tolerance for anyone who threatens the equilibrium and the tranquillity of the Party by his attitude and his ideas, the Communists have him cut down pitilessly. Here Wright shows that the primary aim of Communism is to own the individual, or to kill him if he does not want to act according to Marxist precepts.

In his long diatribe against every form of tyranny, Cross Damon is sincere and reveals his great love of freedom. This speech is an existentialist commitment on the hero's part since he affirms his way of thinking and living:

Those few strong men who do not want to be duped, and who are stout enough in their hearts to accept a godless world, are quite willing, aye, anxious to let the masses of men rest comfortably in their warm cocoons of traditional illusions. Men are more easily and cheaply governed when they fear ghosts more than guns! The real slaves of the twentieth century are not those sharecroppers who wince at the stinging swish of a riding boss's whip; the slaves of today are those who are congenitally afraid of the new and the untried, who fall on their knees and break into a deep sweat when confronted with the horrible truth of the uncertain and enigmatic nature of life...[11]

The violent death which delivers Cross from an aimless and meaningless life shows that total freedom is impossible to attain.Isolated and misunderstood, the hero does not succeed in doing what he wished. He dies because of those who refuse to permit him to enjoy that freedom.

Similar to Meursault in L'Étranger, Cross does not conduct himself according to the norms of the society that produced him and which he does not respect.[12] He tries, nonetheless, to understand the moral problems of this society that has lost all sense of the sacred and in which everything is permitted since traditional values no longer exist. That is why he declares his innocence to Ely Houston a few seconds before dying. Far from being the source of great joy, the freedom enjoyed in New York had driven Cross to be nauseated by life, especially after Eva's suicide. This feeling of disgust closely resembles that of Antoine Roquentin in La Nausée and shows the extent to which Wright had applied himself to following Sartre and Camus's existentialist theories in his novel.[13]

The Outsider shows that existentialism, as a philosophy of action, cannot promise to resolve the numerous problems that afflict the modern world. To a great extent, this novel helps one to understand better the exile and solitude of Richard Wright who, far from his country and suspicious of Communism, wanted first of all to assert himself as an artist and a free man. In adapting the existentialist philosophy to his novel, the author wanted to show that he could broaden his vision as a writer while condemning totalitarianism and denouncing tyranny. But the explicit theories and the direct propaganda presented in The Outsider make the novel too didactic and prevent the author from introducing enough realism and naturalism. The novel is especially important because of its ideas and not the scenes described in it. Thought plays a role in it until then unknown in Wright's work.

If the author can skillfully depict and explain Cross Damon and Ely Houston's behavior in The Outsider, it is because he makes clever use of psychoanalysis. These two men have always lived on the fringes of society and know that all means are permitted to them to achieve their ends. If the ravages of society bring them closer in their suffering, their personal goals bring them into conflict. Ely Houston protects the order of things, whereas Cross Damon wants to destroy it.

Richard Wright was to reveal his passion for psychoanalysis more fully in Savage Holiday.[14] This novel is dedicated to Clinton Brewer, a black murderer who had intrigued Wright in 1941 because of his bloody crimes. Influenced by the bizarre conduct of Clinton Brewer, Savage Holiday attempts to explain the reason for it through the intermediary of his hero, Erskine Fowler. Frederick Wertham, a famous American psychiatrist of German origin, had published Dark Legend: A Study in Murder in 1941.[15] This Freudian analysis of matricide captured the attention of Wright, who found in it the way to explain Clinton Brewer's murders. Wright did not write Savage Holiday until eleven years later, between December 1952 and March 1953.

This short novel does not deal in any way with the racial problem in the United States, since the characters are white and the action aims primarily to draw attention to the behavior of a single individual. Savage Holiday shows that Wright had a great interest in psychoanalysis and psychopathology, and that he wanted to familiarize himself better with the reality around him.

The novel takes place during the summer in New York. Begun on a Saturday evening, it ends early the following Tuesday morning. The sixty hours or so which cover the action see Erskine Fowler, a hard-working and religious bachelor, become a dangerous murderer. Although only forty-three years old, the hero of the novel has just reluctantly accepted being pensioned off by the insurance company for which he has worked for thirty years. Since he held an important administrative position, the president of the company got rid of him in order to replace him with his son. Saturday evening, after a farewell dinner given in his honor, Erskine Fowler returns to his Manhattan apartment disgusted by the hypocrisy of his former colleagues. The leisure he thought he would find the following days turns, from the next day onward, into an infernal nightmare.

Sunday morning Erskine Fowler is about to take a shower when he decides to dart out, stark naked, on his landing to get the newspaper. But an unexpected breeze closes his apartment door behind him. Panic-stricken, the hero dashes out onto the balcony in order to reenter his apartment through the bathroom window. His sudden arrival on the balcony surprises a five-year-old neighbor, Tony Blake, who, stricken with fright, breaks the fragile railing and falls into space. Since Erskine Fowler lives on the tenth floor, the child's death is instantaneous. When he talks to the neighbors and to the police, the hero does not say that he was present at the time of the accident. He lets them think this death was caused only by Tony.

But Fowler feels guilty. This feeling of guilt makes its appearance from the beginning of the novel, even before Tony's death, and haunts the hero's conscience. Thus, he says to himself:

> "Yes; insurance was nothing you couldn't just learn out of books, no matter how thick and profound they were. You just had to _know_ in your heart that man was a guilty creature."[16]

Thanks to his vast knowledge of psychoanalysis, Richard Wright must have known that Freud had said that the feeling of guilt experienced by the human species had its origins probably in the Oedipus complex.[17] Wright makes this idea the main theme of his novel.

Thus, scarcely a few hours after Tony's death, Erskine Fowler goes to find the child's mother, Mabel Blake, to offer her his help. This woman is a pretty twenty-nine-year-old war widow who works in a cabaret at night. The hero knows she constantly receives men at her place and that she barely looked after her son. She reminds him a great deal of his own mother, who led the same type of life when he was Tony's age. As his father had died when he was three years old, Erskine Fowler had identified with Tony, whose unhappy childhood had reminded him of his own. Several times before Tony's death, Erskine Fowler had been attracted by Mabel Blake's sensuality. But since she reminded him too much of the contemptible memory of his mother, the hero's puritanical conscience had condemned any relationship, considered incestuous in advance. Because of his mother, Fowler never loved women. That is the reason he sought refuge in religion.

Seized with a great affection for Tony, the hero had tried to please him by buying him toys and ice cream. One day the boy had told him that, when they were naked, men would beat his mother and that he was afraid of them. Fowler had understood that Tony used to see his mother making love to strangers. Here Richard Wright uses a theory of Freud, who says that a child seeing the sex act interprets it as a fight between the man and the woman.[18] The hero realizes that the fright registered on Tony's face on the balcony had been caused by his nudity. The child's fatal fall had been provoked by the fear of being beaten. Erskine Fowler does not feel entirely guilty for the child's death. He is convinced that the accident would not have happened if Tony's mother had not led a corrupt life.

Since he wants to possess a wife he scorns, Erskine Fowler asks Mabel to marry him. By acting in this manner, the hero thinks he is assuring himself of the silence of a person capable of incriminating him in Tony's death. This is his manifest thought, for his latent desire is to punish Mabel for the child's death by subjecting her to his inflexible and tyrannical will. His desire to punish the young woman goes still farther, even if he does not realize it. Thus, after having taken care of Tony's burial, he has a dream in which he sees a pretty woman, dead, in a casket. As Freud said that desires are often at the root of numerous dreams, it is evident that Wright wants to show that his hero unconsciously wishes Mabel Blake's death.[19]

Here, Erskine Fowler wants to fulfill something of a divine mission for the good of humanity. Torn between the jealousy and hatred of a person who reminds him too much of his own childhood, the hero ends up killing Mabel Blake with several stab-wounds in the stomach. It is by killing her that he finds the only way to possess her and punish her. As if to accentuate symbolically the purity of Erskine Fowler's mission, the young woman's murder takes place in the hero's all white kitchen.

One can explain this strange murder by making a psychoanalysis of Erskine Fowler's past. Several times in the novel, especially when he is nervous, the hero touches the four pencils in the inside front pocket of his jacket. He does not know why he has that habit. Here one feels the influence of Freud, who says that forgetting is often caused by the desire to clear the memory of unpleasant memories.[20] After surrendering to the police on Tuesday morning, and while he is waiting in the guard-room of the police station, Fowler suddenly understands the role of this odd nervous habit. Those pencils remind him that one day, when he was little, he had drawn a completely disarticulated doll in order to take revenge on his mother, who did not look after him. He also remembers having dreamed of killing this doll out of hatred of his mother. This desire repressed in an unhappy child's subconscious has driven Erskine Fowler, thirty-six years later, to kill Mabel Blake.

The young woman's murder is not important in itself. Richard Wright wishes especially to show that the dream has become reality. By killing Mabel Blake, Erskine Fowler can finally punish his mother. Tony's mother is only a means that enables the hero to achieve his goal. Such was the author's intention, for before deciding on the title Savage Holiday he had thought of calling his novel "Monument to Memory," "The Wish and the Deed," "The Wish and the Dream," "The Queen Mother," as well as "Guilt" and "Guilty Children."[21]

Richard Wright knows how to describe a psychopath with precision, in the person of his hero. The primary aim of the novel is to show the impossibility of separating reality from dream. The author also knows how to describe the neurosis of a person whose last name seems to be the symbol of a life doomed to failure. Finally, the three parts of Savage Holiday, "Anxiety," "Ambush," and "Attack," enable Wright to devote himself to his psychoanalytical study and, as in "The Man Who Killed a Shadow," give full prominence to the existence of a close relationship between action and imagination.[22]

If Richard Wright makes clever use of Freudian theories in Savage Holiday, he seems, however, to follow them too closely. He even lacks subtlety in the way he applies them. The reader feels that the author had carefully learned Freud's ideas before incorporating them with a precise aim into his novel. The psychoanalytical theories limit the novel in its action. This novel is far from having the naturalness of certain Shakespearean works which reveal expert psychoanalytical analyses in perfect harmony with human experience.

It is not surprising that The Outsider and Savage Holiday were written during the same period. These two novels constitute an important phase in Richard Wright's life. They show that, thanks to existentialism and psychoanalysis, the author had succeeded in seeing himself differently as a black and an American. They also indicate that Wright was attempting to penetrate the mystery of human nature.

NEW DISCOVERIES

Since he had acquired some new views of himself and his racial origin, Richard Wright found it natural to go to black Africa to ponder his past and the future of the immense continent. Black Power: A Record of Reactions in a Land of Pathos, written between September 1953 and May 1954, criticizes with frankness a young developing African nation.[23] This book is divided into three parts and aims primarily to present a detailed analysis of the society, religion, economy, culture, and the politics of the Gold Coast. In his introduction, "Apropos Prepossessions," Wright says that the manner in which he analyzes historical facts is partly Marxist. According to him, it is the best means of fully bringing out certain significant points. He does not exclude any other method, but prefers to use the one he knows in order to highlight important historical events:

> If anyone should object to my employment of Marxist methods to make meaningful the ebb and flow of commodities, human and otherwise, in the modern state, to make comprehensible, the alignment of social classes in modern society, I have but to say that I'll willingly accept any other method of interpreting the facts; but I insist that any other method must not exclude the facts![24]

He hastens to add that Marxism stops there, for the ideas, impressions, and advice his book contains are personal and human.

Black Power tries to see how a feudal culture can rapidly shift to the state of a pre-industrial civilization. Wright also attempts to understand how Kwame Nkrumah's party, The Convention People's Party, can move the Gold Coast directly from colonialism to socialism while also firmly combatting the supporters of capitalism, the orthodox Marxists, and the numerous tribes unwilling to abandon their ancestral customs in order to form a unified nation. Wright shows with precision the destructive effects that British colonialism had within the space of one century on the inhabitants of a colony. He even goes so far as to say that certain damages will remain irreparable.

After ten years spent in the United States and two years in Great Britain, Kwame Nkrumah had come back to his native land. In 1949 he had created the Convention People's Party, a political movement whose goal had been the independence of the Gold Coast. Since his studies, during his long stay in America and in Great Britain, had made him familiar with Communism, Kwame Nkrumah had become a socialist with Marxist tendencies. The desire to see his country achieve independence had first clashed with the opposition of the English and tribes jealous of their autonomy. Unable to oppose the will of determined men, the British had consented to hand over the reigns of power to Kwame Nkrumah and to his party rather than to the various tribes. The British authorities had preferred to trust a black man converted to Western ideas rather than tribes with traditions and customs far too bizarre. In 1957, the Gold Coast officially attained independence while taking the name Ghana. In 1960, the republic was proclaimed with Kwame Nkrumah as President. Having become a Communist autocracy, Nkrumah's regime was overthrown in 1966 by a military coup.

Although Nkrumah met Richard Wright by chance during his stay in the United States, it was especially because of the aid of a very good friend, George Padmore, Kwame Nkrumah's political adviser, that Wright was able to visit the Gold Coast. From the moment he arrived, the author was struck by the poverty and dirtiness of the four million natives, while the four thousand British nationals led a life of leisure. He was also surprised to see that the educated Africans in Great Britain despised their brothers of color and were coldly rejected by the British colonialists. They reminded him of the American black bourgeoisie, which lived alone between a white society that disdains it and the black masses that it hates. But the author was touched by the feeling of nationalism that Kwame Nkrumah tried to breathe into the black masses.

Owing to his twelve-day trip aboard the ship which took him to the Gold Coast, Wright had a general idea of what awaited him. His preliminary remarks and impressions constitute the first part of the book, "Approaching Africa." Thus, the author noted the perfect indifference of the English towards the Africans, though they joined them nonetheless on Sundays to pray to a god that had enabled them to enslave thousands of natives in Africa.

If Wright had begun to realize that religion had been an excellent means used by the British to achieve their selfish colonial ends, he had discovered and understood a hybrid individual upon meeting Justice Thomas, a member of the Supreme Court of Nigeria. Reared in a British atmosphere and an extreme Anglophile, this black man refused to admit to Wright that he was ashamed of being African. During a stop in the Canary Islands, his conduct in a house of prostitution showed the author that he could not choose freely between his dignity as a British magistrate and the satisfaction of his sexual appetites. Richard Wright noted that Justice Thomas was the product of two different but inseparable cultures. A bastard child of the West, this black man could not, however, claim his African rights since he had rejected them. Before even setting foot on African soil, Wright had been able to judge the harmful effect of British colonial policy on the African anxious to resemble his white masters.

The second part of the book, "The Nervous Colony," deals with the seven weeks or so the author spent in the coastal region of the Gold Coast, important figures he saw there, and scenes or situations that intrigued him. A few days after his arrival, Wright came across Kwame Nkrumah and attended an enormous political demonstration of the Convention People's Party near Accra. Wright was able to realize his host's immense popularity among the black masses, whose only desire was to stop dealing with British authorities and to enjoy freedom. Wright understood that the future of any African nation would depend on the close political union of its inhabitants.

Wright noticed that harmony did not prevail among all educated blacks in the Gold Coast. Two eminent and very extreme Anglophiles, Dr.

J.B. Danquah and Dr. K.A. Busia, declared to Wright that Great Britain had betrayed them by siding with Nkrumah, who appealed directly to the black masses and demanded immediate independence. The first, as a lawyer and a philosopher, and the second, as a sociologist, could not imagine the future of their country without the British presence. Like Justice Thomas, they were torn between two cultures they could not do without. After speaking to Dr. Busia, a member of a large indigenous family, Wright thought that maybe one day the dissatisfied sociologist would become the leader of his country. That prediction was to be realized when Dr. Busia was elected prime minister of Ghana in 1969.

If the political life of the Gold Coast seemed destined to follow an uncertain path, Wright was fascinated by the life into which he found himself suddenly plunged. His fundamentally puritan nature forbade him from accepting the almost total nakedness of the natives forced to live in a hot and humid climate. He was horrified by the poverty of certain areas of Accra such as James Town, where the working class lived in the most abject squalor. One evening, he saw a group of men and women dancing there in the round while following the rhythm of drums beaten frenetically. Inquiring about what happened, he was astounded to learn that a little girl had just died. This observation made the author understand that an enormous distance separated him from the vast majority of the inhabitants of the Gold Coast. Only human compassion drew him close to these people whose wretched life reminded him of that life he had led in Mississippi.

That great cultural difference manifested itself again when Wright saw some men dancing together at a public dance. A black person educated in the United States had to explain to him that these individuals were not homosexuals, but people respecting the customs of African tribes in which men dance that way.

Far from seeing his surprise stop there, Richard Wright was revolted by the way Indian, Syrian, and Greek businessmen unabashedly took advantage of the gullibility of the natives. He was also scandalized to notice that the British authorities preferred to endanger the lives of the black dockers rather than install a port in Accra. Those blacks had to brave the dangerous undertow with their frail little boats in order to go look for enormous cargoes on the ships that awaited them offshore. Wright said,

> "The harbor here, I was told, was too shallow to allow ships to dock; they could dock, of course, at Takoradi, 170 miles away, but that would mean that the various shipping companies would have to send their freight by rail to Accra.[25]

Wright understood the British desire to exploit economically and politically the Gold Coast at the least cost, even if it cost human lives of the black race. That was immaterial to them.

This total lack of respect for the life and culture of a black people disturbed Richard Wright, who realized nonetheless that certain aspects of that native culture ran counter to the progress of the population of the Gold Coast. Thus the superstitions of the inhabitants of Accra prevented the governmental authorities from draining a filthy lagoon, under the pretext that a god lived there. Despite that, Wright was convinced that blacks could change, thanks to education. He was also confident that they would learn to know themselves better only after having obtained independence.

Anxious to penetrate the culture of the Gold Coast better, Wright decided to spend about three weeks in the interior of the country. The third part of the book, "The Brooding Ashanti," speaks of this trip to the heart of the former kingdom of the Ashanti. During his ten-day stay in Kumasi, the old Ashanti capital, he came across several chiefs and the king of that region of Africa. He was surprised to learn that the natives still sacrificed human beings with the sole aim of assuring themselves of rest for their ancestors' souls. During an audience with the king of the Ashanti, Wright realized that the superstitions of the Ashanti would have his throat slit right away if the king happened to die suddenly in his presence.

Understanding that the Ashanti saw in the death of one of their people a sign of their ancestors' displeasure, Wright did not approve of human lives being sacrificed to calm an imaginary anger. Great was his surprise when he became aware that every Ashanti village chief had power of life or death over his citizens; he alone is supposed to know and understand the relationships between the living and the dead.

If Wright did not approve of the Ashanti culture in general, he nonetheless did not condemn it. On the other hand, he was offended by the attitude of the British towards the natives. When he visited Samreboi, he was the guest of some Englishmen who did not hide the fact they considered the African a bestial and stupid being. The author explains this British point of view by their total lack of understanding of African culture, which is so different from theirs. This difference prohibited any dialogue but authorized an exaggerated exploitation of those won over to the Christian religion. By adopting Christianity, the blacks had transformed the blind faith of their so-called paganism into resigned adoration of an essentially white civilization.

Several times in his book, Wright criticizes the Catholic church. He declares that missionaries destroyed the native cultures by forcing blacks to accept a religion which sought only to take advantage of them. This attitude is not fair; it is the direct result of the author's prejudices against the Catholic Church. This is what led Michael Clark to write in the New York Times Book Review: "Nothing could be as grossly unfair as his strictures on the subject of Christian missionary endeavor."[26] The scorn and ill will of the English had forced the tribes of the Gold Coast to distrust every foreigner. This is why Wright did not succeed in penetrating the soul of the Ashanti. Only the African intellectuals torn between two cultures were accessible to him.

Although not having succeeded in understanding African life well, Wright remained respectful of it. This lack of understanding earned him a murder attempt, very fortunately failed, in Tokoradi. He had wanted to take some photos of a burial. One of the dancers, taking him for a spy in the pay of the English, had tried to stab him. That incident showed the author that, even if he was black, he had nothing in common with the land of his ancestors. He was American and a man from the West above all. However, he sided with the natives because he could not ignore the suffering of people neglected and oppressed by the British.

Black Power: A Record of Reactions in a Land of Pathos is a very precise work of political journalism whose direct style enables the author to explain and interpret what he sees and what he hears. In his letter addressed to Kwame Nkrumah at the end of the book, Wright advises the prime minister of the Gold Coast to distrust the Western powers, which have made Africa suffer intensely and which would not hesitate, within the framework of their imperialist and neocolonialist policy, to take hold of any young African nation: "I cannot, as a man of African descent brought up in the West, recommend with good faith the agitated doctrines and promises of the hard-faced men of the West . . . . Given the opportunity, they'll pounce at any time upon Africa to solve their own hard-pressing and political problems, just as you well know that they have pounced in the past."[27] Wright also emphasizes that Europe does not want Africa to become aware of its power. That is why the author chose the title Black Power for his book. His intent was to show that the Gold Coast had to and could exercise black, political and state control in its internal affairs.

Wright's profound wish was to see the natives of that colony enjoy the human freedom denied them by tribal laws and English domination. The author invites Nkrumah to mistrust communism and to think only of protecting his country's independence by constituting a solid and unified nation. To this end, he suggests that the tribal powers be reduced and that the inhabitants of the Gold Coast be induced to understand better that only a close national union can protect them from any undertaking on the part of foreign powers. He advises Nkrumah to give his country the form of government dictated by the people's needs and aspirations and not by the outside world.

Wright read a great deal in order to keep abreast of what was happening in the other colonized countries of the Third World. In talking about the Gold Coast, he also wanted to show what was going on in those countries.

He had thus succeeded in indicating that colonization emptied the colonies of their vital forces, and that Christianity weakened the spiritual life of the colonized. He had emphasized, in addition, that the industrialization and urbanization of the colonies contributed to destroying the stable lives of the tribes. While accentuating the strangeness of the African world, Wright was expressing in Black Power the joy of seeing a black nation taking the road to independence. This book is dedicated to the unknown African, who has suffered for centuries because of whites.

The Color Curtain: A Report on the Bandung Conference constitutes a logical sequel to Black Power.[28] In this book, the author analyzes with the precision of a journalist the attitudes, feelings, hopes, and future of twenty-nine young African and Asian nations, come together for the first time at an extraordinary meeting. As he wished to speak freely about what he was going to see and hear in Indonesia, Wright succeeded in getting the Congrès pour la Liberté de la Culture to pay for the trip. The goal of this international organization has always been to protect the intellectual and cultural heritage of the nations of the world. The Color Curtain, written between May and July 1955, develops and interprets the ideas expressed during the Bandung congress. Wright also speaks of the important personalities present and of the attitude of the Third World towards the West in racial and international matters.

The host country of this congress held an important position in the eyes of the world: it had just ended all relations with Holland, whose colony it had been for several centuries. Since no Western nation, nor Australia, had been invited to join this international colloquium, Wright understood that the white man and his past conduct towards Asia and Africa would be strongly attacked by the representatives of more than a billion men of color. For the first time in modern history, the former colonies of the West had decided to consult one another on the attitude to adopt towards a world which had, until then, only tried to take advantage of them. The twenty-nine nations assembled in Bandung represented more than half of the earth's population, and Wright saw in this number a new force full of prospects of success.

The Color Curtain is divided into five parts. Their primary goal is to show that race and religion dominate all aspects of life in countries of the Third World. In the first part,"Bandung: Beyond Left and Right," the author tries to show that race and religion are the two major factors that have enabled the African and Asian nations to be in Bandung. According to him, any other consideration, whether it be political or social, is only secondary. It was first of all because their races and their religions had suffered because of the colonial powers that these new countries wanted to meet. Without any military, political and economic powers, they wanted simply to decide on the direction to take in a world divided between capitalism and communism.

Shortly before his departure for Asia, Wright had interviewed five people in order to get an idea of the type of situation he was going to find in Bandung. After having spoken to a Dutchman born in Indonesia, a Eurasian born in Malaya, a Europeanized Indonesian teacher, an Indonesian student, and a Pakistani, he had concluded that the Western world had succeeded in colonizing the vast territories of Asia by cleverly bringing the natives round to blindly admiring Western civilization and being ashamed of their racial origins. He had also understood that religion had enabled them to maintain a semblance of pride when faced with the arrogance and scorn of whites. Before turning his attention to the Bandung Conference, the author describes to the reader the ravages of the West in Asia, that is, the influence of Dutch colonization in Indonesia.

After more than 350 years of the presence of the Netherlands, Indonesia had declared its independence in 1945. This decision had been made possible by the Japanese presence, which, from 1942 to 1945, had humiliated the Dutch occupants and encouraged the Indonesians to take their destiny into their own hands. But as it did not intend to lose its possessions in the East Indies so easily, Holland decided to retake control of the situation at the end of World War II. After a period of guerrilla warfare, the Hague Conference of August 1949 resulted in the formation of a Dutch-Indonesian union. This union was to be denounced by the Indonesians in 1954. The Republic of the United States of Indonesia had been born with, as president, Dr. Achmed Sukarno, who had assumed, as from the years 1942-1945, leadership of the movement for independence. It was in that capacity that he was to deliver the inaugural address to the Bandung Conference.

As soon as he arrived in Djakarta, Wright realized that President Sukarno was criticized by numerous Indonesians who accused him of organizing the Bandung Conference in order to hide the pitiful state of internal politics in Indonesia. The author understood that the situation in which this young nation found itself flowed from Dutch colonialism. If for nearly four centuries Holland had succeeded in keeping the natives in the utmost ignorance, Sukarno could not educate more than eighty million people overnight. The Moslems, Christians, Buddhists, and Hindus who inhabited the fifteen thousand islands constituting that country had to learn first to place their national sentiment above their religious convictions.

The filth and poverty that Richard Wright saw everywhere reminded him a great deal of the Gold Coast. This state of affairs common to countries of the Third World convinced him that they had the right and the duty to meet in order to discuss their future. Those countries wanted to bring about rapid and effective means of modernization while remaining independent. If their desire was to attain the same economic level as the Western countries, they wanted also to protect themselves against all neocolonialism and all racism.

During his brief stay in Djakarta, Wright lived with an Indonesian engineer, Mr. P., an ardent nationalist. Although having spent sixteen years in Europe, where he had furthered his education, Wright's host had never embraced the European cause in Asia. He had suffered so much from prejudices in Holland that he had done everything in his power to help his country free itself of foreign occupation. Mr. P. was so aware of his race that in the course of a three-month stay in New York, he had avoided going out in order not to suffer any reactions. Thus, having understood that the white race was master at home, this Indonesian engineer wanted to see his own race act in the same manner in his country.

When Wright went to get his press card at the Ministry of Information in Djakarta, he noticed that the Indonesian civil service worker took care of him right away instead of responding to an arrogant and impatient American journalist. That incident showed the author that racism worked against whites in a nation where men of color were the majority.

In the second part of his book, "Race and Religion at Bandung," Wright mentions only the names of nations present at the Bandung

Conference, for his attention is absorbed in Achmed Sukarno's inaugural address. From this speech, the author deduced that if race and religion had caused twenty-nine countries to meet, a common feeling had to have played an important role. He indicates also that Japan's presence lent that conference encouraging support since the Nippon economy equaled that of Western countries. All those Third World countries knew that by becoming modernized they could, sooner or later, compete with the former colonial powers of the West.

Wright had seen correctly that race was the main factor that was going to determine the future political choices and the future emotional reactions of all those young nations. He had understood that for centuries Europe and even America had thought that their economic and political primacy was due to their racial superiority. The author was therefore not surprised to note that the countries represented at Bandung were united by the horror of the West and the desire to become industrialized in order to replace their civilizations destroyed by colonialism.

In the third part of his book, "Communism at Bandung," Wright shows that the two most important personalities at the congress were Nehru and Chou En-lai. The latter, invited by the signatories of the Colombo Pact, merely offered compassion to nations whose diverse religions kept them away from the Chinese Marxist ideology. Chou En-lai stated clearly that only his race had led him to participate in the Bandung Conference. In reality, he had come above all as an observer. The racial solidarity noticed by Wright at Bandung did not succeed in blurring the political, economic, social and religious problems that afflicted each of the countries represented. Nehru desired a close union among the Asian countries. But the differences that existed among certain of them made any close collaboration practically impossible.

Only generous aid from the West would enable the Third World countries to rise from their poverty and their ignorance. From 1950, the Colombo Pact had granted numerous countries of Southwest and Southeast Asia such assistance. But the nations assembled in Bandung feared that the Western countries might take advantage of this pact to enslave the men of color again. Although highly suspicious of Chinese communism, the Third World hesitated to trust the West.

The reservations of the Third World with regard to the West were largely due to the racial inferiority complex that colonialism had given it. In the fourth part of his book, "Racial Shame at Bandung," Richard Wright talks about a Malay grammar, Bahasa Indonesia, originally written for the Dutch eager to learn Indonesian.[29] It is written solely for giving orders. Wright stresses that the attitude of the Dutch had driven the Indonesians to accept a situation that made them out to be inferior.

According to the author, the Asians were so conscious of their race that they scorned one another. A very well-known Indonesian novelist told him one day that he hated the Japanese because they were yellow. The year of the publication of The Color Curtain, Wright had written a book review in which he had explained that attitude in detail. Speaking of

Prospero and Caliban: The Psychology of Colonization by Dominique Mannoni, he had written: "An agony as induced in the native heart, trying to live under a white ruler that mocks it. The more Westernized that heart becomes, the more anti-Western it has to be, for it is now weighing and judging itself in terms of (white) Western values that make it feel degraded."[30] During a conversation with Nehru, Richard Wright learned that the goal of the Indian head of state was to put an end to these negative and dangerous attitudes; otherwise any union among the countries of Asia would be impossible. Wright understood why the natives of Africa and Asia, crazed with rage and anger, had always revolted against the Western occupants. Seeing that they wanted to reduce them to the state of servile animals, they had gone into action to destroy the oppressors.

In the fifth part of the book, "The Western World and Bandung," Wright shows that the Third World wanted, above all, to trust the West, even if it condemned its racial injustice and colonial exploitation. "It was my belief that the delegates at Bandung, for the most part, though bitter, looked and hoped towards the West.... The West, in my opinion, must be big enough, generous enough, to accept and understand that bitterness.[31] Therefore, the final communiqué of the congress was the last appeal issued by the African world and the Asian world to the conscience of the Western world. This appeal asked the Western nations to abandon their racist and imperialist habits and help the Third World to become industrialized. Africans and Asians wanted, for the last time, to permit the West to show proof of its good intentions. If the West did not change its selfish attitude, these young nations were ready to turn to Communist China in order to obtain what they wanted.

Tillman Durdin wrote in The New York Times Book Review that Wright had attributed false racial attitudes to the Africans and the Asians.[32] Durdin is perhaps right, since he had attended the Bandung Conference: the idea of race has always obsessed Wright because of the color of his skin. In The Christian Science Monitor, Takashi Oka points out that Wright does not speak at all about the anti-Communist sentiments, particularly with regard to China, of the countries assembled at Bandung.[33] But if Tillman Durdin adds that "he has no account of the detailed denunciation of Communism by Sir John Kotelawala, Prime Minister of Ceylon, that was one of the highlights of the conference," one understands that Wright's aim in his book was above all to show that the man of color could finally make the entire world feel his presence.[34]

The Western world did not attach great importance to the Bandung Conference. This union of the free countries of the Third World, whose primary goal was to emphasize the new human and international role played by the man of color in the world, indicated also that world peace would depend greatly on the attitude of Africa and Asia towards communism and capitalism.

If in Black Power Richard Wright had advised Kwame Nkrumah to be suspicious of aid from the Western world, he expressly requests, in The Color Curtain, that all Western aid possible be provided to the Third World.

It was perhaps because he knew the harsh ideology of the Communist world well that the author had decided to appeal to the West. His sole aim was, probably, to save the old African and Asian cultures from blind and total destruction by Marxism. After the Bandung Conference, Wright's major interest was no longer the racial situation in the United States, but rather the relationship between Western civilization and the Third World.

Although Spain does not belong to the Third World, Pagan Spain, written between February and July 1956, shows the author's constant concern for human freedom.[35] The idea of this book was given to Richard Wright by Gertrude Stein, who, before her death, had encouraged him to visit the Iberian peninsula. The composition of the book was facilitated by the advice of Alva and Gunnar Myrdal, to whom it is dedicated. The author's main goal is to bring to light the pagan and mystical origins of a decadent country dominated by the Catholic Church and deprived of all freedom. Manifestly pro-Protestant and anti-Catholic, this book criticizes Franco's Fascist dictatorship. The five parts of which it is composed enable Wright to express his views on certain aspects of Spanish life.

Since the end of a bloody three-year civil war in 1939, this country had remained for a long time isolated from the rest of the world. It was only in 1950 that the United States had decided to reopen its embassy in Madrid. Three years later, American military bases were installed in Spain. When Wright entered the Iberian peninsula for the first time, this country had just barely been admitted to the United Nations. It was probably the mystery of Spanish life that had led the author to go gain an awareness of the political, social, and religious situation on the spot.

The first part of the book, "Life After Death," speaks of Wright's first impressions after his arrival in Barcelona, the capital of Catalonia: a region hard hit during the civil war because it sided with the Republicans, who had granted it great autonomy. Therefore, in the final victory, the Nationalists, anxious not to lose the slightest portion of the national soil, ruthlessly crushed any vague desire for independence in Catalonia. Franco, Nationalist leader, had not hesitated to have every person suspected of liberal, therefore anti-Spanish, ideas arrested and imprisoned.

Curious to know the common Spanish people, Wright mingled with the inhabitants from the moment he arrived in Barcelona. In the boarding house where he spent his first days, he met a girl, Carmen, who described to him the unhappy life of the single woman in Spain. In this extremely Catholic country dominated by authoritarianism, the woman had a place only within a family home. This girl gave Wright a political catechism for Spanish girls from seven to fourteen years old and published by the Spanish paramilitary group, La Phalange, which made sure the Franco regime was respected and obeyed.

That little book with a green cover, Formación Política: Lecciones para las Flechas, offers questions and answers dealing with the principles and designs of the Franco regime.[36] Its main goal is to explain to young Spanish girls the ideal of La Phalange. Carmen explained that any person wanting, like her, to leave Spain, had to learn by heart the seventy-seven pages of the book. The discovery of that means of indoctrination enabled Wright to realize the selfishness and harshness of a political system whose sole object was to keep an ignorant people in the utmost submission.

It was thanks to Carmen's brother, Carlos, a horticulturist by profession, that the author began to understand better why Spain was so poor. The vast majority of the arable lands belonged to a few rich people only; it was the same for industry. That was the reason that Carlos could only rent the piece of land near Valencia, where he had a nursery of orange trees. He also told the author that the government controlled all the prices of his sales and purchases, and that it was difficult for him to make any profits. Not only was the individual's thought controlled by an antidemocratic state, but also his standard of living. Wright noted that the austerity of the Franco government, reinforced by an omnipresent army and civil guard, caused terror to reign in Spain. One day, he was suddenly apprehended by the police for having gotten his car washed in the street. He had to pay a fine in order to avoid troubles with the local authorities.

Thanks to Carlos's help, Wright lived for a few days with a middle-class Spanish family. He quickly realized that the oldest daughter, Lola, was insane. After learning that Lola had lost her mind when she saw the Republicans kill her father, Wright understood all the horror of the civil war and he saw that it had left deep marks on Spanish society. This society seemed not to have recovered from the violence endured eighteen years earlier.

Within just a few days of his arrival, Wright had already discovered the poverty and terror in which the Spaniards were forced to live. The prostitution and illiteracy encountered in Barcelona seemed to be wished for by the all-powerful Catholic Church, whose sole aim, according to Wright, has always been to keep the common Spanish people under its threatening shadow. When he went to see the Black Virgin of Montserrat in the mountainous massif of Catalonia, he could not help attributing the presence of the Christian sanctuary to a primitive sex cult because the shape of the rocks reminded him of the male genitals. In trying to link the Catholic religion to pagan origins, Wright wanted to denounce the near-inhuman way millions of souls were treated by the Catholic Church.

Once he had established direct contacts with the Spanish people, Wright tried to penetrate their soul. This is what he does in the second part of his book, "Death and Exaltation."

Here Wright reports conversations held with representatives of all Spanish social classes. After having met the Duke de A., he thought that the ruling class felt only disdain for the Spanish masses. After chatting with a Catalonian barber from Barcelona, the author realized that the Catalonians had not lost the hope of one day becoming independent; even at the expense of privations. Now, Wright had experienced hunger and knew that the human will had limits. That is why the Catalonian cause only aroused doubts in him.

A bullfight seen in Barcelona convinced the author that the blind and fanatical fervor of the Spanish public was due to the daily atmosphere in which it was forced to live.   In the torture applied to the bull, Wright discerned the anger of a people finding there the only means of revolting against oppression.   This very pagan and blood-stained practice led the author to compare the matador to a priest celebrating mass before thousands of tortured souls.   Only the brutal and inhuman sacrifice of a beautiful bull seemed to give back to the Spaniards the strength to endure reality.

Before going to the bullfight, Wright had been invited to lunch by the family of a young Spaniard, André, whom he had come across in Barcelona.   Before the meal, in the course of a conversation about bullfighting, the author revealed to them that "Olé" was of Arabic origin and meant "for the love of God." Seeing their great surprise, he understood that he had disturbed the religious soul of André's family.   Without wanting to, he had revealed the sacred but unknown origin of a word constantly used on the occasion of a barbarian act.

If Wright had seen that, because of the Catholic Church, the Spanish people were not truly living in the twentieth century, he had also realized that the Protestants were suffering.   In the third part of the book, "The Underground Christ," he reports that the vast majority of the Spanish people ignore the existence of some twenty thousand Protestants.   For him, that is due to the state and especially the church.

One evening, in a little town two hundred kilometers from Madrid, he secretly met a Protestant woman who had been imprisoned for having taught the Bible to her children.   The fear in which that woman lived reminded Wright a great deal of the atmosphere that the color of his skin had made him endure in the United States.   He says: "I am an American Negro with a background of psychological suffering stemming from my previous position as a member of a persecuted racial minority.   What drew my attention to the emotional plight of the Protestants in Spain was the undeniable and uncanny psychological affinities that they held in common with American Negroes."[37]   Wright had just found in Spain a group of people persecuted by the Catholic Church because their faith is supposed to be a dangerous heresy.   Although having never professed any religious faith, the author felt great pity for the Spanish Protestant's situation.   It is probably for this reason that in the fourth part of his book, "Sex, Flamenco and Prostitution," he violently criticizes the Catholic Church.   During a trip to southern Spain, Wright was witness to an astonishing paradox in which religion and reality strangely overlapped.

Although he had come across prostitutes in Barcelona who were wearing the medal of the Virgin, the author was still more surprised to discover that, in order to be accepted by all, the Spanish prostitute had to be Catholic.   After having seen André repulse with disgust a prostitute who was not Catholic, he concluded: "To be a prostitute was bad, but to be a prostitute who was not Catholic was worse."[38]   It was not hard for Wright to understand that the Catholic Church exerted a great influence on everything relating to prostitution in Spain.   According to him, the omnipotence of the Church was the direct cause of this activity.   Ready to do everything to survive in an environment that wanted only the total submission of the woman, the prostitutes he came across in Seville, without hesitation, devoted themselves to white slave trade and went to spend a few years in the prostitution houses of North Africa. Wright notes:

> Well, given the conditions, the moral attitude of the Church toward sex, the poverty, the ignorance, this was bound to be. It was all socially determined. The Church could call it sin, but it was something far more awful than that. Crush, inhibit, deny the impulses of man, thwart his instincts, and those instincts would find a devious way out, a way to freedom, and the instincts of women too would find a way.[39]

The author recognizes here that the Catholic Church was not alone in driving numerous Spanish women to prostitution. The true culprit was Franco's dictatorial regime which knew how to manipulate the Spanish clergy cleverly in order to hide a lamentable social and economic situation. That is why, speaking of the idea that the Spaniard has of sin, Wright says:

> Sin exists . . . . Prostitution is sin and proof of sin. So prostitution exists. To account for prostitution in economic or political terms is to be guilty of more sin, that is, flirting with liberal thought which, in itself, is a mortal sin. Therefore this universal prostitution is not something to be grappled with in terms of social or economic engineering; it is not something to be dismayed about or even astonished at; it is not a blight to be eradicated; it is simply an indication that the work of salvation is not yet complete, and that a more strenuous effort must be made to call men to God (and women, too!). And of course, a prostitute can at any time enter a church and gain absolution.[40]

Thus, prostitutes were never considered fallen in the eyes of the Spanish church, which owned them body and soul.

Driven to prostitution because of the poverty of the social class from which they came, these Spanish women were the first to suffer the direct consequences of a selfish dictatorship supported unreservedly by the Catholic Church. Wright correctly summarizes:

> The Spanish mentality, branding prostitution as sin, is capable of dealing with it as a social problem born of economic conditions buttressed by a political system.[41]

If Wright said with good reason that prostitution was the direct result of the social situation in Spain, he did not seem to see that this social situation emanated also from a Latin culture with which he was not at all familiar. He had not clearly understood that, even if they suffered from the way they lived, Spanish prostitutes were an integral part of Spanish society whose values they had always gladly accepted.

Wright, however, realized the privileged position occupied within Spanish society by women who had no reason to prostitute themselves by virtue of their social or economic rank. He cites the case of André's fiancée, who because she was a virgin, was the object of a very religious cult on the part of André and his family. The author concludes that such women lived looking impatiently forward to being married in order to lose their virginity. Fascinated by sex life in Spain, Wright had not seen that the social classes played a determining role in the sexual behavior of the individual. He had not understood that the struggle between the social classes of the European countries forbade or imposed certain attitudes on members of each of these classes.

In the fifth part of the book, "The World of Pagan Power," after having visited in Azpeitia the house of Saint Ignatius Loyola, founder of the Jesuit order, and attended the Good Friday procession in Seville, the author concluded that the Catholic religion in Spain was founded on superstition, paganism, and sexuality. What he had seen in Montserrat had probably helped him to draw such a conclusion. That religious faith, according to Wright, was responsible for Spain's extreme backwardness compared to the rest of Europe, while keeping the Spanish on the fringe of the Western world.

During his last stay in Spain, Wright had met a well-known young Spanish doctor. This doctor's belief in the miracles of Saint Theresa of Avila, had surprised the author. It was difficult for Wright to understand that a man so intelligent could still believe in miracles. The author wanted to show that religion exerted absolute power over Spanish society.

He understood the close relationship between the Spanish clergy and the Franco regime when he learned what they taught young Spaniards: the Head of State was immortal and resembled even God. Thanks to the aid of the state and the army, the Catholic Church could not only terrorize the Protestants, but also reduce to the state of second-class citizens the two thousand five hundred or so Jews who lived in Spain. These Jews could not get married in the synagogue without obtaining a certificate attesting that they had never been baptized by the Catholic Church.

In Pagan Spain, Richard Wright analyzes the atmosphere of Spain in the fifties. The political situation of this country helped him to understand better what he considered a primitive, irrational, and even mystical life. To emphasize that idea, Richard Strout wrote in The New Republic:

> As he sees it the central paradox is the religion of the Spanish: solidly
> Catholic, of course, but so saturated with relics, miracles, processions,
> fetishes and dark mysteries that it seems less Christian than something
> primitive and pagan--a world in which a worshipper of Maya, Isis or
> some ancient fertility cult might soon have found himself at home.[42]

Whence the title given to the book.

If Pagan Spain is interesting from a human point of view and does not conceal the author's admiration for the Spanish woman, the book also contains huge gaps. By repeating several times that there is a striking contrast between the sumptuous riches of the religious buildings and the poverty of the people, the author reveals his total lack of understanding of a religion implanted for centuries. How could he, as a black American coming from an Anglo-Saxon and Protestant environment, penetrate and understand a totally dissimilar culture? How could he understand a people whose language he did not even speak?All the conversations held in English, in French, or through interpreters did not enable him to understand fully the Spanish soul. The very desire to see only sex symbols in the candles burning in the churches shows that the author had not understood everything he had seen.

The long passages of Carmen's little green book, cited too often, make the reading of Pagan Spain difficult: the reader must be careful not to lose the train of thought. But the descriptions of bullfights seen in Barcelona and in Morata de Tajuna, a small village near Madrid, are excellent because of the atmosphere described as well as the details offered on bullfighting. It is here that the author reveals himself as a fine journalist.

This book on Spain is interesting in itself since the author attempts also to turn it into a psychoanalytical study of Spanish life. But this method does not help one to understand Spain, for Wright himself had not understood that country well. Psychoanalysis is at the root of his surprising conclusions concerning the mountainous massif of the Black Virgin of Montserrat and about the candles burning in the churches. The author's attitude towards Spain is negative. In The Christian Science Monitor, Joseph G. Harrison wrote: "In general, it is a cry of condemnation against most of what he saw in Spain."[43] In The Library Journal, Milton S. Byam pointed out: "He has, however, performed a major service in exposing to view the educational techniques of a dictatorship."[44] But Wright does not speak of Spain's great history, which would explain the state in which he found that country. He could have perhaps indicated that it was only after having lost its immense empire that Spain had become what it was in 1955.

Between 1945 and 1956, Wright had given several lectures on the relations between white peoples and peoples of color. In December 1956, encouraged by the Swedish publishing company Bonniers, he had revised four of those lectures slightly and had put them in coherent and clear order. The book thus assembled revealed and explained the man of color to the white man. His text was entitled White Man, Listen![45]

White Man, Listen! marks the anti-colonial phase of Richard Wright's career, just as Native Son had marked its Communist phase and The Outsider the existentialist stage. This collection of essays, dedicated to Eric Williams and the Westernized elite of the countries of Asia, Africa, and the West Indies, is an expert political and psychological study of whites' racial oppression of men of color. While attempting to join two different worlds, these four essays also propose the definition and resolution of numerous problems. The unity and the logic of those essays make White Man, Listen! an important work since it explains in detail Wright's thought at a crucial time in his life as a writer. Their literary value is as great as that of "Blueprint for Negro Writing" or "How 'Bigger' Was Born," works which, each in its time, had enabled the author to expound clearly his views on his works and his time.[46]

In his introduction, "Why and Wherefore," Wright declares that the

political and social ideas developed in his book are strictly personal.[47] He
does not hide the fact that his only desire is to tell the truth about the reality
of the relationships between white men and men of color. He is also eager
to point out that certain of his ideas are due to his past and his
experiences.

The first essay, "The Psychological Reactions of Oppressed People,"
deals with the deplorable consequences of colonization on the Africans and
the Westernized Asians.[48] This essay, written toward the end of 1956,
stresses that the attitude and the conduct of whites have destroyed
numerous religions and ancestral customs in Africa and in Asia. Caught
between the whites who did not want to accept him as one of theirs and his
own brothers of color who no longer recognized him, the Westernized native
was forced to live on the fringe of two cultures. Wright had to have thought
of Kwame Nkrumah when he wrote this essay.

Constantly held up to ridicule by the white oppressor, the
Westernized native was rapidly becoming his most implacable enemy. It
was then that he persuaded his brothers of color to unite themselves in
order to eliminate foreign interference. But, knowing that the independence
of his country could be realized and maintained only through a high degree
of industrialization, the Westernized native then assumed dictatorial power
in order to attain such a goal. Not only did he have to destroy the naïve
attitude of his people towards the West, but he also had to do everything
possible to protect his country from any form of neocolonialism. Wright
shows that a social, cultural, political, and economic revolution results from
such a situation. He also emphasizes that the Third World countries are
experiencing that revolution within the space of a few years, whereas over
four centuries were necessary for Europe to undergo the same experience.

Aware of that state of affairs in the Third World, Wright seeks its
underlying causes. That is the aim of his second essay, "Tradition and
Industrialization: The Historic Meaning of the Plight of the Tragic Elite in
Asia and Africa."[49] Initially, this essay had been read at the First World
Conference of Black Writers and Artists held in Paris in September 1956.[50]
In this essay, the author points out that Europe suddenly embarked on the
conquest of the world for historical and social reasons. He especially
wishes to show that the influence of the religious doctrines of John Calvin
and Martin Luther enabled Europe to free itself from the omnipotence of the
Catholic Church and become a new world. Protestantism enabled
European societies to enjoy a high degree of democracy within the Christian
religion itself and in all other spheres of activity, including the way in which
the Europeans treated the natives of Africa and Asia.

If the whites were led to destroy the religions, customs, and traditions
of the Africans and Asians, they showed them at the same time the road
leading to modern civilization. It is this historical fact that caused Wright to
say that the future and the final goal of the Western world are the same as
those of the Third World:

> *The truth is that our world--a world for all men, black, brown, yellow and*

*white--will either be all rational or totally irrational. For better or worse,
it will eventually be one world.*[51]

All the countries of the free world must now cooperate with a view to working towards the improvement of their lot. The author asks the West not to mistrust Africa and Asia but, rather, to aid these two new giants generously and to trust them in order to protect human freedom. The Bandung Conference had helped him to adopt such an attitude.

Wright wishes above all to show that harmony between white men and men of color will depend greatly upon their conduct. This is what he tries to demonstrate in his third essay, "The Literature of the Negro in the United States," in which he speaks of the human relationships between blacks and whites of the same country.[52] In this essay, written originally in 1944, the author establishes a direct relationship between the literary work and social and political protest.[53] He shows the extent to which Afro-American literature reflects, through the centuries, the attitude and the conduct of the American white towards the American black. It is by basing himself essentially on the poetry of American blacks that Wright succeeds in proving that black American literature reflects the way the black man is treated in America. He explains that "poets and poems have a way of telling a lot in a compressed manner."[54] The poems written towards the end of the nineteenth century are filled with sorrow, whereas those composed during the 1930s are full of hope.

The main concern of the author is to emphasize that the white and the black citizens of the same Western country must learn to know each other, respect each other, and trust each other in order to ensure a stable future for their country. In order to show how much the soul of the American black is a victim of whites, Wright speaks of very popular ballads, commonly called the Dirty Dozens. Those songs openly poke fun at everything that is just, holy, honest, and right because it is precisely everything that is just, holy, honest, and right that is oppressing the black man in America. The desperate revolt of the Dirty Dozens exalts incest, celebrates homosexuality, and questions God's ability to create a rational world.

If, in "The Literature of the Negro in the United States," Wright insinuates that the future of the United States will depend largely on the human relationships between its white and its black citizens, he affirms, in his fourth essay, that the Third World no longer wishes to live under the yoke of whites. The example given is that of the Gold Coast."The Miracle of Nationalism in the African Gold Coast," written during the fifties, shows how Kwame Nkrumah and five of his friends undertook everything in their power to give their country independence by forming a secret group, the Secret Circle, in 1948.[55] After having faced grave dangers and experienced several failures, they succeeded in their endeavor by appealing directly to the black masses and by imposing the law of numbers on the British minority and on the black bourgeoisie.

Thus the United Gold Coast Convention, a timid independence

movement in the Gold Coast, suddenly saw itself greatly surpassed by Kwame Nkrumah's Convention People's Party. In this essay, Wright indicates that the Third World can live without the domination of the Western world. He also points out that the white and black men of color must accept each other as they are and treat each other with equality in order to live in peace; they must also unite in order to find practical solutions to world problems. According to the author, the hatred and the discord that racism creates among peoples cause the world to face a serious danger. Only the white man can spare the world an imminent catastrophe by changing his attitude towards the man of color.

The four essays that comprise White Man, Listen! criticize both the white and the black man of color. If Wright violently attacks white civilization and the Catholic faith of the West, he does not, however, pass over in silence the poverty, political corruption, sickness, and ignorance of numerous Third World countries. Thus Nick Aaron Ford writes in Phylon: "This is a bitterly frank book that will make any reader happy about the past, present, or future."[56] The general idea to be drawn from the book is that the almost divine reign of the white man and his ideologies is over.

A few months before his death, Wright had written in the preface of Pan-Africanisme ou Communisme? by George Padmore: "The black man, even when he embraces Communism or Western Democracy, does not support ideologies; he seeks to utilize instruments . . . to his own ends."[57] White Man, Listen! was published at a very favorable time, for not only was the American black beginning to make himself heard, but also numerous Asian, African, and West Indian countries had just attained independence or were on the verge of doing so.

Richard Wright wanted to trust the Third World and the oppressed peoples. He was certain that a cultural renaissance and revolutionary action could only spring up from their wounded soul. As a man of color and a member of the Western world, the author also desired to play the symbolic role of the American black in the liberation of the Third World and the oppressed peoples. But the unenthusiastic welcome the American public gave Black Power, The Color Curtain, Pagan Spain and White Man, Listen! prevented Wright from launching upon the ideological essay and forced him to seek consolation in the novel and the short story.

The author's sensitivity and his intelligence had placed him ahead of his time. White Man, Listen! would have assumed great political and racial importance in the eyes of America and of the entire world if it had been published during the sixties. The violent race riots which shook America then, and the various independence movements in the Third World countries which weakened the faith the West had always had in itself, would have confirmed this book's value.

NEW PERSPECTIVES

The failure of <u>White Man, Listen!</u> in the Western world showed Wright that, henceforth, any subject dealing with racism should be presented in a much less alarming fashion than previously. His various trips to Europe must also have shown him that the West was not ready to accept the Third World as an equal.

That is perhaps why, between December 1956 and January 1957, Wright wrote a story full of humor. This story, "Big Black Good Man," uses comedy to destroy the West's ideas of white supremacy.[58] The action is set in the summer in Copenhagen, in a small second-class hotel near the harbor. The two main characters are Jim, a black American sailor, and Olaf Jenson, a white Danish receptionist.

As if to give the short story a symbolic meaning, the action always takes place at night. Late one evening, Olaf Jensen is surprised by the sudden arrival of Jim, who is huge and very black. Wright points out that by his general appearance, the American black commands the white receptionist's respect. He represents the man of color whom the West fears and has always mistrusted. Olaf Jensen is close to sixty years old and has traveled extensively. He believes he is free of all prejudices towards men of color. But the American sailor's size and his color arouse anger and hate in him because he feels diminished. His attitude is probably due to the ten years spent in New York, where he had ample time to adopt the prejudices of whites towards blacks. Olaf Jensen feels that his race is threatened by Jim.

That is the reason the Danish receptionist tries, in spite of his timidity, to do everything to prevent the black sailor from staying in the hotel. But Jim's casual and familiar attitude does not allow him to succeed in that endeavor. Upon his host's request, Olaf Jensen reluctantly telephones a blond white prostitute, Lena, to ask her to come spend the night with this man whom he considers a huge black monster. Olaf Jensen is literally frightened by this sailor.

Six days later, he is terrified when, after having paid his bill, Jim places his ebony fingers around his neck. This incident will make the receptionist so sick that he will have to stay home and spend a restless night in bed. A year later, during the same period, the sailor makes another appearance in order to give Olaf six white nylon shirts. He explains that this is to thank him for the six nights he spent with Lena the year before.

The black American sailor is a grateful and warm person. In the eyes of the white receptionist, he represents a dangerous animal. It is only this monster's gesture of gratitude that will enable Olaf to realize that he is dealing with a human being. Whence the title given to the story. Wright wishes to show that the white receptionist, blinded by the color of the black sailor's skin, is unable to communicate normally with him.

After the black man's first visit, Olaf in his delirium, hopes that Jim's freighter will sink on the open sea and that the black man will be devoured by a white shark. The author's psychoanalytical approach shows that the black man is associated with the phallus and that his strength threatens and castrates the Danish man. Olaf wishes the death of Jim, who represents a diabolical penis. This is why the Dane would like the black man to be devoured by a white shark. Here racism is an avatar of sexuality. The shipwreck of the freighter causes the death of white and blond women and children. Olaf thus punishes Lena for having consented to sleep with the black seaman. According to him, the white race must have no contact with the other races if it wishes to remain master of the situation.

The blind and even childish behavior of Olaf Jonson highlights the beauty and pride of the black race which wants to be treated as an equal by whites. By giving the race relations of "Big Black Good Man" a comic tone, Wright succeeds in producing an encouraging effect for the future. Whether he likes it or not, the white man sees here the man of color behaving as his equal in a new order. The humor that dominates "Big Black Good Man" seems to announce that Richard Wright's imaginative work was taking a direction until then unknown.

But between the fall of 1956 and the spring of 1958, Wright had written a novel based on his childhood memories in order to show that the atmosphere in the South of the United States had not changed. The idea of this novel had been suggested to him by the misadventures of an American black originally from Mississippi, Ish Kelly, expelled from France because he had lived many years at the expense of several French women and given three of them children. Wright had found that the one actually guilty of misconduct was the population of the South in the United States. Forced to live far from whites in his own country, Ish Kelly had not learned the proper way to behave with members of the white race at the time of his arrival in France, where he had enjoyed total freedom.

It was that strange affair that led the author to write The Long Dream, in which he wanted to describe the living conditions of the Southern black and indict white racists.[59] Wright also found the opportunity there to turn his attention to a subject he knew well and which, he hoped, would enable him to write a good novel.

The main object of the novel is to show that it is very difficult for the American black to make the distinction between the real and the imaginary, because the life he is forced to lead often borders on the fantastic. Wright had already broached this subject in "The Man Who Killed a Shadow," but The Long Dream was to develop it more fully. The action covers a twelve-year period in the forties and fifties. It is set in Clintonville, Mississippi, a town of fifteen thousand whites and ten thousand blacks. For the first time in his literary work, Wright brings the reader face to face with a family, the Tuckers, who belong to the black middle class. The central subject of the novel is the way a father, Tyree, and his son, Fishbelly, learn to know each other better and trust each other more in the face of the destructive hatred of whites. What Wright wrote in March 1960 in the preface to the novel Tant qu'il y aura la peur, by Françoise Gourdon, may also be applied to The Long Dream. He had said: "Located psychologically on this burning frontier where the universes of the American white and the

American black meet, the scenes of this novel full of sensitivity evoke the reality of that implacable fear of the white world by the black world and inversely."[60]

The three parts which comprise The Long Dream emphasize the evolution of the relations between Tyree and Fishbelly. The first part, "Daydreams and Nightdreams . . . ," describes the childhood and adolescence of Fishbelly between five and fifteen years old. It is made up of episodes that especially influenced the young black during that part of his life. Its aim is to show that Fishbelly grew up under his parents' protection without suffering too much from whites. The second part, "Days and Nights . . . ," describes how Fishbelly discovers the reality of the white world and the black world between fifteen and sixteen years of age. He also discovers a father who teaches him how to behave with whites. The third part, "Waking Dream . . . ," shows Fishbelly, between the ages of sixteen and eighteen, alone battling against the whites in Clintonville. This is so well written that Time said, "There is . . . so much truth in [this] crude, pounding, wrathful book that no honest reader can remain wholly unmoved."[61] Incapable of following his deceased father's advice, Fishbelly leaves the South for France.

By fleeing, Fishbelly indicated that he could not continue his father's work in the dangerous, hate-filled atmosphere of his hometown. Initially protected by his parents, he had not been able subsequently to endure the whites' attitude. Of humble and illiterate origins, his father had had in his favor the experience of learning alone in his youth how to put up with whites. That is why he had succeeded in creating an excellent position for himself within the black community of Clintonville. At the beginning of the novel, Tyree has a big funeral parlor for blacks as well as several apartment buildings occupied by blacks. His wealth makes him respected by the two racial communities of the city. He lives in a beautiful house in the residential section, Addison Addition, of rich blacks in Clintonville. His son, Rex, was nicknamed Fishbelly by his little playmates. His wife, Emma, takes every precaution so that this little boy will not suffer at the hands of whites or black workers and farmers.

As soon as Fishbelly is able to understand them, Tyree and Emma explain to him that he has to be reared well far from the black masses. Thanks to his situation, Tyree lives between the white world and the poor blacks of the city who are the sole source of all his profits. The nickname given to his son has a symbolic value. For if the stomach of a fish is generally white, this color is not noticed on the outside. Wright is suggesting here that Rex Tucker looks at whites' values with the eyes of a black and that he has completely accepted the values of the majority white society in which he lives.

Fishbelly, whom everyone calls Fish, lives in a white world of which he is an integral part but where he is not accepted as the equal of whites. At the age of six, he is initiated into the prejudices of whites towards blacks when a white worker, playing dice for money, forces him to throw his dice. He believes that a hand from a little Negro boy will bring him luck. Wright's aim is to point out that if Fish is not supposed to deal with the working and farming black masses, he is nonetheless at the mercy of any white whatsoever because of the color of his skin. That is the main idea of The Long Dream.

The first part of the novel describes the carefree and happy life of Fish and his three little friends, Zeke, Tony and Sam. Like him, his pals are from middle-class families except Sam whose father, although poor, is a black nationalist. As they grow up, these four friends realize that the white world hates them and does not want them. So they can go to the Clintonville fair only on the day reserved for blacks. And on that day their joy is greatly tempered when they learn that certain stands are forbidden to people of their color. They are horrified when a white dancer shows them her breasts and invites them to go to bed with her. Since they know they must not deal with the white woman in any way, they leave the fair hastily. This incident has spoiled their day and brought them face to face with the white woman, a source of great dangers for their race.

Some time later, when Fish is twelve years old, this danger becomes a reality when a twenty-four-year-old black man, Chris Sims, is savagely lynched by some whites in Clintonville after having been caught in bed with a white woman. Working as a bellhop in a white restaurant, the West End Hotel, Chris Sims had started a love affair with a white woman. Finding herself in an ambiguous situation because she had desired a reprehensible pleasure, the white woman had decided to redeem herself by claiming rape and letting the man to whom she had given herself be lynched.

Fish understands that if Chris is killed mercilessly, the black community of Clintonville is also terrorized by the whites who take advantage of the opportunity to make their racial omnipotence felt by firing shots randomly at blacks. It is from that time on that Fish realizes the true danger the white woman represents for the black man. Thanks to his father's advice, he will see that the black man must trust only himself and that lynching is a form of sacrifice that the black community makes from time to time to the white gods in order to calm their anger and their hate.

The brutal death of Chris Sims did not directly affect the way of life of Fish, who is constantly protected by Tyree. Three years later, he is, however, arrested by the police for trespassing on private property. The twenty-four hours he spends in prison, and the treatment he experiences, bring him face to face with a world he did not suspect. He manages to get out of prison only because of Tyree's humiliating playacting in the presence of the chief of police, Gerald Cantley.

Dumbfounded by his father's conduct, Fish is ashamed of him. He even accuses him of being afraid of whites. Within the space of a few hours, he makes the discovery of the brutality of the white world and realizes that he does not have the strong and courageous father he thought he had. His father teaches him then that in order to succeed in the South, the black man must always weep or smile before the white man and never reveal his true intentions to him. Thus he says, "Fish, the only way to get along with white folks is to grin in their goddamn faces and make'em feel good and then do what the hell you want to behind their goddamn backs!"[62] The incident will draw the father and son closer and will make Fish discover the unknown world of his father.

Tyree tells him that the secret of his success is to take advantage unashamedly of the poor blacks in Clintonville, since he can expect nothing from the whites. Fish will understand that the one thousand or so blacks who form the black middle class in Clintonville live at the expense of the nine thousand other blacks, without resources, who live in the poor section of Ford's Ride of which Bowman Street is the main artery and where Tyree's apartment buildings are located.

The very evening of the day his son leaves prison, Tyree takes him to a house of prostitution on Bowman Street. This first sexual experience is, for Fish, the crowning achievement of an adventure which, in a few hours, advanced him from an adolescent to a man. Fish has suffered intensely from the treatment of white policemen who, after arresting him, had amused themselves by threatening to emasculate him with a knife. No sooner had he gotten out of prison than the young black had slit the throat of a wounded dog he had found in the forest, then jointed it. In killing the dog, he had shown that he preferred death to suffering and humiliation. Faced with this choice, numerous blacks think only of suicide. But Fish's gesture was also an affirmation of virility, of an awareness of a new stage of his life, which later took the form of a sex act.

Fish discovers a little more about his father's mysterious world when he learns that the house of prostitution belongs to Tyree. He thus sees that if his father lives primarily on the embalming of dead blacks, he also profits from the business of their sex relations. Fish notices more and more that Tyree is unscrupulous in regard to blacks. He remembers that at the age of seven he had caught him making love to a white woman. As she did not have enough money to pay for her deceased mother's coffin, the young woman had yielded to Tyree's advances in order to obtain what she wanted at little cost. The same thing had happened to Chris Sims's tearful mother.

The first part of The Long Dream, above all, exposes Tyree's complex personality as Fish grows up. If Fish believes he knows his father well, he is very surprised when, at the age of sixteen, a terrible fire reveals to him new secrets about his father's affairs. This fire puts a brutal end to Fish's happy life. The second part of the novel covers two phases of Fish's life: before the fire and after the fire. Before the fire, Fish meets his father's mistress, Gloria Mason, a beautiful mulatto who is almost white and well educated. The young black man notices the importance that blacks attach to the color of their skin. They wish it as white as possible because they want to look like whites. Shortly after this encounter, Fish meets a black prostitute, Gladys. He is attracted to her because she is almost white and because he wants to imitate his father. This young black woman is a member of a group of about twenty girls who work in a nightclub, the Grove, frequented by blacks in Clintonville and managed by a black man, Fats Brown.

Dazzled by the life-style his father can provide him, Fish decides to interrupt his studies at the black high school and work for his father. Tyree fiercely opposes this decision at first because he wishes to send his son to the university to ensure a good future for him. But he ends up giving in to the insistence of a son who wants to earn his living.

The young black man's work consists, then, of collecting each week the rent from tenants in Tyree's apartment buildings. Fish also has to get Maud Williams, the black woman who runs the house of prostitution, to hand over a large sum of money. This money is to be shared by Tyree and the chief of police who has permitted this illicit business to go on for a long time. If Fish realizes the corruption of the police, he pays no attention to the matter, for he knows he is protected by his father. His work enables him to discover the poverty in which the vast majority of Clintonville blacks live. He quickly understands that religion, alcohol, and sexual debauchery are the only means that enable the poor blacks of his city to endure their life.

It is perhaps because he feels guilty of human degeneration that Fish decides to make every effort to come to Gladys's aid. That black woman became a prostitute because the color of her skin attracts black men and because she can thus earn a living easily. The day Fish tells her he can be her sole support, the unfortunate girl perishes in the flames of the Grove with about forty other persons and the manager. It is July 4. There Fish was supposed to meet Zeke and Tony, four years older than he, before their departure for military service.

This fire has deep repercussions which affect both blacks and whites, for they want to find the guilty one right away. Since the firemen in Clintonville had warned Fats Brown on several occasions that his establishment had to be better protected from fire, the city authorities are trying to ascertain why the manager never paid attention to those warnings. Fish discovers that his father and a black doctor, Dr. Bruce, ran the black nightclub indirectly. To avoid trouble with the police, each week they gave the police chief a certain sum of money.

This situation shows Fish that, unwittingly, he had taken advantage of Gladys. The money he had given her had been taken by his father who, in his turn, had put a part of it into the receipts of the Grove, where the prostitute worked. Tyree and Dr. Bruce had to manage an establishment unlawfully in order to maintain a standard of living that their position alone could not afford them because their black clientele was too poor.

As he has been receiving each week for ten years, a check for two hundred dollars for his tacit aid in Tyree's fraudulent affairs, Gerald Cantley comes to see him in order to assure himself that the canceled checks have been destroyed. He has endorsed and cashed each of them and does not want to be compromised in the Grove affair. Tyree makes him think all the checks have been burned. This part of the novel is excellent, for it brings face to face two people who hate each other and who, nevertheless, must get along with each other. This is what led Robert Hatch to say in The Nation: ". . . it is a tableau of the two races meeting on their only common ground--corruption."[63] The chief of police wants to avoid scandal and Tyree does not want to be imprisoned and lose all his belongings. During the meeting between Tyree and Cantley, Fish has ample time to observe how his father lies to the white man.

As he knows his trial is inevitable, Tyree asks the chief of police to help him in selecting a jury of six blacks and six whites. He is convinced that, in such a case, he will be acquitted, for he knows that the black jurors will not render a guilty verdict against him. But the reaction of the white mayor of Clintonville, Wakefield, shows Tyree that whites want only his ruin. That is why Tyree plays his last card and gives a white liberal of the city, Harvey McWilliams, the canceled checks of the past five years. His sole aim is to denounce the police corruption. These checks are mysteriously stolen and Tyree is lured into a trap set in Maud Williams' establishment. He is ruthlessly cut down by Cantley's men, in punishment for his betrayal.

Tyree's violent death enables Fish to see that his father would have done anything to ensure a lasting future for his family. By avoiding a costly trial which would probably have landed him in prison, Tyree achieves a victory over the chief of police whose sole aim was to strip him of his possessions. If the second part of the novel ends with Tyree's murder, the third part emphasizes that Gerald Cantley will not rest until he has found the checks received during the first five years of his transactions with Fish's father. He does everything to find out where those checks are located. Cantley is no longer chief of police because of the scandal caused by the Grove fire. But he has been replaced by a good friend. The same thing has happened to Mayor Wakefield. This change shows that if a few whites have been affected by the events, their institutions and their racist attitudes have not suffered from them.

As he suspects that Fish knows something about the checks, Cantley has him put behind bars under the pretext that he tried to rape a white woman. Tyree's son knows where the checks are. But he also realizes that to say anything would condemn him to certain death. He has sworn to Cantley that the checks have been destroyed. Fish will spend two years in prison. He will say nothing about the checks despite the brutality and the ruses employed by the police in order to make him talk. As soon as he is released, he will leave for France from where he will send Harvey McWilliams the checks, hoping to get Cantley and his accomplices punished.

During his stay in prison, Fish had heard from Zeke, who was doing his military service in France. From the details given by his friend on the French, Fish had concluded that he would prefer the French atmosphere to that of Clintonville. He decides to go to France in order to certify on the spot that all whites are not like those in Mississippi. Wright's aim is to show that the American black is so conditioned by racism and segregation that it is difficult for him to believe in a free and different world. The Long Dream wishes to bring to light the human degradation of blacks. This novel analyzes in detail the complexity of race relations between Tyree and Cantley. Fish's father is the symbol of the economic power of the black community in Clintonville, whereas the chief of police represents the legal and political power of whites who want to take advantage of blacks as much as possible. Both proud and humble, fearful and courageous, frank and crafty, Tyree is clever enough to escape domination by whites. It is his changing personality that saves him. Here Wright makes skillful use of psychology. Robert Hatch rightly said, "The two sides of Tyree, the flashing shift from agonizing clown to contemptuous brigand, is a brilliant study in the art of survival."[64] Tyree is never direct with Cantley, of whom he has always been suspicious, whereas he unreservedly depicts for Mr. McWilliams the most delicate aspects of racial segregation. He tells him:

> *Mr. McWilliams, I ain't corrupt. I'm a nigger. Niggers ain't corrupt.*
> *Niggers ain't got no rights but them they buy. You say I'm wrong to*
> *buy me some rights? How you think we niggers live? I want a wife, a*
> *car, a house to live in. The white man got 'em. Then how come I can't*
> *have 'em? And when I git 'em the only way I can, you say I'm corrupt.*
> *Mr. McWilliams, if we niggers don't buy justice from the white man,*
> *we'd never git any . . . . Sure, I did wrong. But my kind of wrong is*
> *right; when you have to do wrong to live, wrong is right . . . .*[65]

Fish is incapable of such an attitude towards whites because he does not know them as well as his father. But the racist atmosphere of Clintonville forces him, overnight, to become a man.

Shortly after Tyree's death, Dr. Bruce flees to the North with Gloria Mason. Despite their insistence, Fish decides not to follow them and to stay in order to continue his father's work. If Cantley and his friends make the black doctor bear all the responsibilities for the Grove fire, Fish tries to combat them by saying nothing about the checks. This display of courage will be made in vain, for he will also have to flee a world he has never understood. His father had decided to remain at all costs to fight against the white enemy with all the means at his disposal. Tyree was from the South, where he had grown up and where he had had to face grave dangers in order to succeed finally in carving out a beautiful niche for himself. Clintonville was both his past and his future. He had not thought one second about leaving his hometown.

Fish is not as involved as his father in the life of Clintonville. He leaves the South with no regrets. Before releasing him, Cantley makes it clear to him that he wants to receive the same bribes as in the past. The unchanged attitude of the former chief of police tells the young black man that he risks suffering the same fate as his father. He is thus driven to run away. He was kept in prison a long time because Cantley does not know him and does not trust him. These two people belong to two different generations. Wright wishes to stress that Fish will not be the man of compromise that his father had had to be. Fish exhibits reverse racism. It is not surprising that after having read The Long Dream, William Dunlea declared in Commonweal that this novel was the most racist of all of Wright's imaginative works.[66]

The primary aim of The Long Dream is to expose to view the racial segregation imposed by whites. That is why the author does not clutter his novel with the judicial interventions of the National Association of Colored People or even of the federal government after the Grove fire. He simply depicts in its crudest details an atmosphere whose real hero is Tyree. The title of the book has a symbolic meaning and applies quite specifically to Fish's father. Wright wishes to make it clear that if the American black expects to be able to enjoy the rights that the Constitution of his country confers upon him, he risks being killed. The black man's desires are a dream.

The Long Dream is a negative book which does not take into account the improvement of the racial situation in the United States. The American public violently criticized this novel, provoking its literary failure. Thus two black Americans, Nick Aaron Ford in Phylon and Saunders Redding in The New York Times Book Review, strongly advised Wright to come back to the United States if he wanted to continue to write about the American race problem.[67] At the time of the publication of the text, certain noticeable progress had been made in the domain of racial integration.

America had not understood that the author wanted to revive in his novel a past which had marked thousands of blacks whose memory did not always forget the insults, humiliation, and brutality of the racist South. Wright wanted to emphasize that the slight progress made within a few years could not erase at one go more than three hundred years of hell. In a sense, he wanted to recommend prudence to the American black while reminding him not to trust whites too much.

It could be that, far from his country for over ten years, the author had actually been unable to realize the changes that had taken place in America during his absence. But when he describes Tyree's funeral and the victims of the Grove, Wright forcefully revives the religious atmosphere of a black church. The funeral oration of the black minister, the Reverend Ragland, possesses a depth of soul that gives the scene an authentic character. When he wrote The Long Dream, Wright knew that the racial situation in America had begun to change. His own experiences could not let him forget a past which had forced him to adopt a negative attitude towards white America.

This novel is, to a large extent, the romanticized version of Black Boy: A Record of Childhood and Youth.[68] Richard Wright's father and Fish's are both reprobates, with the difference that the author tried perhaps to describe in Tyree the type of father and companion he would have liked to have. Then, Wright and Fish's childhood and adolescence are only a long succession of nightmares lived through in a dangerous atmosphere. Finally, Wright and Fish are forced to flee an environment that stubbornly insists on treating them like inferior beings. Nevertheless, and this is an indication of Wright's attitude towards his country at the time of the writing of The Long Dream, Fish leaves America instead of seeking refuge in the North. By making Fish leave the American territory, Wright seems to indicate that American whites from the South and the North are all racists, and that the black man cannot endure his country's atmosphere.[69]

In The Long Dream, Wright wanted to put his black fellow countrymen on guard against the lies of the American government and incite them to preserve jealously the few rights already won. The events of the sixties showed the world that the author had described in his novel a true situation: Southern whites put up a fierce resistance to the civil rights movements that wanted to change their life-style.

The five published episodes of "Island of Hallucinations" seem to indicate that the novel which follows The Long Dream abounds in love and political intrigues among American blacks in Paris.[70] In these five episodes, the emphasis is placed above all on the dialogue and the action. The first two episodes are continuous and show Fish battling against a world that treats him with dignity. The last three episodes have no continuity of action, but the presence and the explanations of a certain Ned in each of them enable Fish to understand better the environment in which he lives.

The first episode takes place shortly after Fish's arrival in France. He has been so conditioned by racism and segregation in Mississippi that he is afraid to venture out into the streets of Paris. Encouraged by the kind attitude of Mme Couteau, the owner of the hotel where he is staying, he decides to go out, after dressing elegantly and putting on a very American plumed hat.

Scarcely is he in the street when he witnesses an anti-American student demonstration. The students are not long in noticing his hat, making fun of him, and jostling him. Gripped by fright of lynching, Fish goes back to his hotel as fast as his legs can carry him, pursued by the students. The crowd of whites, and the policemen who have a smile on their lips, remind him only too well of his native South in which whites always agree on lynching a black. But thanks to Mme Couteau, Fish understands that the students have something against only his hat. He gladly leaves it to them. This incident shows Fish that, although being of the white race, France does not resemble the South in the United States.

Since emotion has given him a real appetite, Fish goes into a little restaurant. At the beginning of this second episode, he must wait until an elderly lady has left the table they assign to him. Under the pretext that they have not given her her change, and while furtively looking for something under the table, the old woman refuses to leave the restaurant. Despite her protests, she is put out.

After taking his seat, Fish finds a dental plate under the table and rushes to take it to the poor woman who, as a reward, only gives him a slap in the face. Reading the humiliation and shame in the old lady's face, Fish remembers that he had experienced the same feelings in the presence of whites in Mississippi. He begins to realize that the suffering of the American black is universal. Fish is nevertheless too young to understand fully what is happening around him. This is why Ned, a black American lawyer living in Paris, appears from the third episode onward. To a great extent, Wright speaks through Ned.

In the third episode, Fish and Ned come across an American black of about thirty years old, Woodie, who has lost his mind because he is afraid of returning to the United States and racial prejudice. Wright's psychoanalytical study stresses here that after having enjoyed great freedom in France, the American black can be easily driven to madness and even suicide at the mere thought of being treated again like an inferior being because of his race. Woodie has been in France for five years. He has obtained a law degree at the Sorbonne. As the date of his departure approaches, he is convinced that something terrible is going to happen.

The fourth episode depicts a black American woman, Irene Stout, who is making every effort not to return to the United States. Since she had found herself short of money, she had pretended to be sick and had gone to spend some time at the American hospital in Paris. From her bed, she had written more than a thousand letters to all American whites in Paris. She had asked them to be so kind as to send her a little money so she might return to America. These letters had brought her in more than four million francs and had enabled her to stay in France.

Basically cynical, Irene Stout had played the role of the ignorant and poor Negress in her letters. Alarmed by her financial situation, numerous whites had rushed to make generous gifts to her. Here Wright shows that it was above all because they were driven by a sense of racial guilt towards American blacks that the whites had reacted so nobly. That black American woman had become a professional beggar who lived at the expense of American whites in Paris.

If Irene Stout had decided to take advantage unashamedly of the American colony in the French capital in order not to return to the United States, Jimmy Whitfield in the fifth episode had had to break French law in order to achieve the same goal. Given notice to leave France within twenty-four hours because he had been denounced to the French authorities as an exploiter of overly trustful white American women, he had taken a brick and had gone to break the display window of the most beautiful jewelry store on la rue de la Paix. Immediately after committing his act, he had been handed over to the French law, which had condemned him to six months in prison, then had released him, without nonetheless forcing him to return to the United States. Jimmy Whitfield had preferred to spend a few months in a French prison, rather than return to America and face a racist law which would have probably condemned him to several years of detention.

That the five published episodes of "Island of Hallucinations" are full of irony and humor is undeniable. But it turns out that if they find great freedom in their exile, Fish, Ned, Woodie, Irene Stout, and Jimmy Whitfield still lead a life in which dreams and nightmares mingle and succeed one another.

Their life abroad is not only lonely but filled with constant hallucinations, as the title of the novel suggests. Wright also indicated that the American black, even if he deeply hated America, could not repudiate his culture and become integrated into the life of another country.

Wright had emphasized in <u>Black Power: A Record of Reactions in</u>

a Land of Pathos that if the American black was different from the white American majority because of the color of his skin, he nonetheless belonged to the Western world and not to the Third World. In order to highlight the gulf that separates the Western world from the Third World, Wright had written a radio play, Man, God Ain't Like That . . . , in late 1957.[71] It is the ironic story of an African, Babu, converted to Christianity and convinced that his white master, John Franklin, is Christ. As he believes that whites have reached a much more advanced civilization than that of the Africans because they killed the son of God, Babu severs John Franklin's head in cold blood, hoping that Christianity will permit the Africans to develop, in their turn, a civilization similar to that of whites.

Babu had been educated by white missionaries who had given him some books describing Christ as a white man with blue eyes and wearing a red beard. When he accidentally meets John Franklin in the jungle in Ghana, Babu believes he is dealing with Christ, for the white man closely resembles the picture he has always had of the son of God. In the African's eyes, Christianity and the white world form a whole. That is why he humbly submits to the white man. We have here an idea already developed by Wright in Black Power: A Record of Reactions in a Land of Pathos in order to emphasize that whites had succeeded in enslaving millions of African natives by using the Christian religion.

As he is a painter, John Franklin does several paintings of Babu. The latter is delighted to pose and at the same time to sing Christian hymns for the one he believes to be Christ. Taken to Paris by his master in order to give more color to the exhibition of the paintings, Babu is dazzled by the modern city that he discovers. After having found, at a secondhand bookseller's shop, a painting of his master posing as the son of God, the African decides to kill him.

Babu's bloody act is the direct result of a half-understood Christian religion and the influence of African ancestral traditions. After the encounter with John Franklin, Babu had sacrificed some chickens in memory of his deceased father in order to thank him for having made him find God and to ask him to be able to remain ever close to him. Once in France, Babu decides to be Christian if he wants to execute his plan and give Africa the ultramodern civilization that he has just discovered. The human sacrifice that he makes takes on, in his mind, a deeply religious and Christian meaning. He is sure that John Franklin will rise from the dead to help him.

If Babu has only half understood the value and meaning of Christianity because of his African roots, the fault may be traced back to the selfishness and blindness of the Western world, which has never tried to understand the psychology of the man of color. This is the state of affairs that leads Babu not to believe his master when he says he posed for the painting for Christ when he was a penniless student. It is this same situation that causes the French police not to believe Babu when he says he killed the painter for religious reasons. Taken for a madman, he is sent back to Africa, where he founds a new religious cult. Following very Western logic, the police inspectors suspect rather a former mistress of

John Franklin of being the author of the crime.

Babu means "ancestor" in Swahili. But Swahili is not at all known in Ghana, for it is a Bantu language of East Africa. In giving such a name to his African character, Wright aims perhaps to make an allusion to all of Africa and its secular traditions, which whites have always treated with scorn. This play for radio should be seen as a warning given to the Western world. It is through his negligence and his errors with regard to the Third World that the white man will bring about his destruction. James Baldwin said concerning this radio play: "it . . . is an unsparing indictment of the frivolity, egotism, and wrongheadedness of white people."[72] The sarcastic humor of Man, God Ain't Like That . . . enables Wright to explain a dangerous contemporary situation.

This situation does not apply only to the attitude of the Western world towards the Third World. It is found also in the United States, where, thanks to the color of his skin, the black man can often deceive whites. That is the subject of Wright's second radio play, Man of All Work, written in two months in the spring of 1959.[73] It had been inspired by an article Wright had read in the black magazine Jet several years earlier. It is the story of a white woman, Mrs. Fairchild, who, jealous, shoots and wounds her black maid, Lucy Owens, because she finds her husband making passes at her. But the injured person is a man, Carl, who, having been unable to find a job as a cook, had dressed in his sick wife's clothes in order to work for the white family.

Here Wright wishes to emphasize the economic powerlessness of the black man, incapable of supporting his family because of racial discrimination. He also stresses how much the black family unit suffers from this situation. Carl and Lucy Owens have neither work nor money and wonder how they are going to be able to feed their two children. Moreover, they have to find a hundred dollars in order to pay for their house, which they risk losing. It is this situation which drives Carl to stake his all in order to earn the money he needs so much.

Wright's primary goal in Man of All Work is to indict the sexual attitude of whites towards blacks. By changing sexual roles, Carl discovers a new world. James Baldwin said rightly concerning this: "Wright uses this incredible situation to reveal, with beautiful spite and accuracy, the private lives of the master race."[74] It is precisely its strange situation that gives this racial drama a comic tone which achieves the effects desired by Wright. The writer satirizes the sexual behavior of the white man with black women when Mr. Fairchild makes advances to Carl. Wright wishes to emphasize that, in the eyes of the white man, the black woman is only a sex object. This attitude brings out the vulnerable position of the black woman before the white man in America.

Only Carl's original situation enables one to give another aspect of race relations in the United States an amusing rather than a dramatic color. Mrs. Fairchild asks Carl to come wash her back in the bathroom. Brought face to face with a stark naked white woman, Carl understands that he is violating a racial taboo forbidden to the black man. But the women's clothes he is wearing cause him to be mistaken for just a black maid. This situation makes it more obvious that whereas the black woman possesses no other means of defense against the advances of white men, the purity of the white woman is jealously protected from black men by a society and its racist laws. The irony of Man of All Work would have it that the white woman is jealous of the black woman's sexuality. Usually, it is always the white man who is suspicious of the black man and his sexuality.

This radio play highlights the hell that must be endured for several hours by a black man whose sole desire is to provide for his family. He must not only repulse Mr. Fairchild's advances, but also answer cleverly the questions asked by his daughter, Lily. This child, who is just six years old, does not stop making embarrassing remarks about Carl's rather masculine appearance.

After Mrs. Fairchild has shot Carl, she thinks she has killed him. Frantic, Mr. Fairchild appeals to a doctor, who reveals to them their domestic's true identity and sex. Anxious to avoid a scandal because he holds an important position in a bank, Mr. Fairchild agrees to give Carl a check for two hundred dollars and to pay for all the medical attention required by his injury. Since he only has a slight thigh wound, the hero of Man of All Work will have basically gotten the better of the white world and obtained what he wanted. The situation in which he had found himself was very dangerous and delicate.

If this radio play is original and full of wit, this does not mean that Wright wanted to forget the serious aspect of race relations in the United States. The first name given to the white family's daughter and the last name of that family seem to be symbols of an especially racist society.

The twenty-three Japanese haiku poems by Richard Wright, published up until the present, show that the author had gone back to the source of that poetry raised to the level of a literary genre, in the seventeenth century, by the Japanese bonze Matsuo Basho. That poetry did not indicate that the author had abandoned the struggle against racism and injustice. It gave him rather the spiritual strength indispensable for combatting reality better.

Wright made a laudable effort to respect the rigid form of the haiku, which requires that the seventeen syllables which comprise it be divided into three lines in blank verse and that the first and the third lines be of five syllables each and the second line of seven syllables. According to Japanese tradition, Wright tried to concentrate the essence of each of his haikus in the first two lines and to insert an implicit or explicit allusion to one of the seasons of the year.

The primary goal of the haiku is to link closely emotion and sense of description. The delicate painting of a landscape, of the elements of nature, of a plant, an insect or an animal is supposed to evoke certain aspects of human destiny. The haiku is a simple personal notation symbolically evoking a fleeting feeling.

Struggling unrelentingly and fiercely against physical exhaustion and illness, Wright found in the haiku the literary means of freeing himself from his anguish. Inspired by nature, his sensitivity enables him to express his feelings gracefully. Thus in:

> In the falling snow
> A laughing boy holds out his palms
> Until they are white,[75]

the author probably is making an allusion to the little black boy who is trying to forget his race by hoping that racial equality will reign once everyone is covered with snow.

In:

> Whose town did you leave
> O wild and drowning spring rain
> And where do you go?[76]

Wright speaks of the carefree haste of youth. It was perhaps the speed with which the flower of youth withers that inspired him to write:

> The spring lingers on
> In the scent of a damp log
> Rotting in the sun.[77]

In this haiku, spring, summer, and fall are intimately united and seem to represent symbolically a life which is discovering the threshold of old age. That subject is taken up again more forcefully in order to show the isolation and even the selfishness of man towards the end of his life when Wright writes:

> The crow flew so fast
> That he left his lonely caw
> Behind in the field.[78]

But love of nature and its inhabitants makes the writer turn to insects and animals. In

> Make up your mind, snail!
> You are half inside your house
> And halfway out![79]

Wright enjoys simply observing a snail. Nevertheless, this simple child's game is tinged with humor when Wright says of a bull:

> Coming from the woods
> A bull has a lilac sprig
> Dangling from a horn.[80]

Nevertheless, the future seems to torment Wright when he writes:

> *Keep straight down this block*
> *Then turn right where you will find*
> *A peach tree blooming.*[81]

This haiku seems to describe the state of mind of the author at a critical time in his life when he did not know exactly what orientation to give his literary career. Here Wright is probably in search of better days and new horizons. The interpretation of this very symbolic haiku depends very much on the feelings of the author and the reader. This typically Japanese characteristic shows the degree to which Wright had perfected the haiku. But:

> *I am nobody*
> *A red sinking autumn sun*
> *Took my name away*[82]

describes the powerlessness of man before his destiny. In addition:

> *It is September*
> *The month in which I was born*
> *And I have no thoughts,*[83]

seems to reflect the tired and depressed author's despair.

Those few examples of haiku poems show that Wright's writings and political and polemical activities had not affected his sense of poetry. This form of poetry admirably expressed the feelings of a sensitive and wounded soul. This is what led Michel Fabre to say: "At the final stage of his evolution, at a moment when nature and the individual played an increasingly important part in his thinking, the poet developed a taste for these intimate tercets in which he could condense the quintessence of his art."[84] A psychoanalytical study of the few published haikus of Wright reveals that unconscious desire to recapture the innocence and purity of his childhood. Thus this desire manifests itself clearly when the author writes:

> *The green cockleburs*
> *Caught in the thick wooly hair*
> *Of the black boy's head.*[85]

The image is simple: one hot summer day a young black man suddenly appears covered with cockleburs after a wild race in the fields. This haiku describes the little black boy who had been Wright when he capered about in the country with his friends in Jackson.[86]

According to what Michel Fabre says in The Unfinished Quest of Richard Wright, "A Father's Law" seems to indicate that Richard Wright had finally recognized that the racial situation had evolved in America since his departure since the main character of the unfinished novel, the Chicago chief of police, is black.[87] Aside from that, the novel offers nothing original. The writer uses the tools with which he is most familiar. Thus crime and the study of the individual's relations with society form the structure of "A Father's Law." Wright seemed to have reached an impasse in the composition of an imaginative work that he knew well and was repeating in a different form.

In fleeing the American environment, Wright had lost all direct contact with the best source of inspiration for his imaginative works. Incapable of following closely the evolution of the race problem in the United States, the author could no longer talk about it with authority. But by going to France, Wright had acquired completely new perspectives on his literary future, the man of color, and life.

NOTES

1. Richard Wright, The Outsider (New York: Harper and Brothers, 1953). All other references to this book will correspond to the Harper and Rowe edition published in 1965. Richard Wright, Native Son (New York: Harper and Brothers, 1940). All other references to this book will correspond to the Harper and Row edition published in 1966.

2. Albert Camus, L'Homme révolté (Paris: Éditions Gallimard, 1966), p. 92.

3. Richard Wright, Lawd Today (New York: Walker and Co., 1963); and "The Man Who Lived Underground," in Cross Section, edited by Edwin Seaver (New York: L. B. Fischer Publishing Corporation, 1944), pp. 58-102, and published under the same title in Eight Men (Cleveland and New York: World Publishing Co., 1961).

4. Wright, The Outsider, p. 135.

5. Donald B. Gilson, "Introduction," in his Five Black Writers (New York: New York University Press, 1970), p. xv.

6. Robert Bone, Richard Wright (Minneapolis: University of Minnesota Press, 1969), p. 37.

7. Wright, The Outsider, p. 133.

8. The Outsider, p. 421.

9. Richard Wright's aim was perhaps to describe in the novel the type of woman that he had chosen as a wife. He seemed at the same time to mean that the black woman could not equal the qualities of the white woman.

10. Cross Damon's speech covers fifteen pages in The Outsider, pp. 353-367.

11. The Outsider, p. 361.

12. Albert Camus, L'Étranger (Paris: Librairie Gallimard, 1957).

13. Jean-Paul Sartre, La Nausée (Paris: Editions Gallimard, 1966). This is probably what led Granville Hicks to say: ". . . this is, so far as I can recall, one of the first consciously existentialist novels to be written by an American."Granville Hicks, "The Portrait of a Man Searching," The New York Times Book Review, March 22, 1953, p. 1.

14. Richard Wright, Savage Holiday (New York: Avon Publications, 1954). All the other references to this book will correspond to the Award Books edition published in 1969.

15. Frederic Wertham, Dark Legend: A Study in Murder (New York: Duell, Sloan and Pearce, 1941).

16. Richard Wright, Savage Holiday, p. 30

17. Sigmund Freud, A General Introduction to Psychoanalysis (New York: Washington Square Press, 1961), p. 341.

18. Freud, A General Introduction, p. 327

19. Freud, A General Introduction, p. 150

20. Freud, A General Introduction, p. 70.

21. Michel Fabre, The Unfinished Quest of Richard Wright (New York: William Morrow and Company, 1973), pp. 379-380, 605.

22. Richard Wright, "The Man Who Killed a Shadow," Zero 1(Spring 1949): 45-53, published under the same title in Eight Men.

23. Richard Wright, Black Power: A Record of Reactions in a Land of Pathos (New York: Harper and Brothers, 1954). All the other references to this book will correspond to the Greenwood Press edition published in 1974.

24. Wright, Black Power, p. xiii.

25. Wright, Black Power, p. 121.

26. Michael Clark."A Struggle for the Black Man Alone?", The New York Times Book Review, September 26, 1954, p. 26.

27. Wright, Black Power, p. 345.

28. Wright, The Color Curtain: A Report on the Bandung Conference (Cleveland and New York: World Publishing Co., 1956). All the other references to this book will correspond to the Dennis Dobson Press edition published in 1956.

29. S. van der Molen, Bahasa Indonesia, a textbook of elementary Indonesian Malay adapted for the use of English speaking students by Harry P. Cemach (The Hague: W. van Hoeve, 1949).

30. Dominique O. Mannoni, Prospero and Caliban: The Psychology of Colonization (New York: Frederick A. Praeger, 1956); published for the first time in French under the title of Psychologie de la colonisation (Paris: Éditions du Seuil, 1950).Richard Wright, "The Neuroses of Conquest," The Nation, October 20, 1956, p. 331.

31. Richard Wright, The Color Curtain: A Report on the Bandung Conference, op. cit., p. 170.

32. Tillman Durdin, "Richard Wright Examines the Meaning of Bandung," The New York Times Book Review, March 18, 1956, p. 33.

33. Takashi Oka, "What Happened at Bandung," The Christian Science Monitor, April 4, 1956, p. 9.

34. Durdin, "Richard Wright Examines the Meaning of Bandung," p. 33.

35. Richard Wright, Pagan Spain (New York: Harper and Brothers, 1957).

36. Formación Política: Lecciones para las Flechas, 9th ed. (Madrid: Sección femenina de Falange Española Tradicionalista y de las Juntas Ofensivas Nacional-Sindicalistas, no date. Information furnished by Mrs. Ellen Wright in her letter of October 10, 1975, to Jean-François Gounard. The publication date appears nowhere in the book. But one may surmise that this ninth edition appeared in the early fifties.

37. Richard Wright, Pagan Spain, p. 138.

38. Pagan Spain, p. 21.

39. Pagan Spain, p. 186.

40. Pagan Spain, p. 152.

41. Pagan Spain, p. 190.

42. Richard Strout, "Richard Wright's Spanish Excursion," The New Republic, February 18, 1957, p. 18.

43. Joseph G. Harrison, "Richard Wright on Spain," The Christian Science Monitor, February 21, 1957, p. 13.

44. Milton S. Byam, The Library Journal, February 15, 1957, p. 553.

45. Richard Wright, White Man, Listen! (New York: Doubleday and Company, 1957). All other references to this book will correspond to the Doubleday and Co. edition published in 1964.

46. Richard Wright, "Blueprint for Negro Writing," The New Challenge 2 (Fall

1937): 53-65, and "How 'Bigger' Was Born," in Native Son, p. vii-xxxiv.

47. Richard Wright, "Why and Wherefore," in his White Man, Listen!, pp. xv-xvii.

48. Richard Wright, "The Psychological Reactions of Oppressed People," in his White Man, Listen!, pp. 1-43.

49. Richard Wright, "Tradition and Industrialization: The Historic Meaning of the Plight of the Tragic Elite in Asia and Africa," in his White Man, Listen!, pp. 44-68.

50. Then the title had been "Tradition and Industrialization: The Plight of the Tragic Elite in Africa." It was first published under this title in Présence Africaine 1 (June-November 1956): 347-360. This essay was included in White Man, Listen! after having undergone slight revisions.

51. Richard Wright, White Man, Listen!, p. 64.

52. Richard Wright, "The Literature of the Negro in the United States," in his White Man, Listen!, pp. 69-105.

53. It was published for the first time under the title of "Littérature Noire Américaine," in Les Temps Modernes 4 (August 1948): 193-221. Richard Wright revised it slightly before including it in White Man, Listen!

54. Richard Wright, White Man, Listen!, p. 69.

55. Richard Wright, "The Miracle of Nationalism in the African Gold Coast," in his White Man, Listen!, pp. 106-137.

56. Nick Aaron Ford, "Blunders and Failures of the White Man," Phylon 29 (Spring 1958): 126.

57. George Padmore, Pan-Africanisme ou Communisme: La prochaine lutte pour l'Afrique, with a Preface by Richard Wright (Paris: Éditions Présence Africaine, 1960), p. 11.

58. Richard Wright, "Big Black Good Man," Esquire, November 1957, pp. 76-80.(Published under the same title in Eight Men).

59. Richard Wright, The Long Dream, (New York: Ace Publishing Corporation, 1958).

60. Françoise Gourdon, Tant qu'il y aura la peur, with a Preface by Richard Wright (Paris: Flammarion, 1961), p. 10.

61. "Tract in Black and White," Time, October 27, 1958, p. 96.

62. Wright, The Long Dream, p. 130.

63. Robert Hatch, "Either Weep or Laugh," The Nation, October 25, 1958, p. 297.

64. Hatch, "Either Weep or Laugh," p. 297.

65. Wright, The Long Dream, p. 249.

66. William Dunlea, "Wright's Continuing Protest," Commonweal, October 31, 1958, p. 131.

67. Nick Aaron Ford, "A Long Way From Home," Phylon 19 (Winter 1958): 436; Saunders Redding, "The Way It Was," The New York Times Book Review, October 26, 1958, p. 38.

68. Richard Wright, Black Boy: A Record of Childhood and Youth (New York: Harper and Brothers, 1945).

69. This discouraging attitude towards America was probably the direct result of the Richard Gilson case and the actions taken by the Central Intelligence Agency in order to tarnish the author's reputation.

70. Richard Wright, "Five Episodes," in Soon, One Morning, edited by Herbert Hill (New York: Alfred A. Knopf, 1963), pp. 140-164.

71. Richard Wright, Man God Ain't Like That . . . , in his Eight Men.

72. James Baldwin, "Eight Men," in his Nobody Knows My Name (New York: Dell Publishing Co., 1964), p. 150.

73. Richard Wright, Man of All Work, in his Eight Men,

74. Baldwin, "Eight Men," p. 149.

75. Richard Wright, "Hokku Poems," in American Negro Poetry, edited by Arna Bontemps (New York: Hill and Wang, 1963), p. 105.

76. "Hokku Poems," p. 105.

77. "Hokku Poems," p. 105.

78. "Hokku Poems," p. 105.

79. "Hokku Poems," p. 104.

80. Richard Wright, "Fourteen Haikus," Studies in Black Literature 1 (Fall 1970): 1.

81. Wright, "Hokku Poems," p. 105.

82. "Hokku Poems," p. 104.

83. Michel Fabre, The Unfinished Quest of Richard Wright, p. 513.

84. Michel Fabre, "The Poetry of Richard Wright," Studies in Black Literature 1 (Fall 1970): 21.

85. Constance Webb, Richard Wright: A Biography (New York: G. P. Putnam's Sons, 1968), p. 394.

86. After having chosen and organized all of his haikus with great care, the author tried to get them published in the form of a book in July 1960. But his efforts were vain. This failure did not demoralize him beyond measure, since he began to write "A Father's Law."

87. Michel Fabre, The Unfinished Quest of Richard Wright, pp. 512-514.

5

CONCLUSION

This research on Richard Wright stresses that the author always tried to understand and explain the facts concerning his time. If the novels, short stories, and essays written after 1950 are perhaps inferior in quality to those preceding that date, it is proper to recognize in these later works the personal feature always contributed by the author. The course of events had made his thought more universal. The evolution of his thought concerning the black American problem had been influenced by the various stages of his life in the South of the United States, in the North of the United States, and in France. That is why this study analyzes his works as they were written. At the time of his death, Wright had not only numerous plans in mind, but also his inspiration and his literary tastes seemed to have taken a completely new direction.

Through his work, Wright had tried to make himself understood by the greatest number of people possible. Jean-Paul Sartre had realized that when he wrote in 1947 that Wright "is addressing educated blacks in the North and American whites of goodwill (intellectuals, leftist democrats, radicals, A.F.L.C.I.O. union members," and in addition, "Illiterate black farmers and Southern planters represent a margin of abstract possibilities around his real public . . . ."[1] Wright's main goal was to touch the human conscience, whatever it might be. Thus Mississippi Senator Theodore Bilbo's anger after the publication of Black Boy: A Record of Childhood and Youth marked, in a sense, a great victory for the black race, until then scorned and unworthy of the least interest on the part of whites.[2] It also gave new importance to the work of an American black and made people recognize the existence of an Afro-American literature. The publication of Native Son a few years earlier had probably helped to open the eyes of the most stubborn Negrophobes.[3]

Certain critics have often said that Wright had chosen exile because he hated blacks and, as a result, because he hated himself. Robert Bone wrote: "Wright suffers, no doubt, from rootlessness, but the source of that rootlessness is self-hatred."[4] This statement is not completely accurate, for it seems not to take into consideration Wright's designs and literary aspirations for blacks. In 1945, he had written to a childhood friend:

> *There is a great novel yet to be written about the Negro in the South;*
> *just a simple, straight, easy, great novel, telling how they live and how*
> *they die, what they see and how they feel each day; what they do in*
> *winter,spring, summer and fall. Just a novel telling of the quiet ritual of*
> *their lives. Such a book is really needed.*[5]

Wright was proud of his race and knew that he could never forget his humble origins, even if they had been the cause of mental and physical sufferings during his youth. Robert Bone may just possibly be right if one thinks that instead of fleeing America, Wright could have shown his great love for the black masses by staying with them. But in that case, he could not have become the great writer of international renown that he was after his settling in France.

Despite the opposition of whites, Wright had succeeded in tearing himself away from the destitution of the black masses. The freedom of expression found in the Northern United States, and especially in France, permitted him to tell how difficult it had been for him to become a writer. It also allowed him to speak openly about his people forced by racism to lead a life of despair. Added to his privileged position as a black writer was the duty to do everything to improve the condition of American blacks.

To say that Richard Wright hated the Southern United States is perhaps correct, but to maintain that he hated blacks is not exact. Without whites, the black American problem would never have existed. In "Big Boy Leaves Home" and in "Long Black Song," Big Boy and Sarah live, happy and carefree, in the earthly paradise that we know the author's native South to be.[6] But this wonderful dream is destroyed by the fatal intrusion of the white man; Big Boy has to flee suddenly to the North, and Sarah witnesses, powerless, the violent death of her husband. These two examples show that Wright loved his people very much and that he was very attached to his native land. When he left the United States, he was fleeing the inhuman atmosphere created by whites, but in his heart he forever reserved a special place for his brothers of color.

If Wright hated a certain category of blacks, it was the black who, through his apathy, humbly accepted his tragic and inhuman lot. For the writer, this black was as guilty as his white torturers, for he makes himself a party to his own humiliation. Tom, in "The Man Who Saw the Flood," represents this type of stupid black, always submissive to the all-powerful will of whites.[7]

Towards the end of his life, Richard Wright had adopted a more tolerant attitude towards human life. For the first time, nature played a subtle and valuable role in his haiku poems. His Marxist poems of the thirties, although full of proletarian propaganda, had shown that he was very sensitive to poetry.[8] Thus in "Transcontinental," the lyric movement of the poem, very varied in ideas and descriptions, contributes to producing a very symphonic unity.[9] In "We of the Streets," Wright uses distichs evoking very much Walt Whitman's style in Leaves of Grass.[10] In short, most of the author's Marxist poems are written in free verse in order to play on the expressive character of the rhythm of the vowels and consonants. It is therefore not surprising that Wright studied nature when he turned again to poetry.

If nature played a new role in Richard Wright's work, the five known episodes of "Island of Hallucinations" show that irony and especially humor had taken their place in a mind until then pessimistic.[11] The writer was revealing the amusing side of the black problem in "Big Black Good Man."[12] Man God Ain't Like That . . . and "Man of All Work" included a deeply comic element.[13]

Also a part of that new comic vision of the world, Daddy Goodness presented the burlesque side of religion as certain American blacks see it and practice it.[14] In this play, Daddy Goodness passes for a saint. He takes advantage of the naïveté and credulity of those around him in order to lead a carefree and happy life. In taking this theatrical work as an example, one would be tempted to think that the American theater would have gained a great deal if Wright had specialized in the dramatic and humoristic Afro-American genre. But the manner in which Wright presented his works was not important in itself; his only aim was to draw the world's attention to the man of color's condition.

Eight Men is dedicated to the Bokanowskis, a French family that Wright knew well, in the following manner: "To my friends, Hélène, Michel, Thierry, Maurice Bokanowski whose kindness has made me feel at home in an alien land. . . ."[15] This dedication seems to indicate that the writer liked France but that he had also remained fundamentally very American on that foreign soil. He knew that he could never identify with the French people. His French was halting and William Gardner Smith said that he was really at ease only when he was in the company of American blacks.[16] The future of America and of American blacks was too close to his heart for him to think for a moment about giving up his American citizenship.

Eight Men strongly evokes the five short stories of Uncle Tom's Children: Five Long Stories, but it does not possess their maturity and balance.[17] In Uncle Tom's Children the reader can follow, from one short story to the other, the social evolution of the American black from the South. Eight Men, on the other hand, is presented as a test tube in which the author tries in vain to fuse five short stories, two radio plays, and an autobiographical essay written between 1934 and 1959. The great variety of situations and characters in Eight Men reflects Wright's eventful literary career at an important moment in his life.

"A Father's Law" seems to indicate that the author had realized the social and racial changes that had occurred in America since the beginning of his exile in France. But he also knew that the position of the American black in his country was very vulnerable and that it would only take the slightest incident to make the white man suddenly put him back in his place. Wright was convinced that it would be necessary to wait a long time before the black man was really treated humanely. This same attitude applied also to the natives of the new independent countries of Asia and Africa. He had always put them on guard against the neocolonialist politics of their former white masters.

Around the late twenties and in the early thirties, Wright took refuge in reading and learned little by little to create an imaginary world for himself by writing. To a great extent, this new world enabled him to control the reality that made him suffer. Wright even succeeded in avenging himself for it. In "The Man Who Lived Underground," Fred Daniels enjoys trampling on diamonds and playing with stolen jewels.[18] In composing this part of the novel, the author had to have remembered life in Jackson and in Memphis, where he had worked in an optical goods establishment. In "Island of Hallucinations," the writer presents characters and situations closely resembling the people and the atmosphere that had involved him in the Richard Gilson case. According to Michel Fabre in The Unfinished Quest of Richard Wright, it is impossible to identify the characters, but it is obvious that Wright makes them do what he wishes.[19]

This way of deforming reality in order to write a novel or a short story was a common technique of the author, who based his imaginative works on his experiences and on personal observations. His goal was to depict reality in its bluntest trueness to life. After beginning to read A Book of Prefaces by H. L. Mecken, Richard Wright had realized that:

> ... this man [Mencken] was fighting, fighting with words. He was using words as a weapon, using them as one would use a club.[20]

He hardly suspected then that he would one day do the same thing to those who had tormented him.

The beginning of Wright's literary career was strongly influenced by Edgar Allan Poe. That is especially apparent in his first imaginative works and more specifically in "Superstition" and in Native Son.[21] Before 1940, Richard Wright had almost no knowledge of literary theories. It was only during the forties and fifties that he gained his knowledge of psychology, psychoanalysis, sociology, criminology, and philosophy. The Outsider, Savage Holiday, and The Long Dream show the pronounced influence of psychology and psychoanalysis.[22]

At the age of fifty-two, after having protested openly against the unworthy treatment endured by the man of color in America and in the world, Wright seemed to have found a certain degree of serenity and equilibrium. But death prematurely cut his life short.

If Wright's protest was always controlled or, at least, dominated by reason, today American blacks have gone beyond that stage in order to express themselves in a violent manner if necessary. In the forties and fifties, Wright tried to reason with the white man. After his death, during the sixties, the American black lost patience and decided to use force. In White Man, Listen!, there is still a glimmer of hope, whereas in Black Power: The Politics of Liberation in America, by Stokely Carmichael and Charles V. Hamilton, and in Soul on Ice, by Eldridge Cleaver, hope no longer exists.[23]

Nevertheless, despite this anger and this aggressiveness, nothing has changed for blacks in the 1980s and 1990s. Thus, the black middle class has become more powerful than before by taking advantage of the gains acquired by the Black Power movement, and nearly a third of the black population is out of a job and lives in poverty. That is why numerous blacks think the American system of government must change. Certain ones, like LeRoi Jones, alias Imamu Amiri Baraka, call for the total destruction of American capitalism in order to replace it with Marxist socialism.[24] Others, like the officials of the National Association for the Advancement of Colored People, believed that the Carter administration intended to improve the lot of the black masses by creating new federal aid programs. That is what Carter had promised them during his electoral campaign. But he did not keep his promise. These leaders felt deceived by Carter because they had encouraged the black masses to elect him President in 1976.[25] More than 90 percent of blacks had voted for him. The extreme-right in the 1980s proved equally ineffectual. The American government is well advised to listen attentively to the advice of black leaders if it does not want the United States to be torn suddenly by a civil war of which the sixties would have been only a weak precursor.

If today the American black does not hesitate to judge his country or his government severely, Richard Wright also had his special way of criticizing what was displeasing to him. Words were for him the ultimate weapon. In Black Power: A Record of Reactions in a Land of Pathos and in The Color Curtain: A Report on the Bandung Conference, he angrily and indignantly accuses British and Dutch colonialism of having let millions of human beings grovel in ignorance and poverty in order to take advantage of them and their lands unashamedly.[26] The prejudices and the racist politics of the British and Dutch colonizers are cleverly ridiculed and refuted. In Pagan Spain, he violently attacks Franco's authoritarian and Fascist regime. He also denounces the omnipotence of the Catholic Church in a country in which Protestants and Jews form two oppressed and despised minorities.[27] In White Man, Listen! Wright advises the white man to accept the man of color as his equal.

It would seem, according to Wright, that race and religion are at the root of the evils that afflict the peoples of the earth. He suggests that man, whatever he may be, should watch himself in order to avoid engendering suffering around him. In each of these four books, Wright takes sides with the weak and the persecuted in order to analyze the motivations of those who make them suffer. Black Power, The Color Curtain, Pagan Spain, and White Man, Listen! reveal the author in search of an orderly and sensible world where hatred and violence can no longer exist.

If Wright had made himself the spokesman for the oppressed man, his deep desire was above all to see the improvement of the American black's lot. This is not to suggest that he had not seen the future of America in the event the white man should continue to turn a deaf ear to the black man's demands. In 1945, he had written in his introduction to Black Metropolis:

They [St. Clair Drake and Horace R. Cayton] willingly shouldered the risks of having gross and fantastic motives imputed to them, for they know that violent events will soon flare forth, prompted either by whites or blacks; and they know that white Americans will stand transfixed in bewilderment at the magnitude and sanguinity of these events.[28]

This prophetic statement shows that Wright wanted America to accept reality as quickly as possible before it was too late. But his advice and his predictions of the following years were not heeded, since they came from a black man who no longer lived on American soil and who had not dared to encourage his brothers of color to resort to violence and fear in order to assert their rights as full citizens.

NOTES

1. Jean-Paul Sartre. Situations, II: Qu'est-ce que la littérature? (Paris: Éditions Gallimard, 1948), p. 126 and 127.

2. Richard Wright, Black Boy: A Record of Childhood and Youth (New York: Harper and Brothers, 1945). All other references to this book will correspond to the Harper and Row edition published in 1966.

3. Richard Wright, Native Son (New York: Harper and Brothers, 1940).

4. Robert Bone, Richard Wright (Minneapolis: University of Minnesota Press, 1969), p. 44.

5. Richard Wright, Richard Wright: Letters to Joe C. Brown, edited by Thomas Knipp (Kent, Ohio: Kent State University Libraries Occasional Papers, 1968), p. 13.

6. Richard Wright, "Big Boy Leaves Home", in Alfred Kreymborg et al., editors, The New Caravan (New York: W. W. Norton and Co., 1936), pp. 124-158 and "Long Black Song":, in his Uncle Tom's Children: Four Novellas (New York: Harper and Brothers, 1938).

7. Richard Wright, "The Man Who Saw the Flood," in his Eight Men (Cleveland and New York: World Publishing Co., 1961).

8. Only eighteen of these poems have been published so far.

9. Richard Wright, "Transcontinental," International Literature 5 (January 1936): 52-57.

10. Richard Wright, "We of the Streets," New Masses, April 13, 1937, p. 14. Walt Whitman, Leaves of Grass (New York: Aventine Press, 1931).

11. Richard Wright, "Five Episodes," in Soon, One Morning, edited by Herbert Hill (New York: Alfred A. Knopf, 1963), pp. 140-164.

12. Richard Wright, "Big Black Good Man," Esquire, November 1957, pp. 76-80.

13. Richard Wright, Man, God Ain't Like That .... and "Man of All Work," both in his Eight Men.

14. Richard Wright, Daddy Goodness, a play performed in New York in 1968 at the St. Mark's Playhouse by the Negro Ensemble Company. The details concerning the play are based on the review by Edith Oliver published in The New Yorker, June 15, 1968, p. 65.

15. Richard Wright, Eight Men. Mrs. Hélène Bokanowski had done an excellent translation of The Long Dream, published in April 1960 by Juillard, in Paris, under the title of Fishbelly.

16. William Gardner Smith, "The Compensation for the Wound," Two Cities 6 (Summer 1961): 68.

17. Richard Wright, Uncle Tom's Children: Five Long Stories (New York: Harper and Brothers, 1940).

18. Richard Wright, "The Man Who Lived Underground," in Cross Section, edited by Edwin Seaver (New York: L. B. Fischer Publishing Corporation, 1944), pp. 58-102.

19. Michel Fabre, The Unfinished Quest of Richard Wright (New York: William Morrow and Co., 1973), p. 279.

20. Henry Louis Mencken, A Book of Prefaces (New York: Alfred A. Knopf, 1922). Richard Wright, Black Boy: A Record of Childhood and Youth, p. 272.

21. Richard Nathaniel Wright, "Superstition," Abbott's Monthly, April 1931, pp. 45-57, 64-66, 72-73.

22. Richard Wright, The Outsider (New York: Harper and Brothers, 1953); Savage Holiday (New York: Avon Publications, 1954); and The Long Dream (New York: Doubleday and Co., 1958).

23. Richard Wright, White Man, Listen! (New York: Doubleday and Co., 1957); Stokely Carmichael and Charles V. Hamilton, Black Power: The Politics of Liberation in America (New York: Vintage Books, 1967). Eldridge Cleaver, Soul on Ice (New York: Dell Publishing Co., 1968).

24. Amiri Baraka, "Why I Changed My Ideology: Black Nationalism and Socialist Revolution," Black World July 1975: y pp. 30-42.

25. See "A Fallout Between Friends", Time August 8, 1977, pp. 27-28.

26. Richard Wright, Black Power: A Record of Reactions in a Land of Pathos (New York: Harper and Brothers, 1954); and The Color Curtain: A Report on the Bandung Conference (Cleveland and New York: World Publishing Co., 1956).

27. Richard Wright, Pagan Spain (New York: Harper and Brothers, 1957).

28. St. Clair Drake and Horace R. Cayton, Black Metropolis: A Study of Negro Life in a Northern City, with an Introduction by Richard Wright (New York: Harcourt, Brace and Co., 1945), p. xxviii.

II
James Baldwin

"James Baldwin," woodcut by Sue Smock. Used with
permission.

6

THE LIFE OF JAMES ARTHUR BALDWIN: THE FORMATIVE YEARS (1924–1970)

James Arthur Baldwin was born in a Harlem hospital on August 2, 1924. His mother, Emma Berdis Jones, originally from Deals Island, Maryland, married a certain David Baldwin in 1927, which seems to indicate that James Baldwin spent the first three years of his life without paternal protection.

We have scant information about his real father because of the author's silence concerning this matter. In <u>Go Tell It on the Mountain</u>, an autobiographical novel, the writer talks about a certain Richard who, at the point of despair, commits suicide shortly before a faithful friend gives birth to a son.[1] Baldwin always said that this father was imaginary. But, nonetheless, the character Richard, and the role he played in the novel, seem to respond to the writer's desire to have had a strong and firm father. Now, the David Baldwin that James Baldwin's mother married in 1927 was a sick man on one hand and fearful of the white world on the other.

At home, James Baldwin's stepfather was a tyrant. A native of New Orleans, where his mother had been born in slavery, without a goal in a cruel life that made him unhappy, David Baldwin worked all his life as a manual laborer in a New York factory. Older than his wife, since she had been born in 1902, he already had a son, Samuel, nine years older than James Baldwin. In all probability, this son, born in 1915, was descended from a first marriage. Samuel, James Baldwin's half-brother, was an object of profound adoration on the part of his father. The latter wanted him to become, like him, a pastor and a preacher. Unfortunately, at the age of seventeen, Samuel, who hated his father, left the house suddenly, swearing to come back only for this despotic father's burial. Thus, James Baldwin found himself alone to suffer the hatred of a scornful stepfather. In addition, he had to take care of his three brothers and five sisters while his mother worked late in the evening waxing the parquet floors of big Manhattan offices. She continued this hard and thankless labor until 1962.

That tormented and unhappy youth gave Baldwin an unpredictable temperament. It made him a sensitive and nervous person. Thus the

Some minor changes and additions were made to Chapter 6 by Joseph J. Rodgers, Jr., following the death of James Baldwin in 1987. These revisions were made with the full agreement of the author, Jean-François Gounard.

slightest event could have surprising effects on him. He intensely distrusted America in general and whites in particular. This attitude may be explained by the fact he was born in a Northern black ghetto, where he lived through some difficult years.   It was, in fact, in Harlem that Baldwin attended elementary school, Public School No. 24, then Frederick Douglass Junior High School. In the latter establishment, known also by the name Junior High School No. 139, Baldwin met the black poet Countee Cullen, then a teacher. Since he possessed precocious talents as a writer, young Baldwin was not long in becoming responsible for the high school newspaper, The Douglass Pilot, for which he wrote a few articles. It is to be noted that when he was little, Baldwin was ugly and suffered harshly from it. Not only did his stepfather repeat it constantly, but also his little friends never missed the opportunity to remind him of his unattractiveness. This unfortunate situation caused him to hate himself and to despair of everything. Isolated, alone, and misunderstood, he did not manage, despite his efforts, to please and be appreciated.

That is perhaps the reason that from the summer of 1938 to the spring of 1941, the future writer was both a pastor and a preacher in a "holy roller" church, The Fireside Pentecostal Assembly in Harlem.   There, sheltered from the hatred and cruelty of the world, young Baldwin found, for a while at least, the peace and rest his soul needed so much. However, this religious retreat of nearly three years made him understand his hate and his need to wreak vengeance upon whites and even God. Here again, and although he tried to please his stepfather by entering heart and soul into a religion that he did not really understand very well, James found only jealousy and icy coldness in David Baldwin. The stepfather did not have as much success as his stepson. Thus, at seventeen years old, the future writer emerged from a human and personal experience completely transformed. In The Negro Novel in America, Robert Bone writes that James Baldwin underwent two important crises in his life: one religious at the age of fourteen, the other antireligious at seventeen.[2] These two crises, says Robert Bone, are complementary and enabled the black author to write his first novel, Go Tell It On The Mountain, and his first play, The Amen Corner.[3]

In the meantime, and seeing that he had no other choice except to face the reality of the world, Baldwin had entered DeWitt Clinton High School, in the Bronx, in September 1938. It was there that he made some very good white and Jewish friends, like Richard Avedon and Emile Capouya, with whom he maintained an excellent friendship. There again, the future writer was in charge of the newspaper, The Magpie. He began at that time to exhibit very promising talents. Although he had not received any good grades, except in English, Baldwin succeeded in obtaining his diploma in January 1942. Realizing that his stepson's literary gifts were full of promise, David Baldwin did all he could to discourage young James Baldwin. Very fortunately for the latter, all attempts failed.

James Baldwin's stepfather was a Baptist pastor, failed and embittered, paranoid and jealous. This situation was all the more painful for him since he realized it. He died of tuberculosis, abandoned by all, in a Long Island hospital, on July 29, 1943. That day, in another hospital, his youngest daughter, Paula Maria, was born. By a strange chance, death and birth manifested themselves brutally the same day in the same family. In his essay Notes of a Native Son," James Baldwin speaks of the death of this unloved stepfather who believed he was persecuted and who did not stop saying his family wanted to poison him.[4] The day of the burial, August 2, 1943, James Baldwin celebrated his nineteenth birthday. He showed little interest and grief at his stepfather's funeral. Samuel, the son adored by David Baldwin, came to pay his last respects to a father that he had sworn to see again only dead.

Thus, after that sudden disappearance, more or less expected and even hoped for, young Baldwin found himself placed at the head of a large family. The oldest of three brothers, with five sisters, James Baldwin had to face the harsh reality of the world with courage in order to support a family of which he was very proud. In Notes to a Native Son, he remembers, however, that as a child, he never liked to see his mother leave for the maternity hospital, for she always came back with a new little brother or a new little sister. Nevertheless, Baldwin adored his brothers and sisters. He felt great tenderness and deep affection for them as a big brother. George, born in 1927, looked after the family when James was in France; he even sent him some money. Barbara was born in 1929 and Wilmer in 1930. David, born in 1931, was very close to James; he looked a lot like him. He often managed the affairs of his oldest brother, whose complete confidence he enjoyed. Gloria, born in 1933, also looked after James Baldwin's affairs, as his faithful secretary. Divorced, she remarried, taking as a husband a representative of Sierra Leone to the United Nations, Frank Karefa-Smart. Ruth was born in 1935 and Elizabeth in 1937. Paula Maria, the youngest child in the family, was born June 29, 1943. That date, as we saw earlier, has a very special meaning for the Baldwin family. It was James who gave his youngest sister that first name. She spent some time with him in Paris in 1961. She feels the greatest admiration for her big brother.

We have seen that, disappointed by the harshness of life, Baldwin dedicated himself for some time to a religious and pious life--after which the future writer abandoned all hope of finding consolation and courage in a faith which did not respond at all to his aspirations. It was his stepfather's death that forced him to face the harsh reality of life despite his nineteen years of age. In his first play, The Amen Corner, Baldwin describes with precision the type of father he would have liked to have. The respect and the admiration usually felt by a son for his father were never a part of the feelings experienced by James Baldwin for his stepfather. In his first aforementioned novel, Go Tell It on the Mountain, Baldwin imagines the father that he would have liked so much to know. The young black author had already begun to write that novel as early as 1942. He had originally called it "Crying Holy," a title which, to a certain extent, seems to indicate the strong psychological influence he was under at the time of his religious experience.

After having left DeWitt Clinton High School in January 1942, the young black writer set out in search for work. He found various more or less long-lasting jobs in factories and restaurants in the New York area. In Notes of a Native Son, he relates that when he worked for a railroad factory in New Jersey in 1942, in a fit of blind anger provoked by segregation and prejudice, he almost, killed the young waitress at a restaurant in Trenton. It was a Saturday evening, and after having heard the girl say that the restaurant did not serve blacks, Baldwin, crazed with anger, had thrown a pitcher of water in her face with all his might. By a hair's breadth, she had managed to escape the murderous projectile, but whites in the restaurant chased Baldwin. After succeeding in escaping them in the night, he promised himself never to react so violently, for that act could have cost him his life. As his family's sole support, Baldwin was not drafted during World War II. However, to ensure his brothers' and sisters' subsistence, he exhausted himself at work and had to agree to ply all kinds of trades. During the winter of 1945, when he worked as a cook in a little restaurant in Greenwich Village, he had the opportunity and especially the great joy of being able to go visit Richard Wright, then living in Brooklyn.

Some time afterward, Baldwin sent a part of his novel, "Crying Holy," retitled "In My Father's House," to his idol, from whom he was not long in receiving wise advice and great encouragement. It was through Richard Wright that he obtained from the Eugene F. Saxon Trust his first scholarship, which he badly needed. Still with Richard Wright's aid, he received, in 1948, another scholarship, this time from the Rosenwald Foundation. It enabled him to take the plane to France. On November 11, 1948, Baldwin had left the United States without any intention of coming back. This more or less sudden departure had been caused, to a certain extent, by the death of one of his three good friends, Eugene Worth, who had committed suicide by jumping into the Hudson. Like him, the young author had endured hunger and destitution in New York. Feeling threatened by the same gloomy fate, Baldwin had decided to leave America as fast as possible. "I left because I wanted to live," he declared on several occasions, particularly in 1971 to Margaret Mead, the well-known American anthropologist.[5]

His first years in Paris were not the easiest, since he spent a week in prison in December 1949, for a sheet that he had not stolen. This harsh initiation enabled Baldwin to strengthen his character and his personality. At the very beginning of his stay in France, he had met a young Swiss from Lausanne, Lucien Happersberger. From that time on, a true friendship was established between the two young men. In the spring of 1949, "Everybody's Protest Novel" appeared.[6] In this essay, James Baldwin violently attacked Richard Wright, brutally ending their friendship. This resounding literary debut was obvious proof that the young black writer from Harlem had already begun to reflect on himself in particular and on the black problem in general. The European atmosphere momentarily detached him from the American environment while enabling him to see it objectively.

Baldwin spent some time, at the very beginning of 1952, in a little chalet in the Swiss Alps, in Loeche-les-Bains, belonging to Lucien Happersberger. It was there, in the calm and solitude of the mountains, that he finished Go Tell It on the Mountain in February 1952. In the summer of the same year, he mustered enough courage to return to New York. He spent three months there. Having come especially to see his family again and in order to be best man at his brother David's wedding, James Baldwin was very disappointed with an unchanged New York. As soon as he was back in Paris, he began to write a novel which would not be published until 1962, under the title of Another Country.[7] From the summer of 1952 to the end of 1953, Baldwin lived in Gallardon, a little village in the Chartres region. It was there that he learned of the publication of Go Tell It on the Mountain, dedicated to his stepfather and his mother. Still in 1952, the young black author began to write The Amen Corner.

Towards the end of 1953, Baldwin decided to live in the South of France and reside in a little village, Les Quatre Chemins, located near Cannes. There he wrote and finished his second novel, Giovanni's Room.[8] Emboldened by his discoveries concerning the complexity of man, he returned to the United States, where he lived from the summer of 1954 to the spring of 1955. This brief nine-month stay in America was productive, since The Amen Corner, a one-act play, appeared in July 1954 and was staged by black students at Howard University, in Washington, D.C., in the spring of 1955. It was during the same period that appeared his first collection of essays, Notes of a Native Son, dedicated to Paula Maria. This second return to America was provoked in all likelihood by the award of a scholarship from the Guggenheim Foundation. Giovanni's Room, dedicated to Lucien Happersberger, appeared in 1956 and made James Baldwin better known to the American public. During the same year, the black author received the National Institute of Arts and Letters Prize and a scholarship from the bimonthly magazine Partisan Review.

During those long years spent in France, Baldwin avoided all contact with American blacks living in Europe, his aim being to strive to know himself better and to discover the profound and human meaning of life. That is the reason he isolated himself often in the silence and calm of the Swiss Alps in Loeche-les-Bains. The songs and blues of Ray Charles and Mahalia Jackson, he said, helped him a great deal, during those voluntary retreats, to understand himself and especially to accept himself fully.

From October 1956 to July 1957, Baldwin spent nearly nine months near Calvi, Corsica. He continued to write Another Country there. Since he was having trouble getting a good grasp on his characters, and describing them, he thought he had to go to the scene itself. In July 1957, he therefore decided to return to the United States definitively. Thus, after spending nearly eight and a half years in France in voluntary exile, Baldwin was in New York in order to understand America better as well as make it better understand him. In his numerous speeches, essays, and articles, the black author was always inclined to speak for all Americans. He was constantly afraid of being misunderstood. He feared the American black middle class. He dreaded contradiction and criticism. In other words, he never forgets who he was, from where he came, and the kind of life he had to lead in order to succeed. Too often disturbed or even depressed when he lived in the United States, Baldwin was forced to seek refuge abroad in order to be able to write and reflect in peace. The travels sustained his morale and his writing capacities.

As soon as he returned to the United States, Baldwin went for the first time in his life to the South. That trip to North Carolina at the age of thirty-three, in the fall of 1957, made him discover a new feeling: fear. That new experience enabled the author to feel pride and esteem for people of his race, particularly by becoming personally aware of the poverty and sufferings of the vast majority of Southern blacks. It was from that moment that he became interested in the civil rights movement with a view to gaining some ideas for the advancement of blacks.

Between 1958 and 1959, attempts were made to stage Giovanni's Room. James Baldwin was strongly opposed to the idea. It was during one of the numerous theatrical meetings that the black author met a young Turk, Engin Cezzar. A sincere friendship was established between the two men. They saw each other often, since James Baldwin made frequent trips to Istanbul. Thus, when Engin Cezzar married a young Turk, Gulriz, Baldwin did not hesitate to go to Turkey for the wedding.

During the summer and fall of 1959, he was back in Paris, where he lived in a small apartment in order to be able to focus his attention better on Another Country. In order to recapture the atmosphere he so badly needed to finish his novel, he was in New York again at the beginning of 1960. He delivered several addresses on the race problem that year, particularly at San Francisco State College on October 22 and at Kalamazoo College on November 21. Richard Wright's sudden death, on November 28, 1960, made James Baldwin the leading spokesman for American blacks in America and in the world. He was going to fulfill his mission already begun.

In 1961, his second collection of essays, Nobody Knows My Name, appeared, dedicated to his three brothers, George, Wilmer, and David.[9] That year, the writer was very busy between speeches, meetings, and literary work. The years from 1961 to 1964 marked the period of his true literary debut. Finally, all of America was listening to him because he was offering love and understanding and not hatred and rancor. The United States was, at that time, violently shaken by innumerable civil rights demonstrations, and Baldwin took advantage of that situation in order to make himself heard. In 1961, the black writer received a subsidy from the Ford Foundation which enabled him to devote more time to his work. Finally, he could make America understand that his own experience was also that of every American black. Baldwin was becoming the spokesman for blacks in particular and for America in general.

This very hectic life-style only accentuated the disorderly fashion in which Baldwin organized his days. He often worked all night long, traveled a lot, and frequently went to live with friends who were willing to offer him peace and quiet. From February to July 1961, for example, Baldwin stayed with the writer William Styron in Roxbury, Connecticut. In September of the same year, he went to Paris, then on to Israel and Turkey. It was in Turkey that he finished <u>Another Country</u>, in December 1961. He continued his travels and spent Christmas with Mary Painter, an American economist he knew very well. At the very beginning of 1962, he made a movie for Swiss television. This film, based entirely on the essay entitled "Stranger in the Village," was filmed in Loeche-les-Bains and in the chalet of Lucien Happersberger's parents.[10]   On June 25 of the same year appeared <u>Another Country</u>, dedicated to Mary Painter.

Since he did not wish to linger in the United States after the publication of his third novel, Baldwin left with his sister, Gloria, for a long ten-week trip to Africa. During a short stay in Dahomey now he was amused, even flattered, by a group of Africans who did not know him and did not want to believe he was American. He insisted above all on being considered a human being and not a representative of America. In 1963, he received an honorary doctorate in letters from the University of British Columbia in Canada. It was around the same time that his third collection of essays, <u>The Fire Next Time</u>, completed in Istanbul after his trip to Africa, appeared.[11] In the spring of the same year, Baldwin had been unanimously designated to be honored as the outstanding former student of the Frederick Douglass Junior High School in Harlem, which he had attended in his childhood. The official ceremony had taken place before all the young students. Among them his nephew, James Mitchell, to whom <u>The Fire Next Time</u> was dedicated. A few months earlier, in January, the writer had gone to Jackson, Mississippi, where he had come across Medgar Evers, a representative of the National Association for the Advancement of Colored People. The latter was brutally killed a few months later. He had also met James Meredith, wounded in 1966. Knowing that the Southern black lived in a virtual human hell, Baldwin wanted to know, in detail, the circumstances of the tragic death of the young black, Emmett Till, killed in cold blood in 1955. His curiosity had been aroused by the fact that the white murderer had confessed his crime to the journalist William Bradford Huie after his acquittal. For Baldwin, this case was blatant proof of the blind and pitiless racism of whites.

On April 4, 1963, Baldwin received a scholarship from the George Polk Trust for his excellent articles which had appeared in the American press. Having become a well-known and well-listened-to literary personality, Baldwin was invited on Thursday, May 13, 1963, to have breakfast with Robert F. Kennedy, then U.S. Attorney General. That first encounter in the state of Virginia was only the prelude to another, more important meeting held in the afternoon of the next day in New York, in Robert F. Kennedy's apartment. Organized by Baldwin to help the U.S. Attorney General better understand the black problem in America, that meeting brought together about ten black personalities, among whom were Harry Belafonte, Lorraine Hansberry, and the psychologist Kenneth B.

Clark. Nothing unfortunately came of it by virtue of the misunderstanding between Robert F. Kennedy and Baldwin's guests. On May 17, <u>Time</u> published a long article on the black author with his photo on the first page.[12] Thus, at the age of thirty-eight, James Baldwin was the best-known American citizen in America.

However, his private life and his numerous activities began to be an object of close surveillance. The F.B.I., for example, tried one day to enter his New York apartment during his absence. His telephone was also bugged. Seeking rest and tranquillity, Baldwin went to spend three months in May and June in Puerto Rico, where, with his childhood friend Richard Avedon, he began to write <u>Nothing Personal</u>.[13] In the summer of the same year, Baldwin was in Paris, where on Sunday, August 18, 1963, he delivered a sermon in the American church. The main subject of this sermon was the great civil rights movement which then united thousands of Americans. A few days later, on Wednesday, August 21, the black writer led five hundred or so Americans to the United States Embassy to show their keen interest in the various civil rights movements. A week later, on August 28, Baldwin was in person by the side of Martin Luther King for the huge march on Washington. These numerous activities, of course, did not permit him to dedicate himself entirely to his literary work. He managed to finish, in October, his play, <u>Blues for Mister Charlie</u>, written for the most part in Istanbul at the home of his friend Engin Cezzar.[14] During the same month, Baldwin was in Selma, Alabama, in order to get blacks registered to vote. Although accompanied by his brother David, he could not help but feel fear and anguish at the mere idea of dying a violent death at the hands of whites opposed to the black vote. This vague and obscure foreboding materialized when, on November 22, 1963, President John F. Kennedy was cowardly assassinated in Dallas, Texas. James Baldwin was depressed and grieved by this senseless murder, even if he was not convinced that John F. Kennedy had been a friend of blacks.

<u>Blues for Mister Charlie</u> appeared in 1964. The first performance took place on April 23 of the same year at the Anta Theater in New York. For financial reasons, the last performance took place on August 29. In that play, dedicated to the memory of Medgar Evers, David Baldwin played the role of Lorenzo. Without the financial aid of Mary Strawbridge and Ann Pierson, daughters of Rockefeller, who had each donated five thousand dollars, <u>Blues for Mister Charlie</u> would not have lasted a long time. This substantial and invaluable aid enabled Baldwin to see his play performed longer than he expected. In the summer of the same year, the black author and his sister Gloria took a long trip to Europe which took them all the way to Istanbul. At the same time, his friend Lucien Happersberger married Diana Sands, the black actress who played the role of Juanita in <u>Blues for Mister Charlie</u>. As one can see, James Baldwin was always surrounded by faithful friends and brothers and sisters, who constantly watched over him. This intensely family atmosphere and his heavy responsibilities as the oldest brother perhaps explain the reason the author never married. He was always ready to take part in nonviolent civil rights demonstrations

during which he often spoke in order to make Americans better understand America.   In an interview published in Esquire in July 1968, Baldwin declared his intention to act always in order to help improve the deplorable racial situation in the United States.[15]

Towards the end of the summer of 1964, James Baldwin came across Richard Avedon in Finland, where they had decided to meet in order to finish Nothing Personal, which appeared at the end of the year. That fourth collection of essays by Baldwin is illustrated with striking photos by Richard Avedon. Seeing that he could work in peace only outside of the United States, the black author bought, in October 1964, an apartment in Istanbul and another one is Paris. Around the same time, he was elected a member of the National Institute of Arts and Letters in America. In November 1964, Baldwin came back to New York, where he lived in his immense Manhattan apartment which he, in fact, kept only from 1963 to 1966. Since he was both everywhere and nowhere, the black writer, strictly speaking, had no fixed address, which was quite disconcerting for those who wanted to follow him closely. In 1965, he participated in the March on Montgomery, Alabama.

As he had decided to devote himself entirely to his literary work, he began, from that time on, to live continually outside the United States, where he could not really find the peace every writer needs. He divided his life between Stockholm, Jerusalem, Paris and, above all, Istanbul. In a discussion with the American anthropologist, Margaret Mead, James Baldwin declared that he was not at home anywhere, for America does not want him nor people of his race.[16] In 1965, Going to Meet the Man, a collection of short stories dedicated to Beauford Delaney, appeared.[17] The latter is a black American painter, a native of Tennessee, settled in Paris for a long time, and a friend of James Baldwin's. The same year The Amen Corner, now a three-act play, was performed on stage in New York.[18] Outside the literary world of which he was a part, Baldwin also likes to get involved in his country's politics. Therefore, he did not hide the fact that he was against the senseless war that America waged in Vietnam.

In 1968, Tell Me How Long the Train's Been Gone, James Baldwin's fourth novel, dedicated to Engin Cezzar, David Baldwin, and David Leeming, appeared.[19] Since that time, Baldwin worked on a new novel, "When the Rest of Heaven was Blue," retracing the life of two American families, one black, the other white, through a period extending from the Civil War to World War II. In addition, he began two plays, "The 121st Day of Sodom" and "Our Fathers".   The latter which has musical accompaniment, takes place in Greece with two black American soldiers and a young Greek woman as main characters. In short, the author continued to devote himself to numerous literary plans.

As we have seen earlier, Baldwin was often outside the United States. Thus, for example, Tell Me How Long the Train's Been Gone was written in New York, Istanbul, and San Francisco between 1965 and 1968. Besides his constant traveling, the black writer led an unenviable life: he smoked and drank, hardly ate, slept little, and worked at impossible hours.

Nervous by nature, he liked to talk a lot and to be surrounded by friends. The idea of touching others fascinated him enormously. To him, that was very important. In this connection, he stated: "Not touching a person is a way of rejecting him. And it is also a way of being rejected."[20] In 1970, Baldwin directed the production of the play by John Herbert, Fortune and Men's Eyes, which depicts the deplorable living conditions in Canadian penitentiaries.[21] All the performances were given in a little theater in Istanbul. His Turkish friend, Engin Cezzar, played the leading role.

Baldwin's desire to be constantly busy intrigued numerous people. David Littlejohn said on the subject:

> Each book is a renewed effort to stay alive and upright through the finding and placing of perfect words. Each book is a staving off of death, a matter of survival.[22]

This explains perhaps Baldwin's attitude in declaring:

> I know something about whence I came. If you forget that then forget about everything, the party is over. I'm a black funky raggedy ass shoeshine boy. If I forget that, it's the end of me.[23]

The certainty of knowing oneself well and the desire never to forget from where he came and who he was, never prevented Baldwin from following a very distinct evolution in his literary career. The progressive change of his ideas seems to have gone through three very distinct stages. In each one, he adopted a special attitude toward life and the American people.

In the first stage, the black author accepted his condition as a black in order, next, to speak of it freely to the white American world. In an interview published in Esquire, Baldwin declared he was completely on the side of Stokely Carmichael and the black militants, and that the white world found itself confronted with both a new and a disturbing force.[24] After having thus recognized the group to which he belonged, Baldwin went through a difficult stage, that of the acceptance of American life with all its complex forms. This acceptance, which required maturity and courage, made him feel deeply the kind of personal identity he was duty-bound to accept. That is perhaps the reason, in most of his essays, he very often uses the first person singular in order to explain better an idea relative to a problem that is close to his heart. As one can see, here we are very close to a definitive position, a commitment, of James Baldwin's. This is the third stage in which the writer hesitated between two roles to play, prophet or artist.

In the first case, we know that Baldwin had already worked hard for civil rights but he preferred to dedicate more time to his job as a writer. In the second case, one knows that Baldwin was deeply interested in man and his problems. Here there is little difference between the prophet and the spokesman for civil rights as he revealed himself in The Fire Next Time, and the artist discovered in Go Tell It on the Mountain. It would be fitting nonetheless to recognize that Baldwin was above all an excellent essayist. As a playwright and a novelist, he was considered of secondary importance. But the author's race embraced all his works, since a dominant Afro-American characteristic constantly manifests itself through the omnipotence of sexuality over his ideas and his characters.

James Baldwin died of cancer on December 1, 1987, in Saint Paul de Vence, France. He was 63 years old.

NOTES

1. James Baldwin, Go Tell It on the Mountain (New York: New American Library, Signet Books, 1963). (All other references to this book will correspond to this edition. Published for the first time in New York by Alfred A. Knopf in 1953). The numerous biographical details are based for the most part on the autobiographical essays of James Baldwin published in Notes of a Native Son, Nobody Knows My Name, and The Fire Next Time. The Furious Passage of James Baldwin (New York: Evans and Co., 1966) by Fern Marja Eckman was also highly useful.

2. Robert A. Bone, "Postscript" in his The Negro Novel in America (New Haven, Connecticut: Yale University Press, 1965), p. 216.

3. The Negro Novel in America, p. 216. James Baldwin, The Amen Corner, Zero 6 (July, 1954): 4-8, 11-13. (Act 1 of a quite obviously longer work.)

4. James Baldwin, Notes of a Native Son (New York: Bantam Books, 1964), pp. 71-95. All other references to this book will correspond to this edition. Published for the first time in Boston by Beacon Press in 1955.

5. Margaret Mead and James Baldwin, "A Rap on Race," McCall's, June 1971, p. 150.

6. James Baldwin, "Everybody's Protest Novel," in his Notes of a Native Son, pp. 9-17.

7. James Baldwin, Another Country (New York: Dell Publishing Co., 1964). All other references to this book will correspond to this edition. Published for the first time in New York by Dial Press in 1962.

8. James Baldwin, Giovanni's Room (New York: Dell Publishing Co., 1964). All other references to this book will correspond to this edition. Published for the first time in New York by The Dial Press in 1956.

9. James Baldwin, Nobody Knows My Name (New York: Dell Publishing Co., 1964). All other references to this book will correspond to this edition. Published for the first time in New York by The Dial Press in 1961.

10. James Baldwin, "Stranger in the Village," in his Notes of a Native Son, pp. 135-149.

11. James Baldwin, The Fire Next Time (New York: Dell Publishing Co., 1964). All other references to this book will correspond to this edition. First published in New York by The Dial Press in 1963.

12. Time, May 17, 1963, pp. 26-27.

13. James Baldwin, Nothing Personal (Harmondsworth, England: Penguin Books, 1964). Date of the first publication. All other references to this book will correspond to this edition.

14. James Baldwin, Blues for Mister Charlie (New York: The Dial Press, 1964). First publication date. All other references to this book will correspond to this edition.

15. James Baldwin, "How can we get the Black People to Cool it?", Esquire, July 1968, pp. 49-53, 116.

16. Margaret Mead and James Baldwin, "A Rap on Race," pp. 152-153.

17. James Baldwin, Going to Meet the Man (New York: The Dial Press, 1965). First publication date. All other references to this book will correspond to this edition.

18. James Baldwin, The Amen Corner (New York: The Dial Press, 1968). First publication date. All other references to this book will correspond to this edition.

19. James Baldwin, Tell Me How Long the Train's Been Gone (New York: The Dial Press, 1968). First publication date. All other references to this book will correspond to this edition.

20. Margaret Mead and James Baldwin, "A Rap on Race," p. 85.

21. John Herbert, Fortune and Men's Eyes (New York: Grove Press, 1967).

22. David Littlejohn, "Baldwin," in his Black on White (New York: Grossman Publishers, 1966), p. 120.

23. Dan Georgakas, "James Baldwin . . . in Conversation," in Black Voices: An Anthology of Afro-American Literature, edited by Abraham Chapman (New York: New American Library, Mentor Books, 1968), p. 667.

24. James Baldwin, "How can we get the Black People to Cool it?", pp. 49-53, 116.

7

CONDITIONS

THE WHITE WORLD

For James Baldwin, the Christian religion and the white world are synonymous since they are both harmful to the American black. Baldwin often reminded us that the conversion of the Africans to Christianity made them lose all notion of freedom and pride. In other words, Christian, for Baldwin, means betrayals and sufferings for the man of color.

The intimate as well as disappointing experience of the Christian faith led Baldwin to recommend a modification of that faith. He even goes so far as to suggest its total destruction as the only solution. According to him, the white world must change at all costs its attitude of arrogant superiority towards peoples of color. One understands that reasoning, though it is at first surprising, when one knows that symbolic minor changes would contribute nothing to the sad lot of millions of Africans and Asians. Only a radical disruption of the values of the white world could present a solution to the problems that divide today's world.

Howard Levant describes quite accurately the kind of life led by the black in America. Since he is not a full American citizen, the black must content himself with whatever white American society cares to grant him. That is the reason the vast majority of blacks, both men and women, have only menial and low-paying jobs.[1] Charles English goes so far as to say that the skin of American whites constitutes the barbed wire fences which surround the concentration camps, or ghettos, where blacks are forced to live. The white man takes advantage of the Christian religion in order to strengthen his authority and his superiority. "What he tells us is the story of the greatest perversion of Christianity on record," declares Charles English in talking about James Baldwin's works.[2] Suffering from the attitude of the white world as well as from the Christian religion, although often giving himself heart and soul to the latter, the black man generally ends up destroying himself. The result is that, more and more, the black man is driven to hate whites intensely and to be suspicious of the Christian religion in which he has less and less faith. This great distrust of the Christian religion results from the nonobservance on its part of the great moral principles that it purports to teach. Who could believe in a religion which does not respect its own precepts and principles?

In "Everybody's Protest Novel," Baldwin affirms that the white man cannot perceive the black man as he is because of more than three centuries of segregation.[3] The values, quite puritanical, that the white man attaches to life, prevent him from seeing the true identity of the black man. The latter, who enjoys no freedom, has the rank of an inferior in a society that constantly despises him. In an article, "To Whom It May Concern: Report From Occupied Territory," published in July 1966, Baldwin goes farther, writing that the main role of the American police is to frighten blacks, whose homes may be searched at any hour of the day or night.[4] Through this article, the black author emphasizes the wretched and degrading living conditions of the man of color in the United States.

At the end of "Everybody's Protest Novel," James Baldwin violently attacks Richard Wright by saying that Bigger Thomas is a descendant of Uncle Tom. As one knows, this essay brutally ended the two writers' friendship. The connection that Baldwin sees between Harriet Beecher Stowe's antislavery novel and Native Son is protest.[5] This protest, according to Baldwin, imposes overly rigid limitations on the novels of Harriet Beecher Stowe and Richard Wright and prevents them from exploring in depth as well as describing in detail the complex soul of their hero. This subject was the theme of a longer essay published in 1951, "Many Thousands Gone."[6] But one must note that protest has always played an important role in the novel in general. It is against Richard Wright's narrow and violent naturalism that James Baldwin reacts. His essential aim has always been to reveal the life of the black man in all its forms, no matter how complex it may be. The author's religious experience, as Go Tell It on the Mountain attests, probably played an important role in this domain.[7] Richard Wright had never had this experience.

In "Everybody's Protest Novel," Baldwin says that the white American possesses various and sundry means of exercising extreme control over the black man. The author brings out two attitudes of the American white which, different though they are, produce the same results. The first is the attitude of the white who feels pity for the sad lot of the black entirely subjected to the omnipotence of the white world. The second typifies the white frightened by the violent revolt and reaction of the black who refuses to be enslaved by the white world. In these two conflicting examples of the conception of the black man, we recognize, in the first, Uncle Tom, and, in the second, Bigger Thomas. In the first case, the black man is the symbol of suffering; in the second, he typifies evil. That the feelings of the American white, towards the black man, may go from compassion to terror is something James Baldwin succeeds in making one see and feel clearly. He wishes to show that American society suffers from dangerous, indeed perverse, evils. Thus, no matter what he does, the black man always ends up being humiliated, vexed, and diminished by the white man. James Baldwin is clear on this point: the white man feels neither sincerity nor compassion towards the black who is suffering. This is the white who lets his imagination go to the point of experiencing exaggerated terror in the face of the destructive rage of the black man. Therefore, the black man must be constantly on his guard, even in a situation of complete submission. The least thing, however small it may be, may at any moment degenerate and endanger his life.

Having himself often suffered from the whims of the white world, Baldwin knows of what he speaks. What is the black man to do, one may wonder, when several whites attribute reprehensible and criminal intentions to him? The only solution would seem to be flight, suicide, or even a sudden and fatal attack of insanity. In "Everybody's Protest Novel," Baldwin remarks that blacks and whites, whether they like it or not, are a part of the same society, share the same reality, have the same future, and that any interesting change affects both of them sooner or later. The only advice given to whites as well as blacks is to accept one another without prejudice, without conditions. A society made up of oppressed and oppressors certainly cannot last long. Here, literature and sociology play a dual role in Baldwin's thought. "Everybody's Protest Novel" announced the literary career and especially the social responsibilities that the author was going to manage in the fifties and sixties.

Any so-called protest novel, in its entirety or in part, is not necessarily a literary failure. Contrary to what Baldwin advances in "Everybody's Protest Novel," numerous literary masterpieces are born of protest. Tell Me How Long the Train's Been Gone strangely resembles Native Son and shows that, nearly twenty years after having violently criticized Richard Wright, James Baldwin had to resort to poorly imitating his former master.[8] Tell Me How Long the Train's Been Gone, in effect, is filled with anger, rage, and especially an intense desire for destruction.

This long novel, divided into three parts and cluttered with numerous retrospective scenes, is difficult to read. Book 1, "The House Nigger," certainly the best of the three, contains flashbacks giving an initial general idea of the hero's family, professional, love, and private life. The hero, Leo Proudhammer, represents poorly what Baldwin would like to make of him: a symbol of love and brotherhood but also of hate and disunion. In this novel, written in the first person singular, the author strongly influenced his hero even as far as his own physical description. In other word Baldwin wants to be the spokesman for the militant black, thirsting for vengeance and anxious to make his dangerous and intimidating ideas known to the white world. The hero's last name, Proudhammer, has a very distinctive resonance, in keeping with his personality and his attitude.

From the beginning of the first book, the writer sees a James Baldwin torn, indeed tortured, by his own ideas. Not only do the retrospective scenes add to the confusion, but the author also tries, in vain, to prove that he has literary talent. In addition, he attempts to speak in the name of millions of American blacks in love with justice. Here Baldwin becomes involved heart and soul in a novel from which he wishes to emerge victorious at all costs. Contrary to certain novelists, he is not detached from his work. The result is quite disappointing; objectivity finds no place there. To a certain extent, <u>Tell Me How Long the Train's Been Gone</u> is a success as a propaganda novel, for the author, or Leo Proudhammer, speaks vehemently in the name of American black nationalists. Evoking the force and weight of the arguments used by Baldwin, Granville Hicks said the power of the novel compensates for the weakness of the style and for the general appearance.[9] From the first page, Leo Proudhammer, a famous black actor, is laid low by a heart attack on the stage of a San Francisco Theater. Beginning with that moment, and until the end of the novel, the action takes place in San Francisco during the hero's convalescence, although the many lengthy flashbacks sometimes make it difficult to situate the action and its hero. James Baldwin is a great admirer of the American black actor Sidney Poitier. Possibly, therefore, the author tried to imbue the person of Leo Proudhammer with the great theatrical qualities of his idol and his own ideas. Baldwin denied having had such an intention, but he recognized nonetheless that the American black artist, in general, has heavy responsibilities towards America and that Sidney Poitier was in a good position to assume them.[10]

It is from his hospital bed that Leo Proudhammer relives four scenes from his past. The first one takes place in Harlem where the hero was born and grew up. We are brought face to face with Leo's parents and his brother, Caleb. Leo is ten years old and his brother is seventeen. The destitution of the Proudhammer family is described in detail. From Mr. Rabinowitz, the Jewish landlord to whom they must always pay the rent and who never misses the opportunity to humiliate Leo's father, to Mr. Shapiro, a grocer, who is willing to extend credit to Leo's mother, we intensely feel the little insults heaped upon a young black man whose life is constantly controlled by the white world. Caleb, although still young, already knows all the secrets of life and has no illusions about his future. He even teaches his young brother the proper way to conduct himself with whites. One day they are stopped, brutally questioned, and searched by two white policemen whose sole aim is to frighten them. On this subject, one knows what Baldwin thinks since he declared that white policemen are on duty in black ghettos "to keep the Negro in his place and to protect white business interests, and they have no other function."[11] It is therefore not surprising, given those living conditions, that the head of a black family often seeks consolation and refuge in drunkenness, debauchery, and violence. That is the reason Leo's father, a simple and poor worker originally from the West Indies, indulges in drinking. Baldwin arouses the reader's pity by presenting the moral as well as physical sufferings endured by the Proudhammer family.

Between two flashbacks, Leo, now thirty-nine years old, wakes up on his hospital bed only, later, to fall back into a dream which makes him relive another part of his past. The action takes place in New York, twenty years earlier, where the young actor is trying to succeed in the path he has chosen for himself. We find him in the company of a young white woman from Kentucky, Barbara King, who is already known to us since she was on the San Francisco theater stage when Leo had his heart attack. In this second retrospective scene, Barbara and young Proudhammer go to a reception where they come across some people, in high places, capable of helping them in their future theatrical career. Lola and Saul San-Marquand, artistic directors of the Actor's Means Workshop, are very much more interested in Barbara than in Leo. The latter, depressed and discouraged, lets himself go singing some blues for the guests. If this musical form, typically Afro-American, permits Baldwin to show the pain of a person thirsting for pity and human compassion, it also reveals Leo Proudhammer's lack of courage and endurance. Leo is content with being near Barbara, as if this white woman's presence were a source of life, protection, and consolation. Between this and Harriet Beecher Stowe's novel there is little difference. Whether we have a Leo or an Uncle Tom, the white woman still exerts the same power and the same attraction over the black man.

When he regains consciousness at the San Francisco hospital, Leo Proudhammer finds Barbara at his bedside. Quite obviously, she is his guardian angel. Shortly afterward, he relives another period of his past in New York where he had spoken at a civil rights demonstration. In that retrospective scene James Baldwin's personality is strongly felt. In it we meet for the first time a certain Christopher Hall, a militant young American black man admired by Leo Proudhammer. Although older, Leo is won over to the revolutionary ideas of young Christopher, who could pass for a Black Panther.

The last retrospective scene of Book 1 takes us back to Harlem, where we rediscover the poverty of the Proudhammer family. The father is out of work, Caleb no longer goes to school, and little Leo has become a shoeshine boy. A deep friendship unites the two brothers, who love each other very much. Their tender camaraderie is interrupted abruptly when Caleb is arrested by white policemen who accuse him of stealing in a department store. The arrest, described realistically, even brutally, takes place in a house of prostitution where Caleb has taken refuge. A native of Harlem, it is not difficult for Baldwin to recreate an atmosphere and events he knows well. Furthermore, it is when the action takes place in Harlem, and we also see in other retrospective scenes of the novel, that the author gives his work a powerful breath of air.

Book 2 of the novel, "Is There Anybody There? said the traveler," relates three flashbacks. They follow upon those already seen in Book 1. In the first, Leo, Barbara, and her lover, Jerry, are in New Jersey one summer, where they are working for the theatrical company of Lola and Saul San-Marquand.

Barbara and Leo are preparing and rehearsing a play by Clifford Odets, Waiting for Lefty. They rub shoulders with numerous other actors and actresses who, like them, are doing all they can to succeed in their theatrical career. The Green Barn, a theater in the city, is the center of their activities.

From time to time, and through the character of Leo Proudhammer, James Baldwin reveals his opinion about various points. Thus he explains in detail, and with curiosity, the hesitant and indecisive attitude of a family of Sicilian immigrants towards blacks. This family runs a little restaurant frequented by the actors and blacks in the city. In this second book, Leo Proudhammer establishes a short-lived affair with a divorced white actress, Madeleine Overstreet, after spending an evening with her in a nightclub in the black section.

The attitude displayed by the author towards the Sicilians is filled with scorn because they are without resources. On the other hand, when he speaks of the sexual adventure of young Leo, then nineteen, he does not hide his pride, indeed his arrogance, in a dangerous situation for his hero. It would seem that he is not interested in the human aspect of two situations in which emotions and feelings have a prominent place. As the author makes clear, the action takes place during World War II, a time when whites' attitudes towards blacks was not at all liberal.

Despite the curses and the coarse language in which he seems to take pleasure, it is from Madeleine's bed that Leo Proudhammer remembers the time spent in Harlem. Here we have the second retrospective scene of Book 2. Leo is fourteen years old and Caleb is twenty-one. The latter has just come out of prison, where he has been mistreated by whites. Thus he is embittered and has great apprehensions about his future. His former girlfriend, Dolores, is a streetwalker and all his friends are either in prison or subjected to the yoke of the white world. His parents, for lack of money, are forced to sublet two rooms of their apartment, for his father earns only very little at his new porter's job. Since they have to sleep in the same bed, the two brothers, who love each other very much and who suffer from their life-style, end up having sexual relations. This brotherly affection helps them, for a while, to endure their life. But not wanting to follow the same road as his father constantly humiliated by whites, Caleb leaves for California and an uncertain future. James Baldwin's descriptions of Harlem are both real and moving. From the father who has lost his pride to the two brothers who discover the cruel face of life, the author communicates a deep feeling of powerlessness and humiliation to the reader. At the age of fourteen, young Leo, in search of human protection, finds a few dubious people who, in their way, are willing to take care of him. But it is Caleb's image that he is especially eager to keep intact and pure in his heart.

On this sad memory, Leo Proudhammer wakes up alone in Madeleine's apartment, which he hastens to leave. Sexuality plays an important role in this novel, for the hero has had both homosexual and heterosexual relations. This seems to come from Baldwin's desire to shock, indeed scandalize, puritan and middle class America. If sexuality plays an already important role in the novels published before 1968, it seems to occupy too big a place here. For this novel cannot be based on the sole sexual prowess of Leo Proudhammer. Because of his language and his style, James Baldwin is far from being as good a writer as in Go Tell It on the Mountain, although the descriptions of Harlem are real, as well as lively and human. The author does not need to appeal to his imagination in order to describe the life he experienced in Harlem during his childhood.

In the third retrospective scene of Book 2, Leo Proudhammer, whom some whites saw leaving Madeleine's apartment, is arrested by the police. Knowing that he is in danger, the young black actor pretends not to understand what is going on. For to admit having spent the night with a white woman could incite the white policemen to accuse him of any crime whatsoever in order to keep him in prison. But his friends succeed in getting him out of prison. At this point, Barbara declares her love to him while assuring him she has broken off her relationship with Jerry. It is not out of the question to think that it is through pity that the young white woman from Kentucky has fallen in love with the black man who has just suffered the physical cruelty of white policemen. This protective pity strangely evokes Harriet Beecher Stowe's attitude towards Uncle Tom, with the sole difference that sexuality does not play a dominating role in the antislavery novel.

Later, Barbara and Leo perform <u>Waiting for Lefty</u> before Saul San-Marquand, who does not hide his disappointment at the young black man's performance. Quite obviously, Barbara is much more talented than Leo and nobody doubts her future success. Here again, as in <u>Uncle Tom's Cabin</u>, the white woman wants to protect the deprived black man. Barbara, in fact, declares to Leo she wants to share her life with him. At this stage in the novel, Barbara is on the road to success whereas the young black man seems to have no future. But we know that Leo will succeed, probably after having worked hard. It is fitting to emphasize the use of flashbacks, which enable one to appreciate better and better judge the road traveled by a little black boy from Harlem who became a famous actor.

In Book 3, "Black Christopher," the numerous retrospective scenes tend, despite everything, to make the reading quite difficult because they are too frequent. This is, from the point of view of structure, the weakest part of the novel. Out of the hospital, Leo Proudhammer lives in an apartment chosen by Barbara and he sees his friends again. Here Baldwin interjects the comment that, with the exception of San Francisco, American cities are all ugly. The hero of the novel is now forty years old. His revolutionary ideas about America are even surprising. Now it is the author who, through Leo, is speaking in the novel. During an interview in 1968, James Baldwin declared he was completely on the side of the young black militants and could only encourage them to arm themselves since the white world was armed already.[12] Such ideas are advanced in the novel through Christopher Hall.

Another flashback takes us to the time when Barbara and Leo were working diligently in order to succeed in their theatrical career. Most of the events take place in Greenwich Village, where Leo sees Caleb again. The latter has changed a lot for, after having lived through the ordeal of World War II, he has chosen God. He has become His disciple in a church in Harlem, the New Dispensation House of God. We are in the presence of two brothers now very different from each other. Leo does what he can to make a living, whereas his older brother seems to have found a lasting vocation in religion. Leo works in a little West Indian restaurant for almost six years before being able to make his theatrical talents known. At that date, Barbara is already well known and Caleb married. The rage and the impatience which devour Leo reflect the feelings that Baldwin was so able to reveal in his essays. Unfortunately for the author, these same feelings fail since the hero of the novel seems to be struggling in space and without a precise goal. It is evident that Baldwin is trying to fade into a character in his own image, from the physical as well as the moral point of view.

Still, thanks to the technique of retrospective scenes, we find Leo, at the age of twenty-six, making his official entrance into the theatrical world. His mother dies shortly thereafter, from the aftereffects of a long illness. Whatever the ills that afflict Leo's family may be, Baldwin seems to think that whites and religion are at the root of all their misfortunes. Although there may be a great deal of truth here, one cannot generalize evil and attribute it solely to the white and Christian world. Other very subtle elements also enter into play. It is after a dazzling debut that Leo comes across Christopher Hall, also originally from Harlem. The bond uniting these two individuals is all the more real since it is both ideological and sexual. One can therefore understand well that the two brothers despise everything white and Christian. What intrigues the reader is the way Leo speaks constantly of the beauty and radiance of his mother's near-white skin. In addition, why would he continue to see Barbara King? One may conclude that Leo, or James Baldwin, feels great admiration for a certain member of the white race: the white woman. She always plays an important role in the hero's life. Here again, we find Harriet Beecher Stowe and poor Uncle Tom. According to Baldwin, the black man constantly needs the white woman who, like a guardian angel, watches over and protects him. Proudhammer offers a very disturbing paradox for, on the one hand, he hates the white race and, on the other, his best friends happen to be white.

Tell Me How Long the Train's Been Gone is quite obviously a very clear anti-establishment novel which seems to indicate that in spite of himself James Baldwin was led by circumstances to imitate Richard Wright very badly. It would seem that the black novelist in general cannot escape the anti-establishment novel and that Baldwin does not know how to write such a novel. In Tell Me How Long the Train's Been Gone, he revels in erotic descriptions, thinking that such scenes will help him to make himself better understood by the white world. He is wrong. It is not curses and coarse language that will induce whites to listen to blacks, but rather well-articulated and positive ideas.

At the end of the novel, Barbara admits to Leo that, out of love for him, she seduced Christopher. Baldwin may wish to show the blind passion of the young white woman for Leo; the fact remains nonetheless that such an attitude and such behavior are quite surprising and even rare. Could it be an indication that the black man cannot do without the warm and comforting presence of the white woman? That is what Baldwin seems to want to indicate again. But the novel does not stop there, for

Christopher, who closely resembles Caleb of the past, decides that blacks must arm themselves against whites. It is evident that the aim of James Baldwin's novel is to arouse hate and hostility in both whites and blacks. The lesson to be drawn from this work is far from exemplary. This sudden and brutal stand was caused to a large extent by the violent manner in which Eldridge Cleaver and the black militants criticized James Baldwin in the 1960s. For them, the author is an indecisive man who, in racial matters, is much more attracted to the white world than to the black. In addition, the fate of the Christians persecuted by the Romans is in no way comparable to that of American blacks harassed by whites. Baldwin should not have established that comparison, because it is untenable. Everyone knows that the first Christians had no intentions of annihilating their persecutors and that their sole aim was to convert them by noble and peaceful means. That comparison is therefore very deplorable and unfortunate for James Baldwin.

In this novel, Baldwin's approach is both sterile and negative. Not only is the work profoundly autobiographical, but the author, in his rage and anger, seems to hate himself. To use hate as a political goal and instrument is something practically impossible. Here one may wonder whether Baldwin still had something to say, for his future as a writer seemed quite restricted. Tell Me How Long the Train's Been Gone is severely limited as a novel because of Baldwin's personal interests and racism. This dichotomy prevents the novel from going completely the way Baldwin wanted, and the result is disappointing. The sexuality, hatred, and violence of the novel strangely evoke the tense atmosphere of Native Son. Whether Baldwin likes it or not, the voice of the prophet has become here the voice of the protester, especially in the person of Christopher Hall. Barbara's constant presence clearly indicates that, for the author at least, the black man needs the pity and the encouragement of the white woman in order to be able to live in a world which, after all, as he himself recognizes, is essentially white. James Baldwin, the artist, is surpassed by Christopher Hall's exhortations to violence and Leo Proudhammer's sexual prowess.

Since the beginning of his literary career, Baldwin has always shown a distrust of whites. In an essay "Journey to Atlanta,"[13] the author advises blacks not to trust the white world, even if its intentions seem good. In order to illustrate his case, he speaks of a quartet, The Melodeers, formed by two of his brothers, who, in 1948, had gone to Georgia with the sole aim of giving performances in several black churches in this Southern state. Since the trip was subsidized by the Progressive Party, Henry Agard Wallace's liberal party with Communist tendencies, the four young blacks had first gone to Atlanta where, to their great surprise, they had been asked to work for the party's electoral campaign. The astonished young people had first yielded to the party's demands. But after a few days of hard labor, they remembered the goal of their trip. The anger of the white leaders was such that they sent them, immediately, back home to the North, to Harlem.

This reaction had been provoked by some young blacks from the

North who, in the eyes of Southern whites, had dared to raise their voices and complain. In other words, James Baldwin's two brothers and their two friends had, by their attitude, upset some whites used to being obeyed by blacks without a murmur. Although representing a political party said to be a friend of blacks, these whites had simply tried to use the four young blacks in order to better ensure the success of their leader, a candidate for the presidency of the United States in the 1948 elections.

From this adventure, Baldwin draws an important and beneficial lesson in order to say that the black man cannot trust the white man. This situation, although distinctive, is nonetheless typical of the South, where the white man has no respect for the black whose vote alone is important. Moreover, and with the sole aim of assuring themselves of the votes of the black masses, whites or the political parties they represent do not hesitate to make false promises. The results, as one may suspect, are very disappointing and even dangerous. On the one hand, the blacks display great distrust; on the other, whites do not hesitate to resort to threats and the brutalities of the Ku Klux Klan in order to achieve their ends. James Baldwin has no illusions about the future relations between blacks and whites, having already repeated, on several occasions, that it would take a miracle for whites to accept blacks. He also said that, if blacks revolt, the fault lies entirely with whites, source of all the misfortunes of blacks. In an interview, he even declared that to be white was an attitude whereas to be black represented a condition.[14]

Norman Podhoretz, who is Jewish, said with accuracy that the color of his skin, when he crossed blacks in the street, gave him a sense of superiority and security. Why? Because he belongs to the camp of the strongest and because the police are on his side.[15] If a man as educated as Norman Podhoretz can make such a statement, it is not surprising that the white man, whatever he may be, has an attitude of crushing superiority towards any individual whose skin is black. Thus, blacks are constantly in the position of inferiors. If they want to survive, they can only accept and play the dangerous game imposed by whites. For the slightest prank is likely to cost them their job or even their life. It is not surprising that blacks in the South are afraid to become involved in the political life of their country, since most of their efforts are often sanctioned by very serious penalties. Besides, whites in the South are accustomed to being obeyed by blacks. That is perhaps the reason James Baldwin's two brothers and their friends left Georgia without asking for any explanations.

THE BLACK WORLD

If the white world has its special way of treating and humiliating the black man, the black world, on the other hand, also has a very specific way of acting and thinking within a hostile universe. The life, the habits, and the actions of the black man are determined by the oppression and the tyranny of the white man who believes himself superior and omnipotent in all domains. Whence the wretched condition of the American black forced to live in a world apart, inferior and even often stripped of all human dignity. Nothing is more depressing than to discover this conglomerate of black and unhappy lives: the black ghetto.

In an essay, "The Harlem Ghetto," Baldwin describes with precision the hard life that blacks lead in Harlem.[16] Not only are the rents and food very high-priced there, but also very often, for lack of work or money, the black is forced to live in poverty. Nothing has changed since 1948, the time when James Baldwin wrote that essay. Twenty years later, he had to repeat with more anger that the white man was at the root of all the ills of the blacks. He also had to add that blacks no longer trusted whites, of whom they were more suspicious than ever.[17]

The white, sometimes in the person of the Jew, is constantly near the ghetto black from whom he always knows how to derive the best profit. This daily presence, says Baldwin in his essay, creates a tense atmosphere in which the slightest thing might cause an already dangerous situation to explode. The Jew, whatever he may be and although deeply hated by the black man, plays the only role he can have in a society that despises him and which is above all Christian. In Harlem, ville noire, Michel Fabre said concerning this: "Whether he takes advantage of the situation or not, the Jewish merchant in Harlem is generally thought of as a usurer: he incarnates white economic oppression, whereas he himself has the feeling he is rendering a service to the black community by staying there although he is exposed to multiple dangers."[18] The utmost lack of understanding therefore prevails between Jews and blacks in Harlem. Thus, after riots, murders, and fires, the ghetto is always there with its poverty and its villainous debauchery. Quite obviously, racism plays both a negative and a destructive role here. The only beneficiary of this state of affairs is always the white and Christian majority that has never seen a black ghetto. On the other hand, the Jew with his business and blacks who live there are the first to feel the disastrous consequences of acts committed in rage and violence. The Harlem riots in 1935 and in 1943 illustrate this point well. Nothing seems to be able to resolve such a problem. Like a volcano, the black ghetto often has eruptions as sudden as unexpected.

Baldwin proposes a solution nevertheless by saying that the situation in the ghettos will improve if the form of education changes radically. Such an idea is not to be sniffed at when one knows that the black has officially no place in American history. It is not his fault, but that of the white man who has always treated him like an inferior being unworthy of any attention and who has declared him unfit for any real function. On this point, Baldwin strongly encourages black leaders not to cease their requests, their demands, and their protests to aid the mass of the black population which finds comfort and moral support only in the voices of its representatives. Even if the numerous and difficult steps taken by black leaders are to no avail most of the time, it is nonetheless a fact that their perseverance, despite everything, plays a positive and encouraging role in a world constantly afflicted by poverty, scorn and kept on the sidelines.

The black press, in its desire to acquire a certain notoriety, succeeds only in imitating the failings, shortcomings, and bad examples of whites. It is only a pale reflection of the white press. That is what the author says in his essay of 1948. Forty-four years later, certain organs of the black press still had no fear of expressing hate and violence against the white world. But most of the black newspapers and magazines of today, such as Ebony, seem to have as their main goal to be accepted and even read by whites. Now, the black press rarely gets noticed outside the black ghetto, where it is like a prisoner and incapable of improving the lot of thousands of souls living in desperation.

Abandoned by the government of its own country, and knowing that he has no future in a hostile world, the black man is forced to fight to defend himself and make himself respected. The identity thus created permits him to escape, for a while at least, the role of an absentee which the white world always tries to impose on him. Most often the black sinks in despair, for lack of courage, determination, and tenacity. Thus, thousands of ghetto blacks go to join the ranks of those who believe they have found salvation and protection in religion. Black religious fervor is only the expression of a tortured soul that, no longer believing in life, hopes to find a better world after death. The result of this negative attitude is to create a black universe apart, expecting absolutely nothing more from this world, in which, indifferent, a person subsists from one day to the next. James Baldwin lived blindly like that for nearly three years in the haven of a misunderstood religion. By withdrawing from religion in time, Baldwin had the courage to accept himself as he was in his universe. His first novel, Go Tell It on the Mountain, and his first play The Amen Corner[19] show that the young black author has not only accepted his past but also his present condition. This fact, to a certain extent, enabled him to understand and explain better the sad lot of the American black imprisoned in his ghetto.

In Go Tell It on the Mountain, undoubtedly Baldwin's best novel, the author's preoccupation is essentially human and spiritual. It is in this work that the religious sensitivity of the American black is revealed and described in detail. This book identifies itself entirely with the black community which the author depicts. The action takes place on a Saturday and Sunday in March 1935 and its main theater is a Harlem church, the Temple of the Fire Baptized. The unity of time and that of place are so closely linked that the action reaches an impressive dramatic concentration.

In a store converted into a small prayer room a few blacks, members of the same religious sect, meet to pray to God and especially to give vent to their emotions. In other words, this weekly meeting is an actual spiritual escape from the human hell that these people endure with difficulty and pain all the other days of the week. We are in the presence of blacks who, although realizing their physical and moral poverty, have accepted their sad lot. Only their ardent religious faith enables them to survive.

That weekend of March 1935 is not chosen at random, for it

coincides with the fourteenth birthday of John Grimes, the hero of the novel, who bears a striking resemblance to James Baldwin. The novel is divided into three parts: the first and the third taking place in 1935 whereas the second, composed of three prayers, those of Florence, Gabriel, and Elizabeth, revives events of the past through a stream of consciousness and several retrospective scenes. In these three prayers, the main character is not John Grimes, but his stepfather, Gabriel Grimes. The young hero does not know that Gabriel is not his real father; but all the other people around him, including the reader, know the truth.

The first part, "The Seventh Day," takes place throughout Saturday and shows in detail the life-style of a young adolescent from Harlem. This Saturday, seventh day of the week, has a very special meaning for the Grimes family, for not only is it the day of prayer, but also, and above all, it marks the birthday of a young boy who is not understood by his people. The name of this poor black family has a special meaning since it evokes filth as well as repugnance. It is also the symbol of the shameful thoughts and degrading acts that Florence, Gabriel, and Elizabeth have always tried to hide. Like an ignoble and indelible stigma, that name, Grimes, seems to make sure that everyone who bears it is sooner or later doomed to moral degeneration. It is in prayer and a deep religious fervor that these people try in vain to escape a cruel world that condemns them.

Since it is through the flesh that they have sinned, religion seems to be the only means enabling them to attain a level of moral purity. In so doing, they will find the way to eternal salvation. Aware of the poverty around him, John Grimes, far from giving in to despair, is determined to do everything to succeed in life. It is while crossing Central Park that he feels the powerful attraction that Broadway exerts over him, as opposed to that of the ghetto. Sin and moral life cause the young black to hesitate. He goes nonetheless to see a film forbidden to children of his age with the few cents given by his mother, Elizabeth.

The effects of the narrow and unhappy life that ghetto blacks lead are manifested when, back home, John Grimes learns that Roy, his brother (half-brother for those who know the truth), has been wounded in the head by some white children. The rage and the anger of his stepfather, who adores Roy and hates whites, show clearly that, whatever his life-style may be, man in general, is an imperfect being. Thus Gabriel Grimes believes he is chosen by God and exercises very tyrannical authority over a family more and more difficult to raise: Elizabeth is expecting a fifth child. John Grimes fully realizes that the lack of material comfort and a wretched life drive his fellowmen to seek support and satisfaction in a fanatical religion filled with emotions. He also knows that only Broadway, or the broad way, can offer him a future full of promises and enable him to get out of the narrow and dead-end rut of Harlem. In other words, the young hero is torn between the desire to succeed in the American world even if his soul is doomed to hell, and the far less attractive expectation of leading a bitter and wretched life in the ghetto.

In the second part, "The Prayers of the Saints," the stream of consciousness of Florence, Gabriel, and Elizabeth, and the memories relived from their past, enable the reader to understand the Grimes family better. Although the action takes place in the Temple of the Fire Baptized during Saturday and Sunday night of March 1935, the retrospective scenes relative to these three characters in fact retrace Gabriel Grimes's entire life. Assembled in their little room, the members of this religious sect give free rein to their emotions. These emotions, although seemingly loud and barbarian at first sight, are the only way these ghetto blacks can manifest their Christian faith in an uncertain beyond. This simple, and even primitive, way of praying to God is in fact a spiritual and mental experience of complete purity for people who basically expect nothing more from life. What matters to them is the purity and intensity of the feelings they experience during these weekly meetings.

It is with Florence, oldest sister of Gabriel Grimes, that the prayer of those chosen ones of the Lord begins. A hard and proud woman, slowly dying of cancer, Florence nonetheless lets herself be drawn in by the fullness of the faith and the devotion of the other blacks. Living alone in a furnished little room and horrified at the idea of dying, this sixty-year-old black woman is converted for the second time in her life. This reconversion is not due to a sincere and frank impulse of her soul, but rather to the feverish and emotional atmosphere which surrounds her.

A stream of consciousness and retrospective scenes revive some events from her past. Gabriel, five years older than she, had always been pampered and coddled by their mother. Florence had been jealous. That mother had had to take care of the black children of a white planter whose slave she had been. As for their father, he had disappeared shortly after the birth of Gabriel. Ashamed of her parents and jealous of a brother who was a good-for-nothing, Florence had left the South at the age of twenty-six hoping to find a better world in New York. A few years later she had married a good-for-nothing, Frank, who thought only of having a good time and who, after ten years, had left her for another woman. In World War I he had enlisted in the army and had been killed in France. Embittered and without illusions about life, Florence had continued living and working in New York. Thanks to a childhood friend, Deborah, she had received some news from her native South where Gabriel, in all probability, had changed completely in order to become a well-known and respected preacher. He had married Deborah, eight years older than he, who, despite her ugliness and her sterility, had been a great moral support to him. One of Deborah's letters had informed Florence that Gabriel had had an illegitimate son. Thirty years later, this compromising letter is in the handbag of Florence, who, her face bathed in tears, is sobbing and shouting in the Temple of the Fire Baptized. Contrary to what one might think, this outburst of emotion is not due to rage or any other human feeling. For these poor, simple blacks, who have suffered so much, this is the expression of the ineffable, indeed the sublime before the abyss of eternity.

Only the reader becomes aware here of Florence's intimate past, whereas John is ignorant of his aunt's whole life. The same secret understanding exists between the reader and Gabriel and Elizabeth during their prayers; John knows nothing about his stepfather's or his mother's past. As one may suspect, Florence has totally failed in her life, in which she has tried in vain to reach a certain level of human respectability. From the cream that did not succeed in making the skin on her face whiter, to her reprobate and penniless husband, we have the image of a black woman that the white world has both seduced and rejected.

Following upon Florence's prayer is that of Gabriel. Here again, the reader intensely relives the disorderly youth of this man who is now an obscure deacon in a little church in Harlem, whereas in his youth he had been a famous preacher in his native South. It was his deep religious faith which, at the time, had made him marry Deborah, made sterile following a rape committed by whites. His wife's ugliness and lack of warmth had led the young preacher to meet and seduce a young woman, Esther. She had died while giving birth to a son, Royal. As punishment for his sin, Gabriel had taken as his second wife a fallen woman, Elizabeth. This second marriage, unlike the first, had not been guided by a redeeming faith, but rather by a deep sense of guilt. Thus, by rejecting young John, Gabriel rejects his own guilt. In other words, John is the living symbol of his own sin and Gabriel wants to forget it. An illegitimate son, John, constantly reminds the embittered deacon that he too had an illegitimate son. The irony of fate would have it that John, and not his half-brother Roy, is the one called to become the anointed of the Lord. Roy totally rejects everything which has to do with his parents' religious life. Despite that attitude, Gabriel hopes for a prompt and sincere conversion of a legitimate son and not a bastard one. He would thus continue the worthy and just line of the Grimeses, by dedicating himself heart and soul to a religion which would shelter him from the evil spells of the white world. Gabriel had nourished the same hopes for his legitimate son who had also remained outside of religion until his brutal death in a bloody brawl in Chicago. Thus one can better understand the reason Gabriel withholds tenderness and affection from John, who, however, asks only to be accepted and loved.

Gabriel had confessed his sin to his first wife, Deborah, before she died. These confessions, contrary to what he expected, had found understanding and compassion in an individual who had suffered a great deal. Sometime after Deborah's death, Gabriel had come to meet Florence in New York and had met and married Elizabeth.

Elizabeth's prayer, like Florence's and Gabriel's, reveals secrets. What we learn about John's natural father, Gabriel does not know. Originally from the deep South, brought to the state of Maryland by an aunt after the death of her mother, Elizabeth had grown up without really knowing that warm family affection that every child needs during adolescence. Her father, who nevertheless loved her very much, had not been able to oppose her departure. The house of prostitution that he ran offered only a depraved and ugly image of life. At the age of eighteen, Elizabeth had met Richard, a serious and hard-working young black man.

She had followed him to New York but had settled at a relative's place in Harlem The great desire to conduct herself properly, and not to be in the wrong, had enabled young Elizabeth to work in the same hotel as Richard and to be near him as often as possible. Knowing that, for lack of a good position, he could not marry Elizabeth, Richard had started to take some evening classes in order to be able to assure himself a better future. But their plans and their hopes had been brutally broken when Richard, falsely accused of having committed a robbery in a white man's store, had been arrested, thrown in prison, and savagely beaten by white police officers. It was at that time that Elizabeth had found herself pregnant. She had not spoken about it to Richard, who, just out of prison and despairing of everything, had committed suicide by slashing his veins. The white world had gotten the better of his sensitivity and of him.

John had been born in a hostile and wretched world. In order to subsist, his mother had had to work at night as a maid in the large empty offices on Wall Street. That is how she had come across Florence, another soul in distress. The latter, embittered by a bleak life, had nevertheless taken a liking for Elizabeth, whose moral courage was exemplary. Later, John and his mother had met Gabriel at Florence's house. Stricken with pity for such a young woman and her illegitimate son, Gabriel Grimes, while remembering Esther and Royal, had decided to marry Elizabeth, less out of love than through a deep sense of divine and moral duty. Although she is a repentant and serious sinner, Elizabeth knows nothing about Esther and Royal; for this reason, Gabriel is free to treat John as he intends. Only Florence, who knows her brother's secret sin, can change this unrewarding and harmful behavior. Gabriel Grimes, as selfish as before, through terror imposes his ideas on a family of which he wishes to be the undisputed and almost divine head.

If in the second part of the novel Gabriel Grimes is the main character, in the third part, "The Threshing Floor," it is John who captures the reader's complete interest. The very title of that third part has a special meaning, since this "threshing floor" is the place where John's soul is delivered from its prison. It is evident that John is Gabriel's true spiritual son.

The seven people assembled in the Temple of the Fire Baptized enable us, through their exhortations and their encouragement, to face with courage a spiritual agony from which John Grimes is going to emerge as if he were transfigured:

> *"Rise up, Johnny," said Elisha, again. "Are you saved, boy?" "Yes," said John, "Oh, yes!" And the words came upward, it seemed, of themselves, in the new voice God had given him. Elisha stretched out his hand, and John took the hand, and stood--so suddenly, and so strangely, and with such wonder!--Once more on his feet.*
> *"Lord, I ain't*
> *No stranger now!*[20]

Like the grain freed from its chaff on the threshing floor, young Grimes can finally show the chosen ones that he is one of them. But Gabriel refuses to accept a being that is the fruit of sin. He would like to see him as rarely as possible. John's conversion nonetheless indicates an Oedipal element in young Grimes, who secretly wishes the death of the one he believes to be his natural father. He fully realizes, without nonetheless being able to explain it, that Gabriel does not like him and rejects all his sincere approaches as a faithful son. John Grimes's main goal, basically, is to make himself loved and accepted by his tyrannical father whom he does not understand, but whom he especially wants to please. This explains also, in part, his conversion, since he knows that Roy is not at all interested in religion. Rejected by the one by whom he wants to make himself loved, young John Grimes simply wishes to disappear.

In any case, John seems to have found the way which, for a while at least, is going to ensure a better future for him than life on the streets of Harlem. There does not seem to be any fundamental difference between the temporal and the spiritual for the characters in the novel. For them, the white world is condemned and only the black world still offers hope and salvation. All those anointed of Christ live intensely their deep religious faith, which goes even to the point of fanaticism. Their religious rites are all the more mysterious and astonishing as they are above all the vestige of a long and obscure pagan tradition of African origin. The moans, shouts, and sobs of these beings enclosed in their little room in the Temple of the Fire Baptized are the pure and sincere expression of human and not barbarian feelings.

This novel explores in depth the subtle relationships that exist between the various members of the Grimes family. Although succeeding in it only with great difficulty, John tries to define himself in relationship to the one he believes to be his father. His aunt, Florence, knows what she is doing when she shows Gabriel Deborah's letter concerning his illegitimate son by Esther. It is this very compromising letter, appearing at the end of the novel, that makes one think that the novel itself is not finished. After a long night of prayers, the eight members of the Temple of the Fire Baptized emerge, as though beatified, into the streets of Harlem. It is a Sunday morning; day is scarcely beginning to break. The action of the novel lasted scarcely twenty-four hours and, nevertheless, everything indicates that the future of the characters is still rich in important events. This impression is perhaps due to the fact that the members of that religious sect seem to belong to a primitive people and that such peoples have always had a great mysterious future before them.

In the essay "Notes of a Native Son," Baldwin indeed says, with precision, what he thinks of this type of tyrannical and paranoid father.[21] There is a close relationship between this long essay and Go Tell It on the Mountain. Harvey Breit said that the book entitled Notes of a Native Son has a natural freedom and grace. He also indicates that in this collection of essays, James Baldwin appears as a young writer in search of himself.[22] Notes of a Native Son reveals in detail Baldwin's life-style between 1942 and 1943. Those were two years which marked a great initiation for the young black -- not only because he found himself alone facing the white world, but also and especially because he was going to learn to know himself better. We know that during the summer of 1942, when he was in Trenton, New Jersey, he almost killed the young waitress in a restaurant that refused to serve blacks. Thanks to a white friend's aid, James Baldwin managed to escape the mob that wanted to lynch him. Later, the young author realized that he had acted without thinking; driven only by anger and the pain of having been treated like an inferior being. His brutal act had almost led to his own destruction. This warning always played an important role in the thought and work of James Baldwin. Another element that played a major role in the author's youth was the death of his stepfather in July 1943. This more or less desired disappearance marked young Baldwin's personality profoundly.

The events surrounding the burial of his father have, for Baldwin, always had a special meaning. First of all, the funeral took place on August 2, on the young author's nineteenth birthday, and, second, the burial took place the following day, August 3, after some uncommonly violent riots had torn Harlem apart during the preceding night. One knows that James Baldwin was far from being moved by the death of David Baldwin: his scorn drove him even to get drunk before coming to attend the funeral.

Of particular significance for the author was the fact that his dead father's hate and violence flared forth in Harlem on the very evening of his funeral. For young Baldwin, these observations seem to have had a very special meaning. Since the sad condition of the ghetto black had not improved during his adolescence, Baldwin was fully aware of the hard and barren future that awaited him. In other words, the Harlem riots of 1943 made him better understand the hatred and anger that his stepfather had always felt towards the white world. The concrete result of that death and those riots was to make Baldwin understand that, perhaps one day, he too would be like the one he had hated so much. "Notes of a Native Son" and Go Tell It on the Mountain closely resemble each other since they are both autobiographical. However, the essay possesses discursive and profound thought that the novel does not have. In "Notes of a Native Son," the author speaks directly to the reader, to better explain himself and make himself understood.

The condition and the future of the black in the United States have always preoccupied James Baldwin, who continued to write essays and articles on this subject. All have a common and precise goal: the improvement of the lot and the life of the American black. The author declared on several occasions that the sole fact of blackness was sufficient to frighten the white man and that this color was unfortunately at the root of numerous tragic situations for the American people.[23] In order to help his brothers of color, James Baldwin often requested the benefit of a certain freedom, indeed of great autonomy, for black ghettos. A Harlem watched and controlled by an entirely black police force would be less inclined to get restless than if it were, as it has always been, under the direct and crushing yoke of whites.[24] Such suggestions seem basically very reasonable; but from there to implementing them, there exists a whole secret system of laws that oppose the black man and make him suspicious. This distrust is at the root of the troubles and sorrows of the American man of color. That is why he prefers to stay where he is, rather than risk his life and that of his people. In effect, any attempt at change initiated by a black is always considered a social upheaval by the vast majority of whites. Whence the all-too-familiar vicious circle that often leads the black man to lose all hope and destroy himself. Thus it is not surprising that Baldwin said, "I have known many black men and women and black boys and girls, who really believed that it was better to be white than black, whose lives were ruined or ended by this belief; and I myself carried the seeds of this destruction within me for a long time."[25] Such a statement is sufficient in itself to make all of America realize its present and past mistakes, and try to improve itself at all costs in the immediate future.

James Baldwin's main goal is that the black will be accepted as a full citizen by American society. Unfortunately, this society has not yet been born, for the injustices against the man of color do not cease to multiply; as we have seen in Go Tell It on the Mountain, the only valid and stable help which today's black can get is that of religion.

In 1968, The Amen Corner was published.[26] At that date, this three-act play had already been playing on the stage for three years. Its publication has a special meaning for James Baldwin, since he had started to write it as early as 1952 for two precise reasons. First of all, after the great success achieved by Go Tell It on the Mountain, he had tried to prove he was capable of writing a play. He did not want to go on writing novels repeating the same subject developed in Go Tell It on the Mountain. In addition, he was not at all eager to be known essentially as a novelist. Next, rich from his own personal experiences, he had tried to revive in the theater the kind of intense and deep communion so well known by him when he was a pastor and a preacher in Harlem.

Published rather late, this play forms nonetheless a logical continuation of the author's religious thought. More than sixteen years separate Baldwin's decision to write such a play from his decision to publish it. This observation emphasizes that the American public, the majority of which is white, has always been slow and unwilling to accept the innovative ideas of any black author. In addition, the black author prefers to wait patiently for his turn through fear of provoking a negative reaction to his works.

The very title of this work, The Amen Corner, has a precise meaning in the American black church. In the "Amen Corner" come to sit those among the faithful who are the pastor's most diligent interlocutors. It is they who give him the most fervent responses. One can see the special meaning that James Baldwin wanted to give this play.

The central character is a woman, Margaret Alexander, the authoritarian and despotic pastor of a little church in Harlem. She had chosen that vocation ten years earlier, after having left a reprobate and good-for-nothing husband. From their union had been born a son, David, now eighteen years old and living with her. Another child, Margaret, had died in childbirth. It was that sad event that had driven Margaret to leave her husband. She had thought she saw a divine sign in that death.

The action takes place entirely in Harlem in Margaret Alexander's church and in her apartment, which are both part of the same building. Since each of the three acts takes place on a different day and at irregular intervals, the action lasts a week. Begun on a Sunday morning, it ends early on the following Sunday morning. The main goal of this play is to show that religion is often a simple refuge for blacks. This refuge enables them to live far from reality as well as to forget a painful past. This is the case with Margaret Alexander, who, anxious to live a wholesome and pure life, has decided to devote herself heart and soul to her people's well-being. Her husband's reappearance shows her that she still loves him and that her religious activities have basically never had any meaning. In other words, James Baldwin wants to show that human feelings, and more precisely love, occupy an important place in life. Margaret Alexander's religious experience closely resembles Baldwin's. But here, the author wishes to lay special stress on one very precise fact: that of the black woman forced to play the role of the man, the head of the family, in American society. This situation, unfortunately very common among blacks, is not designed to improve the black man's lot. The black man, treated like an inferior being by everyone, is often without a job and, in order to survive, is forced to ask his wife to work. This automatically puts the black man in an inferior position with respect to his wife. In such cases, despairing of everything, the black man sometimes deserts his family. There is no need to point out the unfortunate effects these situations have on children coming from such homes.

In Margaret Alexander's case, we have the example of a black woman who, disgusted by her husband's debauched life, has decided to take her own life, and her son's, into her hands:

> "She is in the church," Baldwin says," because her society has left her no other place to go. Her sense of reality is dictated by the society's assumption, which also becomes her own, of her inferiority."

And to explain her uncommon attitude, he writes:

> Her need for human affirmation, and also for vengeance, expresses itself in her merciless piety; and her love, which is real but which is also at the mercy of her genuine and absolutely justifiable terror, turns her into a tyrannical matriarch.

The conclusion that the author draws is the following: "In all of this, of course, she loses her old self - the fiery, fast-talking little black woman whom Luke loved." Such is Margaret's situation at the beginning of the play. But at the end, she is very different, as though transfigured. For in accepting her humble condition, she has also accepted her love for Luke:

". . . although she has lost everything," says James Baldwin, she "also gains the keys to the kingdom. The kingdom is love, and love is selfless, although only the self can lead one there. She gains herself."[27] The various clarifications and explanations that the author gives concerning his character are, without a doubt, very precise. But certain details, indeed certain descriptions, of Margaret Alexander's acts escape the nonetheless clairvoyant mind of the author. In short, one can see and interpret The Amen Corner in a different manner.

In comparison to Margaret Alexander, several secondary characters give the play a determined and marked orientation. The role they play is even, at certain times, more important than Margaret Alexander's. In other words, the ideas they represent have as much importance as those of the main character.

In the first act, Mrs. Ida Jackson, a member of the church, asks Margaret Alexander to bless her little boy, Daniel, because he is very sick. Here James Baldwin presents a Margaret in her omnipotence and at the peak of her tyranny. Thus she advises Ida Jackson to leave her husband who, to a certain extent, reminds her of Luke, whom she has not seen for ten years. Ida Jackson has already lost a young child. Margaret explains herself by saying that such a separation is perhaps God's will, But Ida Jackson refuses to leave her husband, replying that he needs her. In the third act, Ida Jackson reappears, all alone this time, to inform Margaret that her son is dead. At this stage, Margaret's attitude has been shaken by various events including, above all, Luke's unexpected arrival.

Ida Jackson's statement concerning the almost sacred aspect of married and family life at the very beginning of the third act already announces the total transfiguration that Margaret is to experience at the end of the play. Margaret recognizes herself in the person of Ida Jackson: a young woman upset by the loss of her two children, but who, however, insists on living by her husband's side.

Jake's return in the first act does not prevent Margaret from attending to her religious affairs and going to Philadelphia to look after a church on the road to ruin. Here, Margaret's religious obligations come again before her duties as a wife. Scarcely having arrived, Luke passed out from exhaustion. But Odessa, Margaret's oldest sister, takes care of him. It is especially David and some of the chosen ones in the church, including Sister Moore and Brother Boxer, who, by their attitude and their remarks, succeed in getting Margaret to face reality.

In the second act, back from Philadelphia where she spent a week, Margaret finds a changed and tense atmosphere. It is tense because the chosen ones of the church feel that her place is with her husband, and changed because the son admits playing the piano for a little band formed with some friends. Furthermore, he tells her he sides with his father who respects the freedom of others and who, in addition, is an excellent trombone player. Before rejoining his wife, Luke had been playing already two weeks in a Manhattan jazz club.

Towards the end of the second act, Margaret tries in vain to convert

Luke to her religious ideas. But he insists on remaining himself, since his love for her has not changed. He is of the opinion that David must choose his own future and that nobody has the right to impose anything whatsoever on him, even a religion. Ida Jackson's resolute attitude at the beginning of the third act only serves to open Margaret's eyes. Finally, the decision of the chosen ones in the temple to strip Margaret of her divine rights, in order to bestow them upon Sister Moore who has no family responsibilities, shows Margaret that life is made up of concrete realities. She knows that she still loves Luke and that, to a certain extent, she left him to punish herself for her little daughter's death. She admits it to him when she tells him: "In my heart, I always knew we couldn't go on like that -- we was too happy."[28] Thus, forced by her fellow-members to face the world, Margaret has to accept herself. This acceptance is made publicly before the whole church assembled on Sunday morning, at the end of the third act; one day after her return from Philadelphia:

> *"To love the Lord is to love all His children -- all of them, everyone! -- and suffer with them and rejoice with them and never count the cost!"*[29]

declares Margaret, the wife, before going to her sick husband's bedside. Although very different from each other at the beginning of the play, Luke and Margaret are united by a humble acceptance and a deep love at the end of the last act.

In July 1954, a one-act play bearing the same title had been published in Zero. On a whole, this one-act play closely resembles the second act of the play which appeared in 1968. There are several minor differences which, to a certain extent, might explain why the author took so much time before deciding that his three-act play could be performed on stage.

The action takes place on a Saturday morning after a sleepless night for Luke. The main characters are the same. But, contrary to the 1968 play, Luke did not come to rejoin Margaret on his own. Odessa went to get him in the Bowery, where he was groveling in drunkenness and squalor. His physical and moral degeneration was complete. From his conversations with Margaret, one learns that when they were younger, they had both enjoyed happiness in Alabama. But Luke's infidelity and his rowdy life had driven Margaret to leave him after their little daughter's death. This aspect is less well explained in the 1968 play, in which the religious theme tends to dominate the play.

In the 1954 version, the contrast between Luke and Margaret is much more striking than in the three-act play. Margaret, in fact, pastors two churches at the same time: the one in Harlem, where the action takes place, and the other in Philadelphia. Luke has absolutely nothing and lives in total poverty; only Odessa's pity causes him to find his wife and his son, David, whom he has not seen in six years. David plays the piano in his mother's church, but he also bought a guitar which he is learning to play with friends. The mother's attitude towards the guitar, as one might expect, is negative. Only his father, who encourages him to play, is accused of being at the root of such a musical corruption. The end of this one-act play finds Margaret trying, in vain, to convert a husband who believes only in a simple and natural life. Sister Moore's attitude seems, in this little play, to be much more convincing than in the 1968 version. Her frank and direct remonstrances give a more concrete aspect to a reality which, differently, would have been too religious. That is perhaps the reason James Baldwin took so long to finish his three-act play and to decide it had a sufficiently religious character. He wanted, above all, to give his play a religious meaning -- a meaning which only the theater, according to him, could communicate.

The Amen Corner, in three acts, provoked quite varied criticisms. Time declared that James Baldwin was far from being a good dramatist and that his characters lacked reality.[30] John McCarten in The New Yorker, on the other hand, wrote that the atmosphere created by James Baldwin was excellent and that his characters' dialogue gave the play a positive meaning.[31]

The theater, for James Baldwin, must play a very special role through the close and profound relationship established between spectators and actors. This, still according to James Baldwin, is a rare and exceptional thing in the American theater. The author speaks here of plays in which the religious atmosphere has a positive and concrete meaning for a majority black public. But even at that, in order to be in such a situation, the black actor must be able to prove himself and determine the type of role that he wishes to play. This free choice is, unfortunately, impossible since the white world imposes its conditions and its views on a situation that should remain black. This is what he explains in the article "James Baldwin on the Negro Actor."[32]

No white can explain the black condition to blacks: much less the profound meaning that religion can have for the black community. Albert Gérard said concerning this matter: . . . "American blacks would have probably perished out of simple weariness of life, as so many Indian tribes did, if they had not found in the Christian message (except in the practical attitude of the Churches) a confirmation of their human dignity, an assurance of transcendent justice and the hope of an ultimate salvation."[33] The American black has given the Christian religion a special meaning. This religious meaning, as in Margaret Alexander's case, often enables him to detach himself from reality in order to live in a world apart.

That the American theater in our time has several good black actors was not sufficient for James Baldwin. He thought that such actors should perform in plays in conformity with the reality of black American life. These plays, of course, would be addressed to black publics. But unfortunately for James Baldwin, this desire is not yet reality. In 1968, he was to declare: "...(black people) find nowhere any faint reflection of the lives they actually lead. And it is for this reason that every Negro celebrity is regarded with some distrust by black people, who have every reason in the world to feel themselves abandoned."[34] As always, the white world is guilty of not wanting to take the black playwright, or even still, the black actor, seriously, under the pretext that black people are basically a primitive people with nothing to offer. This negative and humiliating attitude seems to indicate that the future has practically nothing more to offer the white person. For the black, who must want and hope for everything from the future, the situation is the inverse.

One knows that religion plays an important role in the life of the vast majority of American blacks. In 1965, there appeared for the first time a short story by James Baldwin, "The Rockpile," in the collection of short stories entitled Going to Meet the Man.[35] This short story could have appeared as an introduction, or first chapter, in Go Tell It on the Mountain since the atmosphere, the place, and the characters are the same as in the novel. The only difference is in John Grimes's little brothers and little sisters. In this short story, he has one little brother, Paul, and one little sister, Delilah.

The story takes place in Harlem, on a Saturday, probably during the summer. Gabriel and Elizabeth Grimes have forbidden their children to play in the street and in a vague area where there is a huge rock. But, yielding to temptation, Roy takes advantage of a moment's inattention on his mother's part to go down into the street. John, who saw what was going on, prefers to say nothing since Roy promised to come right back. A few minutes later, Roy, who was having fun on the rock with some other boys his age, is wounded in the head. Bleeding profusely, he is taken back home just before his father comes back from the factory where he works as a laborer. Gabriel's rage and anger are not long in erupting, for, instead of a John covered with blood and rattled by sobs, it is rather his adored and legitimate son that he has before his eyes. John is accused of not having looked after his brother. He is going to be beaten, when Elizabeth intervenes. She, who knows that Gabriel hates this bastard son, is not afraid to speak to him openly. She tells him that Roy is not the nice little boy that he would like so much for him to be. Since he realizes that John, and not Roy, is living up to his desires and his aspirations, Gabriel has nothing to say.

However short this short story may be, John Grimes's moral solitude and his silent suffering are well highlighted. Roy does not hesitate to lie to John, whom he despises, because he knows he is adored and pampered by his father. For Elizabeth, John is the living symbol of the past that she would like to forget. One can therefore understand John Grimes's precarious position within a family which, at bottom, does not want him. That is the reason, in Go Tell It on the Mountain, John attempts to find love and affection outside the family circle.

If John's homosexuality is not revealed in the novel, it does figure in a short story published for the first time in 1951 in New Story and published a second time in Going to Meet the Man.[36] In "The Outing," in fact, John and another boy his age, David Jackson, promise each other eternal love and support during a boating excursion, on July 4, with all the members of a church, the Mount of Olives Pentecostal Assembly. This short story, has the same atmosphere as "The Rockpile," and the same characters as Go Tell It on the Mountain. The only difference is in a few people who do not appear in the novel. In "The Outing," the spiritual head of the church, Father James, reigns like an absolute ruler and Gabriel Grimes, despite his diligent efforts as a devoted deacon, does not succeed in attracting the least attention. Here we have, in the person of John's stepfather, an embittered man, jealous and full of hate. This hatred erupts on the boat's deck when Gabriel believes he sees arrogance in John's attitude.

The principal theme of this short story is especially the awakening of John's homosexual tendencies. Roy is still the same pampered child who, knowing he is adored by his father, believes he is permitted everything. John, more or less despised by all, seeks tenderness and affection in the arms of a little friend. The religious service on the boat, where all the chosen ones of the Lord are singing and shouting, leaves John cold and impassive. For him, these public demonstrations are only the vague expression of savage and beastly feelings. But it is because of John's detached attitude that the author can describe in detail a religious atmosphere completely stamped with human feelings.

Since he has clubbed together with his friends in order to give Sylvia, a girl their age, a little birthday gift, John realizes with amazement that David Jackson is in love with her. Depressed and distressed, he does not know what to do; it is on that note that "The Outing" ends. The trip on the Hudson River and the day spent in nature seem to enable John to know himself better and, especially, to accept himself. His homosexuality surfaces here and he is duty bound to understand better some feelings that are both new and disturbing. "The Outing" would serve as a very good introduction to Go Tell It on the Mountain since, despairing of everything, it is in religion that John Grimes finally finds consolation.

Since the beginning of his literary career, James Baldwin has always wished to play a special role for the American black. This role as spokesman, says Bernard Mergen in "James Baldwin and the American Conundrum," has been played without fear and with frank honesty.[37] In an essay published for the first time under the title "Life Straight in De Eye," in 1955 and published in Notes of a Native Son under the title "Carmen Jones: The Dark is Light Enough," James Baldwin openly attacks the film Carmen Jones, which is supposed to represent the life of blacks.[38] According to Baldwin, the film is far from realistic. That ghetto life as it is represented by Hollywood is, from the language to the characters' attitudes, totally foreign to that which Baldwin experienced during his youth in Harlem. But the author recognizes that between The Birth of a Nation in 1914 and Carmen Jones in 1955, a great deal of effort had been made by the American cinema in its attitude towards the black man. However, the leading role played by Harry Belafonte is completely devoid of the qualities and theatrical talents of the famous black actor. This, explains Baldwin, comes from the fact that the white American public has always greatly feared the sexual attributes of the black man. To the black and frightening beast of 1914, this film responds by portraying a timid and lifeless black.

In 1968, James Baldwin was to write an article, "Sidney Poitier by James Baldwin," in which he praised the talents of the black actor, in Guess Who's Coming to Dinner.[39] That film, according to Baldwin, is of great importance for, here finally, the black man is taken seriously. In other words, this film treats the black man as an individual, not as the vague and feeble reflection of a being that passes for virile.

In Carmen Jones, the feelings and the passions of blacks in the ghetto have no real place--something which is likely to enrage any child coming from such an environment.

In "Sonny's Blues," a short story which appeared in Going to Meet the Man, but was published for the first time in 1957, James Baldwin says that the sufferings, the hate, and the poverty of the ghetto black are often at the root of his most beautiful inspirations.[40] In that short story, we have the example of a young black from Harlem who, after having grown up in the ghetto and after having been arrested for drug traffic, finally finds his expression and his vocation in jazz. This short story is all the more interesting since we have a striking contrast between a well-established older brother, who is a mathematics teacher in a high school, and his younger brother, Sonny. The latter first serves a stint in the Marines, only to go next to lead a bohemian life in Greenwich Village. It is after having spent some time in prison that he finally discovers himself and accepts himself. After having reconciled himself with his older brother, with whom he had been on bad terms for several years, he admits: ". . . it struck me all of a sudden how much suffering she must have had to go through - to sing like that. It's repulsive to think you have to suffer that much."[41] This statement is made after the two brothers have seen and listened to a group of four blacks who were singing religious songs in a street in Harlem.

A few hours later, in a Manhattan nightclub, Sonny will show his older brother that, he too, is capable of discovering himself by playing the piano for a little jazz band. In other words, Sonny has found peace and tranquillity in the world in which he must live. On this subject Marcus Klein said:

> ". . . he has discovered that the same environment contains a music, jazz, and through jazz he is to be provided with the means of reconciliation. The function of Sonny's blues is that it allows him fully to know his racial identity."[42]

The character of Sonny is interesting because we know that one of his uncles loved life very much and expressed that joy by playing the guitar. But this intense desire to live was brutally destroyed, one Saturday evening, when a group of drunken whites hurled their car into the black man and his musical instrument. Fearing that such a thing might happen to Sonny, the older brother does his best to counsel him and protect him.

However, it is while watching Sonny and listening to him play the piano that the older brother finally realizes the goal achieved by his young brother:

> Freedom lurked around us and I understood, at last, that he could help us to be free if we would listen, that he would never be free until we did. Yet, there was no battle in his face now. I heard what he had gone through, and would continue to go through until he came to rest in earth. He had made it his: that long line, of which we knew only Mama and Daddy.[43]

In this short story, despair mingles with indignation in order finally to reach a compromise permitting Sonny to live in an environment which, otherwise, would have destroyed him. In "Sonny's Blues," James Baldwin strongly emphasizes that music is the very soul of the American black and that, through it, his expression is spontaneous, personal, and above all profound.

Only a ghetto atmosphere can forge a personality and an experience unique in their own way.

CHANGES COMMON TO THE TWO WORLDS

In the first two parts of this chapter, we discovered, through a few of James Baldwin's works, the physiognomy of the white world and that of the black world in America. For Baldwin, these two worlds have necessarily some common points for the problem is essentially American; what affects American whites affects American blacks and vice versa.

In "Autobiographical Notes," an essay that appeared in 1955 in Notes of a Native Son, James Baldwin rightfully said that every American must accept the past in order to understand it better and in order to draw from it constructive lessons which will help him in the present and future.[44] He also says that every black American writer must accept himself as he is in order to find peace and order in his thoughts. It is without surprise that he informs us that three essential elements influenced his literary career: the Bible, the religious atmosphere in which he was reared, and also and especially, ghetto life as he knew it in Harlem. Although knowing he is a bastard child of the West, he recognizes that he belongs to Western culture and not to that of the African jungle.

We then have the image of a man who, although black, is above all American. "I love America more than any other country in the world, and, exactly for this reason, I insist on the right to criticize her perpetually."[45] For this reason, also, he wants to be a good and honest writer. This attitude is the only one, in his opinion, that will enable him to understand better and explain better the race problem to all Americans. James Baldwin has been strongly criticized in this regard. In Soul on Ice, Eldridge Cleaver accused him of hating himself, of hating the black race, and of adoring everything that was white.[46] Harvey Breit, on the other hand, in "James Baldwin and Two Footnotes," praised the author for his frankness and the intense desire that he has to do battle with American society. Breit also recognizes that Baldwin has always been aware of his social and racial responsibilities, and that for him the future of America comes before any other consideration.[47] A very widespread liberal attitude which numerous whites of the North have adopted towards the black man may be discerned here. But to say that Eldridge Cleaver is right would be to go too far.

To a certain extent, H. Orlando Patterson tries to view James Baldwin as objectively as possible. For him, three important elements find room in the black author's work. These three factors are the autobiography, the article, and the analysis of the first two.[48] This would especially apply to Baldwin's essays, a genre in which the black author excels. But these same elements are found again in James Baldwin's better novels. In other words, James Baldwin, through his subtlety of style, his delicate thoughts, and his skillful way of expressing himself, knows how to make one feel and understand a situation which, despite its racial aspect, is above all human and American.

It was after having spent a few months in France that James Baldwin, because of a stolen sheet, realized the originality of his identity. In the article "Equal in Paris," which appeared for the first time in March 1955 and which was published later in Notes of a Native Son, James Baldwin describes in detail the events that surrounded his unfortunate adventure.[49] From December 19 to 27, 1949, in fact, he experienced all the ugliness of the French prison, not because he was guilty of having stolen that sheet, which in fact had been lent to him by an unknown American white, but because his innocence and his naïveté were especially to blame. Thus, scarcely having arrived in France and barely knowing how to speak French, James Baldwin was suddenly thrown in jail despite all his efforts to convince the French authorities of his innocence. What astonished him most was the indifference of the French police who treated him like a foreigner, American in this case, without taking into account the color of his skin. He realized, during this short stay in prison, that the Arab, especially the Algerian, is in France what the black is in the United States.

It was due to the aid of an American lawyer, whom he knew in Paris, that he managed to get out of prison. When he appeared for his trial, the French judges, after having listened to his story and his explanations, could not help but laugh. James Baldwin thought, for a moment, that they were making fun of him because he was black. But he quickly realized that only the human aspect of his adventure caused the people to laugh. In an interview published in July 1965, James Baldwin was to declare that it was because of his stay in Paris that he ceased to hate the white world.[50] It is basically from that time on that he began to become aware of his true identity.

In the article "A Question of Identity," which appeared for the first time in 1954 and was published later in Notes of a Native Son, James Baldwin develops in greater detail this idea of self-discovery that so many Americans, sooner or later, end up making when they live in Europe, and more specifically in France.[51] According to him, numerous Americans have always sought refuge in France because they imagine finding there the legendary freedom and life-style that foreigners wrongly attribute to that country. Once this dream has disappeared, the individual must discover himself and accept himself. He sometimes then either returns to the United States, or tries to be more French than the French. Unfortunately, says Baldwin, this second option is impossible. For the problem of identity, for every American normal in mind and body, embraces both the United States and Europe, Europe being the place of origin of the vast majority of Americans' ancestors. For Baldwin, Europe and the United States are two inseparable and complementary elements that are an integral part of the personality of the average American. According to Baldwin, the American who wants to be more French than the French exposes himself to a dangerous and destructive hatred.[52]

As for the author, it is evident that his stay in Paris made him discover his true identity and also, and especially, his great mission as a writer and American spokesman. Allan Morrison declared: "His function here is to interpret whites to themselves and at the same time voice the Negro's protest against his role in Jim Crow society." In the first part of his deeply human book Nothing Personal, James Baldwin talks about the American in search of his identity.[53] This identity is common to all those who live in the United States and who are of all origins. Baldwin says what he thinks concerning this matter, without being convincing. He is very objective, whence the title of the book, when he affirms, for example, that Americans are Europeans who tried to recreate themselves in a new world. He does not forget to mention that the American does not like to remember his past and is especially eager to earn a lot of money. He makes an exception on this last point when he speaks of poor Southern whites who, oppressed by the oligarchic class in the South, have been driven to hate blacks. Poor whites and poor blacks, he says, have always been twin brothers in pain and oppression. From that first part of Nothing Personal, one may conclude that America must at all costs find a stable and comfortable identity. To this end, it is proper for the individual to accept reality once and for all. Here James Baldwin emphasizes the great loneliness of the individual, black as well as white, in the United States.

In the essay, "The Negro in Paris," which appeared for the first time in 1950 and was published later in Notes of a Native Son under the title of "Encounter on the Seine: Black Meets Brown," James Baldwin speaks of the numerous problems of identity that American blacks in Paris encounter.[54] Here the author is talking about his own experience and reveals his impressions. According to him, the color of the individual's skin does not count in France, and the American, whatever he may be, is completely bewildered upon his arrival on French soil. It is especially the feeling of being above all a human being which has always fascinated Baldwin when he lived in France. That remark applies undoubtedly to the American citizen, but there is much to be said about the great freedom the man of color can find in France. Let us remember that James Baldwin has already drawn our attention to the sad lot of the Arabs from North Africa who live in France. Be that as it may, for the French in general, the American black is generally thought of as a great martyr and he is treated as such in France. In other words, the American black is above all, for the French, a courageous and proud hero. This attitude is a form of anti-Americanism which Baldwin does not seem to realize, for the European is both suspicious and critical of American capitalism.

The attitude of these same French people changes completely when they are in the presence of a black African. James Baldwin, far from being in full agreement with the French who despise the black African, expresses envy and curiosity with regard to the latter. He is envious because the black African has his country, his language, his traditions and, also, great pride. He is curious because over three hundred years separate the African black from the one in America and they have nothing in common except the color of their skin.

For James Baldwin, Americans, whether black or white, are bound by the same customs and the same traditions. The only great difference is in the pigmentation of their skin. This must in no way cause them to want to destroy one another. According to Baldwin, we have here only citizens and their future. Only patience and time will help them to understand one another better, says the author. For the American black, this patience has lasted for a long time and James Baldwin's prophetic voice has little meaning since slavery was instituted in America over three hundred years ago. It is therefore not surprising that the American black wants to use force in order to make whites understand that he has lost his patience, and that he intends to enjoy his rights immediately.

In the second part of <u>Nothing Personal</u>, which appeared fourteen years after the essay just discussed, James Baldwin seems to respond directly to the doubt expressed above. In this part, he says that the American black knows his white fellow-countryman and that he knows how to thwart his hypocritical and deceptive game. The black man always has the upper hand, although the white man believes the opposite. And the important thing is that James Baldwin affirms that Americans avoid facing reality and that they prefer not to ask direct questions. He makes so bold as to say that whites do not want to deal with blacks. This, unfortunately, is true all the more because the American trusts no one, not even himself, since he does not know himself. The result of this is a highly indistinct personality, reflecting both calculated and selfish attitudes. In "Sidney Poitier by James Baldwin," James Baldwin can say perspicaciously that American whites seem to live in a dream whereas their black brothers constantly struggle against the hideous face of reality.[55] It is this dream, says Baldwin in <u>Nothing Personal</u>, that has enabled America to believe Kennedy's murder was due to an external element, and not an internal one as he believes.

Since violence is admitted by all of America, it is not surprising to observe no social change after that assassination. In his conclusion, James Baldwin seems to generalize, and even exaggerate, when he declares that America is a nation without love and without tenderness. This pessimistic attitude has perhaps a precise goal in the author's mind. That goal is to convince America that blacks and whites must, at all costs, understand one another better in order for the country to have a certain and lasting future. This atmosphere of apathy is very well described by Baldwin in an article that appeared in 1962 in which he says:

> "White Americans know very little about pleasure because they are so afraid of pain. But people dulled by pain can sing and dance till morning and find no pleasure in it."[56]

It is accurate that a great effort to understand is necessary, and even obligatory on the part of all Americans if they want their country to survive the racial troubles of the past, of the present, and even of the future.

We saw, at the beginning of this chapter, that in the essay

"Everybody's Protest Novel," which appeared in 1947, James Baldwin had violently attacked Richard Wright. This scathing criticism was directed at the very limited views of Richard Wright's protest work. According to Baldwin, Wright had not succeeded in revealing entirely the profound soul of Bigger Thomas. Baldwin even insinuated that Wright had in no way been able to improve the sad lot of the black man in his time, and that he had only encouraged whites in their distant and disdainful attitude towards blacks.

Two years later had appeared the essay "Many Thousand Gone," in which Baldwin's attack against Wright had been much more virulent. While placing his ideas in a very precise context, James Baldwin begins by saying that in America a great silence has always reigned over the racial question. Because of this attitude, he continues, the black man has just simply been cast aside, pushed back out of the way, by the American nation. This position of the black man within his own country, says Baldwin, has resulted in making him vulnerable to the prejudices of his white fellow-citizens. For the latter, the black man is a symbol of evil and everything that has to do with violence. What whites do not want to understand and respect, says the author, is the black man's distinct way of living and thinking. This blindness desired and maintained by whites results in placing blacks in a category of inferiors. Whence segregation, which claims that the black man is biologically inferior to the white man.

Over forty years after the appearance of "Many Thousands Gone," the general tendency in America demands that the white man question the various segregationist attitudes in his country. In any case, it is evident that yesterday's Uncle Tom has suddenly been transfigured to become the young Tom who violently rocked America during the sixties. In his essay, James Baldwin uses the first person plural when he speaks of the racial problem in the United States. That seems to indicate above all that, for the author, the black man must be considered a full American and in no way different from his fellow-citizens. That is at least the impression that one gets after reading that essay. That does not mean nonetheless that only the present and the future matter. James Baldwin knows very well that the effects of the past, especially in the history of the American black, will make themselves felt for a long time still.

It is at this point, in his essay, that James Baldwin talks about Richard Wright's famous novel, Native Son. Without beating about the bush, he says simply that this novel marks an era of the past and that it belongs to that past. It is evident that such a novel could not be written today if one considers the social and proletarian atmosphere it reflects and in which it takes place. The result of Bigger Thomas's attitude and his acts, says Baldwin, is to show the white American public a savage and monstrous beast in the person of the black man, a matter which is not likely to improve race relations in the United States. If the murder he commits seems, for Bigger, an affirmation of courage, indeed even of manliness, the fact remains that, for whites, this act is bestial and frightful. James Baldwin is perhaps right. The hatred that Bigger Thomas feels towards whites is also a hatred that destroys him. One knows that he has always been bitter and that he has never expected anything from life.

In Native Son, we have the example of a black man, of a new black man, who decides to react violently to the elements of society that are oppressing him. This type of reaction is repeated at more or less regular intervals in the ghettos of the North. The direct result of such a reaction, although it is partly caused by self-hatred and the hatred of others, is destruction and death. Death is the source of dignity and pride for the individual who is thus destroying himself. But what painful benefit can his fellow-creatures derive from that, if they are constrained to live in a world made more hostile and more cruel by the action of one of their people?

If James Baldwin violently attacked Richard Wright in that essay, it is because he felt that Bigger Thomas belonged to the past and that the future alone could give America a new hope. James Baldwin's goal is to be optimistic and to believe in the goodwill of his human brothers, whoever they may be. Up to the present, scarcely nothing further has come of that hope and it is highly likely this new future, of which Baldwin always speaks, has not yet seen the light of day.

One finds a pronounced sign of optimism in the essay "Stranger in the Village," which appeared for the first time in 1953 and was published later in Notes of a Native Son.[57] In it Baldwin talks about his adventures and his personal discoveries in a little Swiss village where he spent a part of the winter of 1951-1952. The village in question is Loeche-les-Bains in the Swiss Alps, where he lived alone in the chalet of the parents of his Swiss friend, Lucien Happersberger. James Baldwin's first discovery was to note that the inhabitants of that little village had never seen a black man in flesh and blood and that from the moment he arrived, they considered him a strange and unusual being. The children called him "Nigger," which, at first at least, shook the author's sensitive soul. But after a certain time, he quickly realized those children wished him no harm and that this term expressed curiosity as well as friendship. For them he represented an astonishing mystery; that is why he let them touch his black skin and his curly hair.

The attitude of the village people, says Baldwin, had been all the more curious because they had taken up a collection in order to send some money to Africa, to some white missionaries, in order to save the lives of about ten blacks by converting them to Christianity. Realizing that he could not make them understand that he had nothing in common with blacks from Africa, Baldwin was amused by their naïveté and the kind manner in which he was accepted and treated.

The attitude of the inhabitants of Loeche-les-Bains would probably have been very different if Baldwin had settled in their little village with several blacks. Curiosity and friendship would have made room for hatred and hostility. From a human point of view, Baldwin is good at describing the deep and intimate feelings the inhabitants of this little village aroused in him. This discovery, which made him serene again, put him in a position to come back to the United States and face the bitter reality there. For, as far as he is concerned, and no matter what the American white says or does, the black American must be a full citizen. The argument advanced by the author seems to be valid, since he says that white civilization is on the decline, and that, more than ever, American blacks and whites must unite in order to prepare a better future together. He adds that, to a certain extent, that future could save the world from a disastrous apocalypse.

One must recognize the frankness with which Baldwin speaks, especially when he says he is the bastard son of the West and that the Cathedral of Chartres does not have the same meaning for him as for the inhabitants of Loeche-les-Bains. For him, and because of his American experience, it is especially the devil and his evil cruelties that strike his imagination when he looks at the Cathedral of Chartres. One can understand that attitude if one remembers that the American black must constantly fight for his civil rights in a country that would prefer to get rid of him, by whatever means, even by sending him back to Africa.

James Baldwin's style in this essay is both natural and elegant. To say that <u>Nothing Personal</u> is better would be exaggerated. It would seem that the works written after 1955 reflect a deep desire, on the author's part, to respond directly and rapidly to the social and political problems that are presented to him. Whence, consequently, the lack of time to write and describe the truth well in all its details.

That is what one finds in the third part of <u>Nothing Personal</u>, in which Baldwin especially highlights the battle represented by the life of the American black. He speaks of Bessie Smith, that black singer of the twenties and thirties who knew so well how to depict in her blues the wounded and bruised soul of the black person. During his stay in the Swiss village mentioned earlier, the author listened attentively to Bessie Smith's records. Thanks to her, to her rhythmical cadences and profound lyrics, Baldwin succeeded in discovering and in seeing what type of man he was. He said on several occasions that the image he had of himself was not his, but that which whites have of every black. In other words, it was partly due to Bessie Smith that Baldwin managed to accept himself. That discovery was all the easier since the author was in Europe, far from his native soil. The lesson he drew from this experience was that one had to display willpower and determination in order to attain a precise goal.

James Baldwin said that American blacks and whites were unwilling to make the effort to know one another and that, if such a situation were to continue, hatred and violence would be reborn. According to him, this negative attitude must change at all costs, for only human love and a mutual understanding of blacks and whites can save America from an imminent catastrophe. James Baldwin's religious experience could play an important role if the present American context were not what it is. Today, unfortunately, America just makes exhortations to the black author's sacred union.

Nonetheless, Baldwin is practically the only black to have suggested a peaceful solution to the racial problem that afflicts the United States. Very often blind violence, or suicide, ends an unbearable life. Now, the author is firmly opposed to suicide, for human life is too precious. It is after the disappearance of an individual that one realizes the enormous place he occupied within society.

Speaking of America's future, Baldwin affirms that American children know neither respect nor love. Their parents, he points out, are at the root of all the ills that afflict these young people. The writer has a tendency to generalize, for, very fortunately, the vast majority of American youth does have a sense of and a respect for life.

The third part of Nothing Personal shows a preoccupied Baldwin believing himself to be responsible for all the evils that torment America. His role as spokesman and his attitude of a conciliator in search of an impossible appeasement lead one to think that America is on the brink of a bloody and merciless civil war. There are many exaggerations, but the author's words of advice are good and correct. America can no longer live as in the past. It must therefore admit the reality and make its black and white citizens understand the necessity of seeking and acquiring, in stages, the process which must bring about social peace through equality of rights and obligations.

NOTES

1. Howard Levant, "Aspiraling We Should Go," Midcontinent American Studies Journal 4 (Fall 1963): 5-6.

2. Charles English, "Another Viewpoint," Jubilee II (September 1963): 44.

3. James Baldwin, "Everybody's Protest Novel," Partisan Review 16 (June 1949): 578-585. Also in Notes of a Native Son (New York: Bantam Books, 1964), pp. 9-17.

4. James Baldwin, "To Whom It May Concern: Report From Occupied Territory," Nation, July 11, 1966, pp. 39-43.

5. Harriet Beecher Stowe, Uncle Tom's Cabin (New York: The Modern Library, 1938). Richard Wright, Native Son (New York: Harper and Brothers, 1940).

6. James Baldwin, "Many Thousands Gone," Partisan Review 17 (November-December 1951): 665-680. Also in Notes of a Native Son, pp. 18-36.

7. James Baldwin, Go Tell It on the Mountain (New York: New American Library, Signet Books, 1963).

8. James Baldwin, Tell Me How Long the Train's Been Gone (New York: The Dial Press, 1968).

9. Granville Hicks, "From Harlem With Hatred," Saturday Review, June 1, 1968, p. 23.

10. James Baldwin, "Sidney Poitier by James Baldwin", Look, July 23, 1968, p. 58.

11. James Baldwin, "To Whom It May Concern: Report From Occupied Territory," p. 41.

12. James Baldwin, "How Can We Get the Black People to Cool It?", Esquire, July 1968, p. 116.

13. James Baldwin, "Journey to Atlanta," New Leader 31 (9 October 1948): 809. Also in Notes of a Native Son, pp. 61-70.

14. James Baldwin, "How Can We Get the Black People to Cool It?", p. 52.

15. Norman Podhoretz, "My Negro Problem and Ours," in B. Daniel, ed., Black,

White and Gray (New York: Sheed and Ward, 1964), p. 221.

16. James Baldwin, "The Harlem Ghetto," in his Notes of a Native Son, pp. 47-60.

17. James Baldwin, "How Can We Get the Black People to Cool It?", p. 53.

18. Michel Fabre and Paul Oren, Harlem, ville noire (Paris: Armand Colin, 1971), pp. 198-199.

19. James Baldwin, "The Amen Corner," Zero 6 (July 1954) 4-8, 11-13. (Act 1 of a quite obviously longer work.)

20. James Baldwin, Go Tell It on the Mountain, p. 178.

21. James Baldwin, "Notes of a Native Son," in his Notes of a Native Son, pp. 71-95.

22. Harvey Breit, "James Baldwin and Two Footnotes," in N. Balakian and C. Simmons, eds., The Creative Present (New York: Doubleday and Co., 1963), p. 9.

23. James Baldwin, "Disturbers of the Peace," in Black, White and Gray, p. 200.

24. James Baldwin, "Negroes are Anti-Semitic Because They're Anti-White," The New York Times Magazine, April 9, 1967, p. 27.

25. James Baldwin, "Unnameable Objects, Unspeakable Crimes," in The White Problem in America, edited by Ebony (Chicago: Johnson Publishing Co., 1966), p. 176.

26. James Baldwin, The Amen Corner (New York: The Dial Press, 1968).

27. Baldwin, The Amen Corner, p. xvi.

28. The Amen Corner p. 59.

29. The Amen Corner p. 88.

30. "Tardy Rainbow," Time April 23, 1965, p. 59.

31. John McCarten, "Tabernacle Blues," The New Yorker, April 24, 1965, p. 85.

32. James Baldwin, "James Baldwin on the Negro Actor," Anthology of the American Negro in the Theater, A Critical Approach, edited by Lindsay Patterson, (New York: Publishers Co., 1967), pp. 127-130.

33. Albert Gérard, "James Baldwin et la religiosité noire," Revue Nouvelle 33 (1961): 177.

34. James Baldwin, "Sidney Poitier by James Baldwin," p. 56.

35. James Baldwin, "The Rockpile," in his Going to Meet the Man, (New York: The Dial Press, 1965), pp. 15-25.

36. James Baldwin, "The Outing," New Story 1 (April 1951): 52-81; and in his Going to Meet the Man, pp. 29-57.

37. Bernard Mergen, "James Baldwin and the American Conundrum," Moderna Sprak 57 (1963): 397-405.

38. James Baldwin, "Life Straight in De Eye," Commentary 19 (January 1955): 74-77. Also published as "Carmen Jones: The Dark Is Light Enough," in his Notes of a Native Son, pp. 37-44.

39. James Baldwin, "Sidney Poitier by James Baldwin," pp. 50-54, 56, 58.

40. James Baldwin, "Sonny's Blues," in his Going to Meet the Man, pp. 103-141; and in Partisan Review 24 (Summer 1957): 327-358.

41. Baldwin, "Sonny's Blues," p. 132.

42. Marcus Klein, "James Baldwin," in his After Alienation (Cleveland: World Publishing Co., 1964), p. 172.

43. Baldwin, "Sonny's Blues," p. 140.

44. James Baldwin, "Autobiographical Notes," in his Notes of a Native Son, pp. 1-6.

45. Baldwin, "Autobiographical Notes," p. 6.

46. Eldridge Cleaver, "Notes on a Native Son," in his Soul on Ice (New York: McGraw-Hill, 1968), p. 103.

47. Harvey Breit, "James Baldwin and Two Footnotes," in <u>The Creative Present</u>, p. 8 and p. 7.

48. H. Orlando Patterson, "The Essays of James Baldwin," <u>New Left Review</u> 26 (Summer 1964): 35.

49. James Baldwin, "Equal in Paris," <u>Commentary</u> 19 (March 1955): 251-259; and in his <u>Notes of a Native Son</u>, pp. 117-134.

50. James Baldwin with James Mossman and Colin McInnes, "Race, Hate, Sex, and Color: A Conversation," <u>Encounter</u> 25 (July 1965): 55.

51. James Baldwin, "A Question of Identity," <u>Partisan Review</u> 21 (July-August 1954): 402-410; also in his <u>Notes of a Native Son</u>, pp. 105-116.

52. Allan Morrison, "The Angriest Young Man," <u>Ebony</u>, October 1961, p. 24.

53. James Baldwin, <u>Nothing Personal</u> (Harmondsworth, England: Penguin Books, 1964).

54. James Baldwin, "The Negro in Paris," <u>Reporter</u>, June 6, 1950, pp. 34-36. Also published as "Encounter on the Seine: Black Meets Brown," in his <u>Notes of a Native Son</u>, pp. 99-104.

55. James Baldwin, "Sidney Poitier by James Baldwin," p. 56.

56. James Baldwin, "Color," <u>Esquire</u> 58 (December 1962): 252.

57. James Baldwin, "Stranger in the Village," <u>Harper's</u> 207 (October 1953): 42-48. Also published in his <u>Notes of a Native Son</u>, pp. 135-149.

8

NEW BEHAVIOR

THE NEW BLACK

In 1961, James Baldwin published his second book of essays, <u>Nobody Knows My Name</u>.[1] In it he does not talk about the race problem as such but, rather, of its American and human aspect. We shall see that he attacks directly, and on several occasions, Richard Wright for his so-called protest works.

Between the appearance of <u>Notes of a Native Son</u> and that of <u>Nobody Knows My Name</u>, more than six years had passed in the course of which James Baldwin had learned to know himself better, thanks to a prolonged stay in France. In this collection of essays, he talks especially about himself, his ideas, and his own experience. In other words, the racial problem, although very important, takes second place in relation to the importance the author ascribes to the exploration of the human soul. In his brief "Introduction," James Baldwin says these essays mark the end of his early youth since he is now well established as a writer.[2] But what preoccupies him enormously is the desire to continue to discover and know himself. He points out that the numerous trips taken across Europe from 1955 to 1961 made him see and understand the necessity of knowing himself before being able to know his fellow-man. In short, it was after mature reflection that Baldwin deliberately decided to return to the United States, of which he had always been an integral part. His exile in France helped him to make such a decision; it was in that country, in effect, that he became aware of his typically American identity.

That return to American reality, says the author, was a reason for living. Without that, he would not have been in a position to ensure his normal functioning as a writer. His conscience and his aspirations would have prevented him from it. It is good that Baldwin did have the courage necessary to return to the United States and face the fear and anguish that awaited him there. But we shall see, in the next chapter, that the author's literary hopes never approached the level he hoped to attain.

According to Baldwin, that return to the native land was to enable him to find his true identity. During that long stay in Europe, he says, he had noticed that the color of his skin prevented him from knowing himself, and that he needed a greater communication with others in order to continue to write well and to know the world better.

It is certain that such an attitude is likely to lead towards the solution of the delicate American racial problem, provided that whites and blacks show an unequivocal will to move towards that solution. This is James Baldwin's hope; it is also his wish. Unfortunately, the violence and the hatred in the two communities in the sixties were to reduce his hope to nothing.

The first essay appropriate to discuss here is entitled "Notes for a Hypothetical Novel -- An Address."[3] That is the speech that James Baldwin delivered on October 22, 1960, at San Francisco State College during a conference on the role of the writer in America. At that time, Baldwin had already come back to live in the United States, and it is interesting to note what he says. Without explaining why, and right at the beginning of the address, he declares that something very definite and profound unites all Americans, whether white or black. Next, talking about a long hypothetical novel based on his childhood, he discusses in detail certain historical events of the thirties. He does not forget to mention the religious, social, and political atmosphere of Harlem as he had known it at the time. Now, today life in this ghetto is very different from what it was then. Here again, Baldwin stresses the color of Americans' skin. According to him, the American accepts it without going any farther. That is a point dear to Baldwin, especially since his return to America. Basing himself always on his childhood memories, he says that after having left the black world for the white world, he quickly realized one curious thing: like blacks, whites do not know themselves. This theme seems familiar, but, for Baldwin, it is the element that is at the very base of what he calls the American confusion. He advises every writer anxious to write this long hypothetical novel to know himself well and to accept himself as he is. That is perhaps what he tried to accomplish unsuccessfully, moreover, in Tell Me How Long the Train's Been Gone.[4]

From this address a very important element emerges: America must remake itself, and its citizens are alone capable of helping it to achieve this goal. This realistic attitude of James Baldwin relies on the appeal to the conscience of those who call themselves Americans. Unfortunately, whites and blacks have not tried to know one another, much less examine and confront their own thoughts and attitudes. The color of the individual's skin, whether it be white or black, is still today a major obstacle. This obstacle prevents the citizens of the same country from knowing one another, and therefore from understanding one another. Dialogue does not exist. The solution to this problem will require time and patience. In the meantime, blacks suffer from the apathy and contempt of whites.

Whether he likes it or not, James Baldwin is black. The color of his skin has influenced the ideas expressed in his works. That he places America's future above the present condition of black ghettos is a point that has irritated numerous critics; after all, Baldwin is a child of the ghetto. He could perhaps have done more to improve the lot of his people. In "Princes and Powers," the author seems to say clearly what he has always thought concerning the race question.[5] That is at least the feeling he tries to communicate to the reader.

This essay is a report on the Congress of Black Writers and Artists held in Paris from September 19 to 22, 1956. According to James Baldwin, that poorly organized congress lacked unity in the ideas developed by the various participants. In the very first place, the English-speaking lecturers had had far less time than their French-speaking counterparts. In addition, and especially, Richard Wright, who was present, was solicited by the Africans on one side and the American blacks on the other. The American delegation, he continues, was very nervous because the Department of State in Washington had prevented W. E. B. DuBois from coming by refusing to issue him a passport. The principal idea of the congress was to recreate the atmosphere that had prevailed the year before at Bandung. At the congress in Paris, however, only the blacks had been invited; whereas at Bandung all peoples of color, except whites, had been welcomed.

In a very journalistic style, Baldwin speaks in detail of the various lecturers; including Léopold Senghor and Aimé Césaire. When it comes to Richard Wright, it is evident that he feels great mistrust. After Wright had, for example, declared that Europe, to a large extent, contributed to Africa's awakening, James Baldwin, straightaway, denies that assertion or, at least, criticizes it strongly without attempting to explain his attitude. On the whole, this essay is hostile to the ideas expressed during the conference. Those ideas, of course, emanated from human beings eager to make themselves heard. Most of them had not yet had any experience.

However objective this essay may be, Baldwin should have tried to clarify and explain certain points. Eldridge Cleaver, in Soul on Ice, emphasized that in this essay James Baldwin expressed a deep hatred of blacks and blind adoration of the white world.[6] Without going so far, one must say that when William Styron was violently criticized after the appearance of his first novel, The Confessions of Nat Turner, James Baldwin was the first to give him encouragement and moral support.[7] William Styron is a white man from the South and his critics were all of the black race. Baldwin's attitude may be explained by the great literary value he recognized in his white friend's work. But that is a valid argument to advance and support when one knows that American blacks are, in the majority, convinced that no American white is capable of understanding them well.

One must not think that Baldwin wishes at all costs to deny the racial reality in the United States. He wishes, in a sense, to be as optimistic as possible so as to discourage the fiercest attitudes. In "This Morning, This Evening, So Soon," a short story which appeared for the first time in 1960 and was published in Going to Meet the Man, we have the example of an American black who decides to return to the United States after having spent more than twelve years in France.[8] He has become a well-known singer and a film he has just finished has made him even more famous. It was France, we learn, that discovered him and revealed him to the world. His wife, Harriet, is Swedish and they have one son, Paul, who is almost eight. The action takes place two days before his departure for America, where an eager public awaits him.

James Baldwin implies that it was the role of Chico which he played in the film Les Fauves nous attendent that, to a large extent, persuaded him to return to the United States. In this film, Chico is supposed to hate whites and blacks and it was with the aid of the French producer, Jean-Luc Vidal, that the black singer finally found and accepted himself. This acceptance, to a certain extent, was facilitated because he is a native of Alabama, where he saw with pity his poor father suffer in silence from the injustice of whites. There is a close resemblance between James Baldwin and his nameless hero. Thus the author has always felt scorn for his stepfather and made the decision to return to the United States only after having spent ten years in France. In addition, it was his stay in France that made Baldwin's work interesting and original.

Forty-eight hours before his departure for America, the hero of the short story experienced certain feelings of anguish about his future across the Atlantic. He remembers very well that eight years earlier, when he was unknown to the public, he had spent a few months in Alabama and in New York City and that he had almost given up all hope of leading a normal and respectable life. This was because of the way whites had treated him. The only thing that he hopes for is that his son will be able to lead a normal life in the United States and also, and especially, that he himself will never suffer any scorn on the part of his own child. He realizes that there is a great difference between having succeeded in life and making oneself loved and respected by his people.

If the racial atmosphere in America frightens the hero, he gets a general idea of racial prejudice the evening he goes out with Jean-Luc Vidal. This evening is practically his last before the departure, and the two friends go to several nightclubs before coming across an Arab from North Africa whom the hero knows more or less. The Arab, Boona, is soon accused of having stolen ten dollars from a young black American woman, Ada Holmes, known by the two friends. Here Baldwin emphasizes the French producer's extremely cold and distant attitude towards the Arab. In addition, he does not hide the physical and moral destitution in which Arabs live in France. Although he knows that Boona, the Tunisian, stole the money, the hero pretends nonetheless to doubt it and to believe in the innocence of his so-called friend. He knows this theft was caused by despair and that the Arab is ready to do everything in order to survive in a hostile world. Whether the individual is an Arab in France or a black in America, James Baldwin wishes to describe a sad but universal human condition. However, the author shows that there is always a hope if the individual is determined to do everything to change his lot and that of his people. That is at least the case of the hero of this short story who is ready to do anything to protect the life of a wife and a son who have never lived in America.

The very title of this short story, "This Morning, This Evening, So Soon," has its origins in a ballad sung by black slaves, about one Roscoe Bill. The latter, appearing before a judge, had admitted having struck a white man because he did not want to be annoyed for quite some time, morning or evening. Could this be the desire of the hero of the short story? Does he intend to return to his native land to demand, at all costs, that his fellow citizens treat him as their equal? This short story, which appeared at the threshold of the sixties, seems to announce the violence and rage that tore that decade apart. But the hero is ready to try everything in order to ensure a viable and stable future for his people. He has discovered and accepted himself, and his only desire is to live in peace in a country that has nevertheless never wanted him.

This short story strangely evokes an essay by James Baldwin, "The Northern Protestant."[9] It deals with James Baldwin's interview with the Swedish producer Ingmar Bergman in Stockholm. But the famous Swede's thoughts, attitude, and behavior do not fail to intrigue, indeed irritate, Baldwin. From their first encounter, what displeased the black author greatly was the authority with which Ingmar Bergman spoke about his ideas and his future. This type of very strong personality could have quickly ended their conversation. However, Baldwin could not help but admire, and even envy, a man proud of his country and who had no intentions of leaving it. According to the author, Ingmar Bergman is known for his frankness and, for this reason, all those around him know well what he thinks. Without writing it nonetheless, Baldwin implies that he admires the Swede because they have two things in common. The first is that they are sons of Protestant ministers and the second, flowing from the first, is the intense desire to know the truth about everything around them. Quite obviously, Baldwin sees in Ingmar Bergman a person whom he would like very much to resemble. That is probably one of the numerous reasons that prompted him to return to America. It was in his own country that James Baldwin succeeded in making himself heard and, especially, understood.

HUMAN EQUALITY

James Baldwin's goal has always been to be treated humanely by those around him. At the end of the previous chapter, we saw how, during a stay in a little village in the Swiss Alps, he discovered his own identity. In "Stranger in the Village," he concluded that he is above all American and that his place is in America. Far from the familiar and known environment, James Baldwin knew that he could not speak with authority about the black problem for very long.

On November 21, 1960, several months after his return to the United States, the black author was to deliver an address at Kalamazoo College in the state of Michigan. This speech was later published in <u>Nobody Knows</u>

My Name under the title "In Search of A Majority--An Address."[10]   It is, to a great extent, a sequel to "Stranger in the Village," for Baldwin speaks of the American racial problem to an American audience after having made the firm resolution to stay in the United States. The author's courageous attitude is evident from a detailed analysis of his speech. That American majority of whom he speaks has nothing to do with, he says, the power or the number of the individuals concerned. What matters, he declares, is especially the influence that these individuals can exert, however small in number they may be. The examples that Baldwin gives are convincing when he mentions the position, very vulnerable, of the majority black population in South Africa of today and that of the French, in a minority, in North Africa during the Algerian War. It is evident that in this speech the author wishes to be free of all restrictions and that his sole aim is to be human. That is the reason his style is excellent and the very composition of the address is prestigious. He speaks as an American, but an American who has the future of his country at heart. Racial considerations play an important role, for Baldwin recognizes that the black man has always been at the bottom of the social ladder in America. This, he says, must change at all costs for political and economic reasons. American whites and blacks, he affirms, are irremediably linked to each other because they are all members of the same family, whether they like it or not. Thus, in this speech, the author uses the first person plural. That pronoun "we" applies to all Americans, white or black.

According to Baldwin, that American majority must be composed of whites and blacks eager at all costs to face together all situations of the present and the future while taking into account the lessons of the past. For the author, such an association would be the beginning of a great racial harmony within a society wanting to be first of all humane. Such an organization, falling within the province of a utopia, would be applicable to all Americans, whatever their origins. That majority would give America a well-defined identity and could then, according to Baldwin, be proud of the goal achieved.

One must remember that James Baldwin is an American black and that his childhood, his religious experience in Harlem, and his stay in France gave him both a special and an original identity. One can say that his experience is typically American. But can the average American, white or black, understand him?   What he is trying to do, basically, is to emphasize, and to make people respect, the human value of the individual.

This deep and intense desire, on the part of the author, to want to go to the bottom of the human soul and explore all aspects of it, has had a surprising result. Thus his novel, Giovanni's Room, does not deal with the racial problem in America.[11] We shall examine the novel later in this chapter. But one can say, for the moment, that Giovanni's Room is an imaginative work in which all the characters are white and in which the situations and feelings are human.

What interests us is a short story, "The Man Child," which appeared for the first time in 1965 in Going to Meet the Man.[12] In this short story, just as in <u>Giovanni's Room</u>, the racial problem does not appear anywhere. Quite obviously, Baldwin wishes to show that he is capable of describing in detail a situation in which the feelings and the attitudes are only human. He succeeds beautifully at it.

"The Man Child" is the story of an eight-year-old blond boy, Eric, savagely strangled by a friend of his father's whose first name is Jamie. This brutal murder is the end of the short story in the course of which one learns that Jamie has sold all his belongings to Eric's father and that he shares the life of the little boy's parents. Since his wife has left him, his only companion is a poor dog with which he lives in a log cabin located on Eric's father's lands.

We have here two farmers who have known each other for a long time and who often go drinking together in a bar, the Rafters, very near the farm. Characters and events are seen and described through the eyes of Eric who, quite obviously, has a very perceptive mind. His mother plays a secondary role in comparison to Jamie, but her various attitudes denote both a humble and a submissive personality. This woman suffers very much from not being able to express herself freely and, especially, from no longer being able to have children. She has just had a painful miscarriage.

Eric's father is a man who loves to work and who takes care of his farm. He is a proud man fearing nothing but, unfortunately, cannot share his wife's delicate feelings. The only tie that binds them is Eric. In order to highlight fully the two main characters of his short story, Baldwin gives only two names: Eric's and Jamie's. One can understand why, from the beginning of the story, these two individuals are doomed to a tragic end. These two people are simple, but very different. Eric is young and discovers at each instant the strange aspects of life; nature around them reflects his brand-new and curious soul. James Baldwin knows how to convey with charm and delicacy that close relationship which exists between little Eric and the land destined to be his when he is older. Jamie, on the other hand, is the very type of the simple-minded and stupid man who has lost everything and who can no longer hope for anything out of life. He has just turned thirty-four, and Eric thinks he is much older than his father who is thirty-two. One understands the attitude of the little boy proud of a father in whom he senses great courage and a very paternal love.

Jamie is an embittered human wreck with no future. Although he does not possess great intelligence, he realizes his wretched condition. It is on his thirty-fourth birthday, which he celebrates with Eric's parents, that he begins to see what he could do to end his friend's worthy lineage. Jealousy devours him and his own desire is to destroy Eric's father's happiness. The abominable act, of which we spoke earlier, will be its unfortunate and brutal consequence sometime later in the barn on the farm.

In this story, Baldwin displays great freedom of composition in the very choice of the subject about which he wishes to converse with the reader. His characters are human and their feelings are described in detail. The author succeeds in rendering an atmosphere in which racial tension would have no place but in which, especially, whites or blacks could recognize one another. In fact, the subject deals with rural life common to millions of whites and blacks who live in the Southern United States.

If whites and blacks in the South share the same life-style, their relations have always been influenced by compromising and dangerous racial attitudes and prejudices. This is largely due to the numerous years blacks spent in slavery and to their total submission to the will of whites. In the essay "Faulkner and Desegregation," which appeared for the first time in 1956 and was published later in Nobody Knows My Name, Baldwin speaks frankly about a worthy representative of whites in the South.[13] According to him, William Faulkner, no matter what he said about blacks in Mississippi, has always been favorable to whites in the South. Baldwin's aim in this essay is to make whites in the South understand that their dreams of the past can have no place in the present and the future. According to Baldwin, the moderate politics that they have always flaunted is no more and no less than the expression of the deep desire not to see blacks change. However liberal and progressive he might have been, Faulkner was ready to kill the black man if necessary. Baldwin explains that Faulkner had such a negative attitude because, after the Civil War, it was the North, and not the South, that had freed the black man. As he knows that he will never have this privilege, the Southern white desires to annihilate everything he cannot control.

Baldwin even goes so far as to say that the Southern white considers himself a Southerner first and an American second. The Southerner's attitude stems, quite obviously, from the fact that the Confederate states lost a war, whereas the North until now has only known victories. In other words, the South has always had an inferiority complex in relation to the North. This feeling is reflected in its ambiguous conduct with respect to the black man, in whom, basically, it finds its own identity again. Baldwin distrusts Southern whites, in whom he sees no encouraging future. The black man, according to him, is forced to rely on this goodwill of so-called white Northern liberals in order to achieve his ends. One may wonder if Baldwin is correct when one considers the slow progress of the black man in one hundred years of supposedly free life.

It is nevertheless impossible for the American black to be entirely self-sufficient, for he will always have to take into consideration the aid and support of whites. The time when the goodness and charity of whites played a decisive role in the life and future of blacks is now over. Baldwin's essential aim in this essay is to highlight the human aspect of racial relations in the South. To a great extent, the originality of this essay is that Baldwin speaks as an American about various problems concerning the future of a complex country. One would even be tempted to say that, since whites from the North and the South do not really want to help the black man, the latter could at any moment opt for a black nationalism which would enable him to rid himself of white guardianship.

The attraction and the complexity of the United States are highlighted much more when Baldwin speaks of his relations with Norman Mailer. In "The Black Boy Looks at the White Boy," which appeared for the first time in 1961, we have two individuals, one black and the other white, who are trying to understand each other.[14] This understanding is all the more difficult because the first one has been brought up in a very strict and religious atmosphere in a black ghetto, while the second comes from a middle-class Jewish family. They have nevertheless their country in common and this is precisely what caused them to meet by chance for the first time in France during the summer of 1956.

It was at the home of Jean Malaquais, French translator of several works by Norman Mailer, that Baldwin was invited to a cocktail party where he discovered a man both intriguing and interesting. James Baldwin said that he was impressed by Norman Mailer's personality and that he remained in contact with him thereafter. According to Baldwin, Mailer is the very type of the American white who has all sorts of preconceived ideas about the American black man and who, consequently, mistrusts him very much. That does not prevent Baldwin from continuing to admire him for his courage and his tenacity which are, at bottom, ludicrous. However amusing and astonishing Mailer may be in Baldwin's eyes, numerous blacks see in Baldwin's attitude proof of a blind love of everything that is white and a deep hatred of everything that is black. In this essay, Baldwin expresses no feeling of anger in the face of Mailer's boastful and even superior attitude. The only thing he dares to suggest, so to speak, is that the white in general must try to know himself, to find himself, before penetrating the mystery of life. He also says that the black men must follow the same course. In short, everything must begin with the individual, and that is what Baldwin firmly believes in. This attitude was very peculiar to Baldwin, whose nature was very sensitive.

What Baldwin says in this essay reflects the fact that he and Mailer had come across each other, and had lived for some time, in an environment that was not theirs. According to the black writer, such a situation should have caused them to understand their personality better. Here Baldwin wishes to apply his own experience to Mailer, which, unfortunately, does not seem to have been exactly the case, for three years after this first encounter, Mailer was to declare in Advertisements for Myself that Baldwin could not tell the truth when necessary. What Mailer reproached Baldwin for was not coming directly to the facts at the appropriate time. "Baldwin seems incapable of saying 'Fuck you' to the reader," he had declared.[15] Baldwin had no reaction for, he said, Mailer treated him almost like a child and had not understood his ideas. In any case, we have here a black man who accepts the insults of a white man without protesting. To a certain extent, this attitude seems to indicate blind deference to the omnipotent and barbarian white world.

The conclusion that James Baldwin draws from his chance meetings and his relations with Norman Mailer is that the writer, whatever he may be, has a duty towards the future. That future will also depend a great deal on the way the writer himself will be able to see and accept his own truth. According to Baldwin, this truth will enable generations to come to understand themselves better and to build a society in which harmony and understanding will be masters. Here again, Baldwin is concerned about the future whereas it is especially the present that should matter.

It would be interesting to note that, if Norman Mailer's remark amused James Baldwin, the same remark made by a black, such as Richard Wright, would probably have provoked a lively and immediate reaction on Baldwin's part. Baldwin was, in effect, quick to criticize Wright strongly when he realized that his literary future was at stake. Richard Wright had certainly done more to help James Baldwin in his literary career than any white he met by chance at a cocktail party.

James Baldwin is very positive and encouraging concerning the future of America when he says that the American writer, white or black, has a duty towards his country. This duty, he declares, requires frankness with oneself and intellectual honesty. We saw earlier that Baldwin imposed these rules on himself and that he wants Norman Mailer to do the same. One must recognize that it was much more difficult for Baldwin than for Mailer to accept such principles. The reason is the color of his skin.

In the essay "The Discovery of What it Means to Be an American," which appeared for the first time in 1959 and was published later in Nobody Knows My Name, Baldwin says that his stay in France saved his life, enabled him to discover himself, to understand himself better and, especially, to accept himself.[16] Baldwin said and repeated many a time that if he had not left the United States, he would have either committed suicide or found himself in an insane asylum. This would have been the regrettable consequence of the white man's attitude towards the black man. Baldwin left America as soon as he learned that one of his best friends had committed suicide; the same fate was lying in wait for him. When he arrived in France, he had to accept that he was simply an American and, what is more, a black American. The case concerning the stolen sheet in December 1949 is undoubtedly one of the elements that contributed to that awareness and its acceptance. Overnight, Baldwin saw himself advance from the stage of the frightened and fearful black to that of an American aware and proud of his past. Such a transition is not made without difficulty and pain, and Baldwin had to go spend some time in the Swiss Alps. This experience is related in detail in "Stranger in the Village," seen at the end of the preceding chapter.[17] David Levin pays great homage to James Baldwin when he writes that:

> "...the Negro himself must overcome immense pressures and temptations if he is to transcend the fact of color, the hatred of the whites, the restricting bitterness that might keep him from achieving what Baldwin calls his identity."[18]

Such an opinion emphasizes well what Baldwin has always wanted to try to do: know himself so as to know and understand others better.

His prolonged stay in France enabled the author to realize the fundamental difference between American society, which never ceases to change, and established and structured European society. Quite obviously,

Baldwin preferred the second since he returned to Europe, far from the American masses constantly in search of a vague and ill-defined identity. He knew very well that the writer, whatever he may be, needs a precise identity in a calm and stable society. The only reason he chose permanent exile in France is that he wanted to have the peace of mind necessary for every good writer. But the sole fact of not living in America, in an American atmosphere, must have hurt him, for he lost direct contact with the subject that was very dear to his heart. It is precisely that reason which had induced him to return to the United States in 1957.

In Europe, the human being that Baldwin finally discovered in himself helped him to know better those whites and blacks around him. We saw earlier, in "The Man Child," that Baldwin could put in their proper place characters and situations which did not concern the racial problem in America. On the contrary, we have essentially human feelings and attitudes.

Long before thinking of writing "The Man Child," James Baldwin had already, in 1944, written a novel, "Ignorant Armies," in which the main character was a homosexual whose life and acts were greatly based on those of Wayne Lonergan. The latter was a Canadian who had brutally assassinated his young American wife in 1943 and who, subsequently, had been condemned to thirty-five years in prison. "Ignorant Armies" was never published, but the main character is found again trait for trait in the character of David in Giovanni's Room. It was his long stay in Europe that enabled James Baldwin to write a novel in which homosexuality is seen and analyzed in all its details but in which, also, characters and situations have nothing to do with the racial problem. Giovanni's Room is a delicate and courageous analysis of homosexual love and announces to a great extent Another Country, which we shall examine in the next chapter.[19] The author had already started to write Another Country at the time of the publication of Giovanni's Room.

To understand this novel better, it would be necessary to examine the essay written by James Baldwin on André Gide, "The Male Prison."[20] That is at least the title under which it appeared in Nobody Knows My Name. It had been published for the first time in December 1954 under the title "Gide as Husband and Homosexual," when Baldwin was writing Giovanni's Room.[21] In that essay, Baldwin expresses respect and admiration for a man who, basically, had suffered very much but who also, to his mind, should not have talked about his intimate and personal problems. Although he does not consider the situation natural, Baldwin does not hesitate to say that men and women always need one another and that Gide had caused his wife, Madeleine, to suffer too much. According to Baldwin, the homosexual must accept himself without making a display of his condition and harming those around him. One may well wonder if that is not a judgment made by Baldwin concerning himself, given the important place homo- sexuality occupies in his work.

In Giovanni's Room, homosexuality is the sign of pain, of weakness, and, above all, of degeneration, but it also enables the individual to reveal himself entirely. Before the publication of the novel, Baldwin had had many doubts about its success, for, in 1956, the theme of homosexuality was not as widespread as today. It is understandable that Baldwin had not wanted to see his career as a writer ruined from the appearance of his second novel. He encountered numerous difficulties in England and in the United States, but finally got an American publishing company to accept his text. In Giovanni's Room men love one another, hate one another, despise one another, and end up either no longer knowing themselves or destroying themselves. The woman plays no role, except that of the underdog. Whether we are dealing with Hella or Sue, the situation is the same: man's tenderness and his love are denied to them. Which, to a great extent, reminds one very much of what Baldwin says in his essay on André Gide and Madeleine. The type of woman that we have in Giovanni's Room corresponds very closely to that of Madeleine. That is to say, that of a person who sacrifices herself, for a time at least, in order to allow a man to go on leading the semblance of a normal and natural life. This theme is fully developed in Another Country, in which the woman, quite obviously, plays an essential role, indeed vital, in a society in which, without her, life would be devoid of equilibrium and attraction.

In Giovanni's Room, Baldwin wishes to speak of man alone, of his hopes and his disappointments. Giovanni's weakness and his vulnerability replace the female sex. It is perhaps his mood that Baldwin describes when he speaks of the mental tortures endured by Giovanni. For it was during the writing of this novel that the author went through an identity crisis. In any case, the two main characters in the novel, Giovanni and David, however close they may be in their intimate relationships, are very different. The first is a native of a little village in southern Italy where the individual depends essentially on the vines and olives of the region in order to subsist. The people there are very poor and are often reduced to living from day to day. Giovanni left his native village after his wife had given birth to a stillborn child. He took refuge in Paris where, little by little, he met people of dubious morals.

Since he has always lived in extreme poverty, his idea of wealth is only vague and ill-defined. David is, on the other hand, the epitome of the American who, living in a semblance of poverty in Europe, can always ask his family to send him money. He was born in San Francisco and has lived nearly all over the United States. His father now lives in Brooklyn. Having lost his mother at the age of five, he was reared by a very strict aunt, Ellen, and his father who was very oblivious to his paternal obligations. This father, nevertheless, has always done his best to try to understand a son who, basically, despises him. Giovanni and David thus represent two very different worlds. Giovanni has always experienced poverty and human degeneration, whereas David comes from a middle-class environment. In view of these details, one can understand Giovanni's complete and unreserved fidelity to David. This fidelity presupposes an identical and reciprocal attitude on David's part. The latter, unfortunately, has no intention, nor any desire, to give in to the feeling that binds him for a time to a poor Italian alone and without resources. His attitude is hypocritical. It is not new since, as early as age thirteen, he had behaved the same way towards a certain Joey.

David is a homosexual who does not want to accept himself and who, consequently, makes those suffer who share his illicit and reprehensible pleasure. The action takes place in Paris because, undoubtedly, Baldwin lived a long time there and because he knew that city well. The atmosphere of the French capital lends itself perhaps much better to this type of situation than that of any other city. In addition, France enables Baldwin, the American black, to give vent to human feelings and attitudes. David's personality is high-lighted because he is not in a natural and familiar environment. It is the same for Giovanni who is also far from his native land. These two meet by chance in a city which is not theirs, surrounded by so-called friends who enjoy observing them and teasing them maliciously.

Giovanni's Room is composed of two parts. In the first, the author gives details about David's family and about the strange relation-ship he had with his little friend Joey from Brooklyn. Baldwin is already preparing the reader for Giovanni's tragic end. In this first part, we witness David and Giovanni's meeting in a bar frequented for the most part by men with special tastes. This bar belongs to a strange person, Guillaume, who is the very good friend of a certain Jacques. These two people, although around sixty years old, are homosexuals constantly in search of young men like David and Giovanni. David is around twenty-seven and Giovanni is approximately the same age. When David and Giovanni meet at Guillaume's place, David has been in France for two years and, for lack of money, no longer has any shelter.

David despises Jacques, whose only attraction is his wealth. Jacques is an American businessman of Belgian origin. David sees in Jacques only a purely material salvation, temporary and especially devoid of any physical aspect. This is the reason they go to Guillaume's bar together, where Jacques is going to try to find an acceptable procurer.

The second part of the novel deals with the blossoming of the intimate relations between David and Giovanni. Giovanni gives himself entirely to David, whom he allows, on the same occasion, to live in his little room. This room will witness Giovanni's honesty and frankness derided and ridiculed by David's hypocrisy. The latter will wait a month before telling Giovanni he has an American fiancée, on a trip to Spain, who is supposed to come back to Paris soon. He will not say that his father is going to send him money to enable him to live freely and as he pleases. It is evident that David is taking advantage of Giovanni and that he has no intention of taking him seriously. But the very refusal to accept himself also prevents him from having a normal and wholesome relationship with the one he thinks he loves, Hella Lincoln. Hella is a native of Minneapolis and is in France in order to study fine arts. Just like David, she is from a middle-class family for whom the material aspect of life never causes any problems. David met her in a bar on Saint-Germain-des-Prés and, some time later, thought himself in love with her. We are dealing with two Americans who meet on foreign soil and who loved each other more out of loneliness and idleness than through a true and deep feeling. Of the two, Hella is the more frank and the more honest. But, as soon as she returns from Spain, numerous events begin to shake the confidence she has always had in David. Her doubts become reality when, after having looked for David for several days, she finds him in a bar in Nice with a sailor. It is after this incident that she decides to leave David and return to the United States.

The action of the novel takes place in several phases, which reflect the course of the amorous relations between David and Giovanni. These two people meet by chance towards the end of the winter, and their adventure lasts all the following spring and summer. In the autumn, David goes to live in the apartment of Hella, back from Spain. Giovanni, like a human wreck, drifts and, despairing of everything, lives with Jacques, then with another homosexual, Yves, and, finally, kills Guillaume by choking him with the belt of his bathrobe. Shortly after this murder, David and Hella decide to go stay on the French Riviera with the money sent by David's father. It is from the house they are renting near Nice that they hear from Giovanni through the intermediary of Jacques. Given Guillaume's illustrious family background, Giovanni is quickly judged and condemned to death. The date of execution coincides roughly with the first anniversary of David and Giovanni's meeting.

There is a close relationship between the essay "Gide As Husband and Homosexual" and Giovanni's Room. In this novel, in effect, Baldwin has Giovanni play the role of Gide and David that of Madeleine. But, surpassing the character of Madeleine, David takes advantage not only of Giovanni but also of Sue and Hella. He denies Giovanni all support and consequently causes his ruin. Sue is a girl whom David meets by chance during a walk and with whom he has a brief affair. This short-lived relationship takes place while David is still living with Giovanni and while Hella is still in Spain. Quite obviously, David has no respect for Giovanni or Sue, since he knows that Hella is supposed to come back to him. Sue is an ugly girl, accustomed to the animal and sensual approach of men. As he senses it, David does not hesitate to use her with a purely selfish aim in mind. Here remorse has no place.

Since he is totally unaware of the affair between David and Sue, Giovanni's pride is not hurt. David will never tell him anything about his adventure with little Joey. But after a long absence and a long silence on David's part, Giovanni realizes that something is wrong. When they meet again, David informs him that he will no longer have anything to do with him and that he loves Hella. From that moment, Giovanni, crazed with despair, attempts everything to hang on to life. Unfortunately, he ends up committing a murder that leads him to the guillotine.

All these events do not go unnoticed in Hella's eyes, although David does not tell her the truth about his relations with Giovanni. He wishes rather to let her think that Giovanni lived with a mistress while he, David, occupied his room. His lies have a harmful effect on his relations with

Hella. Both from the physical and the mental view- point, they will see their love reduced to nothing. If Giovanni and David are bisexuals, Giovanni is in the literal sense of the word for he has always loved with great frankness and a complete commitment on his part. One could say that David is afraid of his homosexuality; he is even ashamed of it. This difference of attitude, according to Collin MacInnes, is due to Giovanni's Latin origins and David's Anglo-Saxon and puritan roots.[22] One should add that the social origins of these two individuals also play an important role. Money, and the life-style it permits, form and shape the individual's personality.

James Baldwin's aim in Giovanni's Room is to make it understood that man, whatever he may be, must accept himself as he is. He recommends a thorough knowledge of oneself if one wishes to be capable of distinguishing the real from the imaginary. David is a person living in a world apart, a world consisting of dreams and illusions which, to a great extent, has something narcissistic about it. He scoffs at everything people want to offer him; Giovanni is brutally rejected and Hella makes the painful discovery of the homosexuality and the lies of the one she thinks she loves. Giovanni and Hella live in a world devoid of all human love in which loneliness is master. David, because he is selfish, will not have the courage to do anything whatsoever to help them. His pleasure comes before everything else. He is aware of what he is doing and he delights in doing it; but he nevertheless feels no guilt. This type of behavior is, for him, completely natural. Guillaume, on the other hand, is a perverse individual who takes pleasure in making Giovanni suffer. Sometime after having informed Giovanni that he no longer wanted him as a barman, and after having learned of Hella's return to Paris, he lures Giovanni into his room by making false promises to him. He will be brutally choked by Giovanni, crazed with rage at the idea of having been duped again. Nobody had done anything whatsoever to come to the aid of a depressed and penniless Giovanni. Jacques had helped him for some time; but with a sadistic and selfish goal in mind.

Giovanni's Room is a subtle novel in which human nature is explored in all its details. It is by using the technique of retrospective scenes that the author enables David to give a precise account of his eventful story. The theme of homosexuality, as it is described in the novel, is seen in a frank and direct manner. If Collin MacInnes, in 1963, thought, wrongly moreover, that the Anglo-Saxon public was not ready for Giovanni's Room, it is evident that today homosexuality is accepted in America. Plays like Hair and Calcutta, performed on stage in the late sixties, helped homosexuality to be understood better by the American public. Numerous homosexual clubs now exist in most large American cities. The very acceptance of this life-style has enabled America to understand better and, especially, to see the racial problem better.

PASSIVE BEHAVIOR

If during the fifties and sixties America realized the power exerted by the black man, the latter will show that he is capable of using diverse means to achieve his ends. The behavior he adopted was both passive and active. We shall content ourselves in this section with seeing what Baldwin thinks of the passive aspect of the question. Three essays which appeared in Nobody Knows My Name will be analyzed so that we may see the author's attitude clearly.

In the first of these essays, "Nobody Knows My Name: A Letter from the South," written shortly after his first trip to the South of the United States in the fall of 1957, Baldwin speaks to us about what he saw and heard there, and draws conclusions from it.[23] Since he had started this trip in Charlotte, North Carolina, he ended it in Atlanta, Georgia. This was the first time that Baldwin had ventured into the South; he had wanted for thirty years to do so. This journey was, for the author, like a pilgrimage to the land of his ancestors. According to him, Southern whites and blacks of one hundred years ago, and even before, are the ancestors of the Northern black. Nothing can be changed any longer; it is a closed chapter of American history. Although he had never lived in the South before, Baldwin found there both a familiar and a strange atmosphere. It was familiar because, through his parents, natives of the South, he could recognize numerous details; and strange because he was not himself from that environment. This dichotomy in his attitude enabled him, in his works, to make interesting remarks and give original impressions of the South.

According to what he says, the elementary and secondary schools attended by blacks have a very low level of education. School integration, for Baldwin, certainly has a racial aspect; but also the stake is political and, unfortunately, sexual. It is clear, after all, that those who are blinded by the sexual aspect of the matter are ignoramuses belonging to that category of whites threatened by the black mass. What makes them different from blacks, they think, is the color of their skin. Little Rock, Arkansas, was shaken by the violent blind reaction of thousands of whites who refused to see a black pupil enter a white institution. The political system of the South is very powerful; it can, at any minute, manipulate whites as it pleases. Baldwin rightly says that relations between the leaders of the city and those of the state are very tense. It is common to note that the mayor of a city does not have the same views and the same ideas as those of the governor of the state on whom he depends. This situation, quite obviously, creates enormous and dangerous problems.

In fact, in the South, the management of urban centers is dependent on the actions undertaken by the rural white population, especially when the latter maintains close and friendly relations with the governor. The governor can then easily influence the politics of the cities in his state. James Baldwin claims that the South cannot change, and that it is not ready to do so. Whites riot when they see a black child enter a white elementary or high school because they fear that their way of life will be threatened. For them, blacks cannot live like whites; consequently, they must live apart. This attitude of white superiority has deplorable effects on blacks and in particular in black elementary and black high schools. In these institutions, education reflects the negative attitudes of the black teachers who know the situation. Therefore, they communicate their feelings of hate and despair to black children. The latter, never completing their studies, prefer to approach life without any intellectual baggage. The spectacle they offer to whites is that, too well known, of the drugged black living only for alcohol and sex.

Aware of the danger, the black anxious to succeed in life begins by attending a white elementary and a white high school where he is sure to obtain a good education. That is, according to Baldwin, the only reason more and more blacks want to attend a white educational establishment. One understands the violent reaction of Southern whites who refuse to see a black child attend the same school as their children. Black parents, although they know the dangers faced by their children, are the first to encourage them to attend a white educational establishment. They know that therein, and therein only, lies the salvation of individuals who are dear to them. Southern whites try to find all the means possible to stop or, at least, slow down school integration. But they clash with two powerful organizations which blacks know how to use with caution: the clergy and the National Association for the Advancement of Colored People. It is thanks to the diligent and serious work of these two groups that the Southern black is succeeding, little by little, in making himself respected and in obtaining some concessions. Be that as it may, the cities in the South will sooner or later be controlled by blacks as whites take refuge in the large suburbs.

The Southern black's attitude is human since it is a question of survival -- despite the violent opposition of whites blinded by the racial aspect of the question. Baldwin's advice is wise since he recommends a mutual understanding in an environment common to all: America. He is also truly an advocate of a slow but sure evolution of a situation in which whites and blacks have everything to gain. The relentless and delicate work provided by the judges and lawyers of the National Association for the Advancement of Colored People is undoubtedly equal in power and scope to that of the Southern Christian Leadership Conference. The latter group, essentially religious, has the sole aim of making the human rights of the black man respected. Martin Luther King was its illustrious leader.

In the essay "The Hard Kind of Courage," which appeared for the first time in 1958 and was published later in Nobody Knows My Name under the title of "A Fly in Buttermilk," Baldwin presents the special case of a young black who has started to attend a white educational establishment in the South.[24] This young fifteen-year-old adolescent, named G., is not geographically situated by the author. Therefore, he could live anywhere in the South. The author wishes above all to present the situation and all the regrettable consequences to which it can lead. Although with a big family to support, G.'s parents had decided to get him admitted to the white high school in their city for the reasons already described. Knowing that their son was both hard-working and intelligent, they simply wanted to give him a good education. Each year, among the students of the black high school, several girls became pregnant and had to interrupt their studies. Furthermore, many boys G.'s age no longer had a clean police record. According to his mother, G. had begun to adopt bad habits at the black high school. But the entry into the white high school was the beginning of a long and difficult experience for the parents.

G.'s mother received several alarming telephone calls threatening her son's life. Keeping all her calm and her cool, she notified the chief of police, who reassured her. Some time later, G.'s father had to change jobs in order to work in another part of the city. In other words, G.'s family life was disrupted for the sole reason that he attended a white high school. G. himself, from his first day at the high school, had to endure insults and provocations. He did not react and suffered in silence. Despite these problems, he had no regret about having left the black high school. The harassment and the insults which he constantly had to face played, to a great extent, the role of determining catalysts. As he knew he had no choice, G. was determined to do well in his studies. For him, the white high school was an institution which was supposed to ensure a good education for him and a positive future. Already at his tender age, he had understood that he was the only one to determine his destiny.

In this essay, Baldwin wishes to be as objective as possible in presenting the white attitude, represented by the principal of the white high school. This essay was written towards the end of the fifties when school desegregation was going full swing and tempers were often very worked up. Baldwin's interview with the principal of the white high school is interesting because it shows the behavior of a Southern white man who thinks he is a liberal but who, at bottom, does not want to change his racist attitude towards blacks. Concerning the insults and vexations suffered every day by young G., the principal explains that that is the custom and that white children do the same thing among themselves. Quite obviously, he refuses to recognize the racial element in a situation dangerously laden with hatred and anger. At that time, in fact, school integration had just reached the high school of a Southern white principal concerned about not having any trouble with the local authorities.

During the conversation, Baldwin realized that the white principal knew nothing about blacks, about their way of living and thinking. The conclusion that he drew from it was that Southern whites and blacks had nothing in common and that they were all satisfied with this situation. If black parents' attitude towards school integration is human, that of whites, on the other hand, is blinded by insurmountable prejudices. Thirty years after the writing of this essay, it is unfortunate to note that the situation has not improved, but that from the South it has spread to the rest of the United States. The courage and the willpower of black parents are to be admired because it is a question of life or death for their children.

In "A Fly in Buttermilk," Baldwin exposes the typical situation of a young black in the South eager to take advantage of school integration in order to attend a white high school. His attitude and that of his parents, both resigned and firm, brings clearly to light the type of constant battle fought today by millions of American blacks. This struggle is characterized by great determination, fierce willpower, and complete silence. Only whites succeed in changing it into bloody conflict.

The fate of thousands of young blacks who attend black educational establishments in the South is the same as that which lies in wait for their brothers in the Northern ghettos. In "Fifth Avenue, Uptown: A Letter from Harlem," which appeared for the first time in 1960 and was published later in Nobody Knows My Name, Baldwin attacks the North fiercely.[25] He affirms that if the condition of the American black is to change, it is in the North that everything must begin. Quite obviously, the Northern white does not wish to know the black man and does not want to deal with him. That is the reason the Northern black is forced to live in a ghetto, separated from the white. In other words, the Northern white is unaware that the black exists. The Southern white, on the other hand, has always been aware of the existence of the black man, since he had to endure severe sanctions after the Civil War. These sanctions, to a great extent, were caused by the presence of the newly-freed black man. Before that conflict, black slaves were so numerous that fearful whites organized themselves in order to control them better. Today, the situation is the same, with the sole difference that the black man is supposed to enjoy great freedom. But by virtue of his permanent presence, his control is both more rigid and easier than that to which he is subjected in the North. In short, the white in the South sees him continually, and everywhere, and thus exercises a constant surveillance.

Therefore it is erroneous to claim that the Southern black leaves the hell in the South in order to find freedom and respect in the North. The Jim Crow life of the South changes into a concentration camp as soon as he arrives in a ghetto in the North. Numerous are the blacks who prefer the Southern way of life, for there, at least, they know where they stand and what role to play. In the ghetto, they live withdrawn into themselves and have no direct contact with whites. A great number of them, according to Baldwin, abandon all hope, and if they do not go mad or die as a result of bloody brawls, spend the whole day in search of drugs. The others, trying to live honestly, accept minor and humiliating jobs that the white world is willing to concede to them.

This depressing way of life offers the ghetto black no hope. No matter what efforts the municipal authorities of the city make in order to improve the lot of these poor wretches, the ghetto is still there. According to Baldwin, the black in the ghetto has no respect for the new apartment houses built for him. Within a very short time, these beautiful buildings become as dirty, ugly, and repulsive as those they had replaced. The only effective solution to the problem would be the total elimination of the ghetto.

But first it would be advisable to note a radical change in the attitude of whites towards blacks. At present, this change is not possible, for the

Northern white does not want to deal with the black man in order to safeguard his position, his way of life. Whence the presence of so many white policemen in the black ghettos. One knows only too well the tendency of these white policemen to take advantage of the situation. Their attitudes and their acts, of an annoying nature, very often provoke violent reactions on the part of those they are watching. The riots of the sixties often originated in such a situation. Baldwin is a child of the ghetto; it is thus with full knowledge of the facts that he openly attacks the murderous hypocrisy of the Northern white and the scarcely concealed hatred of the Southern white.

Strictly speaking, one cannot say that there exist any black ghettos in the South of the United States. In a small Southern town, the black neighborhood is most of the time on the other side of the railroad track. This part of town is always poor, filthy, and badly kept. This state of affairs indicates the low priority it rates in municipal affairs. In a large urban center in the South, such as Atlanta, the downtown area is occupied by blacks whereas whites live on the periphery, the outer suburbs. In most cases, these urban centers are badly kept, and poverty and fear reign supreme. In short, in the North as well as in the South, and wherever the black lives, the white always operates in such a way as to deal with him the least possible.

James Baldwin came from a poor family and, when he speaks of the black man, he speaks of the one who, like him, has experienced fear, hunger, and cold. Nevertheless, one must not forget the existence of a considerable black middle class in the United States. Baldwin came across this category of blacks, in the South as well as in the North. According to him, these blacks think only of themselves and absolutely do not want to deal with other blacks. It is regrettable that Baldwin had this attitude, for those blacks have often contributed to the improvement of race relations in the North and in the South. One must not forget that, for the white, a black, whatever he may be, is always a black and that he is descended from servitude and slavery. These middle-class blacks, whom Baldwin distrusted very much, are often in the ranks of the National Association for the Advancement of Colored People. The author reproached them for not being as radical in thoughts and in deeds as their brothers of color who live in the ghetto. Such a thing is impossible given the enormous gap separating these two groups. One could perhaps say that Baldwin cannot or does not want to understand this black middle class whose life-style is very different from that he knew in Harlem. Nevertheless, these blacks have also experienced, without exception, the bitterness of racial prejudice and it is certain that they do their best to combat it in all their undertakings and their actions. Thus they send their children to the best educational institutions and universities in the United States, in order to ensure a stable future for them. At the same time, they are working for a better future for their race of which they have always been an integral part.

If religious sects as varied and disparate as the holy rollers and the Black Muslims are born in the ghetto, let us remember only that there we have the result of a long human agony. The holy rollers give themselves totally to religion, hoping to find a better world in the beyond. Black Muslims, on the other hand, reject everything that has to do with the white world. In both cases, reality is avoided. This type of attitude accepts the image that the white has of the black. This image, unfortunately, has no human quality.

ACTIVE BEHAVIOR

Given the very precarious position of the American black in the United States, it is not surprising that often his behavior is both ambiguous and confused. That is at least the impression that he gives the white, with the aim of protecting himself and not revealing his true intentions.

We have just seen that, thanks to a patient and passive attitude, the black succeeds sometimes in obtaining concessions from the white world. Often this attitude is not sufficient. Then the black moves to a more active phase. In the essay "East River, Downtown: Postscript to a Letter From Harlem," published in Nobody Knows My Name, but which appeared for the first time a few months earlier under the title of "A Negro Assays the Negro Mood," Baldwin talks about the violent reaction of some American blacks to the announcement of Patrice Lumumba's death.[26] Those blacks demonstrated noisily in the United Nations Building in New York, with the sole aim of showing their discontent after the political assassination of an African who had a brilliant future ahead of him. The goal of this violent demonstration was also to reveal the hypocritical attitude of the United States concerning the independence of the new African countries. At the time, America had preferred to abstain from voting for the independence of Algeria. American blacks have always interpreted every negative decision of their country regarding Africa as a step backwards in their struggle for civil rights.

Numerous American blacks saw in Patrice Lumumba's murder the well-known and familiar action of the white man who does not hesitate to destroy everything that the black man may have as a source of pride. That the American press reported the incident by saying that these few blacks were Communists is not surprising. For, according to what most American whites think, the American black is supposed to be pleased with his lot. Only outside and foreign elements can drive him to anger and revolt. This attitude is, quite obviously, dangerous since the American black is today one of the last black peoples still under the surveillance and dependency of whites. Seeing the African countries attaining independence, the American black man often wonders when his turn will come. Or, at least, he wonders when he will be able to enjoy the respect and dignity that nationals of African countries visiting the United States already enjoy. It is very common that, on American soil, the African is better treated than the American black. One can understand, in part, the reason that, in the sixties, the black ghettos of the North and the black communities of the South were violently shaken by rage and anger. Realizing that he had nothing more to lose, the black man had decided to take by force what had been denied him: his human dignity.

One should not believe that the black man acted without knowing what he was doing. In his essay, James Baldwin speaks of two diverse civil rights movements that nevertheless pursue the same goal. The Student Nonviolent Coordinating Committee and the Black Muslims want the black man to be treated with respect and humaneness. In order to understand these two movements better, we shall take a detailed look at their origins and their evolution and compare them to the National Association for the Advancement of Colored People and to the Southern Christian Leadership Conference. That is a way of understanding Baldwin's thought better, for he has always been interested in their activities. These four black groups are among the most important and best known in the United States; but their actions may be as peaceful as bellicose. All depends on the direction taken and the goals sought by each of them.

The Student Nonviolent Coordinating Committee is an organization of students, for the most part black, with the primary goal of making the rights and the humanity of the American black citizen respected. Its members consider themselves full American citizens. Baldwin, who has often worked for that organization, has said on several occasions that it was the only black American movement anxious to make itself known and respected in a national context -- on condition, of course, that its members in particular and blacks in general are treated humanely and equitably by the rest of the American nation.

The members of that organization are young and still maintain the hope that America is a country of which they can be proud. Their public demonstrations, whatever they may be, are peaceful, but always aim to break down racial barriers that imprison the black man. It is because of that organization that, for example, racial segregation no longer exists in numerous restaurants and common carriers in the South. The sit-ins and the freedom rides of the sixties were mainly organized by its members. The Student Nonviolent Coordinating Committee, more commonly known as SNCC ("Snick"), is undoubtedly a part of the great American civil rights movements. But it is different from the others because it wants to be, first of all, American, and especially, optimistic. That is the reason Baldwin considers it both a positive and a constructive organization.

It often happens that, as a result of physical and moral sufferings inflicted by the white world, the American black decides no longer to deal with a country that does not want him. He then rejects everything that binds him to America by undertaking to live in a world apart. The case of the Black Muslims is a striking example. They founded the Nation of Islam and their sole aim is to have several states of the United States given to them in order to establish their own country there. The gift of these few states would be, according to them, the only way whites could compensate them for three hundred years of slavery. The Black Muslims are of the

Islamic faith and learn Arabic at their university in Chicago as well as in their schools, which are located all over the United States. Their life-style is strict and, since they do not wish to have any contact with the white world, great silence always surrounds their activities.

It is not surprising that Baldwin was interested in this deeply religious and closed sect. He saw in it a movement constituted by reaction to the negative and destructive actions of the white man with regard to the black man. Although he thinks the Black Muslims have no future, Baldwin appreciates the beautiful example of courage and pride given to American blacks who have lost all hope.

In addition to their strict religious organization, the Black Muslims have a small army, or police, called the Fruit of Islam. Its role is purely defensive and it is supposed to intervene only when the provocation is blatant and direct. The Black Muslims want to protect themselves from the white Christian world that they say is doomed to an imminent and total end. The Black Muslims inspire respect and have the secret admiration of millions of American blacks. Living on the fringe of American society and despising everything having to do with the white world, the Black Muslims ardently hope for the union of all American blacks with a single and salutary goal: that of their survival in a world which is to disappear shortly. Malcolm X, their famous spokesman before his assassination in February 1965, clearly explained their views in several speeches and interviews. But they claim that it was the spiritual and religious head of the Black Muslims, Elijah Muhammad, that had Malcolm X executed. The latter seemed to talk too much and, in addition, wanted to create an independent movement less strict than the Black Muslims'.

This is not to suggest that the Black Muslims are the first independent black movement that has ever existed in the United States to give American blacks courage and hope. In the twenties, the Universal Negro Improvement Association (UNIA) rallied millions of American blacks to its cause. Its goal was to create a stable and solid economy which would enable American blacks to leave America to go settle in Africa. Its leader, Marcus Garvey, was unfortunately implicated in some fraudulent affairs and the UNIA saw its dreams and its ambitions fail lamentably. The difference between the Black Muslims and the UNIA is important since, in addition to their economic and social role, the Black Muslims have adopted a religion which has nothing to do with the Christian world. It is that religion which makes the way of life of the Black Muslims so different from that of the rest of the American population and which intrigued Baldwin. It is doubtful that the Black Muslims have a great future, unless America suddenly finds itself in a very vulnerable position and has to yield to the territorial demands of this organization.

In "East River, Downtown" Baldwin cites SNCC and the Black Muslims as the two opposite poles of the various black American movements. This essay was published in 1961. Since, individuals, attitudes, and situations have indeed changed, especially where the SNCC is concerned. In the sixties, numerous members of this organization were disappointed and wounded by the conduct of the white man. Certain of them, such as Stokely Carmichael and H. Rap Brown, decided then to move to a more active phase so as to make themselves better heard and understood. Then, in 1967, the Black Power movement grew to an immoderate extent and whites began to realize the power the black could exert. Approximately at the same time, other young blacks, such as Huey Newton, Bobby Seale, and Eldridge Cleaver, began to attract attention. They had just founded a revolutionary organization, the Black Panthers, whose sole aim was the immediate improvement of the American black's lot. The ten-point program they established and published left no doubt about their distrustful attitude towards the white world. The advocates of Black Power as well as those of the Black Panthers knew that only force could intimidate and even frighten the white. Baldwin undoubtedly followed the evolution of the events favorably, for he admires Christopher Hall very much in his novel, Tell Me How Long the Train's Been Gone. Christopher is converted to the ideas and principles of the Black Panthers.

The Black Power Movement, as it has been described by Stokely Carmichael in Black Power: The Politics of Liberation in America, wants the black to realize his power by making common cause with all other blacks.[27] That is the reason thousands of blacks rallied to that movement which, basically, had no precise rules. What it had to offer above all was dignity and pride to people who up until then had never heard of black power. The Black Panthers, on the other hand, are ready to defend themselves if necessary. There was a time when they did not move without being armed. On several occasions, they exchanged gunfire with the forces of law and order; these confrontations cost them deaths and casualties.

Black Power and the Black Panthers are almost no longer heard of today. Their leaders are either in exile, in prison, or dead -- or else they have given up their demands in order to cooperate with the white world. Such is the case, for example, with Bobby Seale. Thus, whatever their demands and requirements may be, the American black always ends up accepting the power of the white world. The latter makes concessions to him, concessions which, to some extent, enable him to integrate himself better into American society. Only the Black Muslims resist the assaults of the white world from which they want absolutely nothing, except a part of its territory. SNCC, Black Power, and the Black Panthers have always demanded the rights of a full citizen for the American black. These demands will be met, for otherwise the American black will never fully enjoy the rights that the Constitution of his own country grants him. One would be tempted to side with the Black Muslims who simply want a total secession.

Other black organizations in the United States, far from being as bellicose as the Black Panthers, know that patience and Christian love do not know any barriers. These include the National Association for the Advancement of Colored People and a religious group, the Southern Christian Leadership Conference. These two organizations recruit blacks especially, but gladly accept all aid, physical as well as moral, that the white world cares to give them. They purport to be first of all Americans, and their primary goal is the recognition of the human and civil rights of the American black. The means used to achieve such ends vary greatly from one organization to the other.

The National Association for the Advancement of Colored People is a conservative association and is well organized from a political point of view. Numerous whites are members of it since, in the beginning, it was liberal whites from the North who founded the organization in 1910. But the soul of the movement was a black man, W. E. B. DuBois, who, as early as 1905, had created the Niagara Movement. His organization's goal was to oppose segregation firmly and to criticize the politics of gradualism of a black from the South, Booker T. Washington. The latter wanted the black to content himself with his lot, while humbly accepting the role of worker or farmhand that the white wanted to see him play in American society at that time. In addition, Booker T. Washington accepted and even encouraged the policy of segregation as it was practiced in the South. The fundamental difference between these two men was that one came from a middle-class black family and the other had lived through slavery in the South. Moreover, W. E. B. DuBois was far better educated than Booker T. Washington. We shall see later that Booker T. Washington's attitude is reflected, to a certain extent, in that of the SCLC. DuBois's radicalism gave the NAACP an impetus and a vitality very profitable for the American black.

The National Association for the Advancement of Colored People does not profess violence or force but, above all, patience. Its primary goal is to find blatant cases of segregation or discrimination and to have them abolished, thanks to decisions taken by the state or even federal courts. Its action often requires much time before ending in a positive result. School desegregation, for example, was for the most part engineered in a direct, constant, and judicious manner by that association. The NAACP has representatives everywhere in the United States. They are supposed to detect cases of racial discrimination in order to point them out to leaders of the association.

It is evident that the NAACP does not have the aggressiveness, nor the dynamism, of the Black Panthers. But if its process is slow, it is, in spite of everything, sure. Its members claim that, in numerous cases, rage and force are harmful to the black and his status as a free man for which he toiled and worked so hard over the years. In other words, this association is first of all interested in the legal aspect of every action taken for the greater welfare of the American black.

The Southern Christian Leadership Conference, on the other hand, is essentially a religious association uniting the black communities of the South. One must say that the Southern black is very religious and that his life has always depended on the spiritual head of his church. The SCLC was founded with the aim of uniting the greatest possible number of black Christian leaders in the South so as to enable them to make common cause in their demands. After his resounding victory in the Montgomery, Alabama, bus boycott in 1956, Martin Luther King, Jr., became the undisputed leader of the movement.

As he was himself a Baptist minister and a native of the South, Martin Luther King possessed an exceptional gift for speaking to the millions of blacks who admired him. In addition, through his education acquired in a white Northern university, he was convinced that violence and rage would never work in favor of the black. Deeply impressed and influenced by Gandhi's philosophy, Martin Luther King believed that nonviolence and love would finally triumph over the American white. This is the reason that, during the sixties, he organized marches and mass meetings in which order and calm reigned supreme. Only the whites, for whom this attitude was new, reacted with agitation and even violence. Martin Luther King and several of his co-religionists were beaten and thrown in prison many a time, which provoked the indignation of millions of whites in the North and around the world. Since Martin Luther King's assassination, the SCLC has lost much of its dynamism although Ralph Abernathy, who succeeded Martin Luther King, did his best. In fact, the personality and influence of Martin Luther King, Jr., had succeeded in uniting the vast majority of black religious communities in the South. One must understand that the spiritual leaders of these communities are very jealous of their congregations and are often unwilling to share their powers. The SCLC does not have the rigid and orderly character of the NAACP. Although the goals of these two groups are similar, the peaceful means employed are, quite obviously, very different.

From this brief review of the black American civil rights movements, it is clear that only the Black Muslims and the NAACP have a certain future. The first group does not want to deal with America, and its sole desire is to live apart. The isolation of the Black Muslims, and the mystery surrounding them, makes them both uncontrollable and almost invulnerable. One might say that the American white is suspicious and afraid of them. The second group, on the other hand, is well known to whites who, especially in the North, help it considerably. So there is here, on the one hand, complete and desired segregation on the part of the black and, on the other, cooperation with the white world. Since the majority of American blacks want to be full American citizens, it is evident that the NAACP can count on their aid and support. The American black, today, realizes more and more that he belongs to the United States rather than any other country. This is what Baldwin wanted; he claimed, rightfully, that the American black has long since earned the right to be a full American citizen. For his life and his future form a symbiosis both effectively and legitimately with other American citizens. Do they not have more rights than the white immigrants of the great and recent periods of migration to the United States?

It is understandable that those Americans of the black race seek and put into practice all possible means of persuasion in order to make themselves heard, understood, and, finally, recognized by Americans of the white race.

NOTES

1. James Baldwin, Nobody Knows My Name (New York: The Dial Press, 1961).

2. James Baldwin, "Introduction," in his Nobody Knows My Name (New York: Dell Publishing Co., 1964), nátions pp. 11-13. All other references to this book will correspond to this edition.

3. "Notes for a Hypothetical Novel-An Address," in Nobody Knows My Name, pp. 117-126.

4. James Baldwin, Tell Me How Long the Train's Been Gone (New York: The Dial Press, 1968).

5. James Baldwin, "Princes and Powers," Encounter 8 (January 1957): 56-60. (Also in Nobody Knows My Name, pp. 24-54.)

6. Eldridge Cleaver, "Notes on a Native Son," in his Soul On Ice (New York: McGraw-Hill, 1968), p. 99.

7. William Styron, The Confessions of Nat Turner (New York: Random House, 1967).

8. James Baldwin, "This Morning, This Evening, So Soon," Atlantic Monthly 206 (September 1960): 34-52; also published in his Going to Meet the Man (New York: The Dial Press, 1965), pp. 145-193.

9. James Baldwin, "The Northern Protestant," in his Nobody Knows My Name, pp. 133-145. Appeared for the first time under the title of "The Precarious Vogue of Ingmar Bergman," Esquire 53 (April 1960): 128-132.

10. James Baldwin, "In Search of a Majority-An Address," in his Nobody Knows My Name, pp. 107-114.

11. James Baldwin, Giovanni's Room (New York: The Dial Press, 1956).

12. James Baldwin, "The Man Child," in his Going to Meet the Man, pp. 61-80.

13. James Baldwin, "Faulkner and Desegregation," Partisan Review 23 (Fall 1956): 568-573; also published in his Nobody Knows My Name, pp. 100-106.

14. James Baldwin, "The Black Boy Looks at the White Boy." Esquire 55 (May 1961: 102-106. (Also in his Nobody Knows My Name, pp. 171-190.)

15. Norman Mailer, Advertisements for Myself (New York: G. P. Putnam's Sons, 1959), p. 471.

16. James Baldwin, "The Discovery of What it Means to Be an American," The New York Times Book Review, January 25, 1959, pp. 4, 22; also published in his Nobody Knows My Name, pp. 17-23.

17. James Baldwin, "Stranger in the Village," in his Notes of a Native Son (New York: Bantam Books, 1964), pp. 135-149.

18. David Levin, "James Baldwin's Autobiographical Essays: The Problem of Negro Identity," Massachusetts Review 5 (1964): 244.

19. James Baldwin, Another Country (New York: Dell Publishing Co., 1964).

20. James Baldwin, "The Male Prison," in his Nobody Knows My Name, pp. 127-132.

21. James Baldwin, "Gide as Husband and Homosexual," The New Leader, December 13, 1954, pp. 18-20.

22. Collin MacInnes, "Dark Angel: The Writings of James Baldwin," Encounter 21 (August 1963): 27.

23. James Baldwin, "Nobody Knows My Name: A Letter from the South," in his Nobody Knows, pp. 86-99. Appeared for the first time under the title "Letter From the South: Nobody Knows My Name," Partisan Review 26 (Winter 1959): 72-83.

24. James Baldwin, "The Hard Kind of Courage," Harper's Magazine October 1958; pp. 61-65. Also published as "A Fly in Buttermilk," in his Nobody Knows My Name, pp. 75-85.

25. James Baldwin, "Fifth Avenue, Uptown: A Letter from Harlem," Esquire 54 (July 1960): 70-76. Also published in his Nobody Knows My Name, pp. 55-66.

26. James Baldwin, "East River, Downtown: Postscript to a Letter from Harlem," in his <u>Nobody Knows My Name</u>, pp. 67-74. Originally published as "A Negro Assays the Negro Mood," <u>New York Times Magazine</u>, March 12, 1961, pp. 25, 103-104.

27. Stokely Carmichael and Charles V. Hamilton, <u>Black Power: The Politics of Liberation in America</u> (New York: Vintage Books, 1967).

9

DEMANDS

THE AMERICAN HERITAGE

In 1963 appeared <u>The Fire Next Time,</u> a small book comprising two essays published separately by James Baldwin the preceding year.[1] The aim of the first and the shorter of these two essays, "My Dungeon Shook: Letter to My Nephew on the One Hundredth Anniversary of the Emancipation," is to warn a young fourteen-year-old black boy that he has nothing to expect from the white world.[2] For the author, this essay has a special and profound meaning since it is addressed to his nephew whose first name, is James like his.

January 1, 1963, marked the centennial of the emancipation of the American black. This important decision, taken by President Abraham Lincoln alone, was not ratified in the form of a law by Congress until December 18, 1865, eight months after President Lincoln's assassination.

The presidential proclamation of January 1, 1863, concerning the emancipation of the American black had enormous effects on American society. Overnight, the American black went from the status of a slave to that of a free citizen. But not knowing how to protect his rights and his interests, he was reduced to the state of a second-class citizen. Despite the aid of the federal government in the form of the Freedmen's Bureau, the white South, from 1877, had retaken control of the lands as well as its inhabitants. The period 1867-1877 was full of hope for the black in the South, whose sole desire was to be treated humanely. Because of the result of the 1876 presidential election, he was rapidly led back to his old condition as a slave by the landowners in the South, who took advantage of the industrial momentum of the North. Since he was no longer officially a slave, his condition was lowered to the point of total dependence on the white man in order to live and support his family.

Thus the former slaves remained poor farm workers or farmhands laden with debts. The Ku Klux Klan, grouping the vast majority of whites in the South, used threats and terror to keep a fearful and defenseless black in the condition of a slave. So it is natural that, from that time on, thousands of blacks left the South to seek peace and tranquillity elsewhere. The North and its emerging industry attracted most of them. This migration towards the North still continues today at a slower pace. From the moment he arrived in the North, the black is confined within a black ghetto where he has no direct contact with the white world. This condition is quite new since, in the South, the white had always been near him in order to watch over him and take advantage of him better. The constant surveillance in the South and the deep suspicion in the North are the reasons why the American black has always had a tendency to distrust the white.

In "My Dungeon Shook: Letter to My Nephew on the One Hundredth Anniversary of the Emancipation," Baldwin exhorts his nephew to face with courage and firmness the hatred of the white world. He tells him that his grandfather, James Baldwin's stepfather, had believed the white world's lies and that he had died hating everything around him, including his own family and himself. Baldwin demonstrates that it is the blindness and the indifference of whites that hurt blacks. The great ignorance that whites display, he says, enables them to declare themselves innocent of everything that happens to blacks. For Baldwin, this is a crime which must be avoided at all costs and, with this aim in view, he advises his nephew to know and understand the white better by using love. Such a suggestion could appear paradoxical unless one recalls that, according to the author, the black in the United States is above all American and that he will be happy only when whites have accepted his true presence. Force and violence almost never have a positive result. But Baldwin advises his nephew to use force and love to enable whites to understand themselves better and to accept reality. The precise aim of this approach is to destroy the dangerous and harmful prejudices that whites maintain with respect to blacks. In addition, imagination is supposed to have no place; it is what gives rise to prejudices. In any case, this at least is what the black hopes; the white will realize that the black is not an inferior and inhuman being that can be accused of all the evils that afflict American society.

James Baldwin is for integration and, according to him, everything must be done in order to fight against destructive work and segregation. Since 1963, great efforts have been made by American schools and universities with a view to enabling young blacks to be represented and educated better. But this has not affected the Northern ghetto nor the small black city in the South, which continues to live in the threatening shadow of the white world.

Although he desires to be a full citizen of his country, the black knows well that he will never be treated as such as long as the white remains under the influence of his imagination and his prejudices. Whence Baldwin's idea of forcing the white, with love, to face reality. That is what the author thought in 1963, for five years later, he was to admit that some riots in the ghettos were largely due to the indifference of whites and to the total lack of a promising and certain future for blacks. To some extent, he admitted the failure of his message of love and brotherhood.[3] Nevertheless, Baldwin has always succeeded in exposing the delicate aspects of the

American black's condition. In addition, and even until this day, he has known how to trouble the conscience of the white by showing the sensitive points of racial discrimination.

His attitude is simple and clear when he says that if the white is incapable of love, the black can save him by making him discover feelings until then never experienced. This idea, for Baldwin, is completely natural since whites and blacks belong to the same great American family and since they have a common future.

The style of The Fire Next Time is markedly different from that of Notes of a Native Son or even of Nobody Knows My Name.[4] Criticism and analysis in the first two collections of essays yield, in The Fire Next Time, to prophetic language and exhortations to national union that revealed Baldwin to America during the sixties. The essay we have just seen is a beautiful example of this. In a short story, "Previous Condition," published in Going to Meet the Man, but which appeared for the first time in 1948, Baldwin gives a general picture of the baleful effect of the prejudices of whites and racial segregation.[5] The direct consequence of the resultant rage and bitterness is to degrade the individual and make him commit actions that do him harm. It is the story of a black battling against white society which wants at all costs to humiliate him because of the color of his skin. His first name is Peter, and one can easily compare him to Baldwin in the late forties before his departure for France. In this short story, the hero does not leave for a faraway land; but, rather, he is forced to face the reality and the hostility around him. That is, undoubtedly, the type of environment that Baldwin knew in New York before leaving the United States.

We are brought face to face with a twenty-six-year-old jobless and penniless black actor. A native of New Jersey, he was raised in the ghetto and never knew his father. Having left his mother at the age of sixteen, he found himself alone four years later because of her death. His only friends are a Jew, Jules Weissman, and a white woman, Ida, five years older than he. She is married to a rich ballet dancer more interested in his work, and his homosexual relations, than in his own wife.

Although this story was written at the very beginning of Baldwin's literary career, we have all the constituent elements of a segregationist atmosphere. The room that Peter has been occupying in New York for three days was rented by his friend Jules Weissman. It is not supposed to be lived in by a black. As soon as the owner of the apartment building realizes Peter's presence, she does not hesitate to make him leave right away in order to keep a good reputation with her white tenants. According to her, blacks can only live in Harlem. This remark comes from the fact that blacks are supposed to live in the ghettos. In addition, the value of real estate is depreciated by the sole presence of the black man. In other words, the owner of the apartment building reacts to the color of Peter's skin and the threat it represents. It is evident that the individual and his feelings are entitled to no place here. That is what disturbs the young black man. Being as sensitive as he is, he realizes that, in order to survive, he must constantly play the game of the whites and their police.

Ida, his friend, herself from a humble Irish environment in Boston, knows the meaning and the impact that poverty and suffering can have. But, like Jules Weissman, she is white; and this is what Peter envies and reproaches her for. Ida's attitude towards Peter is frank and sincere. The evening of the day he is evicted from his room, Peter has dinner with her in an Italian restaurant in Greenwich Village. Carried away by the anger and hatred of the white race, he cannot help insulting her in front of everybody. Disgusted with everything, he goes to Harlem where, out of spite for his race, he gets drunk in the company of two black prostitutes.

Peter is a delicate person. Although black, he has a pronounced personality. He knows that in America, the color of his skin will always be an obstacle to his hopes and his ambitions. It is not surprising that, exhausted to that extent, the individual has to chose between escape and suicide. Baldwin chooses escape. The bitterness and the hatred of his soul had almost triumphed over his body.

THE NEW AMERICAN SOCIETY

Aware of his condition as a second-class citizen, the American black also knows that America cannot do without him. That is the reason he asks, and even demands, to be treated as equal to whites. This new attitude on his part surprises whites who, until the present, had thought he was content with his lot. The surprise of whites is all the greater because the black has informed them he is ready to use all the means possible to achieve his ends.

We saw, in the previous chapter, the diverse black movements which attracted widespread attention in the sixties. We also saw that, although different from an ideological point of view, the Student Nonviolent Coordinating Committee and the Southern Christian Leadership Conference had a common and unique goal. This goal worries whites, for they realize that blacks have become aware of their place and that they intend to change this society which denies them respect and honor.

During the sixties, Martin Luther King, Jr., knew how to make himself heard by whites and blacks who, haunted by hatred and despair, had turned to him: whites in order to understand better what was going on, and blacks in order to make themselves better heard by whites. Both knew that their society was undergoing some radical and irreversible changes. In an article, "The Dangerous Road Before Martin Luther King," which appeared in 1961, Baldwin gives a precise picture of the situation.[6] Between the author and his subject, we are dealing with two black preachers of very different origins: Baldwin was a preacher for three years in a little church in Harlem, whereas Martin Luther King comes from a respectable line of Southern black ministers. The maternal grandfather of the latter had built, then had pastored, Ebenezer Baptist Church in Atlanta, Georgia. This church was, subsequently, pastored by both Martin Luther King, Jr., and his father.

In his article on Martin Luther King, it is evident that Baldwin is aware of his humble background and that, to some extent, he envies that intelligent man from a middle-class black family. Baldwin does not forget that he came from the black ghetto and that he never had the life-style or upbringing of Martin Luther King. This does not prevent him from speaking frankly about a man he admires. For it is the great difference that exists between Martin Luther King and James Baldwin that enables the latter to make an objective and sensible judgment. They have nevertheless one thing in common: the perfect and clear knowledge of the desires and aspirations of the black masses. Whether he is in Harlem or in Atlanta, the black's only goal is to be treated humanely by America. Therefore, he is constantly in search of a leader and a spokesman who could help him find his pride.

Although Baldwin is deeply suspicious of the black middle class, he admits nevertheless that the children of this middle class have decided to put an end to the hypocritical game of their parents. He explains this by saying that the black middle class lives in an isolated world. This uncommon position comes from the fact, he says, that the white world wants to have nothing to do with the black, in whom he wishes to recognize no class. Rejected by the white world, the black middle class lives withdrawn into itself out of fear of having the slightest contact with the black mass that it despises.

In other words, the middle-class black finds himself caught in a strangle-hold with, on one side, the all-powerful hatred of whites and, on the other, the pain and humiliation of the black mass which, basically, reminds him constantly of his wretched origins. Whence the reaction of a Martin Luther King who, proud of his origins, does not hesitate to speak and to address himself directly to whites in the name of all blacks. But here, Baldwin rightfully says that the role played by Martin Luther King is both dangerous and delicate. Speaking as an equal to whites, King makes them understand that everything will be done so that the black may fully enjoy his rights as a full citizen. Martin Luther King's approach is direct and unequivocal. It has nothing in common with the disturbing and disappointing attitude of Booker T. Washington in 1895. The latter had, in fact, declared that educating the black man had nothing to do with equality of the races. This statement served only to reinforce whites in their racist and segregationist attitude. It also enabled thousands of blacks to educate themselves. Given the violent atmosphere of Booker T. Washington's time, one might wonder, with a few good reasons, if that black leader was not double-dealing with the sole aim of improving the lot of his brothers of color. Tuskegee Institute, the small college he founded in Alabama, is a great university center today.

If whites of Booker T. Washington's time did, or at least believed they were doing, what they wanted with the black, the white of today realizes that the black no longer wishes to play his game. Martin Luther King's position has always been that of the undisputed leader who refused to make any compromise with whites. In fact, this is the way whites have succeeded, until this day, in controlling and manipulating blacks and their spokesmen. Blacks have always had a tendency to want to please their former white masters. It is this attitude that has done them harm. Today's black simply demands what is due him, no more, no less.

In the previous chapter, we saw how blacks used diverse means to achieve their ends. For Martin Luther King, his weapon is love and his sole aim is to cure evil with good. This method is applicable to whites and blacks. Here again, Martin Luther King was careful not to please the black middle class, which, undoubtedly, would have liked to hear him say something else; but he always spoke of the black in general, without mentioning background or social class. What interested him above all was the condition of the American black as it is today. He knows that it is necessary to improve it at all costs, for that is the only way to change whites' attitudes towards blacks.

Unfortunately, Martin Luther King was brutally assassinated on April 4, 1968, while he was in Memphis, Tennessee, in order to help the black sanitation workers of the city who were then on strike. Those, whites or blacks, who had decided on his death had realized the enormous success that he would achieve in the near future. The idea of a rapid and brutal change was sufficient to drive a handful of determined men to end a life full of promises. For if Martin Luther King's movement was of religious inspiration, the young blacks, who demonstrated all over the South, led the black religious leaders to become better aware of their task and their responsibility towards the future of America. By killing Martin Luther King, the assassins of that illustrious black leader aimed to make black youth understand that the same fate awaited them if they did not stop their actions. At the end of his article, Baldwin is careful not to say anything whatsoever about Martin Luther King's future. Perhaps he sensed already that an imminent and inevitable danger was lying in wait for the black leader. Baldwin does refer at one point to this subject when he declares that all futures are difficult. This type of conclusion, although general, enabled the author not to take a position in a situation in which everything could change overnight. A fact which, unfortunately, was confirmed for Martin Luther King and thousands of black admirers.

In the sixties, and long before Martin Luther King's assassination, Baldwin took part in numerous public and peaceful demonstrations in the South. Thus he knew the life-style of the Southern black. Besides, he discovered the tense and dangerous atmosphere in which whites and blacks had to coexist. That is probably the reason he wrote "Going to Meet the Man," a short story which appeared for the first time in 1965 in the collection <u>Going to Meet the Man</u>.[7]

In that story, Baldwin relates the difficulties of a white, Jesse, deputy sheriff of a small city in the South. Quite obviously, Jesse no longer understands the blacks who, through their civil rights demonstrations, have upset the racial equilibrium of his hometown. Since he can no longer understand the blacks, his world crumbles yielding to danger and uncertainty. Has he not always seen the black obedient and respectful towards whites? His anger is all the greater since blacks always demonstrated in a calm and orderly fashion, whereas the whites cause disorder and violence. Jesse is forty-two, perhaps too old to realize that his world is changing. For him, everything must be as before; even if the black must continue to suffer.

At the beginning of the story, Jesse has just spent a hard day with some blacks who wanted to demonstrate peacefully. A number of them, including their young leader, were thrown in prison. This did not prevent them from singing religious songs for the salvation of their persecutors' souls. Crazed with anger, Jesse desperately tried to beat black and blue the already bruised and bloody body of the young leader. Refusing to ask his friends to be quiet, the black man tells Jesse he has known him for a long time. The latter then recalls the time before he worked for the sheriff, when he was a traveling salesman. He used to sell his articles to blacks at high prices; especially to an elderly black woman, old Julia, of whom he took great advantage. She had a grandson, then ten years old, who scarcely liked whites. This grandson is none other than the black man now in prison. This scene repeated itself many a time in the prisons of the South during the sixties, when the demonstrations for new social laws were going full swing. James Baldwin, through this short story, shows that the Southern black is clearly telling the white that everything must change.

In the calm of the night, not knowing what to think of the situation, Jesse plunges into the past in order to relive, with his parents, a memorable day. The action takes place thirty-four years earlier when he was only eight years old. It was around the late twenties, a time when the lynching of blacks was permitted, even encouraged, in the South. Quite obviously, the white man reigned supreme since the black feared him so much. Through this retrospective scene, adroitly handled by Baldwin, Jesse, who cannot calm his rage, hopes to succeed in doing so by recalling a brutal and bloody scene from the past. He thus recognizes implicitly that such a scene would now be almost impossible; it would summon the reprobation of the whole world. When he was eight years old, everything was different, and several hundreds of whites took part in a lynching. That was the practical and direct means used by whites in order to make blacks understand that they were their masters in all domains. The slightest pretext provoked a lynching: a threatening gesture or an insult was all it took to cause the atrocious death of an unfortunate individual. It is clear that the person gravely offended by the black was always an innocent and worthy representative of the white race.

The lynched black before young Jesse had been accused of having struck an elderly white woman, Miss Standish. In such cases, and especially when a black man was implicated, they never tried to prove the facts--much less permit the black man to explain himself. The sacrosanct word of the white was always sufficient. This retrospective scene gives a precise idea of the environment from which Jesse came. His parents, quite obviously, are poor whites who despise blacks; thanks to the color of their skin, they think they are superior to them. The day before and the very day of the lynching, young Jesse is surprised not to see any black on the road or in the countryside; particularly his little black friend, Otis, of whom he is very fond. Unfortunately, and according to what his father's friends say, he quickly realizes that the action of a single individual can affect the life of an entire community. The blacks among whom he has always lived are now hiding at home fearful of incurring the anger of whites.

Since he knew the fate that awaited him, the black man accused of having struck Miss Standish had taken flight. But the whites had quickly caught him in a trap somewhere in the countryside. In this short story, whether the action takes place in the present or in the past, the black man is the symbol of sexuality or of everything that has to do with the degrading and dirty aspect of sexual activity. According to Jesse and his people, the black man belongs to a species that is located between man and animal. The lynching which little Jesse witnesses indicates that man, whatever he may be, always feels a secret joy, both primitive and barbarian, at the sight of a horrible and bloody scene. Baldwin gives a detailed description of the lynching: first, the torture and castration of an individual who is burned alive. As if that atrocious death were not enough to calm their anger, the mob is satisfied only after the bruised and unrecognizable body of the black man is torn to shreds. This lynching scene evokes the one described by Richard Wright in "Big Boy Leaves Home."[8] Although nearly thirty years separate these two stories, the atmosphere is the same and the feelings described are practically identical. This is due to the literary and artistic skill of Baldwin, who knows how to revive an era that he never lived through, but which has always occupied an important place in his work.

Between the pitiless lynching in "Going to Meet the Man," and the ideas developed in the second essay of The Fire Next Time, is located the long and hard road traveled by the American black in one generation. In "Down at the Cross: Letter From a Region in My Mind," Baldwin says that today's black considers himself above all as being an integral part of American society.[9] He does not hide either that the black is ready to do everything to occupy a worthy and respect- able place among the other citizens. Finally, like a prophet, he emphasizes that the future of America will depend greatly upon the direction taken by the American generation of today. By American generation, he means, of course, American whites and blacks closely linked by a common past and a future full of promise and hopes.

This essay closely resembles a monologue. It enables Baldwin to explore in depth the racial problems that afflict America. His ideas and his comments also enable one to understand what is going on in America better. In other words, he is explaining America to Americans. The only way, according to him, to achieve a positive result is to begin by loving one's neighbor and oneself. Nothing is more destructive than blind hatred and rage. This is what the author declares on several occasions in his essay. Thus, the road to integration is wide open to Americans determined to do everything to ensure a stable future for themselves. This attitude is undoubtedly influenced by Baldwin's religious childhood and adolescence. It is that religious strength that, still today, leads him to encourage whites and blacks to remake their society. Very sensitive, and although he knows that everything is the white's fault, Baldwin wishes to trust in a better future. He refuses to believe that all is lost and that America is on the verge of being torn apart by a blind racial war.

Baldwin is sure that the American white, whatever he may be, has always had a feeling of guilt with respect to the black. According to the author, American society must start from this point to transform itself. It is, moreover, this sentiment that leads white society to make more and more important concessions to the black. The various civil rights movements of the sixties were its direct consequence. Before that time, the vast majority of American blacks had always had a very poor opinion of themselves. This opinion had been created by the attitude of the white and also by the living conditions to which the black was subjected.

Baldwin did not claim to have found a miracle solution to the American racial problem. For him, it is especially a question of a humane attitude. Only time and patience can help to resolve such a problem. That is the reason Baldwin uses the term "conundrum" several times in his essay to describe the complexity of the situation he faces. This situation requires that the individual question himself and search himself in order to know and understand better the whole of which he is himself a part.

According to Baldwin, only a handful of determined whites and blacks can bring about a change in American society. The number is not important, for everything would depend on the will and determination of the group in question. This affirmation led him to declare on several occasions that in addition to the Republican Party and the Democratic Party, it would be necessary to create a third party for whites and blacks who desire to change their society. If the Southern states were beaten during the Civil War, the Southern oligarchy is still listened to and even protected by the federal government in Washington. This protection indicates that today the American black must be attentive to the racial policy followed by his government. For him, the Statue of Liberty is a symbol of aggression, falsehood, and oppression: only the white has succeeded in believing and even in realizing the dreams that it promised. The black has always had to content himself with what the white cared to leave him.

Today, aware of his color and his citizenship, the American black intends at all costs to have his rights admitted and respected. He is ready to employ all the means possible to this end. This does not mean that in wanting to improve his condition, the black wants to be an emulator of the white. His sole aim is to have the same rights as the whites. Integration itself has a very different meaning for whites and blacks, and each must define the kind of future that awaits him. According to Baldwin, the black wishes to have the possibility of proving himself in a society that has always denigrated him. That is the reason why thousands of young blacks today attend universities which barely twenty years ago were forbidden to them. This enables blacks to be in direct and daily contact with whites and to experience together the same pattern of thought and a new form of expression. In such conditions, whites and blacks learn to know one another better and also, and above all, to appreciate one another. This situation, which is confirmed at all levels of American society, enables whites and blacks to be closer to one another. It facilitates and even greatly encourages marriages between the white race and the black race. According to Baldwin, the future of the American people is to become a single race in which the mulatto will predominate. This point of view is strongly disputed by millions of whites, who see this as the ultimate goal of black politics; integration at all levels of American society would thus be a fact.

America is very sensitive as far as the sexual aspect of the racial question is concerned. The matter is all the more delicate since America is above all white and puritan. But millions of Americans realize today that things cannot remain where they are and that a change is necessary. The actions of the white policeman in the Northern ghettos or in small Southern black towns are certainly not likely to promote understanding and peace between blacks and whites. Baldwin knows the actions of white policemen in regard to blacks. At the age of ten, he was taken into a deserted lot of Harlem by two policemen who manhandled him and threatened to castrate him. At the age of thirteen, while he was walking to the main library in New York, he was insulted by a white policeman displeased to see a black in a white neighborhood. Such incidents mark the adolescent whose only fault is being black. Fortunately for Baldwin, as he says in his essay, faith in God saved him. The three years spent in a completely religious atmosphere and euphoria enabled him to realize better the dangers that threatened him from both the outside, on the ghetto street, and the inside, from the hypocrisy of the chosen ones of his church. Young Baldwin never preached in his stepfather's church; he had already decided to rely only on himself in order to protect his self-pride.

He abandoned the religious faith because he noticed that everything was controlled by whites and the God worshipped by blacks was white. It was in order to face reality that he decided to come out of his religious isolation and to do without its protection. Since that time, he succeeded in avoiding the numerous traps of a society that seeks the total destruction of the black. Not that Baldwin hates whites and does not want to know them. On the contrary, he says in his essay that one of his best childhood friends is a white with whom he has remained in close contact. Baldwin has always had good white friends; that is the reason he understands the Black Muslims, without however approving their ideas. In his essay, he speaks of his chance meeting in Chicago with Elijah Muhammad. Although realizing that the Black Muslims live on the fringe of America, Baldwin feels that they are nonetheless a part of the society they try so much to avoid. His explanation is simple: without America, there would not be any Black Muslims. In addition, he declares this black religious sect created itself a God and a world in its image: which is designed to arouse the attention and the interest of any poor black subjected to whites. However, Baldwin rejects the segregationist doctrine of the Black Muslims, deeming it as dangerous as the most fanatical white groups. One must nonetheless recognize that the Black Muslims win the respect of a world that hates them but which hesitates to do anything whatsoever in opposition to them owing to the mystery which surrounds them.

The Fire Next Time appeared at the time when Baldwin was in the midst of civil rights demonstrations. The ten years spent in France had taught him that prejudice was a universal thing. Aware of his historical and social past, the author came back to the United States in order to reconcile himself with his fellow citizens. It is perhaps not surprising that the novel Another Country, published after his return to America, presents situations in which love between blacks and whites is homosexual, heterosexual, and bisexual.[10] Another Country reveals clearly a world that is both new and human. We are face to face with several people whose common interest is a young black, Rufus Scott, who commits suicide at the beginning of the novel.

The first chapter of the novel, the best part of the book, relates in detail the last months of the life of Rufus Scott, a character strongly influenced by a black friend of Baldwin's, Eugene Worth. The circumstances that surrounded the tragic death of this man are also those which drive Rufus Scott to jump from the George Washington Bridge into the icy waters of the Hudson.

Rufus Scott, who is twenty-six years old, adores music; he is a musician by profession. He plays the drum in small bands that perform in New York night clubs. This type of activity enabled him to meet people as diverse as they were intriguing. Since he is a native of Harlem, Rufus Scott distrusts by nature all whites with whom he comes in contact. This did not prevent him from getting along well with a white from Brooklyn, Daniel Vivaldo Moore, whom he has known for several years. Their friendship is sincere despite the difference in the color of their skin. They understand each other because both of them came from poor neighborhoods and because they lived through a difficult adolescence.

Although of modest condition, Rufus Scott's family is respectable. Mrs. Scott is a woman of character whereas Mr. Scott is a bitter man without hope. He hates whites and their religion that drove his son to suicide and which also, several years earlier, had caused a white to savagely hammer his father to death. Rufus's youngest sister, Ida, who is twenty-two years old at the time of her brother's suicide, hates whites also. This hatred is all the more intense since she is convinced that the white world is at the root of her adored brother's death. Although she met Vivaldo for the first time when she was fifteen, Ida treats him with great contempt when she sees him again shortly after her brother's suicide. Ida cannot help making Vivaldo suffer because he is white. In other words, Ida is not interested in the individual and his feelings since, quite obviously, she wants to redeem her brother's death by taking revenge on the white man, whatever he may be.

Vivaldo, who has also endured suffering and poverty, understands Ida's actions. He is descended from a poor family which, because it is white, has always believed itself superior to blacks. For him, his own parents are inferior to Rufus Scott's. His father is an inveterate drunkard, whereas his mother does only just what is necessary to keep the family hardware store from being engulfed in debts. As for his brother and his sister, Vivaldo has a poor opinion of them. The things he has always admired in Rufus Scott are that human dignity and that human pride which place the individual above all degrading pettiness. He finds these qualities again in a more pronounced way in Ida. In other words, Vivaldo is a simple and honest person who, by the very nature of his frankness, ends up making himself appreciated and loved by the very ones who hated him because of his race or his origins. He is the center of the novel, just as Rufus is its bond which, even after his suicide, unites the characters and enables them to understand one another better.

Before his death, Rufus Scott knows all the main characters of the novel. The shock of the crisis he is going through, after having made Leona unhappy and insane, is to a certain extent alleviated by the unlimited support that Vivaldo gives him. The latter shows him that the individual can always rise above racial prejudices in order to come to the aid of a loved one. Rufus is incapable of it since he has destroyed an individual, a white woman from Georgia, who loved him with a total commitment. Leona, accused of all the crimes of her race by Rufus, loses her mind and must be confined to a mental hospital. Rufus's unhappy affair with her shows that he is incapable of trusting others entirely, but also that the color of his skin constantly puts obstacles in the way of the world around him. Or, perhaps he wants it that way, for the situation could have been different if he had adopted a new attitude. Quite obviously, Rufus Scott has nothing to lose, since he has nothing in the world even if a person as devoted as Leona must spend the rest of her life in an insane asylum somewhere in Georgia. Baldwin's style is both violent and direct, his aim being to describe a situation as real as possible. Although loneliness and the search for love unite Leona and Rufus for a time, the black man cannot accept the Southern white woman's behavior as sincere. It is through his attitude that Rufus will allow society around him to destroy the little happiness they could have known together.

That Rufus Scott despises, insults, and beats a Southern white woman with whom he has had sexual relations is perhaps surprising, but it also becomes apparent that he has previously had homosexual relations with a white man originally from Alabama. This white man, Eric Jones, has already been in France for two years at the time Rufus Scott has his unfortunate affair with Leona. One might even wonder whether it is out of spite for Eric Jones that Rufus makes Leona suffer so much. For if Eric is a homosexual, he has not yet found a person deserving his complete attention. At least such was his case before he left the United States, because he has now met a young twenty-one-year-old Frenchman, Yves, with whom he is in love. Two years earlier, when he was twenty-nine, Eric had loved Rufus for both natural and personal reasons. Son of a rich banker, he had had his first homosexual adventure at the age of sixteen with a young black, Le Roy, nineteen years old. He had even, as early as age ten, been attracted to Henry, the husband of his parents' black cook. His parents had put an end to the matter by firing the two domestics. It was the life-style he had experienced and practiced that had enabled him, after a certain time, to give free rein to his natural tendencies. He saw his parents only very seldom, and the racial taboos of the South had seemed to him forbidden and tempting fruit.

In his homosexual relations with Eric, Rufus thought he had discovered a true and brotherly love. But Eric's departure for France had dissipated those ideas and left Rufus in a state of great confusion. Although he knows that neither Eric nor Leona has any trace of the racist attitudes of the Southern whites, Rufus Scott refuses to accept the idea that these two individuals are exceptions to the rule. One should perhaps understand his homosexuality as a deep and intense desire to return to a state of pure innocence which would place him above America's social, racial, and sexual norms. After Eric's departure, Rufus Scott must face reality alone. Although he has some very good white friends, such as Vivaldo, Cass Silenski, and Richard Silenski, he hates and despises the white race which is the cause of all his ills. His relations with Leona are affected by the world around them, which will triumph over them and their love.

Vivaldo does all he can to save his friend from the despair and the hate that are devouring him. But all his attempts will be futile. It is white society and its destructive prejudices that drive Rufus to suicide. It is evident that it has destroyed all the human relationships established by this young man whose only mistake is to be black. Numerous critics have said that Rufus's suicide had no reason and that his death was a mystery. Saunders Redding writes that this suicide cannot be explained and that Baldwin, in the person of Rufus, presents the typical image of the poor American Negro who hates himself and who, by committing suicide, does exactly what whites expect of him.[11] If one takes into account the events surrounding Rufus's life, one can see that his suicide has a clear meaning. Thus it would seem that he commits suicide because, on the one hand, he cannot go on living in loneliness and because, on the other, love threatens his independence and his freedom of movement in a society that he hates. Torn between those two choices, Rufus decides simply to take his own life.

Rufus Scott's love affairs are interesting because they reflect his sad condition. But the people he knows, and for whom he plays an important role in the novel, do not forget him after his disappearance. Without him, all these people would be unaware of one another's existence. Thus, for example, one month after his suicide, Ida meets Cass and Richard Silenski for the first time. The Silenskis have known Vivaldo for a long time, since Richard had been Vivaldo's high school English teacher. Through Vivaldo, they had met Rufus. Vivaldo and Richard, who are about ten years apart, are both writers. This element plays an important role in Another Country since the conjugal life of the Silenskis will be destroyed by Richard's attitude toward his novel, and since Vivaldo will develop an intense relationship with

Ida. After nearly fifteen years of hard labor, Richard has just finished a dubious novel that is nevertheless going to bring him instant success. Vivaldo, on the other hand, at the age of twenty-nine, is still writing a novel started twelve years earlier. It is clear that Vivaldo, unlike Richard, is eager to produce a respectable work and that he is ready to do anything necessary to achieve that end. Ida made it clear to him that she expected a great deal from him and that she left him no choice in the matter.

It is the memory of Rufus and of the close relations he had always maintained with them that lead Ida and Vivaldo at first to want to know each other better and then to fall in love. Although there may be a situation made dangerous by its racial aspect, Vivaldo and Ida are the only people in the novel with a positive future. Baldwin's aim in this work is clear, since he shows that a sincere and reciprocal love can always triumph over destructive adversities. Ida's affair with Steve Ellis, an important television personality, is a typical example, even if Vivaldo must suffer from it for some time. Steve Ellis is first interested in Ida because he recognizes her excellent singing talents. Seeing an opportunity to ensure a brilliant career for herself, Ida does not hesitate to give herself to him. But she will quickly realize the total lack of a future, and especially of love, in a relationship with a man who is married and who is as well known as Steve Ellis. In addition -- unlike Vivaldo, who is ready to do everything for her, Steve constantly reminds her that he is white and that she is black. It is that brief affair with Steve Ellis that enables Ida to discover the sincerity of the feelings that Vivaldo shows towards her. She will confess everything in order to be understood and to receive an unreserved pardon. Their love will reemerge stronger than ever. Baldwin indicates here that conjugal life would be possible.

If Ida's sincere confessions enable Vivaldo to love her better, those that Cass makes to her husband, on the contrary, lead to disunion and divorce. It is Richard Silenski's blind and relentless work on his novel that drives his wife to seek affection and tenderness in Eric's arms on his return from France. This novel, <u>The Strangled Men</u>, is mediocre and sacrifices the author's integrity for the benefit of a quick success. Cass, who is thirty-four years old and who has always trusted her husband, feels suddenly betrayed and even deceived by a person that she thought she knew. It is out of contempt for him that she decides to give herself to Eric. Cass comes from a rich New England Anglo-Saxon family, whereas her husband is the son of a poor Polish immigrant. This last detail explains perhaps the reason why Richard Silenski prefers to assure himself success and wealth as quickly as possible. He must perhaps remember the difficulties encountered by his father who, in his trade as a carpenter, struggled to avoid poverty and destitution.

But this is not a sufficient reason to explain Richard Silenski's literary cowardice. Vivaldo, who has also known destitution and poverty, is the first to criticize his former teacher's novel. It is evident that Richard Silenski has not accepted the world around him, and that he thinks that rapid and expeditious means are right and sufficient in order to achieve a profitable end. This attitude goes against the principles of Vivaldo who, by accepting himself, has found peace of mind and success as an artist. This has also enabled him to accept Ida as she is, without wanting to reject her after her brief affair with Steve Ellis. It is especially by accepting reality that Vivaldo can accept Ida.

On several occasions in the novel, Bessie Smith's voice is heard. That queen of the blues has always had a special meaning for Baldwin, for her blues reflect everyday reality for the American black. Baldwin wishes to give these blues a special meaning since it is the memory of Rufus Scott that haunts the novel and since he is the very type of the black man destroyed by a world that never wanted him.

Before leaving the United States for France, Eric had homosexual relations with Rufus. Two years later, upon his return to New York, all those who had known Rufus invite him nonetheless to come to meet him. He does not hide the fact that Yves is soon coming to rejoin him. In the meantime, Cass and then Vivaldo have sexual relations with him. We have already seen that for Cass, it is especially the contempt that she feels for her husband that drives her towards Eric. One could even say that there is something else; for Eric is a very good actor and he has been chosen to perform in a play, Happy Hunting Ground, which is to be presented in a Broadway theater. One may wonder to what extent Cass would be interested in any man whatsoever who is aware of his professional responsibilities. This is not the case at all with her husband. As for Vivaldo, it is especially the memory of Rufus that drives him into Eric's arms. Ida does not like Eric; she knows that he was the cause of her brother's suicide. In addition, she cannot understand the fact that he has consented to have an affair with Cass who is married and the mother of two children. It is clear that Ida has very fixed ideas, which affect her relations with Vivaldo. One might even suggest that Vivaldo makes love to Eric in order to be closer to Ida, for at this point, she has not yet told him the truth about her affair with Steve Ellis.

It emerges from all those homosexual, heterosexual, and bisexual affairs that Eric is the epitome of the universal lover since he is the living link between all those who have known Rufus and also between whites and blacks, men and women.

Just like Baldwin, Eric Jones is back in New York after having spent a few years in France. France is that other country about which Rufus dreamed so much. This autobiographical element contributed to the success of the novel. In effect, Eric Jones, like Baldwin, accepted himself in France and decided to come back to America in order to face a reality he knows only too well.

This reality includes a human truth that man, whatever he may be, must accept under penalty of losing everything he has. Eric is a homosexual and he does not conceal it. Before doing anything whatsoever with Cass Silenski, he tells her about Yves in order to make her understand well that their affair will have no future and that she will have to suffer the consequences. It is that truth which makes Richard Silenski, when he learns that his wife has been unfaithful to him with Eric, decide to leave her and to suspect Vivaldo of being the cause of everything. Even if his literary success was immediate and lucrative, Richard Silenski is jealous of Vivaldo. He knows that he has betrayed his own literary principles, and all those who had confidence in him, by publishing a mediocre novel. It is the remorse which haunts him that prevents him from under- standing his wife's acts and from forgiving her for them. His decision not to live with her any longer could, to a certain extent, be interpreted as a punishment imposed on himself by himself because of his cowardice as an artist and the personal failure he feels. It is even ironic to note that this truth enables Vivaldo to show Ida how much he loves and trusts her. In other words, Cass Silenski's frank confessions bring about the destruction of his marriage, whereas those of Ida reinforce the ties already established with Vivaldo.

In Another Country there is a clear contrast between love and the alienation of hearts. But in addition to human feelings, Baldwin especially wants to describe a situation that is dear to him since it concerns America. In this novel, the black's condition, as it is seen through Rufus Scott, is the very metaphor of the human condition. This fact makes one reflect on the future of American society and think that, perhaps, only frankness and sincerity will enable white and black Americans to understand and respect one another better. In Another Country, the freedom of the characters in their loves and in their sexual relations indicates that, for the author, there exists a good starting point that could lead towards a better future. Or at least it seems to suggest a complete reshaping of the very foundations and norms of the puritanical American society. Without a radical change, the future of American society and its racial issue is far from encouraging.

TODAY AND TOMORROW

The American black of today can assert his rights as a full citizen in several ways if one takes into account that he has a past all his own and typically American. His personality, his language, his very life-style reflect a long history that he alone can understand. This apprenticeship is unique in its kind, since it was accomplished on soil that never wanted him and which has done everything to destroy him.

From this experience, it ensued that American blacks created and developed a way of life which was to enable them to survive in a hostile world. Most blacks who live today in the large Northern centers began to leave the South only during the 1920s. It is not surprising that their children and grandchildren continue to mistrust the world around them since they know that, in the North as well as in the South, everything is hostile to them. The South holds a special place in the heart of all blacks, especially those in the North for whom the South represents the very cradle of their culture and their tumultuous past. It was there that the African slave formed himself a new identity by seeking refuge and comfort in a religion with a profound meaning. The black church has always served as a guide for the fearful and helpless souls of millions of American blacks. Religion is a way of life for Southern blacks; without it life has no meaning. Outside of the black church and its numerous activities, the black finds himself constantly in conflict with the white world. The Southern black communities can easily do without the white world, for they are often important enough to be self-sufficient. They have made it possible to preserve with pride the traditions and customs of black ancestors and, especially, to safeguard that typical manner of speech of the Southern black. This language, to a great extent, reflects the mentality of the black careful not to provoke the white by presenting an image to him of a humble and servile individual. That is now the attitude of the vast majority of Southern blacks, since the end of the civil rights movements in the sixties. As for the black communities in the North, the situation is slightly different since we are dealing with ghettos and since the individual is constantly struggling to survive. But there again, the South still exerts its appeal as the native land, but without having the strong influence that it has on those who still inhabit its lands.

In the North, the black can have all the freedom he desires, whereas in the South his actions are constantly controlled by the community to which he belongs. In other words, the Southern black is protected by the group to which he belongs while in the North he is at the mercy of all, blacks or whites. In "Come Out the Wilderness," which appeared for the first time in 1958 and was published later in Going to Meet the Man, Baldwin talks about a young Southern black woman, Ruth Bowman, who has lived in New York for several years.[12] The title of this story has a special meaning, for we are dealing with a young woman in search of herself following disappointing love affairs and other experiences. Ruth Bowman is twenty-six years old and works as a secretary for an insurance company in Manhattan. She lives in Greenwich Village, in a small apartment which she shares with an unemployed white painter, Paul. He is interested in Ruth only for what she can offer him from a material viewpoint. Their affair is coming to an end, and Ruth no longer knows how to conduct herself with her white lover and the people with whom she works. One must understand that she is from the South and that the white world has always exerted a strong influence upon her. Her parents, like the majority of Southern blacks, live in a religious atmosphere sheltered from the direct and evil action of whites. They have always done their best to protect and counsel their daughter well. But Ruth has constantly been prone to go against their wishes and their hopes.

When she was barely seventeen years old, her brother had caught her in a barn with a boy. Since that time, and although she repeated that she had done nothing wrong, her family had treated her like an impure being. For her family, the sex act was a sacred thing that only marriage could sanction. This situation had driven her, some time later, to go live with a black musician twenty years her senior. A few months later, they had gone to New York, where their affair had ended. Since she found herself in a white environment, deprived of her parents' protection, Ruth had given free vent to her instincts by sleeping with several white men. That is how she ended up living with Paul, in whom she saw more a worthy representative of the white race than an imperfect individual.

In this story, Baldwin presents, deliberately, a striking contrast between the rigid and even harsh life of the black in the South and that, totally free, of the black in the North. Or at least he tries to show the rapidity with which, far from the restrictions of his native South, a black can change. Although Ruth's conduct, when she lived in the South, indicated the life-style she would have later, Baldwin wishes to stress that the atmosphere in the North is conducive to the free development of her desires. Quite obviously, she is fascinated by the white world with which she is constantly in contact. But, especially, she is eager, at all costs, to be as close as possible to that world. This explains, on the one hand, her deep hatred of Paul the human being and, on the other, the intense desire to be with him because of the race he represents. It would thus seem that she is trying to assert her human rights by using solely the color of her skin. This attitude would explain her numerous, but brief, affairs with several whites. The latter see in her only a black woman of whom they can take advantage.

At the end of the story, a young unmarried thirty-two-year-old black man, Mr. Davis, a high-ranking person in the insurance company, becomes interested in Ruth. The interest she shows in him comes rather from despair than from an emerging love. Here Baldwin indicates that the individual cannot shed his race and forget it. This story marks the change that Baldwin's work underwent when his literary interests assumed a more social aspect. What he wants to bring to light is that black and white Americans have the same rights and that the future can only recognize that state of affairs. That is perhaps why he chose the evocative title of "Come Out the Wilderness" for this short story.

Although he understands whites in his country, Baldwin is nonetheless black and proud to be so. This is what enabled him, in the sixties, to speak in the name of blacks and explain their demands to the American white mass. In other words, he played the role of mediator between two groups who hated and feared each other. Already at that time, he had declared on several occasions that this type of social role scarcely permitted him to fulfill his obligations as an artist and as a writer. But this new experience enabled him to develop a certain respect for those of the whites who have the honesty to admit their prejudices towards blacks. Most of the time, this attitude is accompanied by the sincere wish to change a dangerous situation. Thus Baldwin has always been on very good terms with Jewish American writers, such as Norman Podhoretz, who have never tried to hide their prejudices towards blacks. This attitude, according to Baldwin, is encouraging since those people feel the deep desire to change themselves. In the fourth part of Nothing Personal, the author speaks of generations to come and of the responsibilities that the American of today must have towards them.[13] For Baldwin, the white will not be happy as long as the black is mistreated. With violence yielding here to reason, Baldwin believes that there still remains a hope and that, however weak it may be, America must place its trust in it.

This idea is more detailed and is made more concrete in <u>Blues for Mister Charlie</u>.[14] In this play, American blacks are determined to do everything in order to be treated on an equal footing with whites. The action takes place in a small Southern town, Plaguetown, in which 44 percent of the population is black. The main character, Richard Henry, is murdered at the beginning of the play by a white man, Lyle Britten, who has already killed a black man and who does not hide his hatred for people of that race. In flashbacks the author succeeds in explaining why Richard is murdered and the serious consequences that this death has on Plaguetown. The name of this city was chosen by Baldwin with a precise aim in view for, according to him, the races and the Christian religion are similar to the plague which blindly destroys lives and human relations. That is at least what he says in the introduction to this three-act play which especially highlights the abyss that separates blacks and whites in Plaguetown. In this same introduction, Baldwin declares that his play is more or less based on the circumstances that had surrounded the death of the young fourteen-year-old black boy visiting Mississippi, Emmett Till, savagely murdered in 1955 for having whistled at a white woman in the street. Eight years later, in June 1963, Medgar Evers, a very good friend of Baldwin's, was also assassinated in the state of Mississippi. It was that brutal death especially that persuaded Baldwin to finish <u>Blues for Mister Charlie</u>, begun in 1958.

Although doubting his own talents as a playwright, Baldwin's sole desire is that this play will help future generations to understand better the mistakes of those that have preceded them. According to the author, in effect, the generation of today has no hope of achieving positive results as far as race relations are concerned. Only the descendants of this generation, whites and blacks, will be able to nourish the hope of building a new society devoid of racial prejudices. One can even say that Baldwin, in addition to his optimism for the future of civil rights, hopes that Afro-American literature, no matter how young and hesitant it may be today, will occupy an honorable place in America. Whence this place which the author, like a challenge, throws into the face of his country, always suspicious of everything that emanates from the black world.

This play deals with racism in America and presents a situation that is both dangerous and without a solution. That is not surprising when one considers the author's pessimistic attitude. For today's American, <u>Blues for Mister Charlie</u> offers no hope and, consequently, the feeling experienced is that of discouragement. To a great extent, this play presents a precise racial situation and fuels the passions that usually accompany such a situation. According to Baldwin, only the generations to come will be able to enjoy a humane and egalitarian atmosphere, for today's blacks and whites have already made one another suffer too much to be able to try to understand one another. In other words, today's generation has been abandoned to its depressing fate. This does not mean that Baldwin does

not think of the future of his country and of the various means of making it
better; he has said on several occasions that, if it wanted to avoid an
imminent catastrophe, America should courageously analyze itself in order
to change. It is this change, dear to Baldwin, and without which America
is doomed to its ruin, that Americans of tomorrow will experience.

In the introduction to Blues for Mister Charlie, Baldwin does not attempt
to hide his feelings about the contemporary American theater. These
feelings are negative since, until now, the American black has always
played a secondary role in it. For the author, every social and racial
change in America must also make itself felt in its literature. This change
cannot take place overnight or even within a generation in which blacks and
whites do not trust one another. According to Baldwin, the hope of a better
day lies in the future. That is what he implies in his play.

Blues for Mister Charlie presents a racial situation that is tense and
filled with dangers. In the first two acts, the action takes place in the month
of August and explains in detail how and why young Richard Henry is
murdered by Lyle Britten. In the third act, which takes place two months
later, we attend Lyle Britten's trial. This last act has a special meaning, for
it is in a segregationist atmosphere filled with hate and distrust that blacks
and whites wait for the verdict to be pronounced concerning Lyle Britten's
murderous act.

The sole fact that Britten is declared innocent by a white jury indicates
that the situation of blacks in Plaguetown has scarcely any hope of
changing in the near future. The first two acts take place in the black
church, whereas the third act is set in the hall of justice. But, at the black
church as well as at the hall of justice, it is especially through flashbacks
that Baldwin is able to explain the actions and words of his characters.
That is the way we learn that Richard Henry had left the South eight years
earlier, at the age of fourteen, to go to New York. That unexpected
departure had been caused by the sudden death of his mother, who had
succumbed to the after-effects of a mysterious fall on the stairs of a white
hotel. Convinced that his mother had been pushed by a white man who
had made advances at her, Richard, rather than allow himself to be blinded
by anger, had preferred to leave. Since he was the son of the black
minister, Meridian Henry, of the city and since he understood that any
irrational act could endanger the very life of the black community of
Plaguetown, Richard Henry had taken refuge in the home of an aunt who
lived in Harlem.

The first three years spent in the North had enabled him to discover
himself and to develop talents as a singer and a musician. But the last five
years had been ruined by drugs and prison which, in fact, had put an end
to a promising career. These last few years spent far from the South had
enabled him to know the white world better and to stop fearing it. Besides,
he had violated one of the most sacred rules of the South by sleeping with
several white women. Thus Richard's return to his hometown is surprising
for him and for those who have never left the South and who, consequently,
have not enjoyed the freedom of the North. In addition, Richard is no

longer accustomed to the rigidity of the Southern segregationist laws. This is what allows Baldwin to bring out the striking contrast between Richard's personality and his father's much more conservative one. Both represent two different and very divergent attitudes towards the white world. In the person of Richard, we have the typical image of the Northern black, impatient and fiery, anxious to be treated with respect by whites.

Unfortunately, for Richard, Southern whites have no intention at all of treating him as well as those in the North. At the age of twenty-two, he is already embittered by a life and experience that have made him suffer mentally and physically. Deep down inside, he knows well that he came back to the South because he no longer hopes for anything from the future. Or at least one can say that he came back to his people in order to care for his wounds. No matter what his characters do, or what the situation may be, Baldwin always manages to make segregation and white superiority reign supreme. Thus during Lyle Britten's trial, the reader or the spectator is constantly aware of the physical aspect of segregation; we have the whites on one side of the room and the blacks on the other. Besides -- something that has always offended American blacks when one of theirs is judged -- the jurors are all white.

In this play, Baldwin presents a situation as real as possible, which leaves no room for the hope of a better world for the time being. This play is the very portrait of human cruelty and oppression. It contributes to sustaining the indignity of the racial conflict in America. That is why numerous critics have declared that Blues for Mister Charlie was a lamentable play with no reason for being. One must remember here that the author's idea is to relate facts as they would be in reality, with true feelings. In addition, one must understand that this play does not wish to offer any solution to the racial problem, which is itself, for the time being, without a solution. The author clearly indicates that only the future and new generations will be able to bring some changes to this dilemma.

If Blues for Mister Charlie offers no solution to the racial problem which America faces today, Baldwin is trusting in a better future when he speaks of the descendants of Richard Henry and Lyle Britten. And this is the very basis of the existence of future American generations.

Thus, some time after his return to Plaguetown, Richard meets a childhood friend, Juanita, two years his junior, and falls in love with her. After his death, Juanita hopes with all her heart that she is pregnant and will bear the son that he perhaps has given her during their passionate nights of love. Juanita is a determined girl with a firm character. At the time Richard makes his reappearance in Plaguetown, she has already taken part in several civil rights demonstrations which, unfortunately, came to nothing. That is perhaps because Juanita and her friends, since they are from the South and have never known other environments, know when and where to stop before provoking the anger of whites.

This is not at all true of Richard, who has completely forgotten how to behave with Southern whites. After having been warned about Lyle Britten, Richard decides to provoke him. He goes to his little store, which the blacks are boycotting, and frightens his young wife, Jo. This situation is all the more dangerous since one knows that Lyle Britten has already killed one black, Bill Walker, who opposed his having sexual relations with his young wife, Willa Mae. In any case, it is especially Richard's arrogant and courageous attitude that provokes the rage of Lyle Britten, accustomed to seeing only humility and stupidity in blacks.

If Richard and Lyle Britten's worlds are blinded by prejudices filled with hate, there is one white, Parnell Jones, who tries to aid and understand blacks in Plaguetown. Editor of the local newspaper and son of a respectable family of the city, he is a very good friend of Lyle Britten and is even his young son's godfather. This does not prevent him from seeing his friend's dangerous attitude towards blacks and trying to change or, at least, to improve that situation. Thus he arranges for a warrant to be issued for the arrest of Lyle Britten, shortly after Richard's death, although nothing can be proved. Since he is from Plaguetown, and since he knows his friend well, Parnell has good reason for acting in this manner; Lyle Britten has confessed his crime to him.

Although they realize the effort that Parnell makes in order to help them, the blacks of Plaguetown are intrigued by his attitude. In fact, they do not really know what game he is playing, and that is the reason they are always inclined to doubt him; that is especially the attitude of the young blacks of Juanita's age. The old black generation, represented by Meridian Henry and his mother, Mother Henry, is afraid of provoking the anger of whites by refusing them anything whatsoever or by even doubting their so-called good intentions. Parnell's behavior is explained by the fact that, when he was younger, he had fallen in love with Pearl, a black woman. He told Lyle and Jo Britten about that love affair. Pearl's mother, a maid at Parnell's parents' home, had put an end to the matter by sending her daughter off to the home of some relatives in another city.

Since he was never able to be with the one he loved, one may wonder whether Parnell is seeking a compensation with people of the black race. Baldwin implies that, from a sexual viewpoint, whites are inferior to blacks. Parnell and Lyle had love affairs with black women that strongly influenced their lives. In any case, it is clear that white women are not sufficient for them. Thus, and although he has a white fiancée, Loretta, Parnell does not hide the fact that he is still in love with that black woman he met a few years before.

As soon as he arrives in Plaguetown, Richard tells his grandmother and his father that he has a pistol. He even asks his father to put it in a safe place. After his murder, and when they must appear for Lyle Britten's trial, Meridian Henry and Mother Henry deny knowing anything whatsoever about the firearm. This lie is all the more symbolic since the pistol is hidden under the minister's Bible in his church. This will not prevent the court from acquitting Lyle Britten, for during the entire trial, disproportionate emphasis is placed on the dangerously sexual aspect of Richard Henry's attitude towards Jo Britten. That attitude, of course, would explain Lyle's act as self-defense: he who would have killed Richard in order to avenge, or protect, his wife's honor and virtue. We are in the South, where the white man does not tolerate his wife's being insulted by the black man.

If Meridian Henry and his mother lie during Lyle's trial, they do so with full knowledge of the facts. The American black has always used the Christian religion in order to protect himself from the ravages of the white world. As soon as they learn that Lyle is going to be arrested and judged for the murder of a black man, the whites of Plaguetown do not hesitate to come to offer him aid and moral support. Among those is a minister, the Reverend Phelps, who uses the Christian religion in order to preach hatred and violence against blacks. Thus, from the human as well as the religious point of view, the immediate future of this little Southern town is hopeless. The title of this play, Blues for Mister Charlie, shows nonetheless the trust that today's black has in his future. Mister Charlie is the white man in general, or Lyle Britten in particular, and the blues that the black man sings for him is a monotonous chant filled with sorrow and hope. One might even say that this blues emanates from the tortured soul of Richard Henry and that it is time that Mister Charlie realized the enormity and the gravity of his mistakes with regard to the black race. The son that Juanita is hoping to carry would find himself, if born, in the same situation as young John Grimes of Go Tell It on the Mountain.[15] In both cases, the two fathers are named Richard and die a violent death before their son's birth. It would perhaps be surprising to think that Baldwin always wished he had had such a natural father. His stepfather was far from resembling the character named Richard Henry.

If Richard's death contributes nothing to people of his race, it does exert a strong influence on Parnell. The latter is led to examine himself because of a tragic situation for which he feels partly responsible. Or at least, being white and well known by all the inhabitants of Plaguetown, he decides simply to do his best to improve race relations in his hometown. Blues for Mister Charlie is a realistic drama in which human inequality, discrimination, and prejudices occupy an important place.

Richard Henry, just like Bigger Thomas, dies in revolt. This sterility in protest indicates that Baldwin has taken the same road as Richard Wright. It is evident that there is in this play an inevitable conflict between Baldwin the writer and Baldwin the black spokesman. The theater lends itself very well to the explanation of a human situation in which a black minority group wishes to assert its rights and formulate its demands.

NOTES

1. James Baldwin, The Fire Next Time (New York: The Dial Press, 1963). Previously published as "Letter from a Region in My Mind," The New Yorker, November 17, 1962, pp. 59-144, and "A Letter to My Nephew," The Progressive 26 (December 1962): 19-20.

2. James Baldwin, "My Dungeon Shook: Letter to My Nephew on the One Hundredth Anniversary of the Emancipation," in his The Fire Next Time (New York: Dell Publishing Co., 1964), pp. 13-22. (Appeared for the first time under the title of "A Letter to My Nephew," pp. 19-20.)

3. James Baldwin, "How Can We Get the Black People to Cool It?" *Esquire*, July 1968, p. 349.

4. James Baldwin, Notes of a Native Son (Boston: Beacon Press, 1955). James Baldwin, Nobody Knows My Name (New York: The Dial Press, 1961).

5. James Baldwin, "Previous Condition," in his Going to Meet the Man (New York: The Dial Press, 1965), pp. 83-100. Also published in Commentary 6 (October 1948): 334-342.

6. James Baldwin, "The Dangerous Road Before Martin Luther King," Harper's Magazine 222 (February 1961): 33-42.

7. James Baldwin, "Going to Meet the Man," in his Going to Meet the Man, pp. 229-249.

8. Richard Wright, "Big Boy Leaves Home," in Alfred Kreymborg et al., eds., The New Caravan (New York: W. W. Norton and Co., 1936), pp. 124-158. Also in his Uncle Tom's Children (New York: Harper and Row, 1965), pp. 17-53.

9. James Baldwin, "Down at the Cross: Letter from a Region in My Mind," in his The Fire Next Time (New York: Dell Publishing Co., 1964), pp. 27-141. (Appeared for the first time under the title of "Letter From a Region in My Mind," pp. 59-144.)

10. James Baldwin, Another Country (New York: The Dial Press, 1962).

11. Saunders Redding, "The Problems of the Negro Writer," Massachusetts Review 6 (Autumn-Winter 1964-1965): 68.

12. James Baldwin, "Come Out the Wilderness," Mademoiselle 46 (March 1958): 102-104, 146-154. Also published in his Going to Meet the Man, pp. 197-225.

13. James Baldwin, Nothing Personal (Harmondsworth, England: Penguin Books, 1964).

14. James Baldwin, Blues for Mister Charlie (New York: The Dial Press, 1964).

15. James Baldwin, Go Tell It on the Mountain (New York: Alfred A. Knopf, 1953).

10

CONCLUSION

From this study of James Baldwin, there emerged four essential points that deserve to be discussed in detail. First of all, sexuality plays a distinctive role in his characters. Next, and through his characters, the author establishes special relationships with the world around him. Then, seeing himself caught between the white world and the black world, Baldwin no longer seems to know what role to play. It is here that one might doubt his ultimate value as a writer. Finally, aware of his social responsibilities, the author tried to envisage several solutions in order to resolve the American racial problem. One is inclined here to wonder whether he truly succeeded in the role of a prophet.

The men described in Baldwin's work are rarely comfortable and happy when they have normal relations with the female sex. It would seem that the fear of reality incites them to remain virgins or, at least, to have sexual relations only with the male sex. Homosexuality occupies an important place in Baldwin's work. John Grimes in <u>Go Tell It on the Mountain</u>, David in <u>Giovanni's Room</u>, Yves and Eric in <u>Another Country</u> have almost no heterosexual relationships.[1] It seems clear that in the imaginary world, perhaps real, of Baldwin, it is better to be a homosexual. This situation is all the more interesting because there is no uniformity in the attitudes of these homosexuals towards themselves. If Eric accepts himself, David, on the other hand, tries by all means imaginable to hide his homosexuality. It is likely that, if they accepted all their sensuality and their sexuality, Baldwin's homosexuals could live better with those around them. In other words, the image that they would present would be more in harmony with the environment in which they live. For them, homosexuality is a sign of courage and virility. But for those who observe them from the outside, their behavior is purely homosexual. Elisha and John Grimes in <u>Go Tell It on the Mountain</u>, Giovanni and David in <u>Giovanni's Room</u>, and Leo Proudhammer and Christopher Hall in <u>Tell Me How Long the Train's Been Gone</u> are good examples of this.[2]

This fear, on Baldwin's part, of accepting homosexuality and of exposing it openly, indicates that the author is not sure of himself. He wishes nonetheless to have it play a distinctive and important role. In their heterosexual relations his characters suffer very much. This situation shows that Baldwin cannot go deeper into or enrich the theme of sexuality in his work because he is incapable of it.

In Baldwin's works, the real men, marked by a determined character, are destroyed by adversity and do not occupy much space in the narrative. Richard, in Go Tell It on the Mountain, commits suicide, in desperation at not being able to succeed in a white world that only wants his destruction. Rufus Scott, in Another Country, commits suicide for the same reason. Richard Henry, in Blues for Mister Charlie, is coldly murdered by a white man who insists on showing blacks that the white race intends to remain master of the situation.[3] Virility, as it is understood in the literal sense of the word, does not occupy an analogous place in Baldwin's work. It would seem that the author does not wish to recognize such a quality in the vast majority of the men he depicts. Especially if they are black.

One should establish a connection between the lack of virility that characterizes James Baldwin's black man and the manner in which the author tried to destroy Richard Wright's literary reputation. According to what has just been said, Baldwin's black man, in all probability, must submit to the white world if he does not want to be destroyed. This submission would explain, to some extent, this desire to live withdrawn into himself, far from reality, and also his homosexuality. Richard Wright's black man, on the other hand, is not afraid to face reality and is ready to do everything to protect and affirm his masculinity. Thus, not believing the black man capable of courage and firmness, Baldwin attempted everything in order to destroy Richard Wright and the all-powerful masculinity that pervades his work.[4] It is evident that James Baldwin and Richard Wright are very different and that their personality and their attitude in life influenced their works. But sexuality, and especially homosexuality, gave Baldwin's work an original form. This is what enabled him to establish both tense and close relations with the environment from which he came and, especially, the white world.

In his essays, his novels, his short stories, and his plays, Baldwin is constantly preoccupied with the ravages of the white world and the evil influence it has on blacks. He stresses that the Christian religion belongs to the white world and that it serves that world's sole interests. Thus, according to the author, the white world and the Christian Church must change their attitude towards the black if they wish to avoid an imminent catastrophe. This catastrophe, of course, would affect all the peoples of the earth. What Baldwin ardently desires is a radical change, and as rapid as possible, in the attitude of the white man towards the black man. He wishes above all to point out that, with time, the black man and his attitudes have changed and that these changes should change the attitude of the white man and of the Christian Church towards him. In addition, the Christian Church and the white world must restructure themselves; that, according to the author, is the most difficult thing to accomplish. What he hopes with all his heart is that the black man will be able to experience a completely different life-style in which prejudices, segregation, and contempt would no longer have any place. In order to achieve that goal, he recommends, for example, that black primary schools, high schools, and universities be granted greater autonomy, that the police assigned to patrol black neighborhoods consist only of blacks, and that segregation, rampant in American trade unions, as well as in large industries, be abolished. In short, the way of thinking and the very values of the United States should change completely.

Even if white policemen stopped patrolling within black neighborhoods, it would be necessary, according to Baldwin, for them to learn to know blacks better. The American white is afraid of the black man and always fears unforeseeable reactions on his part. This attitude explains, to a large extent, the violence and blindness with which whites react when a black says or does something original or unexpected.

In his oral and written statements made in the late sixties and the early seventies, Baldwin seemed to delight in the use of coarse and vulgar language. Believing, quite obviously, that it was the only means of making himself understood by the white world, the author, by the same token, did harm to his own reputation. This new way of expressing himself came from the fact that the black population had become aware of its powerful vitality and that Baldwin was doing everything that he would to be its most listened-to interpreter.

James Baldwin's work reflects almost faithfully the evolution of the racial situation in America during the fifties and sixties. Therefore, if during the fifties his approach was calm and objective, the one adopted in the sixties and in the early seventies shows that subjectivity and objectivity are mingled and that he has great difficulty remaining master of himself. The honesty he had so often displayed at the beginning of his career had practically disappeared his last works. One may wonder here whether Baldwin had abandoned all hope for his country or, at least, for white America.

The black author had always done his best to be frank and direct in dealing with the white race. His new attitude would seem to indicate that he was convinced that white America no longer wishes to listen to him. But did not always repeat that the racial future of America would lie in the single race descended from an amalgamation of all the races living on the American continent? Now, whites are not ready to accept this kind of idea; they loathe it. That is the reason Baldwin adopted such a pessimistic attitude.

One must hope that, in order to maintain and preserve good relations with white America, an author will be able to control his emotions and create himself an identity both new and special. Otherwise, the future will consist of innumerable thorny problems in which the racial questions and the American nation will be constantly in contradiction. Fifteen years separate the religious atmosphere and language of Go Tell It on the Mountain from the violence and the vulgarity of Tell Me How Long the

Train's Been Gone. Nonetheless, Baldwin was able to make good use of his experience and maturity in order to speak with assurance and courage to a white world that listened to him and understood him. If the fifteen years that separate these two novels mark an evolution in their author's thought, it would not be surprising if he had developed an attitude better corresponding to the needs of his country. He held an important position between American whites and blacks and had always played an active role within a society constantly torn apart by racial violence.

Baldwin's heavy social responsibilities towards America began to take up all his time and energy and even made his future as a writer and artist doubtful. Although he was an excellent essayist and a very good polemist, by the late seventies Baldwin no longer seemed to know how to define a novel. In Tell Me How Long the Train's Been Gone, there is a huge gap between the author's voice and his feelings, as they are described through Leo Proudhammer and Christopher Hall's militant attitude. In other words, Baldwin the artist and Baldwin the prophet seem, in this novel, to be two people very different from each other. Although Baldwin said he was above all a writer, not a black leader, one noted an inner conflict, indeed a double personality in the author. Thus, still in Tell Me How Long the Train's Been Gone, Baldwin is both a prophet of the racial apocalypse and an explorer of the secret nature of man. One could attempt to explain this position by saying that Baldwin describes and reflects in his entire work an American living in a world of illusions and daydreams. Baldwin's white man, just like the one in reality, is a schizophrenic, and the black man is simply a paranoiac. In other words, blindness and insanity are the two terms describing with precision the current state of American society in Baldwin's work.

Not wishing to remain at an impasse, James Baldwin attempts, in his novels and his short stories, to find a solution to the racial problem which afflicts America. Or at least, he puts into practice ideas already voiced in his essays. In Go Tell It on the Mountain, he tries to describe the deep and complex meaning of being black and living in Harlem. In Giovanni's Room, he attempts to explain love and give it a proper meaning. In Another Country, he shows that through a pure and free love a mutual and human understanding can exist. In addition, he indicates, in the person of Vivaldo, that the individual can, if he wishes, analyze himself, accept himself and, embark without preconditions on a well-defined course.

It is evident that, in his work, Baldwin always ends up in a human problem and that the racial question comes in second place. Therefore, the author considers himself above all American and hopes to win the hearts of his fellow-countrymen by using human arguments. This approach would perhaps lead one to think that James Baldwin is a traitor to his race and to himself, since the individual's humanity, according to him, comes before everything else. This attitude is important, for most of the time his public is predominantly white and not black. Certain blacks have even called him a modern-day Uncle Tom. At any rate, his ideas have always been the same and have represented the same contradictions since the appearance of The Fire Next Time.[5] One might wonder whether Baldwin really has anything else to say as a writer if one considers that he often speaks like a prophet. This role of a prophet, one knows, has never pleased him. He had told Robert Penn Warren so in 1964, while adding, nonetheless, that he believed firmly in the future of a total integration in the United States.[6] But, in the meantime, Baldwin wanted to be first of all a writer.

Six years later, in 1970, Baldwin was to declare to Margaret Mead that he no longer nourished any hope for racial integration in America since most of his friends, including Martin Luther King, Jr., had been killed.[7] He was also to tell her that living conditions in the United States were unacceptable for the American black.[8] That is the reason that, as early as 1970, Baldwin had returned to live in France, in more or less forced exile, in order to write without being disturbed and to preserve his reputation as a writer.

Certain isolated aspects of his work indicate nonetheless the role of a prophet and spokesman that he wanted to play for blacks. Thus, according to the ideas that emerge from Tell Me How Long the Train's Been Gone, Baldwin accepts himself as a representative of the black movement. In this novel, the emotions and the feelings experienced by Leo Proudhammer and Christopher Hall are those of the author.

James Baldwin used the novel in order to develop his personal ideas and in order to give free rein to his literary talents. The rest of his work, and more specifically his essays, helped him to discuss current problems and to speculate about the future of his country. This is what he does in The Fire Next Time, a powerful prophetic exhortation, in which he goes easily from the role of a critic to that of a prophet. But also in this book, the author uses protest in order to make himself understood. Thus, one can say that he cannot be seen, through his entire work, as a prophet of race relations in America.

A few years before the publication of The Fire Next Time, Baldwin had violently attacked anti-establishment literature. Today, he finds himself in the same situation in which Richard Wright found himself before his death. Baldwin had not hesitated then to criticize him openly for his protest attitude. That James Baldwin fell into protest is not surprising, especially if one takes into account the racial climate that has always prevailed in America. But that his voice as an anti-establishment prophet rose after Richard Wright's disappearance is surprising, since he offered no constructive solution to the racial problem that afflicts his country.

James Baldwin's revolt was much more violent and troubled than Richard Wright's. Thus, after he attacked the Christian Church, the black ghetto, the female sex, the white race, and the Christian god that it represents, one may wonder what object could still attract Baldwin's thunderbolts. The author seemed never to be satisfied and, unable to offer solutions to delicate problems, unleashed his anger on everything around him.

It would be mistaken to call this attitude merely negative. We have here a man aware of his social and artistic responsibilities who, in his desire to understand his surroundings better, demanded to have as much freedom as possible. The sole aim of this personal and especially independent attitude of Baldwin's was to respond better to the immediate and future needs of a country that was quite obviously dear to him.

NOTES

1. James Baldwin, Go Tell It on The Mountain (New York: Alfred A. Knopf, 1953); Giovanni's Room (New York: The Dial Press, 1956); Another Country (New York: The Dial Press, 1962).

2. James Baldwin, Tell Me How Long the Train's Been Gone (New York: The Dial Press, 1968).

3. James Baldwin, Blues for Mister Charlie (New York: The Dial Press, 1964).

4. Michel Fabre also rightly says that James Baldwin had tried to destroy Richard Wright because the latter had refused to accept him as a protégé and spiritual son. See Michel Fabre, "Pères et fils in Go Tell It on the Mountain, by James Baldwin," Etudes Anglaises 23 (January-March 1970): 47-61.

5. James Baldwin, The Fire Next Time (New York: The Dial Press, 1963).

6. Robert Penn Warren, Who Speaks for the Negro? (New York: Random House, 1965), p. 298 and p. 291.

7. Margaret Mead and James Baldwin, A Rap on Race (New York: J. B. Lippincott Co., 1971), p. 244.

8. A Rap on Race, p. 221.

GENERAL
CONCLUSION

From this study of the American racial problem, through the works of Richard Wright and James Baldwin, it emerges that the racial situation in America may be seen from two angles: literary and human.

As for the human side of the problem, Richard Wright was the precursor of the civil rights movements which swept through the United States in the sixties. Without his violent protest against the way blacks were treated in America, whites would perhaps not have become aware of the seriousness of their country's racial situation. In the tumult of the sixties, James Baldwin's role was to calm the spirits by preaching love and harmony between black and white Americans who, worried, had turned to him in order to understand what was going on. Without him, the situation could have been more serious than it was. Wright and Baldwin thus complement each other in the role they played to help American blacks have their rights as a full citizen recognized. The first raised a voice filled with anger whereas the second calmed the anger of all.

The fact that Baldwin resorted to protest in the late sixties does not change the role he played with Wright, for American blacks had then obtained to a great extent what they wanted. Whether it was a question of employment, and of numerous other domains of American life, whites had begun to recognize blacks for their personal merits and not out of fear of their color. In this sense, one can say that Richard Wright's work belongs to the past since everything, for him, revolved around the color of the individual. Baldwin was especially interested in the human aspect of the racial problem. He came back to the United States because he was trying to penetrate the secrets of human nature in race relations. On the other hand, for Wright, the atmosphere of the forties drove him to leave America. Since he could not say what he wished about his country's racial situation, Wright had to find a country in which he could express himself freely in order to combat American racism better.

In view of the reason that Richard Wright exiled himself to France, the human side of race relations in America may have a positive future if whites continue to meet the demands of blacks. Whites and blacks must work for the progressive disappearance of black ghettos. That will be possible through a school integration plan accepted by all so that whites and blacks will understand one another better. Little by little the prejudices of each will yield to mutual trust and respect. Whites will not only have to accept blacks as their equals, but also to recognize the existence of an Afro-American culture. That is what Richard Wright and James Baldwin always wished for.

However, the human side of race relations in America may have a negative future if blacks decide to have nothing to do with whites in order to protect their racial identity. The black's temperament is exuberant by nature and forms a striking contrast with the cold and serious one of the white ruling class: the white Anglo-Saxon Protestant.[1] An enormous abyss separates these two groups, and blacks often think that it would be better for them not to mix with whites through fear of losing their identity. That is why the history of the United States has always witnessed black movements favorable to a militant black nationalism. In the sixties, James Baldwin repeated constantly that if white America were unwilling to make concessions to blacks, the vast majority of blacks would end up letting themselves be carried away by a nationalist upsurge. The sudden popularity of Black Power clearly showed that Baldwin had been right.

If the racial situation was not as explosive during the seventies, the fact nonetheless remains that the white world and the black world still live apart in the same country. It was because of the civil rights movements of the sixties that the American black rediscovered his racial pride and realized that he can defend it. Richard Wright had encouraged such an attitude without, however, urging the black man to detach himself from American life.

The literary side of the American black problem is closely linked to its human aspect. It may have a positive future if whites and blacks display honesty in their works. This is what James Baldwin does. He tries to represent reality as it is while attentively studying it at the same time in order to highlight its most promising aspects. Thus his essays reflect a deep desire to see a united and strong America. Despite his doubts about racial integration in the United States, Richard Wright had also displayed such an honesty in The Outsider, in which the hero is in search of his identity.[2] But the fate reserved for Damon Cross seems to show that Wright preferred death rather than accept the role assigned to the black man by whites. Unlike Baldwin, who wants reason to dominate the literary work, Wright especially highlighted the absurdity of the black's condition. Wright's violence and his despair form a definite contrast to Baldwin's optimism. Nevertheless, the frankness with which Wright and Baldwin express their ideas sets their works within the same sphere because their inspiration is derived from the same source.

By saying with sincerity what they thought about the American racial problem through their works, Wright and Baldwin were hoping for a dialogue with white America. They wanted blacks and whites to get along. Like all American black writers before them, Wright and Baldwin were writing for white and black Americans. By drawing closer to the white world in order to make themselves understood better, Wright and Baldwin were becoming somewhat estranged from their black environment. They faced the danger of assimilation by the white culture.

That is why, in the sixties, LeRoi Jones reacted violently to this tendency of the black writer to want to write like whites. It is here that the literary side of the American black problem may have a negative future for, realizing that Afro-American culture risks getting lost in the American melting pot, the black writer could decide to write only for blacks. This black nationalism in literature is not good for the black writer; it does not allow him to give free rein to his sensitivity as an artist in all its forms. Thus the poetry of LeRoi Jones in Preface to a Twenty Volume Suicide Note is profound and filled with melancholy, whereas that which he presents eight years later in Black Magic uses surrealist forms expressed in the black dialect.[3] If black nationalism in literature enables blacks to be proud of their race and their culture, it provides no positive aspect for race relations in America since it contributes to keeping the cultural separation between blacks and whites even greater.

White American literature would have much to gain from the contribution of black literature, and, without getting completely lost in the American cultural melting pot, black literature could help American whites discover new forms of poetry and prose.   One may note that Jewish-American literature helped to enrich American literature without losing its special characteristics. No matter what happens, black literature has already marked American literature; both are closely linked, thanks to the works of writers like Wright and Baldwin.

This study of the American black problem through the works of Richard Wright and James Baldwin presents an important aspect because it is situated on a historical, social, and literary plane as well. During the forties and fifties, Wright emphasized in his works the crisis, fraught with anguish, of the American black who wished to affirm his existence. During the sixties Baldwin showed that he viewed the American racial problem as a human problem. Only brotherly love among Americans, he said, could resolve it. Richard Wright, on the other hand, never succeeded in finding any solution to the American black problem. At the time of his death, he was still searching for its underlying causes.

It would seem that the essential difference between Wright and Baldwin is the acceptance of oneself and one's environment. Wright never achieved this goal, whereas Baldwin attained it after staying a few years in France. They represent two general tendencies among American black writers. Thus, William Gardner Smith published a novel in 1963, The Stone Face, in which the hero goes to France and notices that racial prejudices are not peculiar to America.[4] This discovery permits him better to understand and to combat the behavior of American whites in dealing with blacks. But unlike Baldwin and Smith, the American black does not always need to exile himself for a certain period of time in order to accept himself. In Manchild in the Promised Land, which appeared in 1965, Claude Brown describes his childhood and adolescence in Harlem.[5] In this autobiography he wishes to show that if the individual hopes to succeed in a racist atmosphere, he must first accept himself as he is and accept reality as well. Incapable of such an attitude, Richard Wright took refuge abroad. Unable to endure racial prejudices in his country, the black writer Chester Himes also left the United States definitively some time after Wright's departure.

That the American black accepts his country in order to try later to change it does not mean that he risks losing his own culture at the hands of whites. After William Styron published The Confessions of Nat Turner in 1967, ten black writers reacted immediately by publishing William Styron's Nat Turner: Ten Black Writers Respond in 1968.[6] In their essays, these blacks unanimously say that William Styron is not qualified, either on the historical or the psychological level, to talk about Nat Turner. They even add that those confessions by a white man have nothing to do with those of a black. This reaction emphasizes that American black culture emanates from a people aware and proud of its past. In addition, it shows that black America does not intend to be represented or interpreted by whites. One might then wonder here whether the white man will ever succeed in understanding the black man and in gaining his acceptance.

James Baldwin praises William Styron's book because he saw in it proof of a reconciliation between blacks and whites. It is likely that, if he had been alive at the time the book appeared, Richard Wright would have condemned it as a flagrant example of white paternalism.

The works of Wright and Baldwin reflect the profound desire of the American black to be recognized as a full citizen by whites. If, during the sixties, the American Congress officially recognized that the black man was entitled to a place within American democracy, numerous whites are still reluctant to accept him as their equal. In their book Still a Dream: The Changing Status of Blacks Since 1960, published in 1975, Levitan, Johnston, and Taggart affirm that the situation of the American black has barely changed since 1960.[7] They also stress that the false prejudices of whites are the cause of such a situation. According to what Richard Wright said concerning the integration of the black into American society, it seems that white America will take many years to accept the black citizen. It is to be hoped that Richard Wright's cry of alarm and James Baldwin's words of love and understanding will accelerate the integration, thanks particularly to primary and secondary schools, where black and white children mingle freely with one another today.

NOTES

1. More commonly known by the name of WASPS.
2. Richard Wright, The Outsider (New York: Harper and Brothers, 1953).
3. LeRoi Jones, Preface to a Twenty Volume Suicide Note (New York: Totem Press, 1961); Black Magic (New York: The Bobs-Merrill Co., 1969).
4. William Gardner Smith, The Stone Face (New York: Farrar, Straus and Co.,

1963).

5. Claude Brown, Manchild in the Promised Land (New York: The Macmillan Co., 1965).

6. William Styron, The Confessions of Nat Turner (New York: Random House, 1967). John Henrik Clarke, ed., William Styron's Nat Turner: Ten Black Writers Respond (Boston: Beacon Press, 1968).

7. Sar A. Levitan, William B. Johnston, and Robert Taggart, Still6 a Dream: The Changing Status of Blacks Since 1960 (Cambridge, Massachusetts: Harvard University Press, 1975).

BIBLIOGRAPHY

WORKS BY RICHARD WRIGHT

ARTICLES

1935

"Joe Louis Uncovers Dynamite." New Masses, October 8, pp. 18-19.

1936

"Two Million Black Voices." New Masses, February 25, p. 15.

"A Tale of Folk Courage." Partisan Review and Anvil 3 (April): 31. Also published in Negro Digest 18 (December 1968): 51-52. (Review of Black Thunder by Arna Bontemps.)

1937

"Negro Writers Launch Literary Quarterly." Daily Worker, June 8, p. 7. (On New Challenge.)

"C P Leads Struggle for Freedom, Stachel Says". Daily Worker, August 9, p. 2.

"Huddie Ledbetter, Famous Negro Folk Artist, Sings the Songs of Scottsboro and His People." Daily Worker, August 12, p. 7.

"What Happens in a C P Branch Party Meeting in the Harlem Section." Daily Worker, August 16, p. 6.

"Born a Slave, She Recruits 5 Members of Communist Party." Daily Worker, August 30, p. 2.

"Horseplay' at Lafayette Fun for Children and Grown-ups Alike." Daily Worker, September 11, p. 7.

"Harlem Spanish Women Come out of the Kitchen." Daily Worker, September 20, p. 5.

"Between Laughter and Tears." New Masses, October 5, pp. 22, 25. (Review of These low Grounds by Waters Edward Turpin and of Their Eyes Were Watching God by Zora Neal Hurston.)

"Harlem East Side Honor Hero Who Died in Rescue of Negroes." Daily Worker, December 7, p. 4.

"Gouging, Landlord Discrimination against Negroes Bared at Hearing." Daily Worker, December 15, p. 6.

"Blueprint for Negro Writing." The New Challenge 2 (Fall): 53-65.

"The Ethics of Living Jim Crow: An Autobiographical Sketch." In American Stuff (Anthology of the Federal Writers' Project), pp. 39-52. New York: The Viking Press. Also published in Uncle Tom's Children: Five Long Stories. New York: Harper and Brothers 1940. (Constitutes an integral part of Black Boy: A Record of Childhood and Youth.)

1938

"High Tide in Harlem." New Masses, July 5, pp. 18-20.

"Portrait of Harlem." In New York Panorama, pp. 132-151. Prepared by the Federal
   Writers' Project of the Works Progress Administration of New York.
   New York: Random House. (Does not bear Richard Wright's name.)

1940

"How 'Bigger' Was Born." The Saturday Review of Literature 22 (June 1): 3-4, 17-20.
   Incomplete version of the lecture delivered at the Schomburg Collection
   of Harlem in March 1940. The text of that lecture was published in its
   entirety in July 1940 by Harper and Brothers in the form of a small
   thirty-nine-page book, bearing the same title. (This same text is
   included at the beginning of Native Son, pp. vii-xxxiv. New York:
   Harper and Row, 1966.)

"I Bite the Hand that Feeds Me: A Reply to David L. Cohn." Atlantic Monthly 155
   (June): 826-828.

1942

"What You Don't Know Won't Hurt You." Harper's Magazine 186 (December): 58-61.
   (Adventures of Richard Wright after his arrival in Chicago.)

1944

"I Tried to Be a Communist." The Atlantic Monthly, August, pp. 61-70; September, pp.
   48-56. Published in The God That Failed under the same title, pp.
   115-162. Edited by Richard H. S. Crossman. New York: Harper and
   Brothers, 1949. (Forms a sequel to Black Boy: A Record of Childhood
   and Youth.)

1945

"Gertrude Stein's Story Is Drenched in Hitler's Horrors." P M Magazine, March 11, p.
   m15. (Critique of Wars I Have Seen by Gertrude Stein.)

"A Non-Combat Soldier Strips Words for Action". P M Magazine, June 24, p. m16.
   (Review of The Brick Foxhole by Richard Brooks.)

"Is America Solving Its Race Problem?" America's Town Meeting of the Air Bulletin 11
   (May 24): 6-7. Also published in Negro Digest 3 (August): 42-44.

"Alger Revisited, or My Stars! Did We Read That Stuff?" P M Magazine, September
   16, p. m13. (Review of the novels of Horatio Alger.)

"American Hunger." Mademoiselle 21 (September): 164-165, 299-301. (Forms a
   sequel to Black Boy: A Record of Childhood and Youth.)

"Two Novels of the Crushing of Men, One White, One Black." P M Magazine
   November 25, pp. m7-m8. (Review of Focus by Arthur Miller and If He
   Hollers Let Him Go by Chester Himes.)

"Early Days in Chicago." In Cross Section, pp. 306-342. Prepared by Edwin Seaver.
   New York: L. B. Fischer Publishing Corporation. Published in Eight
   Men under the title of "The Man Who Went to Chicago." (Forms a
   sequel to Black Boy: A Record of Childhood and Youth).

"Introduction." In Drake, St. Clair, and Cayton, Horace R. Black Metropolis: A Study
   of Negro Life in a Northern City, pp. xvii- xxxiv. New York: Harcourt,
   Brace and Co.

1946

"Wasteland Uses Psychoanalysis Deftly." P M Magazine, 17 February, p. m.8. Review
   of Wasteland by Jo Sinclair [pseudonym of Ruth Seid].)

"American G.I.'s Fears Worry Gertrude Stein." P M Magazine, July 26, p. m15-m16. (Review of Brewsie and Willie by Gertrude Stein in the form of a letter addressed to Roger Pipett.)

"Psychiatry Comes to Harlem." Free World 12 (September): 49-51. Reprinted under the title of "Psychiatry Goes to Harlem." Twice A Year 14-15 (1946-47), 348-354.

"How Jim Crow Feels." True Magazine, November, pp. 25-27, 154-156. A shorter version also published under the same title in Negro Digest 5 (January 1947): 44-53. Published for the first time in French under the title of "Je sais reconnaître un nègre du Sud . . ." Paris Matin, June 27, 1946, p. 2. (Trip by Richard Wright to Mexico and to the Southern United States during the summer of 1940.)

1947

"E. M. Forster Anatomizes the Novel." P M Magazine, March 16, p. m3. (Review of Aspects of the Novel by E. M. Forster.)

"Lettre sur le problème noir aux U.S.A." Les Nouvelles Épîtres (Paris), letter 32, dated July 1, 1946. Reprinted under the title of "A World View of the American Negro." Twice a Year, 14-15 (1946-47): 346-348.

"Urban Misery in An American City: Juvenile Deliquency in Harlem." Twice A Year 14-15 (1946-47): 339-346.

"A Junker's Epic Novel on Militarism." P M Magazine, May 4, p. m3. (Review of The End Is Not Yet by Fritz Von Unruh.)

1948

"Littérature Noire Américaine." Les Temps Modernes 4 (August): 193-221. Richard Wright made slight revisions in this essay before including it in White Man, Listen! under the title of "The Literature of the Negro in the United States."

1951

"American Negroes in France." The Crisis, June-July, pp. 381-383.

"The Shame of Chicago." Ebony, December, pp. 24-32.

1953

"From Richard Wright." In The Flowers of Friendship, pp. 379-381. Prepared by Donald Clifford Gallup. New York: Alfred A. Knopf. (Letter addressed to Gertrude Stein dated May 27, 1945.)

1954

"What is Africa to Me?" Encounter 3 (September): 22-31. (Constitutes an integral part of Black Power: A Record of Reactions in a Land of Pathos.)

1956

"Foreword." In George Padmore. Pan-Africanism or Communism?: The Coming Struggle for Africa, pp. 11-14. London: Dennis Dobson. March 2, 1956. (Text revised and translated under the title of "Préface." Panafricanisme ou Communisme: La prochaine lutte pour l'Afrique, pp. 9-12. Paris: Éditions Présence Africaine, 1960. September 10, 1960.)

"Tradition and Industrialization: The Plight of the Tragic Elite in Africa." Présence Africaine 1 (June-November): 347-360. Richard Wright made slight revisions in this essay before including it in White Man, Listen! under the title of "Tradition and Industrialization: The Historic Meaning of the

Plight of the Tragic Elite in Asia and Africa."
"The Neuroses of Conquest." The Nation, October 20, pp. 330-331. (Review of Prospero and Caliban by Dominique Mannoni.)

1958

"Une pièce qui aurait ravi Voltaire . . . " L'Avant-Scène, February 15, pp. 3-4 (Introduction preceding Papa Bon Dieu by Louis Sapin.)

1959

"Spanish Snapshots: Granada, Seville." Two Cities 2 (July): 25-34.

1960

"The Voiceless Ones." Saturday Review, April 16, pp. 21-22. (Review of The Disinherited by Michel del Gastillo.)
"Entretien avec Richard Wright." L'Express, 18 August, pp. 22-23.
"Interview de Richard Wright, by Maurice Nadeau." In Fishbelly, (Translation of The Long Dream, pp. 9-15. Paris: Julliard.)

1961

"Le Jazz et le désir." Les Cahiers du Jazz 4 (Spring): 53-54. (Interview with Richard Wright a few days before his death.)
"Hommage ' Quincy Jones." Les Cahiers du Jazz 4 (Spring): pp. 55-57.
"Préface." In Gourdon, Françoise. Tant qu'il y aura la peur, pp. 9-13. Paris: Flammarion.

1968

"Personalism." In Webb, Constance. Richard Wright: A Biography, p. 138. New York: G. P. Putnam's Sons. (Passage from a lecture delivered in 1936.)
Richard Wright: Letters to Joe C. Brown. Prepared by Thomas Knipp. Kent, Ohio: Kent State University Libraries, Occasional Papers.

1971

"The American Problem -- Its Negro Phase." New Letters 38 (December): 9-16. (Written in the early 1950s. Published for the first time in New Letters.)
"Letter from Richard Wright." New Letters 38 (December): 125-127. (Letter addressed to Owen Dodson dated June 9, 1946.)

1972

"Bibliography on the Negro in Chicago, 1936." New Letters 39 (Fall): 68-75. (Written in 1936. Published for the first time in New Letters.)
"Ethnographical Aspects of Chicago's Black Belt." New Letters 39 (Fall): 61-68. (Written in 1936. Published for the first time in New Letters.)

ESSAYS
1941

Twelve Million Black Voices: A Folk History of the Negro in the United States. New York: The Viking Press. (Photographs by Edwin Rosskam and text by Richard Wright.)

1945

Black Boy: A Record of Childhood and Youth. New York: Harper and Brothers.

1954

Black Power: A Record of Reactions in a Land of Pathos. New York: Harper and
Brothers. Also published at Westport, Connecticut: Greenwood Press,
1974.

1956

The Color Curtain: A Report on the Bandung Conference. Cleveland and New York:
The World Publishing Co. First published in French under the title of
Bandoeng, 1.500.000.000 hommes. Paris: Calman-Lévy, 1955.

1957

Pagan Spain. New York: Harper and Brothers. White Man, Listen. New York:
Doubleday and Co., Inc. (This book includes the following essays:
"The Psychological Reactions of Oppressed People." "Tradition and
Industrialization: The Historic Meaning of the Plight of the Tragic Elite
in Asia and Africa," "The Literature of the Negro in the United States,"
and "The Miracle of Nationalism in the African Gold Coast.")

1977

American Hunger. New York: Harper and Row. (Forms a sequel to Black Boy. Aside
from a few short passages until now never published, the chapters of
the book have already been published in the following autobiographical
essays: "American Hunger," "Early Days in Chicago," and "I Tried to
Be a Communist.")

PLAYS

1941

Native Son, The Biography of a Young American. A Play in Ten Scenes. A play
composed with Paul Green. New York: Harper and Brothers.

1968

Daddy Goodness. Play presented on stage in New York in 1968 at the St. Mark's
Playhouse by the Negro Ensemble Company. (Details on the play are
furnished by the review by Edith Oliver published in The New Yorker,
June 15, p. 65.

POEMS

1934

"A Red Love Note." Left Front 3 (January-February): 3.
"Rest for the Weary." Left Front, no. 3 (January-February), p. 3.
"Child of the Dead and Forgotten Gods." The Anvil 5 (March-April): 30.
"Strength." The Anvil 5 (March-April, p. 20.
"Everywhere Burning Waters Rise." Left Front, no. 4 (May-June): 9.
"I Have Seen Black Hands." New Masses, June 26, p. 16.

1935

"Obsession." Midland Left 2 (February): p. 14.
"Rise and Live." Midland Left 2 (February): 13-14.
"Ah Feels It in Mah Bones." International Literature 4 (April): 80.
"I Am a Red Slogan." International Literature, 4 (April): 35.

"Red Leaves of Red Books." New Masses, April 30, p. 6.
"Between the World and Me." Partisan Review 2 (July-August): 18-19.
"Spread Your Sunrise!" New Masses, July 2, p. 26.

1936
"Transcontinental." International Literature 5 (January): 52-57.
"Hearst Headline Blues." New Masses, May 12, p. 14.
"Old Habit and New Love." New Masses, December 15, p. 29.

1937
"We of the Streets." New Masses, April 13, p. 14.

1939
"Red Clay Blues." New Masses, August 1, p. 14. (Poem composed with Langston
    Hughes.)

1941
"King Joe" ("Joe Louis Blues"). New York Amsterdam Star News, October 18, p. 16.
    Also published in New Letters 38 (December 1971): 42-45. (This blues
    was recorded on Okeh record no. 6475 in October 1941. The music is
    played by Count Basie's Orchestra and the words are sung by Paul
    Robeson.)

1949
"The F B Eye Blues." Blues in nine stanzas located in the library of S.U.N.Y. Buffalo.
    Also published in Richard Wright Reader, pp. 249-250. Edited by Ellen
    Wright and Michel Fabre. New York: Harper and Row, 1978. Written
    in 1949.)

HAIKU POEMS
1961
Harrington, Ollie. "The Last Days of Richard Wright." Ebony, February, pp. 92-93.
    Eight haiku poems. These eight poems have been published under the
    title of "Hokku Poems" in American Negro Poetry, pp. 104-105. Edited
    by Arna Bontemps. New York: Hill and Wang, 1963.

1968
Webb, Constance. Richard Wright: A Biography, pp. 393-394. New York: J. P.
    Putnam's Sons. Four new haiku poems.

1970
"Fourteen Haikus." Studies in Black Literature 1 (Fall): 1. Among the fourteen haiku
    poems published, only eleven of them are new.

1971
"Haiku." New Letters 38 (December): 100-101. Ten haiku poems. These poems are
    not new.

1973
Fabre, Michel. The Unfinished Quest of Richard Wright. pp. 506, 513. New York:
    William Morrow and Co. Four haiku poems. These poems are not new

1978

"Haikus." In Richard Wright Reader, pp. 251-254. Prepared by Wright, Ellen, and Fabre, Michel. New York: Harper and Row. Twenty-three haiku poems published so far.

NOVELS AND SHORT STORIES

1924

"The Voodoo of Hell's Half Acre." Southern Register (Jackson, Mississippi). A lost short story which appeared in three installments in the spring. Exact dates of publication unknown.

1931

"Superstition." Abbot's Monthly, April, pp. 45-47, 64-66, 72-73.

1936

"Big Boy Leaves Home." In The New Caravan, pp. 124-158. Edited by Alfred Kreymborg et al. New York: W. W. Norton and Co., Inc.

1937

"Silt." New Masses, 24 August, pp. 19-20. Published in Eight Men under the title of "The Man Who Saw the Flood."

1938

"Fire and Cloud." Story, March, pp. 9-41.

"Bright and Morning Star." New Masses, May 10, pp.97-99, 116-124. Published in the form of a small book bearing the same title. New York: International Publishers, 1941.

Uncle Tom's Children: Four Novellas. New York: Harper and Brothers. (The short stories included in this book are "Big Boy Leaves Home," "Down by the Riverside," "Long Black Song," and "Fire and Cloud.")

1940

"Almos' A Man." Harper's Bazaar, January pp. 40-41. (This short story represents the last two revised chapters of an autobiographical novel never published, "Tarbaby's Dawn," written between 1934 and 1937 and first entitled "Tarbaby's Sunrise". This short story underwent slight revisions before being published in Eight Men under the title of "The Man Who Was Almost a Man.")

Native Son. New York: Harper and Brothers.

Uncle Tom's Children: Five Long Stories. New York: Harper and Brothers. (This book includes "The Ethics of Living Jim Crow: An Autobiographical Sketch," "Big Boy Leaves Home," "Down By the Riverside," "Long Black Song," "Fire and Cloud," and "Bright and Morning Star.")

1942

"The Man Who Lived Underground." Accent: A Quarterly of New Literature 2 (Spring): 170-176. A pronounced difference from the short story published under the same title in Cross Section. Only represents two short parts of it.

1944

"The Man Who Lived Underground." In <u>Cross Section</u>, pp. 58-102. Edited by Edwin Seaver. New York: L. B. Fischer Publishing Corporation. Published under the same title in <u>Eight Men</u>. (This short story is the third of the three sections of a novel written in 1941 and never published.)

1949

"The Man Who Killed a Shadow." <u>Zero</u> 1 (Spring): 45-53. First published in French under the title of "L'Homme qui tua une ombre." <u>Les Lettres Françaises</u>, October 4, 1946, pp. 1, 10.

1953

<u>The Outsider</u>. New York: Harper and Brothers.

1954

<u>Savage Holiday</u>. New York: Avon Publications, Inc.

1957

"Big Black Good Man." <u>Esquire</u>, November, pp. 76-80.

1958

<u>The Long Dream</u>. New York: Doubleday and Co., Inc.

1961

<u>Eight Men</u>. Cleveland and New York: The World Publishing Co. This book includes "The Man Who Was Almost a Man" (short story), "The Man Who Lived Underground" (short story), "Big Black Good Man" (short story), "The Man Who Saw the Flood" (short story), <u>Man of All Work</u> (play for radio), <u>Man, God Ain't Like That</u> ... (play for radio), "The Man Who Killed a Shadow" (short story), and "The Man Who Went to Chicago" (autobiographical essay). Richard Wright had grouped these articles in that order in 1960.

1963

"Five Episodes." In <u>Soon, One Morning</u>, pp. 140-164. Edited by Herbert Hill. New York: Alfred A. Knopf. (Passages from a novel never published, "Island of Hallucinations," written between March 1958 and February 1959).

<u>Lawd Today</u>. New York: Walker and Co. (Posthumous publication of a novel written between 1931 and 1937.)

BOOKS ON RICHARD WRIGHT

1944

Embree, Edwin Rodgers. "Native Son." In his <u>13 Against the Odds</u>, pp. 25-46. New York: The Viking Press.

1945

Slochower, Harry. "In the Fascist Styx," in his <u>No Voice is Wholly Lost</u> . . . , pp. 75-92. New York: Creative Age Press.

1947

Burgum, Edwin Berry. "The Promise of Democracy in Richard Wright's Native Son" in his The Novel and the World's Dilemma, pp. 223-240. Also in the same book "The Art of Richard Wright's Short Stories," pp. 241-259. New York: Oxford University Press. This last essay was also published in Five Black Writers, pp. 36-49. Edited by Donald B. Gibson. New York: New York University Press, 1970.

1948

Beauvoir, de, Simone. L'Amérique au jour le jour. Paris: Editions Gallimard. (About twenty pages deal with the author's activities with the Wrights in New York between January and May 1947.)

Gloster, Hugh Morris. "Richard Wright." In his Negro Voices in American Fiction, pp. 222-234. Chapel Hill: University of North Carolina Press.

Sartre, Jean-Paul. "Pour qui écrit-on?" In his Situations, II: Qu'est-ce que la littérature?, pp. 125-128. Paris: Éditions Gallimard.

1952

Prescott, Orville. "Power of Environment: Wright Motley, Wolff, Betty Smith." In his In My Opinion, pp. 40-49. Indianapolis: Bobbs-Merrill.

1953

Hughes, John Milton Charles. "Portrayals of Bitterness." In his The Negro Novelist, pp. 41-68. Also in the same book. "Reputation," pp. 197-206. New York: Citadel Press.

Lewis, Sinclair. "Gentlemen, This is Revolution." In Sinclair Lewis Reader, pp. 148-153. Edited by Harry E. Maule and Melville H. Cane. New York: Random House.

1958

Bone, Robert. "Richard Wright." In his The Negro Novel in America, pp. 140-152. New Haven, Connecticut: Yale University Press.

1960

James, Stuart Burke. "Race Relations in Literature and Sociology." Doctoral dissertation. University of Washington. (Ann Arbor, Michigan: University Microfilms No. 60-4-2-88.)

1963

Redding, Saunders J. "The Alien Land of Richard Wright." In Soon, One Morning, pp. 50-59. Edited by Herbert Hill. New York: Alfred A. Knopf. Also published in Five Black Writers, pp. 3-11. Prepared by Donald B. Gibson. New York: New York University Press, 1970.

1964

Baldwin, James. "Alas, Poor Richard," in his Nobody Knows My Name, pp. 146-170. New York: Dell Publishing Co. (Book published for the first time in 1961. This essay includes the following three parts: "Eight Men," "The Exile," and "Alas, Poor Richard".)

Baldwin, James. "Everybody's Protest Novel." In his Notes of a Native Son, pp. 9-17. Also in the same book, "Many Thousands Gone," pp. 18-36. New York: Bantam Books. (Book published for the first time in 1955.)

Baldwin, James. "Princes and Powers," in his Nobody Knows My Name, pp. 24-54. New York: Dell Publishng Co.

Margolies, Edward L. "A Critical Analysis of the Works of Richard Wright." Doctoral dissertation. New York University. (Ann Arbor, Michigan: University Microfilms No. 66-9543).

1966

Brignano, Russell Carl. "Richard Wright: The Major Themes, Ideas and Attitudes in his Works." Doctoral dissertation. The University of Wisconsin. (Ann Arbor, Michigan: University Microfilms No. 66-9887).

"Reflections on Richard Wright: A Symposium on an Exiled Native Son." In Anger and Beyond, pp. 196-212. Edited by Herbert Hill. New York: Harper and Row. Also published in Five Black Writers, pp. 58-69. Edited by Donald B. Gibson. New York: New York University Press, 1970.

Littlejohn, David. "Wright." In his Black on White, pp. 102-110. New York: Grossman Publishers.

1967

Zietlow, Edward Robert. "Wright to Hansberry: The Evolution of Outlook in Four Negro Writers." Doctoral dissertation. University of Washington. (Ann Arbor, Michigan: University Microfilms No. 67-9931).

Cruse, Harold. "Richard Wright." In his The Crisis of the Negro Intellectual, pp. 181-189. New York: William Morrow and Co., Inc.

1968

Britt, David Dobbs. "The Image of the White Man in the Fiction of Langston Hughes, Richard Wright, James Baldwin, and Ralph Ellison." Doctoral dissertation. Emory University. (Ann Arbor, Michigan: University Microfilms No. 68-15747).

Cleaver, Eldridge. "Notes of a Native Son," in his Soul on Ice, pp. 97-111. New York: Dell Publishing Co.

Margolies, Edward. "Richard Wright: Native Son and Three Kinds of Revolution." In his Native Sons: A Critical Study of Twentieth Century Negro American Authors, pp. 65-86. Philadelphia and New York: J. B. Lippincott Co.

Negro Digest 18 (December). Issue devoted entirely to Richard Wright and entitled "Richard Wright: His Life and His Works."

Webb, Constance. Richard Wright: A Biography. New York: G. P. Putnam's Sons.

Williams, John A. The Man Who Cried I Am. New York: The New American Library, Signet Books. (A novel introducing real characters under fictitious names about the life of Richard Wright in France and in Europe.)

1969

Blake, Nelson Manfred. "The Volcano of Anger", in his Novelists' America: Fiction as History, 1910-1940, pp. 226-253. Syracuse, New York: Syracuse University Press.

CLA Journal 12 (June). Issue devoted entirely to Richard Wright entitled "Richard Wright."

Bone, Robert. Richard Wright. Minneapolis: University of Minnesota Press.

Margolies, Edward. The Art of Richard Wright. Carbondale, Illinois: Southern Illinois University Press. (Doctoral dissertation published in book form.)

McCall, Dan. The Example of Richard Wright. New York: Harcourt, Brace and World.

1970

Studies in Black Literature 1 (Autumn). Issue devoted entirely to Richard Wright and entitled "Richard Wright."

Brignano, Russell Carl. Richard Wright: An Introduction to the Man and His Works. Pittsburgh: University of Pittsburgh Press. (Doctoral dissertation published in book form.)

Williams, John A. The Most Native of Sons: A Biography of Richard Wright. New York: Doubleday and Co., Inc.

1971

New Letters 38 (December). Issue devoted entirely to Richard Wright entitled "The Life and Work of Richard Wright, including haiku and unpublished prose." Published in the form of a book under the title of Richard Wright: Impressions and Perspectives. Edited by David Ray and Robert M. Farnsworth. Ann Arbor: University of Michigan Press, 1973.

1972

Baker, Houston A., Jr. "Racial Wisdom and Richard Wright's Native Son", in his Long Black Song, pp. 122-141. Charlottesville, Va.: The University Press of Virginia.

Himes, Chester. The Quality of Hurt: The Autobiography of Chester Himes, Volume I. New York: Doubleday and Company, Inc. (Several pages deal with the relations between Richard Wright and Chester Himes in New York and in Paris. To be completed by the reading of "My Man Himes: An Interview with Chester Himes", by John A. Williams in Amistad I, pp. 25-93. Prepared by John A. Williams and Charles F. Harris. New York: Vintage Books, 1970).

Kinnamon, Keneth. The Emergence of Richard Wright: A Study in Literature and Society. Urbana: University of Illinois Press.

Twentieth Century Interpretations of Native Son. Edited by Houston A. Baker, Jr. Englewood Cliffs, NJ: Prentice-Hall, Inc.

1973

Fabre, Michel. The Unfinished Quest of Richard Wright. New York: William Morrow and Co., Inc.

Margolies, Edward. "The Letters of Richard Wright." In The Black Writer in Africa and the Americas, pp. 101-118. Edited by Lloyd W. Brown. Los Angeles: Hennessey and Ingalls, Inc.

1975

Fabre, Michel. "Richard Wright: Beyond Naturalism?" In American Literary Naturalism: A Reassessment, pp. 136-153. Edited by Yoshinobu Hakutani and Lewis Fried. Heidelberg: Carl Winter-Universitdtsverlag.

1976

Himes, Chester. My Life of Absurdity: The Autobiography of Chester Himes, Vol. 2. New York: Doubleday and Co. (Several pages deal with Richard Wright.)

1977
Fabre, Michel. "Richard Wright's Image of France." In Prospects Vol. 3. An Annual
    of American Cultural Studies, pp. 315-329. Edited by Jack Salzman.
    New York: Burt Franklin and Co, Inc., Publishers.

1978
Wright, Ellen, and Michel, Fabre, eds. Richard Wright Reader. New York: Harper and
    Row.

ARTICLES ON RICHARD WRIGHT
1940
Canby, Henry Seidel. "Native Son." The Book of the Month Club News, February, pp.
    2-3.
Seaver, Edwin. "Richard Wright." The Book of the Month Club News, February, p. 6.
    "Negro Hailed as New Writer." The New York Sun, March 4, p. 3.
Cohn, David L. "The Negro Novel: Richard Wright." Atlantic Monthly, May, pp.
    659-661.
Wyke, Marguerite. "South Side Negro." Canadian Forum, May, p. 60.
Daiches, David. "The American Scene: Review of a Group of Novels (Native Son)."
    Partisan Review 7 (May-June): 244-245.

1941
Ellison, Ralph. "Recent Negro Fiction." New Masses, August 5, pp. 22-26.

1944
Wertham, Frederic. "An Unconscious Determinant in Native Son." Journal of Clinical
    Pathology 6 (1944-1945): 111-115. Published under the same title in
    Psychoanalysis and Literature, pp. 321-325. Edited by Hendrik M.
    Ruitenbeek. New York: E. L. Dutton, 1964.

1945
"Black Boyhood." Time, March 5, pp. 38-39.
Ellison, Ralph. "Richard Wright's Blues." Antioch Review 5 (Summer): 198-211.
    Published under the same title in his Shadow and Act.
Ford, Nick Aaron. "Four Popular Negro Novelists." Phylon 15 (First Quarter): 29-39.
Hardwick, Elizabeth. "Artist and Spokesman." Partisan Review 12 (Summer): 406-407.
    "L'Auteur américain Richard Wright à Quebec." L'Événement-Journal
    (Quebec), June 28, p. 4.

1947
White, Ralph K. "Black Boy: A Value-Analysis." Journal of Abnormal and Social
    Psychology 42 (October): 440-461.

1949
Webb, Constance, "What Next for Richard Wright?" Phylon 10 (Second Quarter):
    161-166.

1953
Smith, William Gardner. "Black Boy in France." Ebony 8 (July): 32-36, 39-42.
Riesman, David. "Marginality, Conformity and Insight." Phylon 14 (September):
    241-257.

Ford, Nick Aaron. "The Ordeal of Richard Wright." College English 15 (October):
    87-94. Also published in Five Black Writers, pp. 26-35. Edited by
    Donald B. Gibson. New York: New York University Press, 1970.
Sprague, M. D. "Richard Wright: A Bibliography." Bulletin of Bibliography 21
    (September-December): 39.

1954

Cary, Joyce. "Catching up with History." The Nation, October 16, pp. 332-333.
Jarrett, Thomas D. "Recent Fiction by Negroes." College English 16 (November):
    85-91.

1955

Ellison, Ralph. "The Art of Fiction: An Interview." Paris Review 8 (Spring): 55-71.
    Published under the same title in his Shadow and Act.)

1956

Scott, Nathan A. "Search for Beliefs: Fiction of Richard Wright." University of Kansas
    City Review 23 (October-December): 19-24.
Davis, Arthur P. "The Outsider as a Novel of Race." Midwest Journal 7 (Winter):
    320-326.

1958

Glicksberg, Charles I. "Existentialism in The Outsider." Four Quarters 7 (January):
    17-26. Hicks, Granville. "The Power of Richard Wright." Saturday
    Review, October 18, p. 13.
"Tract in Black and White." Time, October 27, pp. 94, 96.
"Amid the Allien Corn." Time, November 17, p. 28.

1959

Lehan, Richard. "Existentialism in Recent American Fiction: The Demonic Quest."
    Texas Studies in Literature and Language 1 (Summer): 181-202. Also
    published in Recent American Fiction, pp. 63-83. Edited by J. J.
    Waldmeir. Boston: Houghton Miffin Co., 1963.

1960

Isaacs, Harold R. "Five Writers and Their African Ancestors." Phylon 21 (Fall):
    243-265.
"Obituary." The New York Times, November 30, p. 37.
Bryer, Jackson R. "Richard Wright (1908-1960): A Selected Checklist of Criticism."
    Wisconsin Studies in Contemporary Literature 1 (Fall): 22-23.
Gérard, Albert. "Négritude et humanité chez Richard Wright." La Revue Nouvelle 32
    (No. 10): 337-343.
Widmer, Kingsley. "The Existentialist Darkness: Richard Wright's The Outsider."
    Wisconsin Studies in Contemporary Literature 1 (Fall): 13-21. Also
    published in Five Black Writers, pp. 50-57. Edited by Donald B.
    Gibson. New York: New York University Press, 1970.

1961

Gérard, Albert. "Vie et vocation de Richard Wright." Revue Générale Belge 97
    (January): 65-78.
Baldwin, James. "Richard Wright tel que je l'ai connu." Preuves 11 (February):42-45.
    This article was published in English under the title of "Richard Wright".
    Encounter 16 (April 1961): 58-60 (It was also published under the title

of "The Exile" in Nobody Knows My Name.)

Harrington, Ollie. "The Last Days of Richard Wright." Ebony 17 (February): 83-94.

Baldwin, James. "The Survival of Richard Wright." The Reporter, March 16, pp. 52-55. This article was also published under the title of "Eight Men" in his Nobody Knows My Name.

Smith, William Gardner. "The Compensation for the Wound." Two Cities 6 (Summer): 67-69.

Ellison, Ralph. "That Same Pain, That Same Pleasure: An Interview." December 3 (Winter): 30-32, 37-46. Published under the same title in his Shadow and Act.

1962

Ford, Nick Aaron. "Richard Wright: A Profile." Chicago Jewish Forum 21 (Fall): 26-30.

1963

Charney, Maurice. "James Baldwin's Quarrel with Richard Wright." American Quarterly 15 (Spring): 65-75.

Howe, Irving. "Black Boys and Native Sons." Dissent 10 (Autumn): 353-368.

Ellison, Ralph. "The World and the Jug." The New Leader, December 9, pp. 22-26. (Reponse to "Black Boys and Native Sons" by Irving Howe. Published under the same title in his Shadow and Act. Constitutes the first part of the essay.)

1964

Ellison, Ralph. "A Rejoinder." The New Leader, February 3, pp. 15-22. ("A Reply to Ralph Ellison" by Irving Howe Published in the same issue of The New Leader. Published under the title of "The World and the Jug" in his Shadow and Act. Constitutes the second part of the essay.)

Scott, Nathan A., Jr. "The Dark and Haunted Tower of Richard Wright." Graduate Comment 7 (July): 93-99. Revised version published in Five Black Writers, pp. 12-25. Edited by Donald B. Gibson. New York: New York University Press, 1970.

Ellison, Ralph. "Hidden Name and Complex Fate." In The Writer's Experience, pp. 1-15. Washington, D.C.: Library of Congress. Published under the same title in his Shadow and Act.)

1965

Fabre, Michel, and Edward Margolies. "Richard Wright (1908-1860): A Bibliography." Bulletin of Bibliography 24 (January-April): 131-133, 137.

1966

Green, G. "Back to Bigger." Kenyon Review 28 (September): 521-539.

1967

Ellison. "A Very Stern Discipline: An interview with Ralph Ellison." Harper's 234 (March): 76-95.

Ellison, Martha. "Velvet Voices Feed on Bitter Fruit: A Study of American Negro Poetry." Poet and Critic 4 (Winter 1967-1968): 39-49.

1968

"Whiff of the 'Problem.'" Time, March 22, p. 82.

Oliver, Edith. "Off Broadway." The New Yorker, June 15, p. 65.

Ellison, Ralph. "A Dialogue with his Audience." The Barat Review (Barat College) 3: 51-53.

Sanders, Ronald. "Richard Wright and the Sixties." Midstream 14 (August-September): 28-40.

Pitcole, M. "Black Boy and Role Playing: A Scenario for Reading Success." English Journal 47 (November): 1140-1142.

1969

Webb, Constance. "Richard Wright: A Bibliography." Negro Digest 18 (January): 86-92. (Same bibliography as the one published in his book Richard Wright: A Biography, pp. 423-429.)

1970

Hyman, Stanley Edgar. "Life and Letters: Richard Wright Reappraised." Atlantic 225 (March): 127-132.

Mason, Clifford. "Native Son Strikes Home. Black Fiction: A Second Look." Life, May 8, p. 18.

Reed, Kenneth T. "Native Son: An American Crime and Punishment." Studies in Black Literature 1 (Summer): 33-34.

Fabre, Michel. "The Poetry of Richard Wright." Studies in Black Literature 1 (Autumn): 10-22.

Donlan, Dan M. "The White Trap: "A Motif." English Journal 59 (October): 943-944.

1971

Brignano, Russell C. "Richard Wright: A Bibliography of Secondary Sources." Studies in Black Literature 2 (Summer): 19-25.

Fabre, Michel. "Richard Wright: 'The Man Who Lived Underground.'" Studies in The Novel 3 (Summer): 165-179.

Kinnamon, Keneth. "Lawd Today: Richard Wright's Apprentice Novel." Studies in Black Literature 2 (Summer): 16-18.

Bakish, David. "Underground in an Ambiguous Dream-world." Studies in Black Literature 2 (Autumn): 18-23.

Reilly, John M. "Lawd Today: Richard Wright's Experiment in Naturalism." Studies in Black Literature 2 (Autumn): 14-17.

Fabre, Michel and Edward Margolies. "A Bibliography of Richard Wright's Works." New Letters 38 (December): 155-169.

Fabre, Michel. "Black Cat and White Cat: Richard Wright's Debt to Edgar Allan Poe" - Poe Studies 4 (December): 17-19.

Fabre, Michel. "Wright's Exile" New Letters 38 (December): 128-135.

"Letters to Richard Wright." New Letters 38 (December): 128-135.

1972

McCarthy, Harold T. "Richard Wright: The Expatriate as Native Son." American Literature 44 (March): 97-117.

Fuller, Hoyt W. "Traveler on the Long, Rough, Lonely Old Road: An Interview with Chester Himes." Black World 21 (March): 4-22,87,98.

Tatham, Campbell. "Vision and Value in Uncle Tom's Children." Studies in Black Literature 3 (Summer): 14-23.

Graham, Louis. "The White Self-Image Conflict in Native Son". Studies in Black Literature 3 (Summer): 19-21.

Primeau, Ronald. "Imagination as Moral Bulwark and Creative Energy in Richard Wright's Black Boy and LeRoi Jones' Home." Studies in Black Literature

3 (Summer): 12-18.

Kennedy, James G. "The Content and Form of Native Son." College English 32 (November): 269-286.

1973

Fabre, Michel. "Richard Wright's First Hundred Books." CLA Journal 16 (June): 458-474.

1975

Falardeau, Jean-Charles, to Jean-François Gounard. July 24. (Letter emphasizing Richard Wright's racial phobias regarding the inhabitants of the island of Orleans, during the summer of 1945, in the course of his stay in Canada.)

1977

Grenander, M. E. "Criminal Responsibility in Native Son and Knock on Any Door." American Literature 49 (May): 221-223.

King, J. R. "Richard Wright: His Life and Writings." Negro History Bulletin, September, pp. 738-743.

Stepto, R. B. "I Thought I Knew These People: Richard Wright and the Afro-American Literary Tradition." Massachusetts Review 18 (Autumn): 525-541.

Reilly, J. M. "Richard Wright's Curious Thriller, Savage Holiday." CLA Journal 21 (December): 218-223.

WORKS BY JAMES BALDWIN

ARTICLES

1948

"The Harlem Ghetto: Winter 1948." Commentary 5 (February): 165-170. Published under the title of "The Harlem Ghetto" in his Notes of a Native Son.

"Journey to Atlanta." The New Leader, October 9, pp. 8-9. Published under the same title in his Notes of a Native Son.

1949

"Everybody's Protest Novel." Partisan Review 16 (June): 578-585. Published under the same title in his Notes of a Native Son.

1950

"The Negro in Paris." Reporter, June 6, pp. 34-36. Published under the title "Encounter on the Seine: Black Meets Brown" in his Notes of a Native Son.

1951

"Many Thousands Gone." Partisan Review 17 (November-December): 655-680. Published under the same title in his Notes of a Native Son.

1953

"Stranger in the Village." Harper's Magazine 207 (October):42-48. Published under the same title in his Notes of a Native Son.

1954

"A Question of Identity." Partisan Review 21 (July-August): 402-410. Published under
the same title in his Notes of a Native Son.

"Gide as Husband and Homosexual." The New Leader, 13 December, pp. 18-20.
Published under the title of "The Male Prison" in his Nobody Knows My
Name.

1955

"Life Straight in De Eye." Commentary 19 (January): 74-77. (Published under the title
of "Carmen Jones: The Dark Is Light Enough" in his Notes of a Native
Son.)

"Equal in Paris." Commentary 19 (March): 251-259. Published under the same title
in "Notes of a Native Son" in his Notes of a Native Son.

"Me and My House." Harper's Magazine 211 (November): 54-61 (Published under the
title of "Notes of a Native Son" in his Notes of a Native Son.

1956

"Faulkner and Desegregation." Partisan Review 23 (Fall): 568-573. Published under
the same title in his Nobody Knows My Name.

1957

"Princes and Powers." Encounter 8 (January): 52-60. Published under the same title
in his Nobody Knows My Name.

1958

"The Hard Kind of Courage." Harper's Magazine 217 (October): 61-65. Published
under the title of "A Fly in Buttermilk" in his Nobody Knows My Name.

1959

"The Discovery of What it Means to be an American." New York Times Book Review,
January 25, pp. 4, 22. Published under the same title in his Nobody
Knows My Name.

"Letter from the South: Nobody Knows My Name." Partisan Review 26 (Winter):
72-82. Published under the title of "Nobody Knows My Name: A Letter
from the South" in his Nobody Knows My Name.

1960

"The Precarious Vogue of Ingmar Bergman." Esquire 53 (April): 128-132. Published
under the title of "The Northern Protestant" in his Nobody Knows My
Name.

"Fifth Avenue, Uptown: A Letter from Harlem." Esquire 54 (July): 70-76. Published
under the same title in his Nobody Knows My Name.

"Notes for a Hypothetical Novel." Speech given at San Francisco State College on
October 22. Published under the title of "Notes for a Hypothetical Novel
-- An Address" in his Nobody Knows My Name.

"In Search of a Majority." Speech delivered in the Stetson Chapel at Kalamazoo
College, Michigan, on November 21. Published under the title of "In
Search of a Majority -- An Address" in his Nobody Knows My Name.

1961

"The Dangerous Road Before Martin Luther King." Harper's Magazine 222 (February):
33-42.

"Richard Wright tel que je l'ai connu." Preuves 11 (February): 42-45. This article was also published under the title of "Richard Wright." Encounter 16 (April 1961): 58-60. (It was also published under the title of "The Exile" in his Nobody Knows My Name.

"A Negro Assays the Negro Mood." The New York Times Magazine March 12, pp. 25, 103-104. Published under the title of "East River, Downtown: Postscript to a Letter from Harlem" in his Nobody Knows My Name.

"The Survival of Richard Wright." The Reporter, March 16, pp. 52-55. (This article was also published under the title of "Eight Men" in his Nobody Knows My Name.

"The Black Boy Looks at the White Boy." Esquire 55 (May): 102-106. Published under the same title in his Nobody Knows My Name.

"The New Lost Generation." Esquire 56 (July): 113-115.

"The Search for Identity." In American Principles and Issues: The National Purpose, pp. 459-467. Edited by Oscar Handlin. New York: Holt, Rinehart and Winston.

1962

"As Much Truth as One Can Bear." The New York Times Book Review, 14 January, pp. 1, 38.

"Letter from a Region in My Mind." The New Yorker, 17 November, 59-144. Published under the title of "Down at the Cross: Letter from a Region in My Mind" in his The Fire Next Time.

"Color." Esquire 58 (December): 225-252.

"A Letter to My Nephew." The Progressive 26 (December): 19-20. Published under the title of "My Dungeon Shook: Letter to My Nephew on the One Hundredth Anniversary of the Emancipation" in his The Fire Next Time.

"Theater: The Negro In and Out of it." In The Angry Black, pp. 13-22. Edited by John A. Williams. New York: Lancer Books. Published in Beyond the Angry Black, pp. 2-10. Edited by John A. Williams. New York: Cooper Square Publishers, 1966. Also published under the title of "James Baldwin on the Negro Actor." In Anthology of the American Negro in the Theater, A Critical Approach, pp. 127-130. Edited by Lindsay Patterson. New York: Publishers Co., 1967.

1963

"Letters from a Journey." In Soon, One Morning, pp. 36-47. Edited by Herbert Hill. New York; Alfred A. Knopf.

1964

"The Creative Dilemma." Saturday Review, 8 February, pp. 14-15.

"Disturbers of the Peace." In Black, White and Gray, pp. 190-209. Edited by B. Daniel. New York: Sheed and Ward.

1965

"Race, Hate, Sex, and Color: A Conversation." Encounter 25 (July): 55-60.

1966

"To Whom It May Concern: Report from Occupied Territory." The Nation, July 11, pp. 39-43.

"Unnameable Objects, Unspeakable Crimes." In The White Problem in America, pp. 173-181. Edited by the editors of Ebony. Chicago: Johnson Publishing Co.

1967

"James Baldwin Breaks His Silence." Atlas 13 (March): 47-49 (Interview).
"Negroes are Anti-Semitic because they're Anti-White." The New York Times
     Magazine, April 9, pp. 26-27, 135-137, 139-140.
"L'Explosion noire de l'été 1967." Le Figaro Littéraire, no. 1111 (31 July - 6 August).
     pp. 6-7.

1968

"How Can we Get the Black People to Cool it?" Esquire, July, pp. 49-53, 116.
"Sidney Poitier by James Baldwin." Look, July 23, pp. 50-54, 56, 68.
"White Racism or World Community?" The Ecumenical Review 20 (October): 371-376.
"James Baldwin . . . in Conversation." In Black Voices: An Anthology of Afro-American
     Literature, pp. 660-668. Edited by Abraham Chapman. New York:
     New American Library.

1969

"Sweet Lorraine." Esquire 72 (November): 139-141.

1971

"An Open Letter to my Sister, Miss Angela Davis." The New York Review of Books,
     January 7, pp. 15-16.
"A Rap on Race." McCall's, June, pp. 84-85, 142-154. (Dialogue with Margaret Mead).
"Of Angela Davis and the Jewish Housewife Headed for Dachau--An Exchange--James
     Baldwin--Schlomo Katz." Midstream (June-July): 3-7.

1972

"Why I Left America." In New Black Voices: An Anthology of Contemporary American
     Literature, edited by Abraham Chapman. New York: New American
     Library. Pp. 409-419.

ESSAYS

1955

Notes of a Native Son. Beacon Press.

1961

Nobody Knows My Name. New York: The Dial Press.

1963

The Fire Next Time. New York: The Dial Press.

1964

Nothing Personal. Harmondsworth, England: Penguin Books.   (Photographs by
     Richard Avedon and text by James Baldwin.)

1971

A Rap on Race. New York: J. B. Lippincott Co. (Dialogue with Margaret Mead.)

PLAYS

1954

The Amen Corner. Zero 2 (July): 4-8, 11-13. (Act I of an apparently longer work.)

1964

Blues for Mister Charlie. New York: The Dial Press.

1968

The Amen Corner. New York: The Dial Press. (Play in three acts).

NOVELS AND SHORT STORIES

1948

"Previous Condition." Commentary. 6 (October): 334-342.

1950

"The Death of the Prophet." Commentary 9 (March): 257-261. (Sequel to Go Tell it on the Mountain: John Grimes goes to the bedside of dying Gabriel Grimes.)

1951

"The Outing." New Story 1 (April): 52-81.

1953

Go Tell it on the Mountain. New York: Alfred A. Knopf.

1956

Giovanni's Room. New York: The Dial Press.

1957

"Sonny's Blues." Partisan Review 24 (Summer): 327-358.

1958

"Come Out the Wilderness." Mademoiselle 46 (March): 102-104, 146-154.

1960

"This Morning, This Evening, So Soon." Atlantic Monthly 206 (September): 34-52.

1962

Another Country. New York: The Dial Press.

1965

Going to Meet the Man. New York: The Dial Press. The short stories that constitute this book are "The Rockpile" (first appearance), "The Outing," "The Man Child" (first appearance), "Previous Condition," Sonny's Blues," "This Morning, This Evening, So Soon,"
"Come Out the Wilderness," "Going to Meet the Man" (first appearance).

1968

Tell Me How Long the Train's Been Gone. New York: The Dial Press.

BOOKS ON JAMES BALDWIN

1962

Kazin, Alfred. "The Essays of James Baldwin", in his Contemporaries, pp. 254-258. Boston: Little Brown and Co.

1963

Breit, Harvey. "James Baldwin and Two Footnotes." In The Creative Present, pp. 1-23. Edited by Nora Balakian and Charles Simmons. Garden City, NY: Doubleday and Co.

1964

Harper, Howard Morrall, Jr. "Concepts of Human Destiny in Five American Novelists: Bellow, Salinger, Mailer, Baldwin, Updike." Doctoral dissertation. The Pennsylvania State University. (Ann Arbor, Michigan: University Microfilms No. 65-4380.

Klein, Marcus. "James Baldwin." In his After Alienation, pp. 147-195. Cleveland: World Publishing Co.

Nyren, Dorothy. "Baldwin, James." In his A Library of Literary Criticism, pp. 32-34. New York: F. Ungar Publishing Co.

Podhoretz, Norman. "In Defense of James Baldwin." In his Doings and Undoings, pp. 244-250. New York: Farrar, Straus and Giroux. Podhoretz, Norman. "In Defense of a Maltreated Best Seller." In On Contemporary Literature, pp. 232-237. Edited by Richard Kostelanetz. New York: Avon Books. Podhoretz, Norman. "My Negro Problem and Ours." In Black, White and Gray, pp. 210-225. Edited by Bradford Daniel. New York: Sheed and Ward.

Sayre, Robert F. "James Baldwin's Other Country." In Contemporary American Novelists, pp. 158-169. Edited by Harry Thornton Moore. Carbondale: Southern Illinois University Press.

1965

Bone, Robert. "Postscript." In his The Negro Novel in America, pp. 215-239. New Haven, Connecticut: Yale University Press.

O'Brien, Conor Cruise. "White Gods and Black Americans." In his Writers and Politics pp. 17-22. New York: Pantheon Books.

Dupee, F.W. "James Baldwin and 'The Man.'" In his The King of the Cats, pp. 208-214. New York: Farrar, Straus and Giroux.

Warren, Robert Penn. "James Baldwin." In his Who Speaks for the Negro?, pp. 277-298. New York: Random House.

1966

Eckman, Fern Marja. The Furious Passage of James Baldwin. New York: Evans and Co.

Littlejohn, David. "Baldwin", in his Black on White, pp. 119-137. New York: Grossman Publishers.

1967

Zietlow, Edward Robert. "Wright to Hansberry: The Evolution of Outlook in Four Negro Writers." Doctoral dissertation. University of Washington. (Ann Arbor, Michigan: University Microfilms No. 67-9931.

Cruse, Harold. "Negroes and Jews." In his The Crisis of the Negro Intellectual, pp. 481-491. New York: William Morrow and Co.

1968

Britt, David Dobbs. "The Image of the White Man in the Fiction of Langston Hughes, Richard Wright, James Baldwin, and Ralph Ellison." Doctoral dissertation. Emory University. (Ann Arbor, Michigan: University Microfilms No. 68-15747.

Cleaver, Eldridge. "Notes on a Native Son." In his <u>Soul on Ice</u>, pp. 97-111. New York: Dell Publishing Co.

Margolies, Edward. "The Negro Church: James Baldwin and the Christian Vision." In his <u>Native Son: A Critical Study of Twentieth Century Negro American Authors</u>, pp. 102-126. Philadelphia and New York: J. B. Lippincott Co.

1970

Herton, Calvin C. "A Fiery Baptism." In <u>Amistad I</u>, pp. 200-214. Edited by John A. Williams and Charles F. Harris. New York: Vintage Books.

1973

Macabuh, Stanley. <u>James Baldwin: A Critical Study</u>. New York: The Third Press.

1974

Kinnamon, Keneth, ed. <u>James Baldwin: A Collection of Critical Essays</u>. Englewood Cliffs, N.J.: Prentice-Hall.

1977

O'Daniel, Therman B., ed. <u>James Baldwin: A Critical Evaluation</u>. Washington, D.C.: Howard University Press.

ARTICLES ON JAMES BALDWIN

1946

"Three Writers Receive Eugene Saxton Fellowships." <u>Publishers' Weekly</u> 149 (January 19): 308-309.

1959

Ulman, Ruth. "James Baldwin." <u>Wilson Library Bulletin</u> 33 (February): 392.

1960

Isaacs, Harold R. "Five Writers and their African Ancestors." <u>Phylon</u> 21 (Winter): 322-329.

1961

Morrison, Allan. "The Angriest Young Man." <u>Ebony</u> 16 (October): 23-30.

Gérard, Albert. "James Baldwin et la religiosité noire." <u>Revue Nouvelle</u> 2: 177-186.

Jacobson, Dan. "James Baldwin as Spokesman." <u>Commentary</u> 32 (December): 497-502.

1962

Bobosky, Phillip. "The Negro Writer and Commitment." <u>Mainstream</u> 15 (February): 16-22.

Shayon, Robert Lewis. "T.V. and Radio: An Interview with James Baldwin." <u>Saturday Review</u>, February 24, p. 35.

Gordon, Eugene. "Disturbing." <u>Mainstream</u> 15 (May): 49.

Luce, Phillip Abbott. "Abruptly Banal." Mainstream 15 (May): 45-48.
Ellison, Ralph. "Ralph Ellison talks about James Baldwin." Negro Digest 11 (September): 61.
Finn, James. "The Identity of James Baldwin." The Commonweal, 26 October, pp. 113-116.

1963
"The Rainbow Sign." Time, January 4, pp. 18-19.
Gross, John. "Disorganization Men." New Statesman, February 8, pp. 202-204.
Charney, Maurice. "James Baldwin's Quarrel with Richard Wright." American Quarterly 15 (Spring): 65-75.

Time May 17, pp. 26-27. (Long article on James Baldwin with his photo on the first page.)
Foote, Dorothy Norris. "James Baldwin's Holler Books'." C.E.A. Critic 25 (May): 8, 11.
Hentoff, Nat. "It's Terrifying." New York Herald Tribune Book Review, June 16, pp. 1, 6. (Interview.)
Simmons, Harvey G. "James Baldwin and the Negro Conundrum." Antioch Review 23 (Summer): 250-255.
Lamming, G. "The Fire Next Time." Spectator, July 12, pp. 58-59.
Gross, John. "Day of Wrath." New Statesman, July 19, pp. 79-80.
MacInnes, Colin. "Dark Angel: The Writings of James Baldwin." Encounter 21 (August): 22-33.
"Black Man's Burden." The Times Library Supplement, September 6, p. 672.
English, Charles. "Another Viewpoint." Jubilee 11 (September): 43-46.
Howe, Irving. "Black Boys and Native Sons." Dissent 10 (Autumn): 353-368.
Finn, James. "James Baldwin's Vision." The Commonweal July 26, pp. 447-449.
O'Daniel, Therman B. "James Baldwin: An Interpretive Study." CLA Journal 7 (September): 37-47.
Nichols, Charles H. "James Baldwin: A Skillful Executioner." Studies on the Left 3 (Winter): 74-79. (On Another Country.)
Hagopian, John V. "James Baldwin: The Black and the Red-White-and-Blue." CLA Journal 7 (December): 133-140.
Ellison, Ralph. "The World and the Jug." The New Leader, December 9, pp. 22-26. (Response to "Black Boys and Native Sons" by Irving Howe. Published under the same title in Shadow and Act. Constitutes the first part of the essay.)
Mergen, Bernard. "James Baldwin and the American Conundrum." Moderna Sprak 4: 397-405.
Spender, Stephen. "James Baldwin: A Voice of a Revolution." Partisan Review 2: 256-260.

1964
Schroth, Raymond A. "James Baldwin's Search." Catholic World 198 (February): 288-294.
Ellison, Ralph. "A Rejoinder." The New Leader, February 3, pp. 15-22. (Response to "A Reply to Ralph Ellison" by Irving Howe, published in the same issue of The New Leader. Published under the title of "The World and the Jug," in his Shadow and Act. Constitutes the second part of the essay.)
Graves, Wallace. "The Question of Moral Energy in James Baldwin's Go Tell It on the Mountain." CLA Journal 7 (March): 215-223.

Kent, George E. "Baldwin and the Problem of Being." CLA Journal 7 (March): 202-214.

"Liberalism and the Negro: A Round-table Discussion: James Baldwin, Sidney Hook, Gunnar Myrdal, Nathan Glazer." Commentary 37 (March): 25-42.

Gresset, Michel. "Sur James Baldwin." Mercure de France 350 (April): 653-655.

Coles, Robert. "Baldwin's Burden." Partisan Review 31 (Summer): 409-416.

Cox, C. B., and A. R. Jones. "After the Tranquilized Fifties: Notes on Sylvia Plath and James Baldwin." Critical Quarterly 6 (Summer): 107-122.

Ellison, Ralph. "An Interview with Ralph Ellison." Tamarack Review. 32 (Summer): 3-24.

Patterson, H. Orlando. "The Essays of James Baldwin" New Left Review 26 (Summer): 31-38.

Sontag, Susan. "Blues for Mister Charlie." Partisan Review 31 (Summer): 389-394.

Elkoff, Marvin. "Everybody Knows His Name." Esquire 67 (August): 59-64, 120-123.

Simon, John. "Blues for Mister Charlie." Hudson Review 17 (Autumn): 421-424.

Collier, Eugenia W. "The Phrase Unbearably Repeated." Phylon 25 (Fall): 288-296.

Van Sickle, Milton. "James Baldwin in Black and White." Trace 54 (Autumn): 222-225.

Gross, Theodore. "The World of James Baldwin." Critique 7 (Winter): 139-149.

Lash, John S. "Baldwin Beside Himself: A Study in Modern Phallicism." CLA Journal 8 (December): 132-140.

Levin, David. "James Baldwin's Autobiographical Essays: The Problem of Negro Identity." Massachusetts Review 5 (Winter): 239-247.

1965

Fischer, Russell G. "James Baldwin: A Bibliography, 1947-1962." Bulletin of Bibliography 24 (January-April): 127-130.

Kendt, Kathleen A. "James Baldwin, a Checklist: 1947-1962." Bulletin of Bibliography 24 (January-April): 123-126.

"Tardy Rainbow." Time, April 23, p. 59.

Bryden, Ronald. "Blues for Mister Charlie." New Statesman, May 7, pp. 737-738.

Moore, John Rees. "An Embarrassment of Riches: Baldwin's Going to Meet the Man." Hollins Critic 2 (December): 1-12.

1966

Blount, T. "Slight Error in Continuity in James Baldwin's Another Country." Notes and Queries 13 (March): 102-103.

Jones, B. F. "James Baldwin: The Struggle for Identity." British Journal of Sociology 17 (June): 107-121.

Stanley, F. L. "James Baldwin: The Crucial Situation." South Atlantic Quarterly 65 (Summer): 371-381.

Furay, Michael. "Negritude: A Romantic Myth?" New Republic, July 2, pp. 32-35.

Berry, Boyd M. "Another Man Done Gone: Self-pity in Baldwin's Another Country." Michigan Quarterly Review 4 (Fall): 285-290.

Newman, Charles. "Lesson of the Master: Henry James and James Baldwin." The Yale Review 56 (October): 45-59.

1967

Bigsby, C. W. E. "Committed Writer: James Baldwin as Dramatist." Twentieth Century Literature 13 (April): 39-48.

Gayle, A., Jr. "Dialectic of The Fire Next Time." The Negro History Bulletin 30 (April): 15-16.

1968

Madden, David. "The Fallacy of the Subject-dominated Novel." English Record, April 4, pp. 11-19.

McCarten, John. "Tabernacle Blues." The New Yorker, 24 April, p. 85.

Hicks, Granville. "From Harlem with Hatred." Saturday Review, June 1, pp. 23-24.

"Milk Run." Time, June 7, p. 104. (On Tell Me How Long the Train's Been Gone.)

Long, Robert Emmet. "From Elegant to Hip." The Nation, June 10, pp. 769-770.

Puzo, Mario. "His Cardboard Lovers." The New York Times Book Review, June 23, pp. 5, 34.

Thompson, John. "Baldwin, the Prophet as Artist." Commentary 45 (June): 67-69. (On Tell Me How Long the Train's Been Gone.)

Standley, Fred L. "James Baldwin: A Checklist, 1963-1967." Bulletin of Bibliography 25 (May-August): 135-137, 160.

Howe, Irving. "James Baldwin: At Ease in Apocalypse." Harper's Magazine 237 (September): 92, 95-100.

Richardson, Jack. "The Black Arts." The New York Review Books, December 19, pp. 11-12.

Alexander, Charlotte. "The 'Stink' of Reality: Mothers and Whores in James Baldwin's Fiction." Literature and Psychology, 1: 9-26.

1970

Fabre, Michel. "Pères et fils dans Go Tell It on the Mountain de James Baldwin." Etudes Anglaises 23 (January-March): 47-61.

Adelson, C. E. "Love Affair: James Baldwin's Image of Black Community." Negro American Literature Forum 2: 56-60.

1971

Katz, Shlomo. "An Open Letter to James Baldwin." Midstream 17 (April): 3-5.

McWhirter, William A. "Parting Shots: after years of futility Baldwin explodes again." Life, July 30, p. 63.

Gérard, Albert. "The Sons of Ham." Studies in the Novel 3 (Summer): 148-164.

Foster, David E. "'Cause my house fell down': The Theme of the Fall in Baldwin's Novels." Critique, 2: 50-62.

Mead, Margaret. "A Rap on Race: How James Baldwin and I 'talked' a book." Redbook, September, pp. 70-72, 75.

1972

Fuller, Hoyt W. "Traveler on the Long, Rough, Lonely Old Road: An interview with Chester Himes." Black World 21 (March): 4-22, 87, 98.

Mowe, Gregory and W. Scott Nobles. "James Baldwin's Message for White America." Quarterly Journal of Speech 58 (April): 142-151.

DeMott, Benjamin. "James Baldwin on the Sixties: Acts and Revelations." Saturday Review, May 27, pp. 63-66.

Collier, Eugenia W. "Thematic Patterns in Baldwin's Essays." Black World 21 (June): 28-34.

Standley, Fred L. "Another Country, Another Time." Studies in the Novel 4 (Fall): 504-512.

1973

"The Black Scholar Interviews: James Baldwin." Black Scholar 5 (no. 4): 33-42.

1974

Bell, George E. "The Dilemma of Love in Go Tell It on the Mountain and Giovanni's

Room." CLA Journal 17 (March): 397-406.

1975
Tedesco, John L. "Blues for Mister Charlie: The Rhetorical Dimension." Players, 50: 20-23.
Allen, S. S. "Religious Symbolism and Psychic Reality in Baldwin's Go Tell It on the Mountain." CLA Journal 19 (December): 173-199.

1976
Daniels, Mark R. "Estrangement, Betrayal and Atonement: The Political Theory of James Baldwin." Studies in Black Literature 7 (Autumn): 10-13.
Pratt, Louis H. "James Baldwin and 'The Literary Ghetto.'" CLA Journal 20 (December): 262-272.

1977
Sheed, W. "Twin Urges of James Baldwin." Commonweal, June 24, pp. 404-407.
Coles, Robert. "James Baldwin Back Home." The New York Times Book Review, July 31, pp. 1, 22-24.
Murray, D. C. "James Baldwin's 'Sonny's Blues': complicated and simple." Studies in Short Fiction 14 (Fall): 353-357.

GENERAL WORKS ON THE RACIAL PROBLEM
1933
Raper, Arthur F. The Tragedy of Lynching. Chapel Hill: University of North Carolina Press.

1943
Aptheker, Herbert. American Negro Slave Revolts. New York: International Publishers.

1944
Myrdal, Gunnar. An American Dilemma. New York: Harper and Brothers.

1955
Byrd, James Wilburn. "The Portrayal of White Character by Negro Novelists, 1900-1950." Doctoral dissertation. George Peabody College for Teachers. (Ann Arbor, Michigan: University Microfilms No. 55-680.
Johnson, Beulah Vivian. "The Treatment of the Negro Woman as a Major Character in American Novels, 1900-1950." Doctoral dissertation. New York University. (Ann Arbor, Michigan: University Microfilms No. 55-824.

1956
Warren, Robert Penn. Segregation: The Inner Conflict in the South. New York: Random House.

1957
Butcher, Margaret Just. The Negro in American Culture. New York: Alfred A. Knopf.

1958
Allport, Gordon. The Nature of Prejudice. Garden City, NY: Doubleday Anchor Books.

Bone, Robert A. The Negro Novel in America. New Haven, Connecticut: Yale University Press. (Revised edition published under the same title in 1965.)

Sterling, Dorothy. Tender Warriors. New York: Hill and Wang.

Vander Zander, James Wilfrid. "The Southern White Resistance Movement to Integration." Doctoral dissertation. The University of North Carolina. (Ann Arbor, Michigan: University Microfilms No. 58-5972.

1961

Du Bois, W. E. Burghardt. The Souls of Black Folks. Greenwich, Connecticut: Fawcett Publications.

1962

Nilon, Charles H. Faulkner and the Negro. University of Colorado Studies, Series in Language and Literature, No. 8. Boulder, Colorado: Colorado University Press.

1963

Guérin, Daniel. Décolonisation du Noir Américain. Paris: Les Éditions de Minuit.

Hill, Herbert, ed. Soon, One Morning. New York: Alfred A. Knopf. Also published under the title of Black Voices. London: Elek Books, 1963.

Lomax, Louis E. The Negro Revolt. New York: The New American Library.

1964

Duberman, Martin B. In White America. Boston: Houghton Mifflin Co.

Gregory, Dick. Nigger. New York: E. P. Dutton Co.

King, Martin Luther, Jr. Strength to Love. New York: Pocket Books, Inc.

Lomax, Louis E. When the Word Is Given. New York: New American Library.

Maliver, Bruce L. "Anti-Negro Bias Among Negro College Students." Doctoral dissertation. Yeshiva University. (Ann Arbor, Michigan: University Microfilms No. 64-10006.

Quarles, Benjamin. The Negro in the Making of America. New York: Bantam Books.

Wish, Harvey, ed. The Negro Since Emancipation. New York: Prentice Hall.

Wish, Harvey, ed. Slavery in the South. New York: Noonday Press. (Adapted for publication in French by Michel Fabre under the title Esclaves et Planteurs dans le Sud américain au XIXe siècle. Paris: Juillard, 1970.)

1965

Broom, Leonard, and Norval Glenn. Transformation of the Negro American. New York: Harper and Rowe.

Clark, Kenneth B. Dark Ghetto: Dilemmas of Social Power. New York: Harper and Row.

Hernton, Calvin C. Sex and Racism in America. Garden City, New York: Doubleday.

Miers, Earl Schenck. The Story of the American Negro. New York: Grosset and Dunlap, Inc.

Shogan, Robert, and Tom Craig. The Detroit Race Riot: A Study in Violence. New York: Chilton Books.

Walker, David. David Walker's Appeal. New York: Hill and Wang.

Warren, Robert Penn. Who Speaks for the Negro? New York: Random House.

Williams, John A. This Is My Country Too. New York: New American Library.

1966

Davis, John Preston. The American Negro Reference Book. Englewood Cliffs, N.J.: Prentice Hall.

Gross, Seymour L., and John Edward Hardy, eds. Images of the Negroes in American Literature. Chicago: University of Chicago Press.

Hill, Herbert, ed. Anger and Beyond. New York: Harper and Row.

Hughes, Langston. La Poésie négro-américaine. Paris: Éditions Seghers.

Littlejohn, David. Black on White: A Critical Survey of Writing by American Negroes. New York: Grossman Publishers.

Salk, Erwin A. A Layman's Guide to Negro History. Chicago: Quadrangle Books.

The Negro Handbook. Prepared by the editors of Ebony. Chicago: Johnson Publishing Co.

The White Problem in America. Edited by the editors of Ebony. Chicago: Johnson Publishing Co.

1967

Carmichael, Stokely, and Charles V. Hamilton. Black Power: The Politics of Liberation in America. New York: Vintage Books.

Cruse, Harold. The Crisis of the Negro Intellectual. New York: William Morrow and Co., Inc.

Powell, Adam Clayton. Keep the Faith, Baby! New York: Trident Press.

1968

Britt, David Dobbs. "The Image of the White Man in the Fiction of Langston Hughes, Richard Wright, James Baldwin, and Ralph Ellison." Doctoral dissertation. Emory University. (Ann Arbor, Michigan: University Microfilms No. 68-15747.

Cleaver, Eldridge. Soul on Ice. New York: Dell Publishing Co.

Cruse, Harold. Rebellion or Revolution? New York: William Morrow and Co.

Emanuel, James A., and Theodore L. Gross. Dark Symphony. New York: The Free Press.

Grier, William H., and Price M. Cobbs. Black Rage. New York: Basic Books., Inc.

Kesteloot, Lilyan. "Les Écrivains négro-américains", in Les Écrivains noirs de langue française, pp. 53-82. Parc Léopold: Editions of the Institute of Sociology. (Belgium.)

King, Martin Luther, Jr. Where Do We Go From Here: Chaos or Community? Boston: Beacon Press.

Larner, Jeremy, and Irving Howe, eds. Poverty: Views from the Left. New York: William Morrow and Co.

Margolies, Edward. Native Sons: A Critical Study of Twentieth Century Negro American Authors. Philadelphia and New York: J. B. Lippincott Co.

1969

Goldston, Robert. The Negro Revolution. New York: Signet Books.

Lincoln, C. Eric. The Black Americans. New York: Bantam Books.

1970

"Which Way Black America?: Separation? Integration? Liberation?" Ebony, No. 25 August. (Special issue.)

1972

Dillard, J. L. Black English: Its History and Usage in the United States. New York: Vintage Books.

1973

Shockley, Ann Allen and Sue P. Chandler, eds. <u>Living Black American Authors: A Biographical Directory</u>. New York: Bowker.

1975

Levitan, Sar A., William B. Johnston, and Robert Taggart. <u>Still a Dream: The Changing Status of Blacks Since 1960</u>. Cambridge, Massachusetts: Harvard University Press.

1976

Baker, Houston A., Jr., ed. <u>Reading Black: Essays in the Criticism of African, Caribbean, and Black American Literature</u>. Ithaca, N.Y.: Cornell University, Africana Studies and Research Center.

Barton, Rebecca. <u>Black Voices in American Fiction, 1900-1930</u>. New York: Dowling College Press.

Haley, Alex. <u>Roots</u>. New York: Doubleday.

Perry, Margaret. <u>Silence to the Drums: A Survey of the Literature of the Harlem Renaissance</u>. Westport, Connecticut: Greenwood Press.

OTHER WORKS CONSULTED

1902

Dixon, Thomas Jr. <u>The Leopard's Spots</u>. New York: Doubleday, Page and Co.

1905

Dixon, Thomas Jr. <u>The Clansman</u>. New York: Grosset and Dunlap.

1935

Bonneau, Georges. <u>Anthologie de la poésie japonaise</u>. Paris: Librairie orientaliste Paul Geuthner.

1937

Steinbeck, John. <u>Of Mice and Men</u>. New York: J. J. Little and Ives Co.

1938

Stowe, Harriet Beecher. <u>Uncle Tom's Cabin</u>. New York: The Modern Library.

1941

Brown, Sterling A., Arthur P. Davis, and Ulysses Lee, eds. <u>The Negro Caravan</u>. New York: The Dryden Press.

Wertham, Frederic. <u>Dark Legend: A Study in Murder</u>. New York: Duell, Sloan and Pearce.

1945

Himes, Chester B. <u>If He Hollers Let Him Go</u>. New York: Doubleday and Co., Inc.

1947

Camus, Albert. <u>La Peste</u>. Paris: Éditions Gallimard.

1948
Grene, Marjorie. Dreadful Freedom: A Critique of Existentialism. Chicago: The University of Chicago Press.

1949
Dostoieski, Fédor. Mémoires écrits dans un souterrain. Paris: Gallimard.

1950
Mannoni, Dominique O. Psychologie de la colonisation. Paris: Éditions du Seuil. (Translated into English under the title of Prospero and Caliban: The Psychology of Colonization. New York: Praeger, 1956.)

1952
Fanon, Frantz. Peau noire, masques blancs. Paris: Éditions du Seuil. (Translated into English under the title of Black Skin, White Masks. New York: Grove Press, 1967.)

1953
Goodwin, Ruby Berkley. It's Good to be Black. New York: Doubleday and Co.

1955
Harris, Joel Chandler. The Complete Tales of Uncle Remus. Boston: Houghton Mifflin Co.

1957
Camus, Albert. L'Étranger. Paris: Librairie Gallimard.

1959
Mailer, Norman. Advertisements for Myself. New York: G. P. Putnam's Sons.

1961
Fanon, Frantz. Les damnés de la terre. Paris: François Maspero. (Translated into English under the title of The Wretched of the Earth. New York: Grove Press, 1963.)
Freud, Sigmund. A General Introduction to Psychoanalysis. New York: Washington Square Press.
Griffin, John Howard. Black Like Me. New York: New American Library.

1962
Williams, John A. The Angry Black. New York: Lancer Books, Inc.

1963
Smith, William Gardner. The Stone Face. New York: Farrar, Strauss and Co.
Wagner, Jean. Les Poètes Nègres des États-Unis. Paris: Librairie Istra. (Translated into English under the title of Black Poets of the United States. Urbana: University of Illinois Press, 1973.)

1964
Copans, Sim. Chansons de Revendication. Vol. 1. Paris: Minard.

1965
Brown, Claude. Manchild in the Promised Land. New York: Macmillan Co.
Burns, W. Haywood. The Voices of Negro Protest in America. New York: Oxford

University Press for the Institute of Race Relations.
Gover, Robert. Here Goes Kitten. New York: Dell Publishing Co.
Himes, Chester. A Rage in Harlem. New York: Avon Books.
Martin, Ralph. Skin Deep. New York: New American Library.

1966
Camus, Albert. L'Homme révolté. Paris: Éditions Gallimard.
Camus, Albert. Le Mythe de Sisyphe. Paris: Éditions Gallimard.
Copans, Sim. Chansons de Revendication. Vol. 2, Paris: Minard.
Haley, Alex. The Autobiography of Malcolm X. New York: Grove Press, Inc.
Sartre, Jean-Paul. La Nausée. Paris: Éditions Gallimard.

1967
Dommergues, Pierre. Les U.S.A. à la recherche de leur identité: Rencontres avec 40 écrivains américains. Paris: Éditions Bernard Grasset.
Fabre, Michel. Les Noirs Américains. Paris: Armand Colin.
Sartre, Jean-Paul. L'Existentialisme est un humanisme. Paris: Les Éditions Nagel.
Styron, William. The Confessions of Nat Turner. New York: Random House.

1968
Blaustein, Albert P., and Robert L. Zangrando, eds. Civil Rights and the American Negro: A Documentary History. New York: Washington Square Press.
Clarke, John Henrick, ed. William Styron's "Nat Turner": Ten Black Writers Respond. Boston: Beacon Press.
Dunbar, Ernest, ed. The Black Expatriates: A Study of American Negroes in Exile. New York: E. P. Dutton and Co.

Ussher, Arland, Journey Through Dread: A Study of Kierkegaard, Heidegger and Sartre. New York: Biblo and Tannen.
Williams, John A. The Man Who Cried I Am. New York: New American Library.

1969
Brown, H. Rap. Die Nigger Die! New York: The Dial Press.
Cook, Mercer, and Stephen E. Henderson. The Militant Black Writer in Africa and the United States. Madison: University of Wisconsin Press.
Cronon, E. David. The Story of Marcus Garvey and the Universal Negro Improvement Association. Madison: University of Wisconsin Press.
Lester, Julius. Look out, Whitey! Black Power's Gon' Get your Mama! New York: Grove Press.
Pantell, Dora and Edwin Greenidge. If not now, When?: The Many Meanings of Black Power. New York: Dell Publishing Co.
Robinson, A. L., C. C. Foster, and D. H. Ogilvie. Black Studies in the University: A Symposium. New York: Bantam Books.
Scheer, Robert, ed. Post-Prison Writings and Speeches by Eldridge Cleaver. New York: Random House.
Skolnick, Jerome H. The Politics of Protest. New York: Ballantine Books.
Toomer, Jean. Cane. New York: Perennial Library.
Solotaroff, Theodore, ed. Writers and Issues. Toronto: The New American Library of Canada Ltd.

1970
Austin, L. J., L. H. Fenderson, and S. P. Nelson. The Black Man and the Promise of America. Glenview, Illinois: Scott, Foresman and Co.

Marine, Gene. The Black Panthers. Toronto: The New American Library of Canada Ltd.

Miyamori, Asataro. An Anthology of Haiku--Ancient and Modern. Westport, Connecticut: Greenwood Press.

Smith, William Gardner. Return to Black America. Englewood Cliffs, N.J.: Prentice Hall.

1971

"American Negro Novelists." Studies in the Novel 3 (Summer). (Special issue.)

Davis, Angela Y. If They Come in the Morning. New York: New American Library.

Fabre, Michel, and Paul Oren. Harlem, Ville noire. Paris: Armand Colin.

1973

Young, James O. Black Writers of the Thirties. Baton Rouge: Louisiana State University Press.

1974

Brignano, Russell Co. Black Americans in Autobiography: An Annotated Bibliography of Autobiographies and Autobiographical Books Written Since the Civil War. Durham, N.C.: Duke University Press.

Godman, Peter. The Death and Life of Malcolm X. New York: Perennial Library.

Whitlow, Roger. Black American Literature: A Critical History. Totowa, N.J.: Littlefield, Adams.

1975

Heiss, Robert. Hegel, Kierkegaard and Marx. New York: Delacorte Press, Seymour Lawrence.

ARTICLES

1963

Ford, Nick Aaron. "Walls do a Prison Make: A Critical Survey of Significant Belles-Lettres by and about Negroes Published in 1962." Phylon 24 (Summer): 123-134.

Levant, Howard. "Aspiraling We Should Go." Midcontinent American Studies Journal 4 (Fall): 3-20.

"Les Problèmes de l'écrivain noir aux États-Unis." Les Lettres Nouvelles, October, pp. 69-79.

Lomax, Louis E. "A Phony Islam's Unveiled Threat." True, December, pp. 14-28.

1964

Geismar, Maxwell. "The American Short Story Today." Studies on the Left 4 (Spring): 21-27.

"Civil Rights." Time, 27 July, pp. 25-26.

King, Martin Luther, Jr. "Negroes-Whiters Together." Amsterdam News, August 15, p. 18.

Brower, Brock. "Of Nothing But Facts." American Scholar 33 (Autumn): 613-614, 616, 618.

Malcolm X. "Malcolm by Himself." Post, September 12, pp. 30-53.

Huie, William Bradford. "A Ritual 'Cutting' by the Ku Klux Klan." True, October, pp. 23-36.

Warren, Robert Penn. "Who Shall Overcome?" The New York Review of Books, October 22, pp. 8-9.

King, Martin Luther, Jr. "Negroes are not Moving too Fast." Post, November 7, pp. 8-10.

Duke, Paul. "Southern Politics and the Negroes." The Reporter, December 17, pp. 18-21.

Gordon, Caroline. "Letters to a Monk." Ramparts, December, pp. 4-10.

Redding, Saunders. "The Problems of the Negro Writer." Massachusetts Review 6 (Autumn-Winter): 57-70.

1965

Gregory, Dick with Robert Lipsyte. "Nigger." True, January, pp. 42, 109-123.

Martin, Harold H., and Kenneth Fairly. "The KKK: We Got Nothing to Hide." Post, January 30, pp. 26-33.

Harris, Louis. "The Negro in America." Newsweek, February 15, pp. 24-28.

Barnette, Aubrey with Edward Linn. "The Black Muslims are a Fraud." Post, February 27, pp. 23-29.

Parks, Gordon. "The Violent Death of Malcolm X." Life, March 5, pp. 26-31.

Warren, Robert Penn. "The Negro Now." Look, March 23, pp. 23-31.

1966

Leonard, George B. "Not Black Power but Human Power." Look, September 5, pp. 40-43.

Redding, Saunders. "The Negro Writer and American Literature." In Anger and Beyond, pp. 1-19. Edited by Herbert Hill. New York: Harper and Row.

1967

McBee, Susanna. "A Long Void is Filled at Last." Life, January 13, pp. 32-33B.

Comer, James P. "The Social Power of the Negro." Scientific American, April, pp. 21-27.

"Which Way for the Negro and his Leaders Now?" Newsweek, May 15, pp. 27-34.

1968

Le Clec'h, Guy. "Pour les Noirs américains la confession de Nat Turner n'est pas celle de William Styron." Le Figaro Littéraire, March 3-9, p. 24.

Kanters, Robert. "La Révolte de l'oncle Tom." Le Figaro Littéraire, April 7-13, pp. 19-20.

Gross, Theodore L. "Our Mutual Estate: The Literature of the American Negro." Antioch Review 28 (Fall): 293-303.

1969

Ricks, T. "Black Revolution: A Matter of Definition." American Behavioral Scientist 12 (March): 21-26.

Meyer, P. "Aftermath of Martydom: Negro Militancy and Martin Luther King." Public Opinion Quarterly 33 (Summer): 160-173.

Howe, Irving. "New Black Writers." Harper's Magazine, December, pp. 130-146.

1970

Farley, R. "Changing Distribution of Negroes Within Metropolitan Areas: The Emergence of Black Suburbs." The American Journal of Sociology 75 (January): 512-529.

Young. V. H. "Family and Childhood in a Southern Negro Community." American Anthropologist 72 (April): 269-288.

Baird, K. E. "Semantics and Afro-American Liberation." Social Casework 51 (May): 265-269.

1971
Udry, J. R. "Skin Color, Status, and Mate Selection." American Journal of Sociology 76 (January): 722-733.
Bullock, H. A. "Black College and the New Black Awareness." Daedalus 100 (Summer): 573-602.
Baraka, Imamu Amiri. "The Ban on Black Music." Black World 20 (July): 4-11.
Jiobu, R. M., and H. H. Marshall. "Urban Structure and the Differentiation Between Blacks and Whites." American Sociological Review 36 (August): 638-649.
Lapham, V. "Do Blacks Pay More for Housing?" Journal of Political Economy 79 (November): 1244-1257.

1972
Heiss, J. "On the Transmission of Marital Instability in Black Families." American Sociological Review 37 (February): 89-92.
Bell, D. "Occupational Discrimination as a Source of Income Differences: Lessons of the 1960's." American Economic Review: Papers and Proceedings 62 (May): 363-372.
Gayle, Addison, Jr. "The Politics of Revolution: Afro-American Literature." Black World 21 (June): 4-12.
Taylor, Clyde. "Black Folk Spirit and the Shape of Black Literature." Black World 21 (August): 31-40.
Morris, M. D. "Black Americans and the Foreign Policy Process: The Case of Africa." Western Political Quarterly 25 (September): 451-463.
Power, J. "On the Economic Progress of Black America." Encounter 39 (October): 79-84.
Walton, Eugene. "Will the Supreme Court Revert to Racism?" Black World 21 (October): 46-48.

1973
Anderson, W. A. "Reorganization of Protest: Civil Disturbances and Social Change in the Black Community." American Behavioral Scientist 16 (January): 426-439.
Aldrich, H. E. "Employment Opportunities for Blacks in the Black Ghetto: The Role of White-owned Businesses." American Journal of Sociology 78 (May): 1403-1425.
Taylor, Prentiss. "Research for Liberation." Black World 22 (May): 4-14, 65-72.
Lieberson, S. "Generational Differences Among Blacks in the North." American Journal of Sociology 79 (November): 550-565.
Strickland, William. "Watergate: Its Meaning for Black America." Black World 23 (December): 4-14.

1974
Clarke, John Henrik. "The Afro-American Image of Africa." Black World 23 (February): 4-21.
Lincoln, C. E. "Power in the Black Church." Cross Currents 24 (Spring): 3-21.
"Ishmael Reed on Ishmael Reed." Black World 23 (June): 20-34.
Dance, Daryl C. "Contemporary Militant Black Humor." Negro American Literature Forum 8 (Summer): 217-222.
Washington, J. R., Jr. "Shafts of Light in black religious awakening." Religion in Life

43 (Summer): 150-160.

Whitlow, Roger. "Black Literature and American Innocence." Studies in Black Literature 5 (Summer): 1-4.

Willis, Robert J. "Anger and the Contemporary Black Theater." Negro American Literature Forum 8 (Summer): 213-215.

DeBaggio, T., and J. Aldridge. "Black News Services: Dying of Neglect?" Columbia Journalism Review 13 (July): 48-49.

Baraka, Imamu Amiri. "Toward Ideological Clarity." Black World 24 (November): 24-33, 84-95.

Simkins, Edward. "Black Studies-Here to Stay?" Black World 24 (December): 26-29.

1975

Abrahams, R. D. "Negotiating Respect: Patterns of Presentation Among Black Women." Journal of American Folklore 88 (January): 58-80.

DeGraaf, L. B. "Recognition, Racism, and Reflections on the Writing of Western Black History." Pacific Historical Review 44 (February): 22-51.

Barksdale, R. K. "White Triangles, Black Circles." CLA Journal 18 (June): 465-476.

Baraka, Amiri. "Why I Changed My Ideology: Black Nationalism and Socialist Revolution." Black World 24 (July): 30-42.

Waniek, Marilyn Nelson. "The Space Where Sex Should Be: Toward a Definition of the Black American Literary Tradition." Studies in Black Literature 6 (Fall): 7-13.

Baraka, Amiri. "Statement on the National Black Assembly." Black World 24 (October): 42-43.

Strickland, Bill. "Black Intellectuals and the American Social Scene." Black World 25 (November): 4-10.

1976

Diggs, Congressman Charles C. "Viewpoint: The Afro-American Stake in Africa." Black World 25 (January): 4-8.

Hare, Nathan. "Division and Confusion: What Happened to the Black Movement?" Black World 25 (January): 20-32.

Fuller, Hoyt W. "The Angola Crisis and Afro-Americans." Black World 25 (March): 24-25, 72-73.

1977

Barbour, James, and Robert E. Fleming. "A Checklist of Criticism on Early Afro-American Novelists." Studies in Black Literature 8 (Spring): 21-26.

Thornton, J. "U. S. Black Leadership--Now Going Collective." U.S. News and World Report, July 4, pp. 53-54.

"A Fallout Between Friends." Time, August 8, pp. 27-28.

1978

Zashin, E. "Progress of Black Americans in Civil Rights: The Past Two Decades Assessed." Daedalus 102 (Winter): 239-262.

Aldridge, Delores P. "Interracial Marriages: Empirical and Theoretical Considerations." Journal of Black Studies 8 (March): 355-368.

Wright, W. D. "DuBois' Theory of Political Democracy." Crisis, March, pp. 85-89.

Lester, J. "And Innocence Shall Be No More." Essence, May, pp. 72-73.

Berry, B. "Interracial Marriages in the South." Ebony, June, pp. 64-66.

INDEX OF AUTHORS
AND WORKS CITED

JEAN-FRANÇOIS GOUNARD is Director of International Student Affairs and Adjunct Assistant Professor of English at the State University College at Buffalo. Dr. Gounard specializes in Afro-American literature and Francophone African literature. He has also co-edited *Commentaries on a Creative Encounter: Proceedings of a Conference on the Culture and Literature of Francophone Africa.* His most recent article was entitled "Developing a Course on the Literary Figures of the Francophone African World."

JOSEPH J. RODGERS, JR., is the Chairman of the Department of Languages and Linguistics, Chairman of the Humanities Division, Professor of Romance Languages, and Director of the Critical Languages Center at Lincoln University, Pennsylvania. He is presently working on a methodology textbook entitled *Demystifying French Grammar.* His previous volumes include *Afrique: Face à la Modernisation* and a critical edition of Chateaubriand's *Essay on English Literature.*